FEMINIST INTERPRETATIONS OF SIMONE DE BEAUVOIR

RE-READING THE CANON

NANCY TUANA, GENERAL EDITOR

This series consists of edited collections of essays, some original and some previously published, offering feminist reinterpretations of the writings of major figures in the Western philosophical tradition. Devoted to the work of a single philosopher, each volume contains essays covering the full range of the philosopher's thought and representing the diversity of approaches now being used by feminist critics.

Already published:
Nancy Tuana, ed., *Feminist Interpretations of Plato* (1994)

FEMINIST INTERPRETATIONS OF SIMONE DE BEAUVOIR

EDITED BY MARGARET A. SIMONS

THE PENNSYLVANIA STATE UNIVERSITY PRESS
UNIVERSITY PARK, PENNSYLVANIA

Library of Congress Cataloging-in-Publication Data

Feminist interpretations of Simone de Beauvoir / Margaret A. Simons, ed.

    p.   cm. — (Re-reading the canon)
Includes bibliographical references and index.
ISBN 0-271-01412-1 (cloth)
ISBN 0-271-01413-X (paper)
  1. Beauvoir, Simone de, 1908–86 —Political and social views.
2. Feminism and literature—France—History—20th century. 3. Women
and literature—France—History—20th century. 4. Beauvoir, Simone
de, 1908– —Philosophy. 5. Existentialism in literature.
6. Feminism—Philosophy. I. Simons, Margaret A. II. Series.
PQ2603.E362Z673 1995
848'.91409—dc20   94-20972
                                                      CIP

Published by The Pennsylvania State University Press,
University Park, PA 16802-1003

Contents

Preface

Take into your hands any history of philosophy text. You will find compiled therein the "classics" of modern philosophy. Since these texts are often designed for use in undergraduate classes, the editor is likely to offer an introduction in which the reader is informed that these selections represent the perennial questions of philosophy. The student is to assume that she or he is about to explore the timeless wisdom of the greatest minds of Western philosophy. No one calls attention to the fact that the philosophers are all men.

Though women are omitted from the canons of philosophy, these texts inscribe the nature of woman. Sometimes the philosopher speaks directly about woman, delineating her proper role, her abilities and inabilities, her desires. Other times the message is indirect—a passing remark hinting at woman's emotionality, irrationality, unreliability.

This process of definition occurs in far more subtle ways when the central concepts of philosophy—reason and justice, those characteristics that are taken to define us as human—are associated with traits historically identified with masculinity. If the "man" of reason must learn to control or overcome traits identified as feminine—the body, the emotions, the passions—then the realm of rationality will be one reserved primarily for men,[1] with grudging entrance to those few women who are capable of transcending their femininity.

Feminist philosophers have begun to look critically at the canonized texts of philosophy and have concluded that the discourses of philosophy are not gender-neutral. Philosophical narratives do not offer a universal perspective, but rather privilege some experiences and beliefs over others. These experiences and beliefs permeate all philosophical theories whether they be aesthetic or epistemological, moral or metaphysical. Yet this fact has often been neglected by those studying the traditions of philosophy. Given the history of canon formation in Western philosophy, the perspective most likely to be privileged is that of upper-class, white males. Thus, to be fully aware of the impact of gender biases, it is imperative that we re-read the canon with attention to the ways in which philosophers' assumptions concerning gender are embedded within their theories.

This new series, *Re-Reading the Canon*, is designed to foster this process of reevaluation. Each volume will offer feminist analyses of the theories of a selected philosopher. Since feminist philosophy is not monolithic in method or content, the essays are also selected to illustrate the variety of perspectives within feminist criticism and highlight some of the controversies within feminist scholarship.

In this series, feminist lenses will be focused on the canonical texts of Western philosophy, both those authors who have been part of the traditional canon, as well as those philosophers whose writings have more recently gained attention within the philosophical community. A glance at the list of volumes in the series will reveal an immediate gender bias of the canon: Arendt, Aristotle, Beauvoir, Derrida, Descartes, Foucault, Hegel, Hume, Kant, Locke, Marx, Mill, Nietzsche, Plato, Rousseau, Wittgenstein, Wollstonecraft. There are all too few women included, and those few who do appear have been added only recently. In creating this series, it is not my intention to reify the current canon of philosophical thought. What is and is not included within the canon during a particular historical period is a result of many factors. Although no canonization of texts will include all philosophers, no canonization of texts that exclude all but a few women can offer an accurate representation of the history of the discipline as women have been philosophers since the ancient period.[2]

I share with many feminist philosophers and other philosophers writing from the margins of philosophy the concern that the current canonization of philosophy be transformed. Although I do not accept the position that the current canon has been formed exclusively by power relations, I do believe that this canon represents only a selective history of the tradition. I share the view of Michael Bérubé that "canons are at once the location, the index, and the record of the struggle for cultural representation; like any other hegemonic formation, they must be continually reproduced anew and are continually contested."[3]

The process of canon transformation will require the recovery of "lost" texts and a careful examination of the reasons such voices have been silenced. Along with the process of uncovering women's philosophical history, we must also begin to analyze the impact of gender ideologies upon the process of canonization. This process of recovery and examination must occur in conjunction with careful attention to the concept of a canon of authorized texts. Are we to dispense with the notion of a tradition of excellence embodied in a canon of authorized texts? Or, rather than abandon the whole idea of a canon, do we instead encourage a reconstruction of a canon of those texts that inform a common culture?

This series is designed to contribute to this process of canon transformation by offering a re-reading of the current philosophical canon. Such a re-reading shifts our attention to the ways in which woman and the role of the feminine is constructed within the texts of philosophy. A question we must keep in front of us during this process of re-reading is whether a philosopher's socially inherited prejudices concerning woman's nature and role are independent of her or his larger philosophical framework. In asking this question attention must be paid to the ways in which the definitions of central philosophical concepts implicitly include or exclude gendered traits.

This type of reading strategy is not limited to the canon, but can be applied to all texts. It is my desire that this series reveal the importance of this type of critical reading. Paying attention to the workings of gender within the texts of philosophy will make visible the complexities of the inscription of gender ideologies.

Nancy Tuana

Notes

1. More properly, it is a realm reserved for a group of privileged males, since the texts also inscribe race and class biases that hereby omit certain males from participation.

2. Mary Ellen Waithe's multivolume series, *A History of Women Philosophers* (Boston: M. Nijhoff, 1987), attests to this presence of women.

3. Michael Bérubé, *Marginal Forces/Cultural Centers: Tolson, Pynchon, and the Politics of the Canon* (Ithaca: Cornell University Press, 1992), 4–5.

For Mika

Acknowledgments

I would like to express my appreciation to the Department of Philosophical Studies at Southern Illinois University at Edwardsville, and its chair, Carol A. Keene, for providing me with reassigned time to complete this project. I owe special thanks to Debbie Mann for advice on French translation and to Julie Ward and Debra Bergoffen for their critical readings of the manuscript, and for reminding me of the pleasures of doing philosophy with friends. Nancy Tuana, who conceived of this fine series and encouraged me to undertake the volume on Beauvoir, has my deepest respect and gratitude for her vision, patience, and good humor. Her encouragement and the enthusiasm of the wonderful authors with whom it has been my pleasure to work on this volume have brought me the unexpected joys of participating in a growing community of feminist scholars interested in Beauvoir's philosophy, a community crossing disciplinary boundaries and rooted in both the Society for Women in Philosophy as well as the Simone de Beauvoir Society of the Modern Language Association. I am grateful as well to Mary Thomason, whose intelligence and wit made the task of preparing the manuscript much easier, and, at Penn State Press, to Cherene Holland, for her editorial skills, and to Sanford Thatcher without whose flexibility and goodwill this project could not have been completed. Finally I acknowledge my profound debt to Sylvie Le Bon de Beauvoir, whose meticulous and courageous work in preparing her adopted mother's notebooks and letters for posthumous publication has inspired many of the feminist reinterpretations of Beauvoir evident in this volume.

A longer version of Jo-Ann Pilardi's "Feminists Read *The Second Sex*" appeared in *History and Theory: Studies in the Philosophy of History*, vol.

32, no. 1 (1993), and is reprinted with revisions by permission of Wesleyan University.

An earlier version of Céline Léon's "Simone de Beauvoir's Woman: Eunuch or Male?" appeared in *Ultimate Reality and Meaning: Interdisciplinary Studies in the Philosophy of Understanding*, vol. 11 (1984), and is reprinted with revisions by permission of the International Society for the Study of Human Ideas on Ultimate Reality and Meaning, Toronto.

Sonia Kruks's "Simone de Beauvoir: Teaching Sartre About Freedom" was first published in *Sartre Alive* (1991), edited by Ronald Aronson and Adrian van den Hoven, and is reprinted with revisions by permission of Wayne State University Press. An earlier version of Kruk's paper was published in French as "Simone de Beauvoir entre Sartre et Merleau-Ponty," *Les Temps Modernes*, vol. 45, no. 520 (November 1989). The author's name was erroneously printed as Sonia Kraüs.

A longer version of *"The Second Sex*: From Marxism to Radical Feminism," by Margaret A. Simons, will appear in *Selected Studies in Phenomenology and Existential Philosophy*, vol. 20: *Political Theory*, edited by Lenore Langsdorf and Stephen Watson (Albany: State University of New York Press, forthcoming).

Michèle Le Doeuff's "Simone de Beauvoir: Falling into (Ambiguous) Line" was first published as "Simone de Beauvoir, les ambiguïtés d'un ralliement," in *Magazine Littéraire*, no. 320 (April 1994), and is reprinted by permission of the author.

Introduction

Biographical Background

Simone de Beauvoir was born in Paris in 1908 to an atheistic father with aristocratic pretensions and a deeply pious, overbearing mother devoted to shaping the lives of her two daughters, Simone and her younger sister, Hélène. Simone received a classical education in a conservative Catholic girls' preparatory school where she was attracted to an exuberant classmate, Zaza, the first love of her life. A series of financial crises following World War I impoverished Simone's family and left her without a dowry. Increasingly set apart from her classmates who were being groomed for arranged marriages, Beauvoir prepared for a career, recalling later in *Memoirs of a Dutiful Daughter* (1958) that she identified with women novelists and dreamed of becoming a writer herself one day. Claude Francis and Fernande Gontier, in their biography *Simone de Beauvoir: A Life, A Love Story* (1987), report that Beauvoir passed her baccalaureate in 1925 with honors in Latin and literature, and highest honors in basic mathematics. Against the wishes of her mother, who despaired of her future, but under pressure from her antifeminist father to mask the dishonor of a career by accumulating degrees, Beauvoir pursued three *licences:* in literature, philosophy, and mathematics. A *licence,* the rough equivalent of a master's degree, was composed of four *certificats,* which were usually completed at the rate of one, or at best two, a year. The *licence* was followed by both the *diplôme d'études supérieures* and, for students who wanted to become tenured lycée professors, the highly competitive national exam called *l'agrégation.*[1]

To prepare for her *certificat* in general mathematics, Beauvoir enrolled in courses at the Catholic Institute. Her courses in literature, including

Greek and Latin, were at the private Ecole Normale Libre in Neuilly, where she came under the influence of two teachers. The first was Robert Garric, a leftist Catholic literature professor whose organization, Equipe Sociale, enabled student volunteers to teach workers in the poorer districts of Paris. Beauvoir's participation in this organization encouraged the commitment to social justice evident in her later anticolonialist and feminist writings. It was also at Neuilly that Beauvoir worked with Mademoiselle Mercier, one of the first women to pass the philosophy *agrégation* exam, who encouraged Beauvoir to devote herself to philosophy (see Francis and Gontier 1987, 51). Beauvoir's interest in modern literature led her to Adrienne Monnier's combination bookstore and salon, La Maison des Amis du Livre, where James Joyce read from *Ulysses* and dadaist texts first became available, and to Sylvia Beach's neighboring bookstore, Shakespeare and Company, the celebrated haunt of expatriate American writers such as Ernest Hemingway and Gertrude Stein. Beauvoir read modern literature avidly and, rebelling against the confines of her conservative culture, was drawn to surrealism.

In the spring of 1926 she completed her *certificat* in literature summa cum laude, as well as *certificats* in general mathematics and Latin, and began preparing for her *certificats* in logic and the history of philosophy by reading Plato, Schopenhauer, Leibniz, Hamelin, and Bergson (Francis and Gontier 1987, 159). In June 1927 Beauvoir was one of the top three recipients of the *certificat* in general philosophy, preceded by Simone Weil and followed by Maurice Merleau-Ponty, who became her friend and guide to the prestigious and, until that year, all-male Ecole Normale Supérieur, where he (along with Jean-Paul Sartre, Claude Lévi-Strauss, and Simone Weil) was a student. Not having attended the special preparatory classes for the Ecole Normale Supérieur, Beauvoir registered for classes at the Sorbonne, and wrote a lengthy essay on "the personality" for Jean Baruzi, who "congratulated her publicly and announced that he saw in it the seeds of a major work" (Francis and Gontier 1987, 67). Also in 1927 Beauvoir began working on a novel and earned money by teaching Mademoiselle Mercier's philosophy classes at the private Institute Sainte-Marie. She completed her *certificat* in the history of philosophy and debated philosophy with her classmates at the Sorbonne, becoming friends with a group of young left-wing intellectuals, which included Henri Lefebvre, a follower of both Descartes and Marx, and Georges Politzer, author of a 1928 work on psychology, which replaced the Freudian unconsciousness with *le vécu*, a concept akin to that of "lived experience" in phenomenology, and which Beauvoir later employed in *The Second Sex* (Francis and Gontier 1987, 69).

After completing her degree in philosophy in the spring of 1928, Beauvoir decided to write her graduate thesis, earn the *diplôme d'études supérieures*, and prepare for the *agrégation* competition at the same time. Fortunately for Beauvoir she had participated in one of Léon Brunschvicg's seminars. A noted Kant scholar who was a dominant figure in French philosophy, Brunschvicg was also a feminist and the husband of the French suffragist Cécile Brunschvicg. Léon Brunschvicg agreed to direct Beauvoir's thesis and gave her the topic "The Concept in Leibniz."[2] Beauvoir attended lectures in psychology by Georges Dumas at the Salpêtrière Hospital, and in the spring of 1929 did her teaching apprenticeship, along with Claude Lévi-Strauss and Maurice Merleau-Ponty, at Lycée Janson-de-Sailly, where she became the first woman in France to teach at a boys' *lycée*.

The essay topic for the written portion of the philosophy *agrégation* exam in 1929 was "freedom and contingency," an apt assignment for both Beauvoir and a fellow student with whom her name would be linked for the rest of their lives, Jean-Paul Sartre. Sartre, who was older than Beauvoir, was repeating the written exam after having failed it the previous year. They met when Sartre invited Beauvoir to join his study group to prepare for the orals of the *agrégation* and help them learn Leibniz. The judges for the orals, Georges Davy and Jean Wahl, ranked Sartre first and Beauvoir second, although another student reported that "everyone agreed that *she* was the true philosopher" (Francis and Gontier 1987, 92).

After successfully completing her degree, Beauvoir's career was slow to establish itself, as she recovered from both the frenetic pace of her student years and the sudden death in November 1929 of her close childhood friend, Zaza, who fell ill in the midst of what Beauvoir saw as a struggle to escape an arranged marriage.[3] Throughout her life, and in her philosophy, Beauvoir saw the self as inextricably linked to others and defined through personal relationships, as Carol Ascher points out in *Simone de Beauvoir: A Life of Freedom* (1981). Beauvoir would write years after Zaza's death that she felt that her own freedom had been won at the cost of her friend's life.

Beauvoir tutored students in philosophy and taught Latin for a year before beginning her career as a lycée philosophy teacher, first in Marseilles, then in Rouen (where her intimate relationship with a former student, Olga, soon became a trio including Sartre), and finally in Paris. Her first novel, *When Things of the Spirit Come First*, was completed in 1937 (but not published until 1979), and she continued teaching philosophy until her contract was terminated in 1943 by a Nazi-controlled administration after a complaint about Beauvoir by the mother of one of her female students. In order to survive, Beauvoir began working later that year as the writer-producer of a program on medieval France for the Nazi-controlled French radio. Her first published novel, *She Came to Stay* (1943), appeared during the Occupation when publication was prohibited for Jews, a less than honorable wartime record that may have fueled her postwar political engagement and work in ethics.[4] Reinstated to the faculty after the war, Beauvoir never returned to teaching, but supported herself as a writer.

Although Beauvoir was deeply interested in philosophy, she was an outsider in this male domain, which may have encouraged her to conceive of philosophy in literary form, an approach she explains in her 1946 essay "Literature and Metaphysics." In *She Came to Stay*, which became the subject of Merleau-Ponty's 1945 essay "Metaphysics and the Novel," Beauvoir addressed epistemological issues that located consciousness in the world and formulated what she called "the problem of the Other," laying much of the philosophical foundations in literary form of what would later become known as Sartrean existential phenomenology (see Fullbrook and Fullbrook 1994).

World War II and the Nazi Occupation transformed Beauvoir's outlook, inaugurating a period of intense reflection that she described as the "moral period" in her writing, the time when she defined a social ethics for existentialism. Her only play, *Who Shall Die* (1945a), was written during this period, as were her novels *Blood of Others* (1945c) and *All Men Are Mortal* (1946b), and several essays on ethics, politics, and social philosophy published in *Pyrrhus et Cinéas* (1944), *L'Existentialism et la sagesse des nations* (1948b), and *Privilèges* (1955b), many of which remain untranslated. In 1945, during the immediate postwar period, with Sartre, Merleau-Ponty, and others, Beauvoir co-founded the journal *Les Temps Modernes*, in which they published fiction from such writers as Richard Wright and Violette Leduc, as well as philosophy and cultural criticism, reflecting their concept of a literature of political engagement.[5] It was during this period that Beauvoir wrote *Ethics of Ambiguity* (1947), the culmination of her work to formulate an abstract moral philosophy. In *America Day by Day* (1948), Beauvoir, influenced by the African-American writer Richard Wright, presented an analysis of the American system of racist segregation which provided a model for her analysis of women's oppression in *The Second Sex* (1949). In this, her best-known text, Beauvoir placed existentialist ethics within a historical and political context and laid the philosophical foundations for radical feminism. In "Must We Burn Sade?" ([1952] 1966), Beauvoir developed her philosophy further in a critical biography.

The angry outcry in France that greeted the publication of *The Second Sex* forced Beauvoir to abandon the cafés where she had done much of her work. But she continued to write. Beginning with *The Mandarins* (1954), her award-winning novel about the disintegration of the leftist political alliance in postwar France, her writing became increasingly contextual and personal. In her best-selling autobiographies, Beauvoir shielded herself from public exposure and attack by cloaking her accounts of her life and work with conventionality. She disguised her lesbian relationships and went along with the critics who described her as Sartre's philosophical follower, depicting her relationship with Sartre as the centerpiece of her life. The first volume, *Memoirs of a Dutiful Daughter* (1958), tells of her childhood; *Prime of Life* (1960) covers her early career as a writer and experiences of the Nazi Occupation; *Force of Circumstance* (1963), the post–World War II years and the Algerian war; *A Very Easy Death* (1964b) tells of the death of her mother; and *All Said and Done* (1972) describes her involvement in the French women's liberation movement and the beginning of her relationship with Sylvie Le Bon, her companion during the last decades of her life.

Her continuing political commitments are reflected in writings such as her 1957 book on China, *The Long March*, and *Djamila Boupacha* (1962), her writings during the Algerian war coauthored with Gisèle Halimi, which contained their defense of a young Algerian woman tortured by French military. In the 1960s her two controversial novels, *Les Belles Images* (1966a) and *The Woman Destroyed* (1968), which expose the inauthenticity and pain in the lives of bourgeois women, met with criticism from the nascent French women's liberation movement for their negative portrayals of women. In 1970 Beauvoir published *Old Age* (euphemistically translated as *The Coming of Age*), where she analyzed the political and social construction of aging from a framework analogous to that of *The Second Sex*. In the 1970s she became an active participant in the French women's liberation movement, co-founding an organization for abortion rights, editing issues of *Les Temps Modernes* on women, and joining the editorial collective, *Questions Féministes*. Her political engagement is also reflected in her prefaces to various books: *Treblinka* (1966b), by Jean-François Steiner, on a rebellion at the Treblinka concentration camp; *Avortement: Une loi en procès; L'Affaire de Bobigny* (1973), on a case in the battle to legalize abortion; *Les Femmes s'entêtent* (1975), from a special 1974 issue of *Les Temps Modernes* on the women's movement; and the *Proceedings of the International Tribunal on Crimes Against Women* (1976).

Beauvoir's publications following Sartre's death in 1980 were devoted to solidifying her account of their relationship, first in *Adieux: A Farewell to Sartre* (1981), which contains a transcript of conversations with Sartre from 1974 as well as an account of his final illness and death, and then in her edition of Sartre's letters, *Lettres au Castor* (1983). But in 1986 Beauvoir died, leaving a legacy of unpublished letters and notebooks that, when published in 1990 by Sylvie Le Bon de Beauvoir, now her adopted daughter and literary executor, would destroy the conventional myths surrounding not only her private life but her contribution to philosophy as well.

Beauvoir and the Philosophical Canon

The encouragement that Beauvoir received from Léon Brunschvicg in writing her graduate thesis in philosophy unfortunately did not reflect the attitude of the discipline as a whole. Indeed the contemptuous dismissal of Beauvoir from the philosophical canon was so complete that the most radical disruption caused by feminist interpretations of Simone de Beauvoir may be in reading her work at all. Despite Beauvoir's contributions to formulating an existentialist social philosophy and ethics, and her post–World War II fame as an existentialist writer, coeditor of *Les Temps Modernes*, and author of *The Second Sex*, by the early 1970s her name had practically disappeared from American histories of existentialism or discussions of French philosophy. Jean Wahl set the tone in his *Short History of Existentialism*: "We might mention, without discussing, Simone de Beauvoir and Merleau-Ponty, whose theories are similar to those of Sartre, though sometimes applied to different domains of experience" (Wahl 1949, 31). In a comparable vein, Walter Kaufmann's popular text, *Existentialism from Dostoevsky to*

Sartre (1956), does not mention her at all, although he includes literary writers such as Rilke, Kafka, and Camus. Not that Beauvoir was unknown to Americans in 1956; her 1947 lecture tour of the United States was well covered by the media. The Philosophical Library published an English translation of her *Ethics of Ambiguity* in 1948, and *The Second Sex* appeared in English in 1952.

Some of the references to Beauvoir in texts by American philosophers make it obvious that Beauvoir's feminism, as well as her gender, was a factor in her exclusion from the canon. Her support for abortion rights, rejection of "maternal instinct," and condemnation of the oppressive nature of woman's traditional role directly challenged a cornerstone of religious conservativism. What Yolanda A. Patterson (1986) has called Beauvoir's "demystification of motherhood" was the focus of William Barrett's anger in his popular study of existentialism, *Irrational Man* (1958). Barrett initially praises Beauvoir with Sartre and Camus as "brilliant and engaging writers" and "leaders" of the "existentialist literary movement." But soon her name disappears from the text. There is, however, an indirect reference to Beauvoir in Barrett's text that is most revealing. The context is Barrett's criticism of Sartre's existential psychology for "not really comprehend[ing] the concrete man who is an undivided totality of body and mind" (Barrett 1958, 231). One of the counterexamples Barrett offers to this Sartrean duality contains a reference to *The Second Sex:* "Consider the psychology of the ordinary woman. Not of the women one meets in Sartre's novels or plays; nor of that woman, his friend, who wrote a book of feminine protest, *The Second Sex,* which is in reality the protest against being feminine" (Barrett 1958, 232). A clue to Barrett's dismissive tone is evident in his own psychology of "the ordinary woman," whom he describes as fulfilled by family and children, not from a conscious choice but rather from the "unfolding of nature through her" (Barrett 1958, 232; see Simons 1990).

Although few histories of existentialism match Barrett's tone, most continue the pattern of either ignoring Beauvoir or reducing her to Sartre (see Collins 1952; Heineman 1958; Blackham 1965; and Breisach 1962). By 1960 Beauvoir finally seems to have learned the lesson herself. In contrast to "Literature and Metaphysics" (1946a), where she writes of taking risks in the "authentic spiritual adventure" of creating a metaphysical novel, fourteen years later in *Prime of Life* (1960) she describes women as ill-suited to philosophy and mocks philosophers' pretentious claims to universal truths (254). In interviews throughout the 1970s and 1980s she would deny her philosophical originality, claiming instead to be Sartre's follower. The sexism in philosophy had left its mark.

There are exceptions to the dismissal of Beauvoir's work by philosophers, including Hazel Barnes's *The Literature of Possibility: A Study in Humanistic Existentialism* (1959). Barnes, the translator of Sartre's *Being and Nothingness*, provides a landmark reading of Beauvoir's first published novel, *She Came to Stay*, and tries to leave open the question of whether it was Beauvoir or Sartre who originated the philosophical framework shared by both the novel and *Being and Nothingness*. A later, and less well known example with contemporary relevance is Albert Rabil's *Merleau-Ponty: Existentialism of the Social World* (1967). Rabil, whose interest in Beauvoir is tangential to his main concern of differentiating Merleau-Ponty from Sartre, argues: "Mlle de Beauvoir did not hold Sartre's view of freedom in the early postwar period. In *The Ethics of Ambiguity*, for example, she outlines a phenomenology of freedom in which approximate realizations of freedom are described and arranged in an ascending order of validity. Here the 'mixture' of man and the world is the point of department" (Rabil 1967, 133).

Unfortunately neither Barnes's nor Rabil's readings prevailed, as is evident in *The Encyclopedia of Philosophy* (1967), an ambitious project in the formalization of the American philosophical canon edited by Paul Edwards. Once again Beauvoir is not included in the index, although she is mentioned in the entry on Sartre, where she is cited with Merleau-Ponty as one of the founders of *Les Temps Modernes*. Of the four French existentialist philosophers mentioned in this entry—Merleau-Ponty, Sartre, Beauvoir, and Camus—only Beauvoir lacks an entry under her own name. Beauvoir is also mentioned in the entry "Existentialism," written by Alasdair MacIntyre, under a discussion of Sartre: "[Sartre's psychological analyses] are employed, too, in the novels of Simone de Beauvoir, whose moral and political writings also use the Sartrean concept of choice" (Edwards 1967, 3–4:150). This is an odd claim since in *The Second Sex*, for example, or even in *Ethics of Ambiguity*, one obvious area of Beauvoir's philosophical difference from Sartre is her rejection of a Sartrean concept of absolute freedom and choice. For Beauvoir, as Rabil noted, freedom is not absolute but limited by one's situation.

The *Encyclopedia of Philosophy*'s "Bibliography of the History of Ethics" includes a mention of Beauvoir's *Ethics of Ambiguity* with the comment:

"Important in its own right and in relation to Sartre" (3–4:116). But in the article itself there is no mention of Beauvoir or her "important" work, although there is a lengthy discussion of Camus. The contrast between the treatment accorded Camus and that given Beauvoir is particularly dramatic in this instance, for the author of the article remarks that "Camus wrote no technical philosophy" (3–4:107). In this case, the author had seemingly better philosophical grounds for including Beauvoir than Camus, but once again, it was Beauvoir who was excluded (see Simons 1990).

Feminist Reinterpretations

With the rebirth of feminism as a political movement in the late 1960s, activist and theorists such as Shulamith Firestone (1970) and Kate Millett (1969) modeled their radical feminism on *The Second Sex*. Feminist philosophers, encouraged by the formation of the Society for Women in Philosophy in 1969, took up the critique of the philosophical canon begun by Beauvoir in *The Second Sex* and began to challenge her exclusion. But integrating Beauvoir into the canon proved problematic. Existential phenomenology could hardly be considered a feminist philosophical tradition, and Sartre's descriptions of the female body in *Being and Nothingness*, often cited as the philosophical foundation for *The Second Sex*, were filled with disgust. Beauvoir herself added to the interpretive difficulties by rejecting efforts by feminist philosophers to define her position as philosophically distinct from Sartre's, a result perhaps of both the years of contemptuous dismissal by philosophers and her affection for Sartre, whose reputation and health were then in decline. By the mid-1970s and with the emergence of a feminist politics based on woman-identity, the relationship of Beauvoir's feminism to male-defined philosophy in general and Sartrean existentialism in particular had become the focus of intense feminist criticism.

The result was an interpretive impasse that was not broken until after Beauvoir's death in 1986. The articles collected in this volume reflect the resurgence of interest in her work that followed her death, an interest generated as well by the popularity of postmodernism, bringing an appreciation for historical-political context, critique of essentialism, and reaffirmation of individualism, all of which encouraged a re-reading of Beauvoir. But, as several of the essays included here will show, the most significant contribution to breaking this interpretive impasse came in 1990 with the posthumous publication of Beauvoir's letters and notebooks by Sylvie Le Bon de Beauvoir. Their publication would provide new grounds to challenge not only conventional interpretations of Beauvoir's personal relationships but historical accounts of her contribution to the philosophical movement known as existentialism as well.

The debates generating the new feminist interpretive paradigms focus on several issues, including the relationship of feminism and existentialism, the nature of philosophy and its relationship to literature, and the charge that the philosophical tradition of existential philosophy in general and Beauvoir's philosophy in particular is masculinist. In Chapter 1, Jo-Ann Pilardi provides a historical context for these debates in a survey of feminist criticism of *The Second Sex*, which, as she notes, encompasses a history of contemporary feminism itself. Her essay defines six issues raised by critics in the 1980s and early 1990s that are addressed by other authors in this volume as well. First, regarding the relation of *The Second Sex* to existentialism, some critics who have assumed a Sartrean foundation for Beauvoir's philosophy have charged that her reliance on Sartrean individualism undermines feminist activism in *The Second Sex*; others have credited Sartre's concept of radical freedom with empowering women's individual freedom. Still other feminist critics have argued that Beauvoir's concept of situated freedom represents a philosophical departure from Sartrean existentialism. Second, Pilardi describes the charge that Beauvoir's philosophy is masculinist, as arising from concern with Beauvoir's distinction between transcendence and immanence in *The Second Sex* and the Sartrean (and Hegelian) dualism it seems to imply. American theorists of gynocentric feminism and French "feminine difference" theorists have argued that Beauvoir's theory is male-identified or phallocentric in privileging male activities, exemplifying transcendence, over traditional female activities, exemplifying immanence.

The charge that the transcendence/immanence dualism led to Beauvoir's failure to value motherhood and incorporate it into a definition of freedom is the focus of Pilardi's third issue. Here critics have variously credited Beauvoir with exposing the effects of oppression on mothers and attacked her for suggesting that maternity is merely biological. The fourth issue identified by Pilardi concerns female sexuality and the criticism that Beauvoir's description of female eroticism is inconsistent, pervaded by a Sartrean disgust for the body in general and the female body in particular, and a "betrayal of her revolutionary discussions of homosexuality."

The fifth issue raised by feminist critics of *The Second Sex* concerns the relationship of Beauvoir's feminism to socialism, an issue complicated by both the historical antagonism between Marxism and existentialism and the appropriation of *The Second Sex* by radical feminists in the 1960s. The final issue identified by Pilardi concerns a charge leveled by postmodern critics of Eurocentrism as well as feminist anthropologists: that Beauvoir falsely universalizes women as a group, ignoring the experience of women outside Europe and the middle class. The positions taken in these debates by the authors in this volume reflect a variety of philosophical methodologies and perspectives. Together they underscore both the shifting political context of interpretation and the increasing subtlety and complexity of contemporary feminist readings of Beauvoir.

In Chapter 2 Karen Vintges addresses two of the issues identified by Pilardi. On the issue of the relation of *The Second Sex* to existentialism, Vintges claims that Beauvoir transforms Sartrean existentialism rather than simply applies it. Vintges locates Beauvoir within the phenomenological tradition defined by Husserl, describing Beauvoir, in *The Second Sex*, as applying the descriptive methodology of phenomenological anthropology, where "the importance of subjectivity" is acknowledged and "immediate experience is decisive." Vintges's specific concern throughout most of the essay is to address a second issue: the charge that Beauvoir has "unleashed male thinking" on the subject of woman through her reliance on Sartre's concept of transcendence. Vintges first challenges the notion that certain philosophical positions are necessarily "masculine" and others "feminine." After reviewing Sartre's representations of women in the subhuman role of being-in-itself, Vintges then argues that Sartre's sexual metaphors about women are not required by his analysis of bad faith.

Vintges looks for confirmation of this reading of Sartre in *The Second Sex* where, she argues, Beauvoir maintains Sartre's philosophical framework while eliminating the representations of woman's body as "the enemy par excellence of transcendence." Vintges focuses our attention on passages in *The Second Sex* where Beauvoir, drawing on the phenomenological tradition, states that "the body is not a thing, but a situation." It is a historically contingent process, not biology, that has made woman the Other, identified with nature and *en-soi*. Thus, Vintges argues, Beauvoir's achievement has been to eliminate the masculinism in Sartre's philosophical framework through her analysis of the historical construction of woman's oppression, while at the same time retaining his metaphysics of authenticity.

Michèle Le Doeuff, whose earlier work (1979, 1989) has described Beauvoir's ingenuous use of Sartre's philosophy of radical freedom in *The Second Sex* to undermine the legitimation of women's oppression, provides in Chapter 3 a new answer to the question of the relationship between Beauvoir's feminism and existentialism. Rejecting efforts such as Vintges's to reclaim a connection between Beauvoir and Husserl, Le Doeuff moves away from Sartre as well. For Le Doeuff, Beauvoir's venture into existentialism and her attempts in *The Ethics of Ambiguity* to define an existentialist ethics and social philosophy are misguided efforts to address a problem that arises from within Sartre's solipsistic metaphysic and not her own. Le Doeuff, who in *Hipparchia's Choice* (1989) used evidence from Sartre's posthumously published *Lettres au Castor* to criticize his efforts to silence Beauvoir as a philosopher, here draws upon Beauvoir's *Lettres à Sartre* in her new interpretation of Beauvoir's philosophy. Disavowing Beauvoir's connection with a philosophical movement extending from Kierkegaard, through Husserl and Heidegger, to Sartre, Le Doeuff uses evidence from Beauvoir's posthumously published letters to argue that it was Hegel's *Phenomenology of the Spirit* that reawakened Beauvoir's need to do philosophy at the beginning of the Nazi Occupation and shaped her most original philosophical writing in *She Came to Stay* and *The Second Sex*.

Eleanore Holveck's impressionistic essay (Chapter 4) on the question of the relationship of Beauvoir to existentialism raises another issue as well, that of the relationship of philosophy to literature. Holveck finds a metaphor for a woman philosopher in a tale familiar to us from antiquity and recounted by Heidegger. In the tale, Thales of Miletus, the pre-Socratic philosopher often described as originating the Western philosophical tradition, is said to have fallen into a well while watching the stars. A servant-woman who was watching laughed scornfully, "wondering how he could claim to know anything about the sky, when he could not even see what was directly in front of his feet." Heidegger, identifying with Thales, defines philosophy as "that thinking with which one can start nothing and about which housemaids necessarily laugh." Holveck invites us to identify instead with the servant-woman, and argues that Beauvoir would not admit to being a philosopher because "the philosophy she studied and taught spent too much time on nothing."

Holveck notes that Beauvoir, in words reminiscent of Husserl's *Cartesian Meditations*, scorns the pretense of "universal" claims actually based in the consciousness of some individual thinker. Instead, Holveck writes, Beauvoir, like Sartre, "wrote her philosophy in literature," an interpretation Holveck supports with discussion of Beauvoir's essay "Literature and Metaphysics" (1946a). Holveck, like Le Doeuff, also finds evidence of Hegelian influence in Beauvoir's philosophy, specifically in her construction of the problem of intersubjectivity in her novel *She Came to Stay.*

In her discussion of *The Second Sex,* Holveck joins Vintges in challenging the canonical view of Beauvoir as a Sartrean, arguing instead that Beauvoir's philosophy "owes as much, if not more to Edmund Husserl." According to Holveck, Beauvoir made extensive use of Husserl's method of phenomenological *epochē,* that is, bracketing all claims about reality to consider an object simply in relation to consciousness, and eidetic reduction (varying the individual object to expose its essential structure). In *The Second Sex* Beauvoir used the method in appealing to the concrete, lived experiences of women in order to expose the prejudices about women embedded in ordinary language and taken up by the sciences. Responding to Beauvoir's ideal that women from as many cultures as possible articulate their own lived experiences, Holveck contributes a personal account of how she herself became a philosopher, "a guest at the master's banquet table." At the conclusion, Holveck describes herself leaving the master's banquet table for the kitchen, where she serves as a kitchenmaid to Beauvoir, "a story-telling cook who peels the layers of vegetables so that we might taste every distinct ingredient in the stew of our existence," and remembers "our great, great . . . grandmother, that housemaid who laughed at Thales."

Sonia Kruks, in Chapter 5, challenges even further the canonical Sartrean interpretation of Beauvoir, arguing that Beauvoir, drawing on insights by Merleau-Ponty, originated a different philosophy in *The Second Sex,* one that Sartre himself would adopt in his later writings. Kruks argues that Sartre, in his *Critique of Dialectic Reason* (1960), modified the absolute and radically individualist notion of freedom he had elaborated in *Being and Nothingness* and replaced it with a concept of freedom as relative and socially mediated as Beauvoir's of the late 1940s. Although Sartre credited Merleau-Ponty with teaching him about history, politics, and the social dimensions of human existence, Kruks argues that as early as 1940 Beauvoir had herself "insisted against Sartre that 'not every situation is equal' from the point of view of freedom." Furthermore, in a *Les Temps Modernes* review of Merleau-Ponty's *Phenomenology of Perception* (1945b), Beauvoir contrasts Sartre's philosophy to Merleau-Ponty's, revealing, according to Kruks, that she had grasped "earlier and perhaps better than Sartre" the implications of Merleau-Ponty's view that "history is incarnated in a body which possesses a certain generality, a relation to the world anterior to myself."

In contrast to Le Doeuff's reading of *Ethics of Ambiguity*, Kruks reads Beauvoir's description of the interdependence of freedoms in her existential ethics as quietly subverting Sartre's conception of freedom, thus anticipating her own analysis of oppression in *The Second Sex*. In this later text Beauvoir distinguishes "relations of otherness between social equals" where "otherness is 'relativized' by a kind of 'reciprocity' . . . mediated through institutions" and relations of otherness involving social inequality, where "reciprocity" is replaced by oppression, and freedom itself undergoes modification. Kruks points out that, for Beauvoir, the relation of husband and wife is defined by the institution of marriage, just as the female body is defined as "inferior other" by the social constructions placed on it, none of which can be accounted for in Sartre's *Being and Nothingness*.

According to Kruks, a central problem in Sartre's early work is the discontinuity "between on the one hand, discrete, individually constituted meanings and, on the other, the existence of social and historical wholes." Beauvoir's analysis of women's situation—a human creation that a woman may frequently experience without "bad faith" as a "destiny"—points a way beyond Sartre's dilemma, a solution most fully mapped out in Merleau-Ponty's *Phenomenology of Perception*. In her conclusion Kruks calls for "a detailed comparison" of Sartre's *Cahiers pour une morale* (published posthumously in 1983) and Beauvoir's contemporary works from the late 1940s. Her own examination of the texts reveals that Sartre, struggling to reconcile a radical individualism with history, was "mired in difficulties that do not arise for Beauvoir." That Beauvoir, as well as Merleau-Ponty, led him out of these difficulties is supported by Sartre's account of the subject as embodied—as an agent of praxis—in his *Critique of Dialectical Reason*. In that later text, "Sartre uses the term 'destiny'—Beauvoir's term from *The Second Sex*—to describe such a praxis alienated from itself" "by oppression," and bases his fullest discussion of "destiny" on a woman, a low-paid woman factory worker.

Kate and Edward Fullbrook, in Chapter 6, provide the most radical challenge to the canonical interpretation of Beauvoir's relationship to existentialism, arguing that Beauvoir, in her novel *She Came to Stay*, created the existential philosophy made famous by Sartre in *Being and Nothingness*. The Fullbrooks, authors of a 1994 biography of Beauvoir and Sartre, describe the research on Sartre's posthumously published *War Diaries* and Beauvoir's *Lettres à Sartre* that led to their discovery of Beauvoir's influence. Drawing on an analogy with science, the Fullbrooks describe how various anomalies led them to reject the traditional theory of the Beauvoir/Sartre relationship—including the theory of Beauvoir's intellectual subservience. Intrigued by evidence in the letters that popular theories about their intimate lives were not true, the Fullbrooks were led to consider a reinterpretation of their intellectual relationship as well.

Convinced by scholarly evidence of Beauvoir's philosophical influence on Sartre's postwar social philosophy, the Fullbrooks began looking for evidence that Beauvoir had contributed, even if in a minor way, to the philosophical system found in Sartre's *Being and Nothingness*. They used Sartre's *War Diaries* and the correspondence to construct a "calendar" of the development of "Sartrean" existentialism, determining that "the great watershed in the development of his philosophical system had come at the end of February 1940, in the week and a half immediately following his return from an eleven-day army leave in Paris," a leave during which Sartre read the manuscript of Beauvoir's novel *She Came to Stay*.

The Fullbrooks were already curious about this novel because of an anomaly they had discovered regarding its genesis. In *The Prime of Life* (1960), Beauvoir described *She Came to Stay* as being well under way in 1938, an account confirmed by other sources. But in an interview near the end of her life, Beauvoir claimed that she had barely begun the novel at the time of Sartre's February leave. Beauvoir's *Lettres à Sartre* confirms that her account in *The Prime of Life* is the truthful one and that Beauvoir had drafted at least five hundred pages of her novel by the time of Sartre's leave. When reading *The Prime of Life* in the late 1950s, the Fullbrooks argue, few people were "predisposed to believe in the possibility of a woman creating one of the major philosophical systems of her century. There was, therefore, no need for her to take pains to hide their ultimate secret. . . . But by the 1980s the climate of belief was changing." In the face of challenges by feminist scholars, Beauvoir was forced to take more aggressive evasive action.

In their conclusion, the Fullbrooks call for a scholarly decoding of Beauvoir's philosophy in *She Came to Stay*, a task begun in their own book with a detailed analysis of Beauvoir's first chapter and discussion of her contribution to "philosophy's two most central and intractable problems: the conceptual gap between appearance and reality, and the question of the existence of other people as conscious beings whose consciousnesses act on one another." Thus in an interesting historical twist, the Fullbrooks' return to *She Came to Stay*, the subject of Merleau-Ponty's essay "Metaphysics and the Novel" (1945a), provides a surprising answer to the question first posed by Hazel Barnes in 1955: Who authored the philosophy found in both the novel and Sartre's *Being and Nothingness?*

In Chapter 7, Jeffner Allen, who addresses all three issues debated in this volume—that is, Beauvoir's relationship to existentialism, the phallocentrism of philosophy, and the relation of philosophy to literature—focuses on what she calls Beauvoir's myth-making activities. Fullbrook and others exposed two myths about Beauvoir: (1) that she was heterosexual, and (2) that she was not a philosopher and had no philosophical influence on Sartre. Allen recognizes a third myth, dispelled by Francis's and Gontier's 1985 biography, that Beauvoir had grown up living a bourgeois life; and then she adds a fourth as the principal concern of her essay: that "[Beauvoir] was never discriminated against as a woman." In Allen's view the myths are Beauvoir's attempt to protect herself against the public's "peculiar hostility" to women's "mobility" that Beauvoir once described in an essay on Brigitte Bardot. Allen compares Beauvoir's relationship with Sartre, with existentialism, and with the "lineage of white European-born male philosophers" to the bitter, confined life of the married woman described by Beauvoir in *The Second Sex*. Leaving her letters for Sylvie Le Bon de Beauvoir to find strikes Allen as an angry, "naphthalenic gesture" akin to an embittered housewife's heedlessly flinging household chemicals about the house.

Reminding us that Beauvoir dedicated many of her books to women, and felt a deep sense of connection to women, Allen criticizes the Fullbrooks for characterizing Beauvoir's relationship with Zaza as an "allegorical device," despite the evidence in the notebooks and letters of Beauvoir's bisexuality, and argues that "Beauvoir's relation to a male lineage need not be, is not always, paramount." Understanding Beauvoir requires that we understand the complex dialectic of women's oppression and nurture women's ability to overcome it, which for Allen entails moving away from both "the heterosexual contract by which female becomes woman" and the philosophical canon, which offers little nourishment to women "as we witness this dialectic and as we heal within it and from it."

Allen asks: What account, then, can we give of Beauvoir's relationship to existentialism? She finds the Fullbrooks' evidence that Beauvoir had already produced a full statement of "Sartrean" existentialism in *She Came to Stay* convincing. But, since Sartre changed Beauvoir's ideas often beyond recognition, and denigrated others, as in *Being and Nothingness*, where woman's sexuality and nature become "holes and slime," Allen suggests that we "liberate Beauvoir from her intellectual marriage to Sartre" and find another context for reading her philosophy. Allen considers reading Beauvoir within the context of the broader existentialist movement, and suggests how such a project might proceed, noting, with Vintges and Holveck, Beauvoir's use of Husserl. But Allen ultimately rejects efforts to place Beauvoir within a philosophical movement that exploited and silenced her. Allen urges instead that we read Beauvoir in the context of her relationships with women, a project that requires that we "give up artificial distinctions between 'thinker' and 'literary writer,' " and abandon the drawing of disciplinary lines that "effects the conversion of assorted individuals from a movement into a canon."

Céline Léon (Chapter 8) provides both a clear statement of the charge of phallocentrism leveled against Beauvoir and a postmodernist critique of the "feminine difference" theories that first posed it in France. Léon focuses on Beauvoir's ambivalent stance toward sexual difference. Beauvoir criticizes Freud's view that "anatomy is destiny," as a basis for her claim that "one is not born a woman; one becomes a woman." But elsewhere in *The Second Sex,* as Léon points out, Beauvoir contradicts this denial of sexual difference by calling for "a healthy sense of alterity" and denouncing women who deny their femininity to assert themselves qua men.

Léon charges that Beauvoir's ambivalence toward sexual difference is compounded by her own puritanical attitude toward the body, her reliance on Hegelian dualisms devaluing immanence, and Sartre's neurotic influence. Léon describes Beauvoir's depictions of women's sexuality as "fictions of pollution, mutilation, humiliation, defilement, and wounded shame" that reflect Sartre's neurotic fear of the female body. Léon also criticizes Beauvoir for failing to appreciate the "glorification of the Feminine" found in writers such as Hélène Cixous, who believes that woman's voice must "displace the sterile echo of Western man's monologue." Beauvoir denounces this call for a specifically feminine discourse as "imprisonment of women in a ghetto of difference/singularity." But when she herself is forced to recognize the existence of feminine specificity, Beauvoir, according to Léon, "hesitates, goes this way and that, and, when cornered, runs to the masculine camp."

Léon's ultimate assessment, one influenced by Derrida, is that "Beauvoir finds herself trapped in phallocentrism and her feminism is nothing but the operation of a woman who aspires to be like a man and whose voice is that of the ventriloquist's dummy." But Léon criticizes écriture féminine for relying on the same masculine/feminine dualism found in Beauvoir and antifeminists. Her alternative is the dream of "an economy which, transcending the male/female, phallus/uterus opposition, would exalt the individual beyond all sexual differentiation." Referring to contemporary feminists as Electras who wish to murder their sexist mother, Léon acknowledges Beauvoir's contribution: "At least, there has begun a dialogue where there used to be a monologue—that of man with himself."

Kristana Arp agrees with Léon that Beauvoir's descriptions of female biology, as passive and immanent, are problematic. But, in an interesting turn that brings her closer to Vintges on this issue, Arp argues in Chapter 9 that we should discount these descriptions in the light of Beauvoir's "incisive account" of how female bodily experience is constructed through social or ideological means. Since immanence and transcendence are ontological attributes for Beauvoir, Arp argues, they cannot be manifested in biological structures. Thus the passivity of the female body is a social construction, the result of a social process of alienation. For support of this reading and her claim that Beauvoir escapes the Sartrean dualism at the heart of Léon's critique, Arp points (as Vintges and Kruks do) to Beauvoir's roots in the phenomenological movement, especially Merleau-Ponty's concept of the "lived-body." According to Arp, Beauvoir uses this concept to ground her critical appreciation for Freud, but differentiates her position from that of Merleau-Ponty by her claim that, while woman, like man *is* her body, her body is something other than her; that is, that woman is alienated in her body.

That women must accede to playing alienating roles implies that they might resist it in some fashion, which suggests to Arp that bodily alienation is "not originally a biological phenomenon" for Beauvoir but a social one. For evidence of women's agency under patriarchy, Arp looks at Beauvoir's example of female narcissism as an "attempt to realize the union with one's own body—one's own self—which has been denied through the process of bodily alienation." Further challenging the canonical reading of The Second Sex as Sartrean, still evident in Léon, Arp argues that it is not Sartre's concept of the Look that founds Beauvoir's theory of how a woman's body is objectified, but an alternative theory of how historically men have oppressed women as the Other. The female body as a real material presence becomes the site where oppression takes hold, as Beauvoir's study of myths and a glance at the depiction of women's bodies in advertising continues to show.

In an innovative reading of Ethics of Ambiguity and The Second Sex in the context of Beauvoir's later essay, "Must We Burn Sade?" Debra Bergoffen (Chapter 10) challenges both the charge of Beauvoir's phallocentrism and that she merely applied Sartre's philosophy. In a densely packed analysis Bergoffen argues that Beauvoir developed a set of philosophical principles in Ethics of Ambiguity that she used to understand the existential meaning of the concrete, whether in the individual existence of the particular man, the Marquis de Sade, or in the more diffuse particular circumstances of women, as in The Second Sex. Bergoffen carries forward the project of differentiating Beauvoir's philosophy from that of Sartre, emphasizing, as did Holveck, Beauvoir's use of Husserl and her methodological focus on concrete experience; focusing, as did Vintges, on Beauvoir's view of the body as situation; and arguing, as did Kruks but against Le Doeuff, that Ethics of Ambiguity is a key text for understanding Beauvoir's original contribution to philosophy.

In Ethics of Ambiguity Beauvoir, following the phenomenological tradition, defines consciousness as intentionality. Permeated by desire, consciousness is always of an object. In Bergoffen's reading, Beauvoir's break with Sartre comes in her identification of two moments of intentionality: the moment of disclosure of the object, and the moment of the desire to be the disclosed object. For Sartre, consciousness is immediately ensnared by the anxiety of freedom in this second moment, the moment of bad faith. But Beauvoir identifies a relationship between freedom and desire other than one of anxiety: the delight and joy to be found in disclosure itself. Beauvoir provides an original account for the continuing lure of bad faith, according to Bergoffen, not in ontology but history, as nostalgia for the securities of childhood, an explanation that, as Bergoffen points out, "empowers the situation in ways foreign to the analysis of *Being and Nothingness.*"

Tracing Beauvoir's account of relations with others not to Sartre's account of the Look, but (here siding with Le Doeuff) to Hegel's consciousnesses who seek each other's death, Bergoffen identifies two directions in which the desire to dominate the other struggles against itself. First, consciousness recognizes its disclosures as always grounded in a world already there, in a world opened up to us by our ancestors. Second, consciousness recognizes that without the other to challenge the meanings of my freedom, I risk forgetting the subjective source of my values. Following Husserl, Bergoffen argues, Beauvoir grounds her ethics in the intentionality of consciousness, which links it to the Other as fundamentally as it links it to the world.

In "Must We Burn Sade?" what interests Bergoffen is the tension between the Beauvoir "who claims to be Sartre's shadow" (affirming his affirmation of autonomy) and the Beauvoir "who moves out on her own" (undermining this affirmation, speaking against the domination of lucidity). Beauvoir respects Sade's effort to transform his sexuality from a given into an ethic, but she sees him as someone who understood but never experienced the ambiguity of the human condition in the erotic intoxication "where consciousness gives up its lucidity and intersects with the body to become flesh." Beauvoir's *The Second Sex,* according to Bergoffen, situates Sade's ethics of the erotic against another (feminist) ethics grounded in the courage to accept the risks of subjectivity and guided by the desires of disclosure and relation.

In *The Second Sex* Beauvoir's efforts to understand woman's complicity with domination, according to Bergoffen, uncover a different ontological dimension of being—the desire for reciprocity and the value of the bond. For Beauvoir, erotic love is a privileged human relationship where one lives out the strange ambiguity of existence made body, either in sadism/masochism as Sartre suggests, or as a consenting voluntary gift, in which my body is not the tool of domination but the passivity of my subjectivity. Thus, for Beauvoir, the Hegelian transcendence/immanence dichotomy is transformed, collapsing into "the ambiguous fluidity of all embodied subjects." In Bergoffen's interpretation of Beauvoir's philosophy, "the body could become the ground of a new social order, that draws upon the value of the bond without submitting to the alienation of bondage."

In Chapter 11, Barbara Klaw maintains the focus on female embodiment but employs the methodology of literary criticism in responding to criticisms that Beauvoir perpetuates patriarchal stereotypes of feminine sexuality. In a definitive reading of Beauvoir's philosophy of the erotic in the novel *Les Mandarins*, Klaw argues that Beauvoir presents sexuality from the point of view of a woman trying to express her desires within the confines of a culturally repressive world. Stereotypes are thus represented, but in order to be violated. According to Klaw, for Beauvoir female sexuality is active, bisexuality is a real possibility, and each woman has numerous erogenous zones that comprise her erotic pleasure. Beauvoir's violation of patriarchal stereotypes is evident in the novel's plot, textual strategy (for example, the central female character, Anne, accounts for 61 percent of the novel's second volume and has the last word), derisive allusions to Freud (for example, Anne is a psychoanalyst who ridicules Freud and focuses on her own pleasure in her love scenes), compromising situations for both men and women, her mockery of myths and stereotypes, and objectification of the male body and subjectification of the female.

One of the most interesting elements of Klaw's strategy for reading *Les Mandarins* is her use of postmodern theorists such as Irigaray, and Beauvoir's posthumously published letters and notebooks to understand how women "assume their gender" under patriarchal culture. Klaw agrees with Allen that Beauvoir's experiences and representations of her sexuality reflect her oppression as a woman. Klaw uses examples from Beauvoir's letters describing her sexual experiences with her female lovers to suggest how Beauvoir's treatment of her female characters provided her with an opportunity to represent sexual feelings and experiences she could not include in her autobiographies. In a dramatic challenge to accounts such as Léon's, Klaw reads Beauvoir, with Bergoffen, as glorifying lovemaking and revalorizing the female body. "Through the concrete examples of the awareness of all senses, the poetic description of the body, the use of voice, and reference to creation myths, *Les Mandarins* suggests the myriad ways woman as opposed to man has a more authentic experience of the sexual self," a judgment Beauvoir had defended in *The Second Sex*.

Julie Ward, in Chapter 12, also rejects the charge of phallocentrism leveled against Beauvoir. Using a methodology of philosophical analysis in contrast to the phenomenological approach we have seen in several of the other chapters in this collection, Ward sides with Klaw against both Léon and Arp in denying that Beauvoir's depiction of the female body reflects a negative, and thus "masculinist," stance. She also rejects the claim that Beauvoir's remarks on women's biology constitute biological reductionism or determinism as many critics charge. Ward's response to the apparent contradictions that troubled Léon in Beauvoir's account of women's biology is an attempt to reconcile them, taking the structure of the work as central to its interpretation. Ward finds that Beauvoir employs two distinct levels of analysis in *The Second Sex.* In volume one, the level of abstract constructs with which male thinkers theorize about women; and in volume two, the level of women's experience under patriarchy. Since the myths and theories in volume one constitute a part of the theoretical framework of patriarchy, which Beauvoir explicitly criticizes, Ward argues that it would be naive to assume, as gynocentric critics do, that Beauvoir subscribes to them. Thus Ward concludes that Beauvoir is not committed to the negative views of woman's body that she mentions, which is why Beauvoir distinguishes the "biological" treatment of the body from her own way of accounting for it.

Beauvoir's account employs two senses of the body: a Cartesian sense of the body as a thing, a biological mechanism, which she rejects; and a second, anti-Cartesian sense of the body as experienced, as "an historical idea, not a natural fact." Thus Ward, with Vintges and Arp, reads Beauvoir's view of the body not as biological reductionist or determinist but as social constructivist, a view as influenced by the analysis of determinacy found in historical materialism as the description of choice found in existentialism. According to Ward, Beauvoir's most controversial account of female experience, that of maternity as "enslavement to the species," is a description of the female body under patriarchy. The value of maternity and pregnancy depends upon the *situation* of the woman; that is, her political, economic, social context. For Ward, as for Holveck, Beauvoir's project in *The Second Sex* is to appreciate the plurality, heterogeneity, and complexities of women's experience, a project that makes Beauvoir a precursor of Léon's individualist stance as well.

My own essay (Chapter 13) shares an analytic philosophical methodology with Ward but addresses another issue defined by Pilardi: the relationship of Beauvoir's feminism to socialism and the charge by socialist-feminist philosophers that Beauvoir's text is philosophically and historically insignificant, unrelated to the development of either socialist feminism or radical feminism. I argue on the contrary that *The Second Sex* laid the philosophical foundation for radical feminism, and that Beauvoir's theory, rather than being irrelevant to contemporary socialist feminism, actually defined many of its points of differentiation from traditional Marxist analysis. Drawing on a recent history of the 1960s radical feminist movement for a definition of radical feminism, I argue that Beauvoir's philosophy in *The Second Sex* meets the criterion: Beauvoir argues that women's oppression is irreducible to any other form of oppression, a position that draws on an analogy with racial oppression and defines the central tenet of radical feminism.

Beauvoir's perspective was shaped by an awareness of the African-American struggle against racial oppression and a critical, leftist engagement with Marxism, as well as a critique of Freudian psychoanalysis, a political and ideological context shared by later radical feminists of the 1960s. My article lends support to the interpretive consensus emerging in this volume that Beauvoir was a social constructionist. Indeed, I argue that she explicitly denied that sexual dimorphism had any ontological foundation. I also agree that her philosophical methodology privileges descriptions of women's experience as the basis for her rejection of the prejudiced accounts of women's "nature" in science, and the feminist views that women's oppression is historically unchanging or absolute, or that feminism is a commitment to an essentialist definition of woman-identity. I emphasize the transgressive elements of Beauvoir's philosophy in calling for collective struggle by women and, with Klaw, note how Beauvoir's analysis undermines normative heterosexuality. In conclusion I argue that feminists searching for an alternative to essentialist politics in radical feminism should consider the historical and philosophical foundation of many of its limitations and merits in *The Second Sex*.

Julien Murphy addresses in Chapter 14 the final issue identified by Pilardi, the charges against Beauvoir of ethnocentrism and false universalism, as well as the issue of Beauvoir's relationship to philosophy, in this case postmodernism as well as existentialism, in her discussion of Beauvoir's development of a postcolonial ethic. Like Bergoffen, Murphy analyzes a little-known text, in this case a book on the 1954–62 Algerian war, which Beauvoir coauthored with Gisèle Halimi, *Djamila Boupacha* (1962). According to Murphy, the Algerian war, which marked the end of French colonialism, also marked Beauvoir's transformation into a politically engaged intellectual. One might argue, as I do in my chapter, that writing *The Second Sex* marked an earlier act of Beauvoir's political engagement. But Murphy identifies two factors that make Beauvoir's Algerian writings unique: (1) neither the Nazi Holocaust nor American racism threatened her sense of identity as did the atrocities committed in Algeria by France, and (2) it was during the Algerian war that Beauvoir first became a political activist in an organized movement.

Murphy argues that Beauvoir's Algerian writings reflect the development of a postcolonial ethics anticipated in *Ethics of Ambiguity,* an ethics that sets her war writings philosophically apart from those of Sartre as well as from other writers, such as Camus, who refused to support Algerian independence. The focal point of Beauvoir's involvement was women in the Algerian war, and her most explicit political action was taking up the case in 1960 of Djamila Boupacha, a young Algerian Muslim student who was accused of planting a bomb and was arrested, tortured, and raped with a bottle by French officials who forced her confession. Murphy reports that Boupacha would have undoubtedly been executed had it not been for the efforts of Halimi, her lawyer, and Beauvoir, who wrote an article for the French newspaper *Le Monde* filled with moral outrage in her defense. The French government ordered the seizure in Algeria of all copies of the paper containing her article, provoking an international response in support of Boupacha. Beauvoir formed and chaired a political action committee that petitioned for the adjournment of the trial and made the public aware for the first time of the French army's routine use of torture and rape.

According to Murphy, Beauvoir's political writings on the war, which have been overlooked by scholars, contribute to the development of Beauvoir's concrete view of freedom, as situated within an intersubjective context, and subject to political and social limitations begun in *Ethics of Ambiguity* and *The Second Sex.* In addition, they differentiate her philosophically from Sartre, for whom the gaze of others objectivized us and limited our possibilities. For Beauvoir, Murphy reminds us, "the gaze afforded moral possibilities and gave moral content to subjectivity." Beauvoir was moved to moral outrage and political action after imagining how Algerian rebels must have perceived her, a French woman. Her attitude was not detached and distanced, but personal; her writings became autobiographical: the war led her to look back nostalgically on the middle-class French culture of her past and "say good-bye to it forever."

Murphy's analysis of how various identities are represented and deconstructed by the Boupacha case and its representations is the subject of her interesting concluding section, which locates a shared political context for reading Beauvoir's writings and the postmodern philosophy of deconstruction. Murphy examines the politics of representations of Boupacha in Halimi's and Beauvoir's writings and their dominant discourses on virginity and torture as they tried to make Boupacha, a Muslim woman, visible but not as the hated Other. As Beauvoir and Halimi constructed representations of Boupacha, Murphy argues, they were also aware of "how their own identities were undone by the war." Recognizing the difficulty of cultural identity in a postcolonial context, Murphy observes that "It is no surprise that a new philosophy, deconstruction, would emerge from France after the war." Deconstruction, founded by a former Algerian Jew, Jacques Derrida, can be easily applied to Beauvoir's own situation, according to Murphy, since her own identity was deconstructed by the war. Murphy implies several reasons that Beauvoir, instead of being philosophically surpassed by the emergence of deconstruction, might contribute to it: (1) deconstruction moves us to a more ambiguous concept of liberation "compatible with Beauvoir's description of subjectivity"; (2) Beauvoir saw her life as shaped, not by stages of biological development, but "by historical moments. . . . Part of her radical perspective is her belief that historical events of our time are rites of passage for us"; and (3) the deconstruction of cultural identities by war "presents us with moral and political challenges" to which Beauvoir's philosophy responds by indicating "possibilities for reconstruction through recognizing our bonds to others."

The new interpretations of Beauvoir's philosophy offered by the authors in this collection (and there are more that could have been included) have raised more questions than they have settled. Nor do the new readings made possible by the posthumously published letters and notebooks always show Beauvoir in a positive light. The early period of uncritical feminist identification with Beauvoir is over. Now, aided by Beauvoir's decision to preserve her notebooks and letters, and by Sylvie Le Bon de Beauvoir's courageous decision to publish them, scholars have largely abandoned the matricide described by Léon, for an effort to understand Beauvoir, for the person she was and the philosophy she created.

Notes

1. I am indebted to Francis and Gontier (1987, 49) for this explanation of the French educational system. It was Francis and Gontier who first reported evidence of the impoverishment of Beauvoir's family after World War I and made use of the Nelson Algren correspondence housed in the archives at Ohio State University.
2. See Deirdre Bair's *Simone de Beauvoir: A Biography* (1990, 654n) for a discussion of Léon and Cécile Brunschvicg. Bair's biography contains a wealth of information, much of it gathered from interviews, but unfortunately it is plagued by errors.
3. See Lacoin (1991) for Zaza's notebooks and letters, including those to her friend, Simone de Beauvoir.
4. See Susan Rubin Suleiman (1992) for a critical discussion of Beauvoir's activities during the Occupation.
5. See Isabelle de Courtivron (1986) for a discussion of Beauvoir's relationship with Leduc, whose earliest publications are in the first volume of *Les Temps Modernes*. Beauvoir also wrote a preface to Leduc's novel *La Bâtarde* (1964a).

References

Ascher, Carol. 1981. *Simone de Beauvoir: A Life of Freedom*. Boston: Beacon.

Barnes, Hazel. 1959. *The Literature of Possibility: A Study in Humanistic Existentialism*. Lincoln: University of Nebraska Press.

Barrett, William. 1958. *Irrational Man: A Study in Existential Philosophy*. Garden City, N.Y.: Doubleday.

Beauvoir, Simone de. 1943. *L'Invitée*. Paris: Gallimard. Translated as *She Came To Stay*, by Y. Moyse and R. Senhouse. Cleveland: World Publishing, 1954.

———. 1944. *Pyrrhus et Cinéas*. Paris: Gallimard.

———. 1945a. *Les Bouches inutiles*. Paris: Gallimard. Translated as *Who Shall Die*, by C. Francis and F. Gontier. Florissant, Mo.: River Press. 1983.

———. 1945b. "*La Phénoménologie de la perception de Maurice Merleau-Ponty.*" *Les Temps Modernes* 1:363–67.

———. 1945c. *Le Sang des autres*. Paris: Gallimard. Translated as *The Blood of Others*, by Y. Moyse and R. Senhouse. New York: Knopf, 1948.

———. 1946a. "Littérature et métaphysique." *Les Temps Modernes* 7:1153–63. Reprinted in *L'Existentialisme et la sagesse des nations*, 89–107. Paris: Nagel, 1948.

———. 1946b. *Tous les hommes sont mortels*. Paris: Gallimard. Translated as *All Men Are Mortal*, by Friedman. Cleveland: World Publishing, 1955.

———. 1947. *Pour une morale de l'ambiguïté*. Paris: Gallimard. Translated as *The Ethics of Ambiguity*, by B. Frechtman. New York: Philosophical Library, 1948.

———. 1948a. *L'Amérique au jour le jour*. Paris: Mohrien. Translated as *America Day by Day*, by P. Dudley. New York: Grove. 1953.

———. 1948b. *L'Existentialisme et la sagesse des nations*. Paris: Nagel.

———. 1949. *Le Deuxième Sexe*. 2 vols. Paris: Gallimard. Translated as *The Second Sex*, by H. M. Parshley. New York: Knopf, 1952.

———. [1952] 1966. "Must We Burn Sade?" In *The Marquis de Sade*, translated by A. Michelson, New York: Grove Press.

———. 1954. *Les Mandarins*. Paris: Gallimard. Translated as *The Mandarins*, by L. Friedman. Cleveland: World Publishing, 1956.

———. 1955a. "Merleau-Ponty et le pseudo-Sartrisme." In her *Privilèges*, 203–72. Paris: Gallimard. Translated as "Merleau-Ponty and Pseudo-Sartreanism," by V. Zaytzeff and F. Morrison. *International Studies in Philosophy* 21, no. 3 (1989): 3–48.

———. 1955b. *Privilèges*. Paris: Gallimard.

———. 1957. *La Longue Marche: Essai sur la Chine*. Paris: Gallimard. Translated as *The Long March*, by A. Wainhouse. Cleveland: World Publishing, 1958.

———. 1958. *Mémoires d'une jeune fille rangée*. Paris: Gallimard. Translated as *Memoirs of a Dutiful Daughter*, by J. Kirkup. Cleveland: World Publishing, 1959.

———. 1960. *La Force de l'âge*. Paris: Gallimard. Translated as *The Prime of Life*, by P. Green. Cleveland: World Publishing, 1962.

———. 1963. *La Force des choses*. Paris: Gallimard. Translated as *Force of Circumstance*, by R. Howard. New York: Putnam, 1965.

———. 1964a. Preface to *La Bâtarde* by Violette Leduc, 7–18. Paris: Gallimard.

———. 1964b. *Une Mort très douce*. Paris: Gallimard. Translated as *A Very Easy Death*, by P. O'Brian. New York: Putnam, 1966.

———. 1966a. *Les Belles Images*. Paris: Gallimard. Translated as *Les Belles Images*, by P. O'Brian. New York: Putnam, 1968.

———. 1966b. Preface to *Treblinka*, by J. Steiner, 7–11. Paris: Arthème Fayard.

———. 1968. *La Femme rompue*. Paris: Gallimard. Translated as *The Woman Destroyed*, by P. O'Brian. New York: Putnam, 1969.

———. 1970. *La Vieillesse*. Paris: Gallimard. Translated as *The Coming of Age*, by P. O'Brian. New York: Putnam, 1972.

———. 1972. *Tout compte fait*. Paris: Gallimard. Translated as *All Said and Done*, by P. O'Brian. New York: Putnam, 1974.

———. 1973. Preface to *Avortement: Une Loi en procès; L'Affaire de Bobigny*, 11–14. Association Choisir. Paris: Gallimard.

———. 1975. "Présentation." *Les Femmes s'entêtent*. Paris: Gallimard, 11–13.

———. 1976. Preface to *Crimes Against Women: Proceedings of the International Tribunal*, xiii–xiv, edited by D. H. Russell and N. Van de Ven. Millbrae, Calif.: Les Femmes.

———. 1979. *Quand prime le spirituel*. Paris: Gallimard. Translated as *When Things of the Spirit Come First: Five Early Tales*, by P. O'Brian. New York: Pantheon Books, 1982.

———. 1981. *La Cérémonie des adieux*. Paris: Gallimard. Translated as *Adieux: A Farewell to Sartre*, by P. O'Brian. New York: Pantheon, 1984.

———. 1990a. *Journal de guerre: Septembre 1939–Janvier 1941*. Edited by Sylvie Le Bon de Beauvoir. Paris: Gallimard.

———. 1990b. *Lettres à Sartre*. 2 vols. Edited by Sylvie Le Bon de Beauvoir. Paris: Gallimard. Translated and edited as *Letters to Sartre*, by Quintin Hoare. New York: Little, Brown, 1992.

———, and Gisèle Halimi. 1962. *Djamila Boupacha*. Paris: Gallimard. Translated as *Djamila Boupacha: The Story of a Young Algerian Girl which Shocked Liberal French Opinion*, by P. Green. New York: Macmillan, 1962.

Blackham, H. J. 1965. *Reality, Man and Existence: Essential Works of Existentialism*. New York: Bantam Books.

Breisach, Ernst. 1962. *Introduction to Modern Existentialism*. New York: Grove Press.

Collins, James. 1952. *The Existentialists: A Critical Study*. Chicago: H. Regnery.

Courtivron, Isabelle de. 1986. "From Bastard to Pilgrim: Rites and Writing for Madame." In *Simone de Beauvoir: Witness to a Century*, edited by Hélène Wenzel. Special Issue of *Yale French Studies* 72:133–48.

Edwards, Paul, ed. 1967. *The Encyclopedia of Philosophy*. 8 vols. New York: Collier Macmillan.

Firestone, Shulamith. 1970. *The Dialectic of Sex: The Case for Feminist Revolution*. New York: Bantam Books.

Francis, Claude, and Fernande Gontier. 1987. *Simone de Beauvoir: A Life . . . A Love Story*. Translated by L. Nesselson. New York: St. Martin's.

Fullbrook, Kate, and Edward Fullbrook. 1994. *Simone de Beauvoir and Jean-Paul Sartre: The Remaking of a Twentieth-Century Legend*. New York: Basic Books.

Heineman, F. H. 1958. *Existentialism and the Modern Predicament*. New York: Harper and Row.

Kaufmann, Walter, ed. 1956. *Existentialism from Dostoevsky to Sartre*. Cleveland: World Publishing.

Kojève, Alexandre. 1969. *Introduction to the Reading of Hegel*. Translated by J. Nichols. New York: Basic Books.

Lacoin, Elisabeth. 1991. *Zaza: Correspondence et carnets d'Elisabeth Lacoin, 1914–1929*. Paris: Seuil.

Le Doeuff, Michèle. 1979. "Operative Philosophy: Simone de Beauvoir and Existentialism." *Ideology and Consciousness* 6:47–57. Reprinted in *Critical Essays on Simone de Beauvoir*, edited by Elaine Marks, 144–54. Boston: G. K. Hall, 1987. A revised version, "Simone de Beauvoir and Existentialism," was published in *Feminist Studies* 6, no. 2 (Summer 1980): 277–89.

———. 1989. *L'Etude et le rouet*. Paris: Seuil. Translated as *Hipparchia's Choice: An Essay Concerning Women, Philosophy, Etc.*, by T. Selous. Cambridge, Mass.: Basil Blackwell, 1991.

Merleau-Ponty, Maurice. 1945a. *Phénoménologie de la Perception*. Translated as *Phenomenology of Perception*, by C. Smith. New York: Humanities Press, 1962.

———. 1945b. "Le Roman et la Métaphysique." *Cahiers du Sud*, no. 270 (March) Translated as "Metaphysics and the Novel," by H. Dreyfus and P. Dreyfus, in *Sense and Non-Sense*, 26–40. Evanston: Northwestern University Press, 1964.

Millett, Kate. 1969. *Sexual Politics*. Garden City, N.Y.: Avon Books.

Patterson, Yolanda A. 1986. "Simone de Beauvoir and the Demystification of Motherhood." In *Simone de Beauvoir: Witness to a Century*. Special issue of *Yale French Studies* 72:87–105.

Rabil, Albert, Jr. 1967. *Merleau-Ponty: Existentialist of the Social World*. New York: Columbia University Press.

Sartre, Jean-Paul. [1960] 1976. *Critique of Dialectical Reason*. Translated by A. Sheridan-Smith. Edited by Jonathan Rée. London: NLB.

———. 1983. *Lettres au Castor*. 2 vols. Edited by Simone de Beauvoir. Paris: Gallimard. Translated as *Witness to My Life: The Letters of Jean-Paul Sartre to Simone de Beauvoir, 1926–1939*, by L. Fahnestock and N. McAfee. New York: Scribner.

Simons, Margaret A. 1990. "Sexism and the Philosophical Canon: On Reading Beauvoir's *The Second Sex*." *Journal of the History of Ideas* 51, no. 3: 487–504.

———. 1992. "Lesbian Connections: Simone de Beauvoir and Feminism." *Signs: Journal of Women in Culture and Society* 18, no. 1: 136–61.

Spelman, Elisabeth V. 1988. *Inessential Woman: Problems of Exclusion in Feminist Thought*. Boston: Beacon.

Suleiman, Susan Rubin. 1992. "Life-Story, History, Fiction: Reflections on Simone de Beauvoir's Wartime Writings." *Contention: Debates in Society, Culture and Science* 1, no. 2 (Winter): 1–21.

Wahl, Jean. [1947]. *A Short History of Existentialism*. Translated by F. Williams and S. Maron. New York: Wisdom Library.

1

Feminists Read *The Second Sex*

Jo-Ann Pilardi

If we accept as a criterion for a book's being considered a classic that it creates a new paradigm; that is, that it virtually "reorients our most basic way of viewing an object or a concept,"[1] then *The Second Sex* is surely a classic. However, Beauvoir's book did not enjoy the in-depth attention of scholarly analysis, either in France or in the United States (where the first translation of the work appeared), for nearly twenty years following its publication, prior to the feminist movement's attention to it begin-

I would like to thank the Faculty Research Committee of Towson State University for its support; the grant gave me the precious time I needed to begin research for this article. Julia Perkins and Ann-Louise Shapiro, two editors at *History and Theory*, must also be mentioned and thanked for their encouragement and the fine editing they contributed to the original version of this article, which appeared in *History and Theory* 32 (1993).

ning in the 1970s.[2] Before that there were few books and articles published on *The Second Sex*. Since then, however, a body of feminist scholarly writings has developed, a large part of it dating from 1979, when the thirtieth anniversary of the book's publication was honored by a major international conference in New York and by various publications spawned by the conference and anniversary. At present, studies of the book come primarily from feminists, particularly philosophers who identify themselves as feminists, and from biographers and other critics and writers in the literary tradition. With very few exceptions, other philosophers in the philosophic tradition out of which Simone de Beauvoir wrote, existential-phenomenology, have not studied the book.[3]

The power of *The Second Sex* resides in Beauvoir's articulation of a new analysis of woman: the notion that woman is the Other. Her central thesis is that women are patriarchally forced into immanence (the "brutish life of things, the passivity of a pure object"); it is an argument about the denial of the freedom of one subject (or whole group) by another. But because Beauvoir's conception of otherness is dialectical, the book manages not to be about "woman" only, but about "man," about both, about humanity under patriarchy, about "gender" as we have come to understand it since *The Second Sex* was published.

Social theorist Elizabeth Janeway's early and popular book, *Man's World: Woman's Place*, cited the Beauvoirian theory of woman as Other in tracing the connections between female behavior and the behavior of any subordinate group.[4] But the attention of feminists to Beauvoir was expressed as an appreciation not only of her work but of her life, in an interesting reversal of the original French scandal that greeted the book.[5] When Shulamith Firestone dedicated *The Dialectic of Sex* to "Simone de Beauvoir, who kept her integrity," undoubtedly it was the connection of the theories in *The Second Sex* to Beauvoir's personal refusal of both marriage and motherhood, as well as her political activism, to which Firestone referred.[6] In recent years, Beauvoir's life and her relationship to Sartre have come under increasing scrutiny, through Deirdre Bair's biography of her and with the publication of Sartre's letters to her and her letters to Sartre.[7] In a special issue of *L'Arc* devoted to Simone de Beauvoir, French feminist Yvette Roudy noted that *The Second Sex* "constitutes, for American feminists, a veritable Bible, of the same sort as the writings of Engels."[8] Beauvoir herself was careful to distinguish her book's importance to feminists from the question of the *origin* of contemporary American feminism and maintained that the movement's real source was the "anti-imperialist movement" (the outcry against the war in Vietnam).[9] Whether or not we call *The Second Sex* a cause of twentieth-century feminism or simply claim that its discovery by feminists was an *effect* of the emergent feminist movement, its usefulness to the movement was already indisputably accepted in the 1970s.[10]

With the rediscovery of *The Second Sex* by the feminist movement, however, and as feminist issues developed into feminist theory, feminist philosophy, and feminist critique, an increasing gap began to open among the movement, its bible, and its mother. Feminists differed among themselves about the meaning of Beauvoir's discussion of women's biology, worried about the influence of Sartre and the masculinist bias that they thought they saw in some of Beauvoir's work, and struggled to identify both the radical potential in her writing and its limitations. As the field of feminist scholarship has grown, the subtlety of discussion of *The Second Sex* has grown correspondingly. A review of those issues raised by critics of *The Second Sex* during the 1980s and early 1990s represents a cross-section of nearly all of the major theoretical debates within feminism in the late twentieth century. Unable to explore adequately these debates here, I've created a catalogue of the major issues and included what I hope is enough detail and bibliographic information to allow the reader to pursue the important and lively discussions that have arisen in the current dialogues with *The Second Sex*.

The Second Sex and Existentialism

A number of critics have complained of *The Second Sex*'s lack of attention to feminist praxis, that is, to specific plans for accomplishing the liberation of women from patriarchal oppression.[11] Some tie this weakness to the book's connection to existentialism and "male thinking."[12] French philosopher Michèle Le Doeuff was probably the first to begin a detailed study of the connection between *The Second Sex* and French existentialism, particularly the work of Jean-Paul Sartre. Le Doeuff maintained that because early Sartrean existentialism was focused on the individual and the individual's ability to choose her/his actions, it denied that one's acts could be determined; thus it became impossible to conceptualize oppression (for women or any other group). Women's oppression, as described in *The Second Sex*, would have been literally oppression without a cause. With existentialist ethics as her foundation, Beauvoir's position remained in liberal political theory; using theories such as John Stuart Mill's, whom she quoted a number of times, she was able to discuss an oppressed group, women, and their possible liberation.[13]

Contradictions between Sartrean existentialism and the theory of *The Second Sex* have been pointed out by a number of critics studying not only *The Second Sex* but Beauvoir's autobiographies and indeed the whole body of her work, with some suggesting a significant Beauvoir-to-Sartre influence as well.[14] Jeffner Allen, studying existentialism as a variant of patriarchal thought, maintained that *The Second Sex* represented the end of traditional existentialism, because it problematized the well-worked connection among the "existentialist hero," the "god," and the human "existent"; Beauvoir's presentation of the experience of women's lives confused this elementary formula, Allen said.[15] Traditionally, however, critics of *The Second Sex* have assumed that the doctrine of radical freedom contained in Sartrean existentialism led Beauvoir to the conclusion that women were more than their anatomy, that is, that though female biological functions played an important role in women's lives, nevertheless women need not be "determined" by them, nor by any factors.[16] In her study of the concept of "situation" in existentialism, Sonia Kruks differentiated the Beauvoirian brand of existentialism found in *The Second Sex* from Sartre's version in a number of ways; most notably she maintained that Beauvoir's notion of subjectivity stressed situatedness, while at the same time stressing the notion of a "general situation" shared by a group.[17] Along these lines, others have described Beauvoir's innovations in existentialism as the creation of a new concept of the self.[18]

The Second Sex and Dualism: Transcendence/Immanence; Same/Other

Existentialism remained, nevertheless, an ambiguous legacy for feminists. Jean Leighton, for example, objected to Beauvoir's use of the Sartrean dichotomy between transcendence and immanence. Leighton maintained that this not only led her to "destroy motherhood altogether" but to privilege the so-called masculine world of transcendence; it seemed to Leighton that Beauvoir's "scorn for her own sex outweighs her compassion."[19] Both Leighton and Dorothy Kaufmann (McCall) referred to a line in *The Second Sex* that lent credence to an uncomfortable idea that had been developing among feminists: that Beauvoir's thinking was what Americans might call "male-identified" and what French feminists were already calling "phallocentric."[20] In an attempt to explain why women have been the Other throughout history, Beauvoir had said, in a chilling passage: "it is not in giving life but in risking life that man is raised above the animal; that is why superiority has been accorded in humanity not to the sex that brings forth but to that which kills."[21] In this statement, which Beauvoir went on to say held "the key to the whole mystery," she had unquestioningly grafted Sartrean ontology onto her complex social-political-historical-literary study of women. The result was an argument (and one contrary to what Sartrean existentialism maintained) that concluded that there *were* natural hierarchical givens within the human race, that is, that there was a sort of natural order of superiority and inferiority: male and female.

Similarly, Moira Gatens argued that *The Second Sex* contained "a philosophical dualism of the most orthodox kind," in that it presupposed the nature/culture distinction, and located the inferiority of women in female biology, so that women "simply *are* absolutely Other."[22] Charlene Haddock Seigfried, pointing to the problem of an ambiguity in *The Second Sex* between transcendence as male-defined and transcendence as non-gender-specific, called it a "category mistake" that made the creation of specifically female values impossible, since all transcendence would be based on the male norm.[23] Nancy Hartsock described this as a form of "abstract masculinity," a characteristic of the thought of Lévi-Strauss also, noting (as had many others) Beauvoir's assumption of the superiority of "risking life" over giving life.[24]

Shifting the terms of the discussion, Alice Jardine posed the question of dualism differently for American feminists, noting as the significant dualism of *The Second Sex* that of same/other, rather than transcendence/immanence. "Is there a way to think outside the patriarchally determined Same/Other, Subject/Object dichotomies diagnosed as the fact of culture by Simone de Beauvoir thirty years ago, and, in the process, still include woman as a presence?" she asked.[25] Jardine's remarks represented a turn toward postmodernist discussions in which the construction of a different notion of the subject (self) was emerging. Dorothy Kaufmann did a helpful review of the arguments against *The Second Sex* already made by the French "feminine difference" theorists, many of whom had called *The Second Sex* "masculinist." Kaufmann alluded to the Oedipal drama, a favorite of the psychoanalytically oriented "new French feminists," noting that the French "Daughters" were in fact imitating the masculine models (Lacan and Derrida) who had overthrown "Fathers" (such as Sartre), by rejecting the Mother (Beauvoir).[26] Kaufmann suggested connection with, rather than rejection of, "our first generation feminist Mother, even as we move beyond her limitations."[27]

The Second Sex, Biology, and Motherhood

Much of the debate on maternity theory in *The Second Sex* had its origins in arguments about the theoretical implications of the immanence/transcendence dualism for Beauvoir. Canadian theorist Mary O'Brien claimed that *The Second Sex* did not value highly enough women's ability to reproduce, nor did it give enough attention to historical variations of Otherness; rather, a rigid existentialist theory of immanence and transcendence had, she argued, been grafted onto the experience of women and their reproductive histories, so that Beauvoir was locked into a masculinist *anti-physis*, whereby immanence was "natural" and equated with the biological, and whereby a distinctly masculine hierarchy was accepted that assigned greater value to sexuality and sexual freedom than to reproduction, that is, to motherhood.[28]

Yet some feminist writings incorporated Beauvoir's insights on maternity. In *The Mermaid and the Minotaur*, a book that was one of the first to present an American "difference theory," Dorothy Dinnerstein relied heavily on ideas from *The Second Sex*. Beauvoir's analysis of the mythology surrounding the Earth Mother and her descriptions of the hostility within mother/son and mother/daughter relations was useful in making Dinnerstein's case that the female/mother is resented and scapegoated.[29] She disputed, however, Beauvoir's notion of transcendence; Dinnerstein felt it privileged the male world and man's work over the traditional female world of feeling and child care, so that one might conclude that "freedom" as Beauvoir understood it exclusively meant that women must enter the male world.[30]

In contrast to the many early reviewers of the book who had claimed that *The Second Sex* misunderstood maternity, radical feminist Adrienne

Rich began with Beauvoir's discussion of maternity, but with maternal power rather than reproductive maternity. Rich saw an obvious coherence to Beauvoir's claim that patriarchal civilization would include a fear of maternity and maternal power and a consequent need to control it and claim superiority for the male; since "it was as Mother that woman was fearsome, it is in maternity that she must be transfigured and enslaved," Rich remarked.[31] A later critic, reviewing Rich's own book, compared its analysis of motherhood with Beauvoir's analysis in *The Second Sex*, but was not as sympathetic to the book as Rich had been. Criticizing its fundamentally negative description of motherhood, Carol Christ concluded that Beauvoir believed motherhood was essentially a function of the "flesh," and consequently was devalued by Sartrean existentialism.

Because, then, *The Second Sex* had suggested that maternity is merely biological, and as more attention was being given to "maternal practice," feminists in the 1980s and 1990s increasingly challenged this aspect of the book.[32] But even as feminist critics have found much to fault in the analysis of maternity in *The Second Sex*, many continued to acknowledge the political importance of it (in spite of its flaws) in opening the discussion of maternity and maternal instinct, in short, in being one of the first texts to "break the taboo on motherhood."[33]

Love, Sexuality, Even "Marriage," in *The Second Sex*

Some critics have claimed that Sartre's ambivalence and even disgust for sex pervades *The Second Sex*, primarily in Beauvoir's descriptions of sexuality and her discussion of maternity.[34] Others question Beauvoir's consistency in thinking through women's sexuality, suggesting that she was at best inconsistent and at worst phallocentric in her descriptions of female eroticism.[35] An early study by Suzanne Lilar, *Le Malentendu du deuxième sexe* (The Misunderstanding of *The Second Sex*), had raised this issue. Lilar's book maintained that biological differences between the sexes are crucial, and blamed Sartre for Beauvoir's minimization of them.[36] Claiming that for the most part Beauvoir had really said nothing new, Lilar did, however, underline Beauvoir's analysis of female eroticism, especially her claim that there is a certain "aggressive eroticism" that may orient women toward homosexuality. Though sarcastic in tone and excessively harsh toward Beauvoir, Lilar's book was prophetic about the development of ideas from French feminists like Luce Irigaray, Julia Kristeva, and Hélène Cixous, first presented to Americans in the popular anthology *New French Feminisms*.[37]

To some critics, Beauvoir's attention to the heterosexual "couple" in *The Second Sex* seemed a betrayal of her revolutionary discussion of homosexuality (for which she was pilloried by early French critics); in pointing to this problem, Claudia Card suggested that a new vocabulary is needed to describe sexual preference, one in which, for example, "attitude" might replace the simple "free versus determined" dichotomy in which the problem was usually posed.[38] Ann Ferguson, in agreement with Card on the originality of Beauvoir's analysis of lesbianism, nevertheless felt she didn't give sufficient attention to the social and historical meaning of a lesbian identity, since Beauvoir had focused on the existentialist issue of individual choice, thereby diminishing the important aspect of the social and political oppression of lesbians as a group.[39]

Phenomenologist Arleen Dallery noted the lack of gender-specific structures of embodiment in Beauvoir's phenomenological descriptions of the body and suggested the need for new theories of the libido to explain the presentation in *The Second Sex* of female sexuality as passive.[40] Iris Young noted that though Beauvoir had given a critically important discussion of women's situation, she had failed to consider seriously the female body in relation to its surroundings, bodily movement, and orientation, leaving readers of *The Second Sex* with the impression that it is woman's anatomy and physiology *as such* that in fact will (and must) determine her to a life of oppression.[41] Judith Butler, however, reminded feminists of the radical understanding of gender Beauvoir had presented in *The Second Sex*, especially in the well-known statement, "One is not born, but rather becomes, a woman." Regardless of the existentialist/masculinist ontology she sometimes called upon, the book's gift and lesson to feminism was that "anatomy alone had no inherent significance," Butler said, and she herself went on to develop this line of thought by describing the body as "a field of interpretive possibilities."[42]

In recent years, discussions of Beauvoir's ideas on love and marriage have originated not only from feminist scholars but also from those writing outside of the feminist debates, such as Irving Singer.[43] Singer noted that, though many critics over the years have suggested that in *The Second Sex* Beauvoir argued against marriage outright, her arguments were directed to a form of marriage in which the man is dominant and the woman submissive. Yet Beauvoir's notion of genuine (that is, non-inauthentic) love included the possibility of long-term relationships, such as "married love," relationships that are not necessarily legalized by contract and that usually evolve out of romantic love.[44] Beauvoir's ideas remain on the utopian level, Singer believed (as others have also said), because she included no plan for their realization. He also criticized Beauvoir for failing to acknowledge how period-specific the inauthentic romantic love of "the woman in love" was, in that it represents one aspect of the romantic ideology of the West that reached fruition in the nineteenth century.[45]

Marxism/Socialism and *The Second Sex*

Shulamith Firestone's early use of Beauvoir in *The Dialectic of Sex* effected a connection between Beauvoirian theory and the terms "sex class" (or "sex caste") that increasingly represented the radical feminist assertion that the sexual division was the primary patriarchal division. Though Beauvoir had made clear her preference for socialist theory in *The Second Sex* ("in the authentically democratic society proclaimed by Marx there is no place for the Other"), she was also clear that socialist practice had fallen short of its theory.[46] Further, she criticized historical materialism for being reductive of the human being and noted that, though economic equality with, and independence from, men is important to women, the ending of women's oppression required more than economic means.[47] Developing the notion of an "existentialist social-ism," Bob Stone has claimed that the perspective might be traced to Beauvoir, for in both *The Ethics of Ambiguity* and *The Second Sex* she spoke of a "we," a consciousness formed by an oppressed group to counter its oppression.[48] Toril Moi noted that because of Beauvoir's approval of socialism in *The Second Sex*, her most faithful following was neither in France (where a heavily psychoanalytic feminism is in vogue) nor in the United States (ever suspicious of socialism), but in Britain and the Scandinavian social democracies.[49] Zillah Eisenstein, a noted American socialist feminist, had already said that *The Second Sex* was a pioneering work in the creation of a feminist materialist analysis because it was the first to make connections between sexuality and history that showed how a good analysis of women should use economics, sociology, and psychology to interpret biology.[50] Using psychologist Carol Gilligan's two models of moral responsibility ("female") and rights ("male"), philosopher Linda Singer argued that there is a strong difference between Beauvoir's and Sartre's discussions of freedom as represented by the two moral models; Singer claimed that Beauvoir's model of freedom is tied to material conditions, whereas Sartre's is not.[51]

The strongest critique of *The Second Sex* in regard to socialism has come from philosophers Alison Jaggar and William McBride; they claimed that Beauvoir's distinction between reproduction and work was a "conceptual misadventure" similar to that which she herself had detected in Engels, an underestimation of the work of reproduction, a result of her identification of the female with immanence.[52] British sociologist Mary Evans similarly remained unconvinced of the materialist analysis of *The Second Sex*. Evans claimed *The Second Sex* was a work of ideology rather than science, hindered by its existentialism from being a genuine analysis of class or of some other form of determinism such as those made by Marx, Engels, and Freud; though *The Second Sex* was "a call to arms," Evans questioned whether it "pointed towards any clearly defined target."[53]

False Universalism in *The Second Sex*

On an issue which holds great current interest, multiculturalism or "cultural diversity," *The Second Sex* has been found seriously lacking. The problem is sometimes identified as "false universalism." Important critiques have come from anthropology as well as philosophy. In Elizabeth Spelman's analysis of the problem, Beauvoir is given credit for a high level of consciousness about class and race privilege, though it was "sabotaged" by her universalization of women as a group, a problem that feminism continually encounters.[54] In the introduction to a recently published collection of anthropology articles, *The Second Sex* and writings by other feminist scholars were criticized for their claim that a universal sexual asymmetry exists between women and men, specifically that in all cultures the female is secondary and is identified with "nature," and the male is primary and is identified with "culture."[55] Judith Okely, a British social anthropologist, offered a clever analysis of the faults of *The Second Sex* along the lines of false universalism, which Okely called "pan-cultural generalization." She claimed that *The Second Sex* itself was a work of "anthropology"; the ethnographic study it provided was of an urban "village," that is, mid-twentieth-century Paris; the women studied were white and middle-class, like Beauvoir herself.[56] Okely felt that, though it is a good study of the dominant European tradition since the eighteenth century, the book contained sweeping generalizations similar to those in old-fashioned anthropologies like Frazer's *The Golden Bough*, where different customs were connected with no concern for variations in their contexts.[57]

Beauvoir's Legacy

Though the appearance of *The Second Sex* in France in 1949 provoked an onslaught of criticism against it, its fortunes changed once it was published in the United States and England. But in spite of this second and generally positive reception, Beauvoir's ideas lay dormant for nearly twenty years while events in the West advanced toward them. (That *The Second Sex* was written in isolation from a feminist movement and from the intellectual company of women has been appreciated, though not often enough.)[58] Only when feminism emerged in the late 1960s did *The Second Sex* begin the intense dialogue with and influence on its times that marks a book as what we call a "classic." In recent years, as feminist theory has developed its own history, dialogues with the book have intensified, becoming more complex and more profound. But even as its specific faults are being uncovered, *The Second Sex* maintains its high status: first, as the text that fundamentally recast the issue of women's oppression; and second, as a text that can offer insights to the theoretical imagination. What connects many readers to *The Second Sex* is its theory; what binds feminists is more than theory: it is affection, even love.

Notes

1. Seymour Drescher, "Eric Williams: British Capitalism and British Slavery," *History and Theory* 26, no. 2 (1987), 180. See also Thomas S. Kuhn, *The Structure of Scientific Revolutions*, 2d ed. (Chicago, 1970), 1–34, for a discussion of new paradigms.

2. I believe but am not absolutely sure that H. M. Parshley's English translation, done for A. Knopf, was the book's first translation in any language.

3. See Margaret Simons's article, "Sexism and the Philosophical Canon: On Reading Beauvoir's *The Second Sex*," *Journal of the History of Ideas* 51, no. 3 (July–September 1990): 487–504, for a discussion of the studied ignorance of *The Second Sex* in philosophical circles and publications, particularly in existentialist and phenomenological ones. There have been several sessions devoted to Beauvoir and feminism at the Society for Phenomenology and Existential Philosophy meetings (1978, 1986, 1992, and 1994); at least three of these were organized by M. Simons.

4. Elizabeth Janeway, *Man's World, Woman's Place: A Study in Social Mythology* (New York, 1971), 108.

5. For the story of that "scandal," see the original version of this article in *History and Theory* 32, no. 1 (1993): 51–73.

6. Shulamith Firestone, *The Dialectic of Sex: The Case for Feminist Revolution* (New York, 1971).

7. After the publication of Deirdre Bair's biography of Beauvoir in 1990, which revealed the extent of Sartre's sexist behavior and Beauvoir's complicity in it, many women felt that Beauvoir had betrayed them by agreeing to a male-dominated life-style for herself. I think the quality of the Beauvoir–Sartre relationship through the many years they were together (more than fifty) should not be simplistically described, nor should it be reduced to their early years together. See the film/video *Daughters of De Beauvoir* for one example of how they interacted; see also her *Adieux: A Farewell to Sartre*, trans. Patrick O'Brian (New York, 1984) for her narrative of his last years and her interviews of him, to better assess "dependency" or "subordination" in this relationship more thoroughly.

8. Yvette Roudy, "La second révolution des Américaines," *L'Arc* 61, "Simone de Beauvoir et la lutte des femmes" (1975), 68. My translation.

9. See John Gerassi's interview with her for the twenty-fifth anniversary of the publication of *The Second Sex* in *Society* 13 (January–February 1976): 79–85. In this interview Beauvoir did fault Kate Millett for not crediting TSS enough in *Sexual Politics*.

10. See, for example, Catharine R. Stimpson, "Neither Dominant Nor Subordinate: The Women's Movement and Contemporary American Culture" in *Dissent* 27 (Summer 1980): 299–307; Jessica Benjamin and Lilly Rivlin, "The De Beauvoir Challenge: A Crisis in Feminist Politics," in *Ms. Magazine* (January 1980), 48; Sandra Dijkstra, "Simone de Beauvoir and Betty Friedan: The Politics of Omission," in *Feminist Studies* 6 (Summer 1980): 290–303; Mary Lowenthal Felstiner, "Seeing *The Second Sex* through The Second Wave," in *Feminist Studies* 6 (Summer 1980), 271. See also Hester Eisenstein, *Contemporary Feminist Thought* (Boston, 1983), 3; and Rosemarie Tong, *Feminist Thought: A Comprehensive Introduction* (Boulder, Colo., 1989), 6.

11. One of these is Anne Whitmarsh in her *Simone de Beauvoir and the Limits of Commitment* (Cambridge, 1981), 160.

12. Andrea Nye, "Preparing the Way for a Feminist Praxis," *Hypatia* 1 (Spring 1986): 101–5.

13. Michèle Le Doeuff, "Simone de Beauvoir and Existentialism," *Feminist Studies* 6 (Summer 1980): 277–89. This article originally appeared in *Ideology and Consciousness* 6 (Autumn 1979): 47–57. It has also been reprinted in *Critical Essays on Simone de Beauvoir*, ed. Elaine Marks, 144–54.

14. See Margaret A. Simons, "Beauvoir and Sartre: The Philosophical Relationship," in an excellent collection of articles published shortly after her death, *Simone de Beauvoir: Witness to a Century*, ed. Hélène Vivienne Wenzel, special issue of *Yale French Studies* 72 (1986). See also Jo-Ann Pilardi, "Philosophy Becomes Autobiography: The Development of

the Self in the Writings of Simone de Beauvoir," in *Writing the Politics of Difference*, ed. Hugh J. Silverman, 145–62 (Albany, 1991).

15. Jeffner Allen, "An Introduction to Patriarchal Existentialism: A Proposal for a Way out of Existential Patriarchy," in *The Thinking Muse: Feminism and Modern French Philosophy*, ed. Jeffner Allen and Iris Marion Young (Bloomington, Ind., 1989), 78–79. Also see discussion of Linda Singer's interpretation, to follow.

16. Terry Keefe, *Simone de Beauvoir: A Study of Her Writings* (Totowa, N.J., 1983), 98.

17. Sonia Kruks, *Situation and Human Existence* (Boston, 1990), 84, 110–11.

18. Pilardi, "Philosophy Becomes Autobiography," in *Writing the Politics of Difference*, Silverman, ed., 148.

19. Jean Leighton, *Simone de Beauvoir on Women* (Rutherford, N.J., 1975), 29 and 40.

20. Dorothy Kaufmann McCall, "Simone de Beauvoir, *The Second Sex*, and Jean-Paul Sartre," in *Signs: Journal of Women in Culture and Society* 5 (Winter 1979): 209–23.

21. *TSS*, 64.

22. Moira Gatens, *Feminism and Philosophy: Perspectives on Difference and Equality* (Bloomington, Ind., 1991), 2, 58, 127.

23. Charlene Haddock Seigfried, "Gender-Specific Values," *Philosophical Forum* 15 (Summer 1984): 425–42.

24. Nancy C. M. Hartsock, *Money, Sex and Power: Toward a Feminist Historical Materialism* (Boston, 1985), 286–91. See *TSS*, 64.

25. Alice Jardine, Prelude, in *The Future of Difference*, ed. Hester Eisenstein and Alice Jardine (Boston, 1980), xxvi. Also see Eisenstein's introduction in this same volume, for a discussion of the turn toward "difference."

26. Dorothy Kaufmann, "Simone de Beauvoir: Questions of Difference and Generation," *Yale French Studies* 72 (1986): 121–31.

27. Ibid., 131. One recent study of Beauvoir used the "stages of feminism" developed in Julia Kristeva's important article, "Women's Time" to discuss the "masculine discourse" of *The Second Sex*, a work which, though it used the masculine, nevertheless "altered the terms of the discourse on femininity." (Jane Heath, *Simone de Beauvoir* [New York, 1989], 3–14.) Julia Kristeva's article, "Women's Time," trans. Alice Jardine and Harry Blake, was printed in *Signs* 7 (1981): 13–35.

28. Mary O'Brien, *The Politics of Reproduction* (Boston, 1981), 65. O'Brien included a whole chapter on *The Second Sex*: "Sorry, we forgot your birthday," 65–92. For a study of O'Brien contrasted with Beauvoir on motherhood, see Reyes Lázaro, "Feminism and Motherhood: O'Brien vs. Beauvoir," *Hypatia* 1 (Fall 1986): 87–102.

29. Dorothy Dinnerstein, *The Mermaid and the Minotaur: Sexual Arrangements and Human Malaise* (New York, 1976).

30. Ibid., 219–24.

31. Adrienne Rich, *Of Woman Born: Motherhood as Experience and Institution* (New York, 1977), 52. Beauvoir's interpretation of female power was incorporated also into a much-used study of women writers: Sandra Gilbert and Susan Gubar, *The Madwoman in the Attic: The Woman Writer and the Nineteenth-Century Literary Imagination* (New Haven, 1979), 94–95.

32. See Janet Farrell Smith, "Possessive Power," *Hypatia* 1 (Fall 1986): 103–20. Smith approvingly discusses Adrienne Rich's and Sara Ruddick's theories of maternal practice and contrasts these to Beauvoir's. See Ruddick's "Maternal Thinking," in *Feminist Studies* 6 (Summer 1980). Also see Iris Marion Young, "Humanism, Gynocentrism and Feminist Politics," in *Hypatia Reborn: Essays in Feminist Philosophy*, ed. Azizah al-Hibri and Margaret A. Simons (Bloomington, Ind., 1990), 231–48. Young describes this change in feminist theory as a shift from humanist feminism to what she calls "gynocentric feminism." See also Judith Okely, *Simone de Beauvoir* (London, 1980), 89–99, for an enlightening discussion of Beauvoirian ambiguity in regard to "biologism."

Questions have also been raised about the biological data used in *The Second Sex* and Beauvoir's uncritical acceptance of it. See Charlene Haddock Seigfried, "*Second Sex*: Second Thoughts," in al-Hibri and Simons, 305–22.

33. Yolanda Astarita Patterson, *Simone de Beauvoir and the Demystification of Motherhood* (Ann Arbor, 1989), 3. See especially chap. 6, "Motherhood and *The Second Sex*," 115–32, for a discussion of critical reaction to *The Second Sex*.

34. Naomi Greene, "Sartre, Sexuality, and *The Second Sex*," *Philosophy and Literature* 4 (Fall 1980): 199–211.

35. Jo-Ann Pilardi, "Female Eroticism in *The Second Sex*," *Feminist Studies* 6 (Summer 1980) (published as Jo-Ann P. Fuchs), expanded as "Female Eroticism in the Works of Simone de Beauvoir," and printed in *The Thinking Muse*, ed. Allen and Young, 18–34.

36. Suzanne Lilar, *Le Malentendu du deuxiéme sexe* (Paris, 1969). To underscore her point, Lilar ended her book with a scientific essay by Professor Gilbert-Dreyfus, "The Perspective of Endocrinology," which even included a chemical chart.

37. *New French Feminisms*, ed. Elaine Marks and Isabelle de Courtivron (Amherst, Mass., 1980). Beauvoir's introduction to *The Second Sex* is the first selection in the book, which also includes writings by feminists like Monique Wittig who maintained a Marxist-feminist analysis (as Beauvoir herself did) over biology, that is, over the more psychoanalytic and anatomical analyses of the French. American thinkers have developed their psychoanalytically derived ideas as "difference theory," as in Nancy Chodorow's *The Reproduction of Mothering: Psychoanalysis and the Sociology of Gender* (Berkeley and Los Angeles, 1978) or Carol Gilligan's *In a Different Voice: Psychological Theory and Women's Development* (Cambridge, Mass., 1982). Feminist psychoanalysis often stresses the pre-Oedipal stage over the Oedipal stage.

38. Claudia Card, "Lesbian Attitudes and *The Second Sex*," in *Hypatia Reborn*, ed. al-Hibri and Simons, 290–99.

39. Ann Ferguson, "Lesbian Identity: Beauvoir and History," in *Hypatia Reborn*, ed. al-Hibri and Simons, 280–89.

40. Arleen Dallery, "Sexual Embodiment: Beauvoir and French Feminism (*écriture féminine*)," in *Hypatia Reborn*, ed. al-Hibri and Simons, 270–79.

41. Iris Marion Young, "Throwing Like a Girl: A Phenomenology of Feminine Body Comportment, Motility, and Spatiality," in *The Thinking Muse*, ed. Allen and Young, 53.

42. Judith Butler, "Sex and Gender in Simone de Beauvoir's *Second Sex*," in *Simone de Beauvoir: Witness to a Century*, special issue of *Yale French Studies* 72 (1986), 45. A version of this was published later in *Feminism as Critique*, ed. Seyla Benhabib and Drucilla Cornell, 128–42 (Minneapolis, 1987).

43. Irving Singer, *The Nature of Love*, Vol. 3, *The Modern World* (Chicago, 1987). For an article that is in nearly total agreement with Beauvoir's analysis of love, see Kathryn Pauly Morgan, "Romantic Love, Altruism, and Self-Respect: An Analysis of Simone de Beauvoir," *Hypatia* 1 (Spring 1986): 117–48.

44. Irving Singer, *The Nature of Love*, 312–16.

45. Ibid., 313.

46. TSS, 142 and 731–32.

47. TSS, see chap. 3, "The Point of View of Historical Materialism," and 724–26. See also Ellen Willis, "Rebel Girl," an obituary/eulogy for Beauvoir, *Village Voice*, 27 May 1986, 18.

48. Bob Stone, "Simone de Beauvoir and the Existential Basis of Socialism," *Social Text* 17 (Fall 1987): 123–33.

49. Toril Moi, *Sexual/Textual Politics*, 92. Moi is a Norwegian who teaches French literature in England.

50. Zillah Eisenstein, "Developing a Theory of Capitalist Patriarchy and Socialist Feminism," in her *Capitalist Patriarchy and the Case for Socialist Feminism* (New York, 1979), 26.

51. Linda Singer, "Interpretation and Retrieval: Rereading Beauvoir," in *Hypatia Reborn*, ed. al-Hibri and Simons, 323–35.

52. Alison M. Jaggar and William L. McBride, " 'Reproduction' as Male Ideology," in *Hypatia Reborn*, ed. al-Hibri and Simons, 249–69.

53. Mary Evans, *Simone de Beauvoir: A Feminist Mandarin* (London, 1985), 67–75.

54. Elizabeth V. Spelman, *Inessential Woman: Problems of Exclusion in Feminist Thought* (Boston, 1988); see especially chap. 3, "Simone de Beauvoir and Women: Just Who Does She Think 'We' Is?" 57–79.

55. Peggy Reeves Sanday and Ruth Gallagher Goodenough, *Beyond "The Second Sex": New Directions in the Anthropology of Gender* (Philadelphia, 1990), 1–3.

56. Okely, *Simone de Beauvoir*, 71. See also I. Singer, *The Nature of Love*, especially 313.

57. Okely, *Simone de Beauvoir*, 75–78. Historian Gerda Lerner has also remarked on the book's sweeping statements, a function of its ahistoricity, she feels. See Gerda Lerner, *The Creation of Patriarchy* (Oxford, 1986), 3 and 221.

58. Carol Ascher, *Simone de Beauvoir: A Life of Freedom* (Boston, 1981), 146. Ascher's fine book presents a good summary of some of the earliest critical reaction to *The Second Sex*.

2

The Second Sex and Philosophy

Karen Vintges
Translated by Anne Lavelle

The Second Sex[1] has often been weighed against scientific norms and found wanting. According to cultural anthropologist Margaret Mead, "theoretically, the book violates every canon of science and disinterested scholarship in its partisan selectivity" (Mead 1953, 31). Bair (1990) quotes historian Mary Beard's dismissal of the book as "utter nonsense" and "folly" (392). Anne Whitmarsh (1981) also labeled The Second Sex bad science. Beauvoir is said to have attempted to carry out a sociological analysis, but only succeeded in piling up numerous literary examples (149). This criticism assumes Beauvoir's pretensions were of a scientific nature. But is that really true?

Methodological remarks in The Second Sex are rare. In the introduction, Beauvoir states that her intention is to leave behind all earlier debates on the position of woman and to start all over again. She believed that, as a woman, she knew the world of women intimately and could therefore elucidate the problem. She goes on to say: "But it is doubtless impossible to approach any human problem with a mind free from bias" (1972, book 1, 28). Beauvoir then raises the question of her own "ethical background" and states her position is based on existentialist principles. Subsequently, she discusses the specificity of woman's situation; that is, her position as the Other, a position that, in her view, cannot be explained through either psychological, physiological, or economic factors alone, as scientific disciplines attempt to do. Instead we should investigate the *total* situation of woman: "We shall study woman in an existential perspective with due regard to her total situation" (1972, book 1, 83).

This approach can be traced back to an affinity with a phenomenological perspective in philosophical anthropology, which approaches humans as situated beings. Beauvoir shares this approach, which is influenced by Heidegger and others, with Merleau-Ponty, Lévinas, and Sartre. The point of departure of the phenomenological perspective is that humans are always involved in the world, and so can only be understood within the total, very complex context of that world. However, this also implies that humans are seen as beings who continually give meaning to their situation. Thus, humans are objective subjectivity and subjective objectivity. According to this approach, the person should be understood within his or her situation, whereby this situation itself has to be charted in an unbiased manner.

The point of departure here is that reality can be perceived directly if we are open to what the phenomena themselves tell us. Feelings, intuitive understanding, but also critical researches—all are ingredients of this basic approach. This epistemology derives from the thinking of philosopher Edmund Husserl. His aim was the refutation of Descartes's dualistic epistemology, which had introduced a strict distinction between thinking and being, and thus also between knowing subject and known object. Husserl only accepted the world of the phenomenon (*phainomenon*, "that which shows itself"). He argued that objects only exist as objects for a subject. He thus abolished the subject-object dichotomy. Husserl believed that phenomena could be described accurately and without bias, thus revealing their truth. For Husserl, explanatory, scientific theories were of secondary importance; according to him, *Aufklärung* (elucidation) rather than *Erklärung* (explanation) was required. Scientific approaches alone were inadequate, and as such had denied man access to phenomena and hidden reality from view. Philosophical phenomenology reinterprets the sciences by integrating them into a phenomenological total view.

Beauvoir narrates how Sartre turned pale with emotion when he first came across these ideas. "Aron pointed to his glass: "You see, my dear fellow, if you are a phenomenologist, you can talk about this cocktail and make philosophy out of it." That was exactly what Sartre had had in mind for years: "to describe objects just as he saw and touched them and extract philosophy from the process" (1965, 135). On the way home from the cafe, Sartre immediately bought Lévinas's book on Husserl, paging through it as he walked to see if Husserl had already formulated his ideas. Beauvoir concludes her account with the observation that fortunately, this was not the case on a number of essential points (1965, 136). In 1933, Sartre left for Berlin to make a serious study of both Husserl's and Heidegger's work. In that same period, Beauvoir immersed herself in the works of these German philosophers because, she said, she wanted to be able to follow the way Sartre's thinking evolved. Therefore, it is not surprising that from then on we also find traces of this philosophy in her work, and that her thinking shows a clear affinity with phenomenology. Looking back on her discussions with Sartre during this period, Beauvoir recalls: "There was a phrase which we borrowed from phenomenology and much abused during these arguments: 'self-evident truth.' Emotions and all other 'psychological entities' had only a *probable* existence; whereas the *Erlebnis* [experience] contained its own self-evident truth [*sa propre évidence*]" (1965, 258).

In her review of Merleau-Ponty's *La Phénoménologie de la perception* (1945), Beauvoir expresses explicit approval of the "élucidation phénoménologique" method. She calls the abolition of the subject-object dichotomy one of phenomenology's greatest achievements: "it is impossible to define an object by cutting it from the subject through and for which it is object; and the subject manifests itself only through the object with which it is involved" (1945, 363). Thus, our own judgments again acquire the relevance they are due. Through education and morality the child unlearns the ability to take itself seriously as a presence in the world. Phenomenology restores the importance of subjectivity by denying a distinction between objectivity and subjectivity. It gives back to the adult that childlike audacity which allows him to say: "I am here," and to again take seriously his own judgments; an audacity that has to be recaptured from the sciences. These present us with a universe full of "petrified" objects and teach us to perceive ourselves as subject to universal and anonymous laws.

Thus, Beauvoir also criticizes scientific explanations of the world and wants a return to direct observation of the world. Initially, she considered philosophy by definition superior to the sciences:

> The thing that attracted me about philosophy was that it went straight to essentials. I had never liked fiddling detail; I perceived the general significance of things rather than their singularities, and I preferred understanding to seeing; I had always wanted to know *everything*; philosophy would allow me to appease this desire, for it aimed at total reality; philosophy went right to the heart of truth and revealed to me, instead of an illusory whirlwind of facts or empirical laws, an order, a reason, a necessity in everything. The sciences, literature, and all the other disciplines seemed to me to be very poor relations of philosophy. (1963, 158)

However, in *The Second Sex* her approach is more refined; she certainly applies scientific theory here. For example, she incorporates Lévi-Strauss's theories. In a footnote, she thanks him for allowing her to see the proofs of his *Elementary Structures of Kinship* (1949a, 1:16–17). Lévi-Strauss's thesis on exogamy is the point of departure for her chapter on history. She also makes use of Lacanian psychoanalysis when she refers to the mirror stage in the earliest development of the child as basis for her own socialization theory (see 1972, book 2, 297). In general, in *The Second Sex* she applies the perceptions of sciences, such as biology, psychoanalysis, and historical materialism, but criticizes these when they claim an exclusive explanatory power for the position of women, or when they pretend to offer the whole explanation for the historically suppressed position of woman.

In her review of Lévi-Strauss's *Structures*, Beauvoir states that his theories can be placed in a broader philosophical framework (something Lévi-Strauss himself never ventured to do): "Lévi-Strauss never allowed himself to enter the domain of philosophy. He adhered strictly to scientific objectivity, but his thinking is clearly linked to the grand humanist tradition" (1949b, 949).

So there is a question of division of tasks between the sciences and philosophy; the latter places the results of the former in a broader framework. Beauvoir's view in *The Second Sex* is in line with Husserl's on this point. Her point of departure is also the necessity of a broad, direct approach, as opposed to the reductionism of the sciences. Based on the foregoing, the structure of *The Second Sex* now becomes comprehensible. In this work, Beauvoir wanted to chart the whole situation of woman. She believed she knew that situation thoroughly and in the introduction she states that women are best suited to illuminating the situation of women: "we know the feminine world more intimately than do the men because we have our roots in it, we grasp more immediately than do men what it means to a human being to be feminine" (1972, book 1, 27). We should now see this against the backdrop of phenomenological epistemology, in which the immediate experience is decisive. It also gives us insight into how Beauvoir could claim she was beginning "all over again"; the phenomena could be observed and described directly. We also understand now that, in contrast to the sciences, she wanted to examine the *total* experience and circumstances (i.e., situation) of woman, this being the reason why *The Second Sex* became such a lengthy work, exploring such a broad set of aspects of women's lives. As now becomes clear, far from being a clumsy eclectic work, *The Second Sex* is structured systematically as a philosophical phenomenological enterprise. Beauvoir was criticized by Whitmarsh for merely "piling up examples," but this is totally in line with the methodology of philosophical phenomenology; in this approach examples are not used as empirical evidence, but rather as a means to show something, to pass on a specific insight. The Dutch phenomenologist Theo de Boer argues: "It is important that in a philosophical argument examples are chosen with the aim of transferring the spark of insight to the reader. Thus, the philosophical argument does not have the form of a deductive proof or an empiric theory" (1989, 181).

My conclusion is that *The Second Sex* cannot be weighed against scientific norms alone but should be evaluated on its own merits, that is, as a philosophical work. To make a start on this evaluation, I shall concentrate on the way Beauvoir deals with Sartre's philosophy. The general consensus is that *The Second Sex* applies Sartrean theory; I see it, however, as containing a transformation rather than an application of that theory. This transformation can be traced back to Beauvoir's earlier *Ethics of Ambiguity* (1947). This work is a consistent reconciliation of Sartrean thinking with the phenomenological perspective in philosophical anthropology mentioned above, a reconciliation Sartre himself did not achieve. In his *Being and Nothingness*, Sartre states that human beings are always situated and that consciousness does not exist independently from their bodily position in the world. In fact, however, he strongly opposes all bodily incarnation as immanence, and thus bad faith, and advocates lucid, pure conscious existence (i.e., transcendence) as the only authentic human existence. In her *Ethics of Ambiguity*, Beauvoir develops a theory of human beings as essentially ambiguous. As situated beings, they are a psychophysiological unity by which they realize their ontological freedom, transforming their status as pure consciousness (which can never be transformed completely).[2] Phenomenological anthropology, which considers human beings as psychophysiological unities, thus acquires a prominent place in her thinking, and *The Second Sex* is the result of this theoretical reconciliation. But the two works have never been studied simultaneously from such a philosophical point of view. When *The Second Sex* is examined, usually only the Sartrean notions it contains are considered. Because Beauvoir applied these concepts, she is accused of unleashing male thinking on (the subject of) woman. Male values are said to dominate in her work because she is believed to place consciousness above the body, thinking above feeling, activity over passivity and transcendence above nature (see, e.g., Greene 1980, 205; Leighton 1975, 213; Seigfried 1984, 441).

Margaret Walters believes Beauvoir's own life and her view of human history comprise a devaluation of the feminine. In her attempts to escape stereotyping, Beauvoir has lost something (Walters 1977, 377, 359). Mary Evans suggests Beauvoir took her own prolonged student existence as a measure: the values in *The Second Sex* are based on a life as childless, hard-working bachelor (see Evans 1985, 56–57, xi). With *The Second Sex*, Beauvoir is even said to have joined the ranks of our culture's long tradition of misogyny (see Lilar 1970, 9 et passim). All these critics place the blame on Sartre's conceptual framework. Beauvoir's use of the Sartrean distinction between transcendence and immanence and her adoption of his hierarchical relationship between both is said to reproduce the Western rationalistic image of humanity and thus, through the underevaluation of the body, embrace a masculine thinking.

Now, in my view, this kind of strict gender-labeling of a certain philosophic thinking forms a problem in itself. The label is grafted onto socially prevalent definitions of masculinity and femininity: masculinity as consciousness and rationalism, femininity as body and nature. When, based on this, Sartre's philosophy is labeled masculine, the stereotypes that are so liberally available in our culture are only reproduced and what still has to be proven is in fact presupposed.

However, Beauvoir's thinking was not deemed masculine on these general bases alone. Another, more specific reasoning was put forward by Genevieve Lloyd: Sartre's conceptual framework was said to be characterized by a rejection of the female body; in this sense then, *The Second Sex* was also believed to have a masculine content. According to Lloyd (1984), transcendence in Sartre signifies nothing less than an abhorrence of the *female* body. Thus, the masculine perspective was said to have made a definitive mark on the concept. I shall examine this criticism more closely here. Is Sartre's existential philosophical framework sexist, and in *The Second Sex* does Beauvoir adopt and apply it to the subject of woman in an identical manner? Let us first look more closely at Sartre's reasoning in *Being and Nothingness*.

The first woman we meet in this work is the so-called frigid woman. She serves to illustrate Sartre's argument that the unconscious does not exist. According to his argument, the frigid woman consciously ignores the pleasure that she, as her husband testifies [?!], actually experiences in the sexual act. The frigid woman is presented to us as an example of bad faith; by assuming the attitude of frigidity, she falls back on a fixed identity and thus places herself on the side of the en-soi. The second woman we meet is similarly reproached. She has "accepted" a man's invitation to go out with him. So she knows what the man is after, but elects to ignore this for the time being, thus postponing her decision on whether or not to accept his advances. Sartre apparently hates this: according to him, the woman is shirking her responsibilities. In both cases, he cites woman as an illustration of bad faith, implying that she can, in principle, act as free subject, but, in practice, functions as object. So although potentially woman has a consciousness, in *Being and Nothingness* we see her continually in the role of an être-en-soi.

In the final section, which discusses the sexes explicitly, it becomes clear this is no coincidence.[3] Sartre talks here of the threat to the pour-soi from the "slimy," which is said to be a "moist and feminine sucking," a "sickly-sweet, feminine revenge." All "holes" threaten the pour-soi. These are an "appel d'être"; they seduce the subject into becoming flesh and thus fill the hole. And Sartre continues: "The obscenity of the feminine sex is that of everything which 'gapes open.' . . . in herself woman appeals to a strange flesh which is to transform her into a fullness of being by penetration and dissolution. Conversely woman senses her

condition as an appeal precisely because she is 'in the form of a hole.'
. . . Beyond any doubt her sex is a mouth and a voracious mouth which
devours the penis" (1969, 609, and 614 respectively).

How should we think about these sexist passages in Being and Nothingness? Do they mean Sartre's conceptual framework is essentially infected
by masculine thinking, as Lloyd argues, and does The Second Sex suffer
from the same malady? Kaufmann McCall (1979) and Le Doeuff (1979)
also addressed this question. Both distinguish gender-specific and gender-
neutral sections in Sartre's work, and subsequently conclude Beauvoir
took on-board the latter only. Dorothy Kaufmann McCall introduces a
distinction between Sartre's philosophical and 'personal' contributions:

> When Sartre evokes the feminine in Being and Nothingness, his
> language bears more resemblance to the language of his obsessions
> in the novels than it does to the language of his philosophical
> discourse. . . . Sartre's descriptions of "the slimy" and "holes" in
> Being and Nothingness do not derive logically from his analysis of
> the en-soi and the pour-soi. They are not inherent in either his
> ontology or in existentialist thought in general; they are rooted
> in Sartre's particular sensibility. Obsessed with his horror of the
> vital in all its manifestations, Sartre the writer takes over from
> Sartre the philosopher, using words as magical means to impose
> those obsessions on his reader. (1979, 214)

So Kaufmann McCall distinguishes the philosopher Sartre and the
writer Sartre as the objective and subjective Sartre respectively. However, she forgets this distinction is one of philosophy's continually
recurrent problems: What basis can we use for such a distinction?
Kaufmann McCall builds her argument on a premise that in fact forms a
problem in itself.

Sartre's sexual metaphors are probably not so much projections of his
personal Ängste, but, according to Michèle Le Doeuff (1979, 52), more
an indispensable part of his metaphysics of authenticity. Her view is that
the sexual metaphors are not a coincidental appendage, but an essential
tailpiece for Sartre's theoretic system. Woman fulfills the role of unceas-
ingly drawing the pour-soi into the en-soi, so that the pour-soi is forced
continually to transcend anew. According to Le Doeuff, Sartre needs
woman to complete the circle and lend his theory the status of philosophical system.

Now, in my view, this is not the case. The fact that transcendence has to be striven for again and again is explained by Sartre through the constant tendency to bad faith present in every human being, which emerges from his désir d'être. The task of transcendence is completed only on death. So Sartre does not need woman to let transcendence start again and again. Moreover, by considering the sexual metaphors as a tailpiece, Le Doeuff herself introduces a distinction between those metaphors and the so-called real theory. Hazel Barnes also makes a distinction between Sartre's "objectionable images" and his theoretical system; these images only cast a shadow over his work and do not form its substance (Barnes 1990, 346).

The distinction between imagery and theory, however, is in itself problematic, as I suggested above. Wouldn't this be an ideal way to explain away the less agreeable elements in any philosophical work, by characterizing them as literary or metaphorical nonessentials that do not belong to the actual core of the body of philosophical ideas? The sexual metaphors in Sartre's theory specify the characteristics of transcendence and immanence in gender-specific terms. So no other conclusion would appear justified than that Sartre's conceptual framework in *Being and Nothingness* includes a masculine thinking. If, to him, transcendence, consciousness, pour-soi, and being human are equivalents, then by making transcendence and the female body opposites, the latter is brought into line with immanence, nature, matter, en-soi. It would seem then that transcendence is the preserve of people with a male body, and woman emerges as the opposite of transcendence and consciousness.

The question now is in which form Sartre's conceptual framework appears in *The Second Sex*. Is it applied in its original form and is the female body also seen by Beauvoir as the enemy par excellence of transcendence? We have already seen that *The Second Sex*'s central proposition is that man has made woman the Other. Beauvoir argues that an existentialist point of departure can make clear how this happened:

> The female, to a greater extent than the male, is the prey of the species; and the human race has always sought to escape its specific destiny. The support of life became for man an activity and a project through the invention of the tool; but in maternity woman remained closely bound to her body, like an animal. It is because humanity calls itself in question in the matter of living— that is to say, values the reasons for living above mere life—that, confronting woman, man assumes mastery. (1972, book 1, 97).

How should we take this? Does Beauvoir also consider women's anatomy as their destiny? Can their subordinate position in history be traced back to their body? There are passages in *The Second Sex* that would suggest this. In the chapter on history, Beauvoir states literally that the historic position of woman as Other originates in the anatomy of women. In this sense, she talks about the biological advantage of men. We can also find passages where she speaks very negatively about female bodily functions, including those describing menstruation, pregnancy, and labor as extremely painful and disagreeable experiences for women (see, e.g., 1972, book 1, 61–62; book 2, 512–13).

In addition, however, in *The Second Sex* we also find an emphasis on the fact that the body is not a thing, but an always "experienced" reality. Beauvoir states explicitly: "it is not the body-object described by biologists that actually exists, but the body as lived in by the subject" (book 1, 69), and "It is not merely as a body, but rather as a body subject to taboos, to laws, that the subject is conscious of himself and attains fulfilment—it is with reference to certain values that he evaluates himself. And, once again, it is not upon physiology that values can be based; rather, the facts of biology take on values that the existent bestows upon them" (book 1, 68–69).

So according to Beauvoir, the body always has a signifying component. Referring to the insights of Heidegger, Sartre, and Merleau-Ponty, she states that the body is not a thing, but a "situation" (book 1, 66). By doing so, she approaches the body explicitly from the phenomenological perspective discussed above: the perception of the human being as objective subjectivity *and* subjective objectivity. For her, one can never be a mere body; there is always a dimension of meaning. Thus, in *The Second Sex* reductionist biological perceptions of woman are subject to permanent criticism.

Here follows a number of Beauvoir's own comments on this subject:

> [Woman is only a female] to the extent that she feels herself as such. (book 1, 69)

> Woman is determined not by her hormones or by mysterious instincts, but by the manner in which her body and her relation to the world are modified through the action of others than herself. (book 2, 734)

. . . if body and sexuality are concrete expressions of existence, it is with reference to this that their significance can be discovered. (book 1, 77)

It is not nature that defines woman; it is she who defines herself by dealing with nature on her own account in her emotional life. (book 1, 69)

Experience, understanding, meaning, feeling—for Beauvoir the body is always linked to the human experience of it. It is never a separate entity, and woman's historic role as the Other can, therefore, never be determined by pure biology. The biological facts

> are insufficient for setting up a hierarchy of the sexes; they fail to explain why woman is the other; they do not condemn her to remain in this subordinate role for ever. (book 1, 65)

> Thus we must view the facts of biology in the light of an ontological, economic, social, and psychological context. (book 1, 69)

> As we have seen, the two essential traits that characterize woman, biologically speaking, are the following: her grasp upon the world is less extended than man's, and she is more closely enslaved to the species. But these facts take on quite different values according to the economic and social context. In human history grasp upon the world has never been defined by the naked body. (book 1, 84)

> As for the burdens of maternity, they assume widely varying importance according to the customs of the country: they are crushing if the woman is obliged to undergo frequent pregnancies and if she is compelled to nurse and raise the children without assistance; but if she procreates voluntarily and if society comes to her aid during pregnancy, and is concerned with child welfare, the burdens of maternity are light and can be easily offset by suitable adjustments in working conditions. (book 1, 84–85)

If we examine more closely Beauvoir's own explanation for woman's historical position as the Other, then we find she indicates a combination of factors. Human beings find transcendence important; woman, through her greater role in procreation, was more subject to biology. That is why men have been able to appropriate transcendence and postulate woman as its opposite. So the oppression of women is a historical contingent result of a number of factors. Men have *grasped* women's biology to relegate woman to a specific role: the Other. In history, the biology of woman has been assimilated into a process of specific cultural meaning, and as such has caused the development of the asymmetrical relationship between the sexes. So biology certainly has its place in the explanation of woman's oppression, but it is not a unique place, because stating that biology has been used is not the same as stating it is an ultimate cause. Beauvoir's historic explanatory model perceives biology as a factor, but it is not infected by biologism.

Beauvoir claims woman has become the absolute Other through a historic contingent process, but states this is in no way an inevitable consequence of bodily functions. There is no essence in woman, or in her body, which by definition places her on the side of en-soi; in principle, woman can also realize herself as subject, as Self. Beauvoir's thesis is that woman has been the *historic* (contingent) Other, but in no way the inevitable (necessary) Other. Through the central role of this thesis of woman as historic Other in *The Second Sex*, it is clear that whenever Beauvoir talks about the female body, she has the situated body in mind; that is, the body which is embedded in and shaped by sociocultural practices and meanings. Beauvoir (1972) stated literally: "the situation does not depend on the body; the reverse is true" (book 2, 706). The phenomenological-anthropological approach of *The Second Sex*, that is, the approach of woman as a situated human being, made it impossible for Beauvoir to share Sartre's rejection of the female body as such. In *The Second Sex*, Beauvoir removed the female body from Sartre's dualistic ontology and ranked it at a sociocultural level. Thus, Beauvoir has disaggregated Sartre's series of equivalents: nature/female body/immanence/en-soi, breaking down his antagonism between the female body and transcendence.

Whereas Sartre characterized transcendence in sex-specific terms (a transcendence of the female body), we do not find such an explicit characterization in *The Second Sex*. Moving from ontology to a sociological-historic perspective, Beauvoir's approach transformed the very core of Sartre's sexist conceptual framework. *The Second Sex* opposes the traditional situation of woman, not the female body. Beauvoir's negative evaluation of female bodily functions is targeted against the experience of motherhood, labor, and pregnancy which is inherent to a specific objective situation where women have no active control over their own bodies and lives. We occasionally hear some echoes of Sartre's influence, but it is clear they are not the main "sound" of the work.[4] *The Second Sex* is a philosophical work in its own right, articulating the break between a younger and an older, more independent Beauvoir. My conclusion is that criticisms of Beauvoir that claim she is in opposition to the female body as such ignore the main thesis in *The Second Sex*, which we can characterize as the thesis of woman as the historic Other. Beauvoir opposes a specific cultural embedding and organization of the female body that has made it impossible for women to develop and experience themselves—including their bodies—as active subjects. If women have active control over their own bodies and lives, they will also experience their bodies actively, including motherhood, pregnancy, and labor.

Notes

1. As a better alternative is lacking, the Penguin translation of *The Second Sex* by H. M. Parshley (1972) has been used here, although, as Margaret Simons (1983) has pointed out, it often fails to represent accurately the original French, especially from a phenomenological perspective.

Numerous books and articles have been written on Simone de Beauvoir, but few contain a serious attempt to analyze her philosophical attitudes. To most people, her philosophy is no more than a vague reflection of Sartre's thinking. In my *Philosophy as Passion* (Indiana University Press, 1995), I show that Beauvoir definitely had her own original notions. In this chapter, based on my book, I demonstrate that Beauvoir's *The Second Sex* is a phenomenological work that breaks with rather than applies Sartrean concepts.

2. This is all examined in depth in my *Philosophy as Passion*. It will become apparent here that Beauvoir's theoretical approach also reconciles Sartre's notion of the Self–Other structure of human contact with the possibility of love and friendship.

3. Collins and Pierce (1976) and Le Doeuff (1979) have already made extensive mention of the passages from *Being and Nothingness* cited here.

4. Moi (1994) fails to see the importance of Beauvoir's *Ethics of Ambiguity* and therefore sees no theoretical justification for a shift from Sartrean ontology to the sociological perspective in *The Second Sex*. According to Moi, this shift is merely a massive metaphorical operation. Consequently, she approaches the work primarily on the level of rhetoric and style, handling it as prose. Thus Beauvoir's systematic theoretical transformations of Sartrean theory do not emerge.

References

Bair, Deirdre. 1990. *Simone de Beauvoir: A Biography*. New York: Summit Books.

Barnes, Hazel. 1990. "Sartre and Sexism." *Philosophy and Literature* 14:340–47.

Beauvoir, Simone de. 1945. "La Phénoménologie de la perception de Maurice Merleau-Ponty." Les Temps Modernes 1, no. 2:363–67.

———. 1949a. Le Deuxième Sexe. 2 vols. Paris: Gallimard.

———. 1949b. "Les Structures élémentaires de la parenté." Les Temps Modernes 7, no. 49:943–49.

———. 1963. Memoirs of a Dutiful Daughter. London: Penguin.

———. 1965. The Prime of Life. London: Penguin.

———. 1968. The Force of Circumstance. London: Penguin.

———. 1972. The Second Sex. London: Penguin.

Boer, Theo de. 1989. Van Brentano tot Levinas. Meppel: Boom.

Collins, Marjorie, and Christine Pierce. 1976. "Holes and Slime: Sexism in Sartre's Psychoanalysis." In Women and Philosophy: Toward a Theory of Liberation, edited by C. Gould and M. Wartofsky, 112–27. New York: Putnam.

Evans, Mary. 1985. Simone de Beauvoir—A Feminist Mandarin. London: Tavistock.

Greene, Naomi. 1980. "Sartre, Sexuality and The Second Sex." Philosophy and Literature (Fall): 199–211.

Kaufmann McCall, Dorothy. 1979. "Simone de Beauvoir, The Second Sex, and Jean-Paul Sartre." Signs: Journal of Women in Culture and Society 5, no. 2:209–23.

Le Doeuff, Michèle. 1979. "Operative Philosophy: Simone de Beauvoir and Existentialism." Ideology and Consciousness 6 (Autumn): 47–57. Reprinted in Feminist Studies 6 (1980): 277–89. Also reprinted in Critical Essays on Simone de Beauvoir, edited by Elaine Marks, 144–54. Boston: G. K. Hall, 1987.

Leighton, Jean. 1975. Simone de Beauvoir on Woman. Rutherford, N.J.: Fairleigh Dickinson University Press.

Lilar, Suzanne. 1970. Le Malentendu du Deuxième Sexe. Paris: Presses Universitaires de France.

Lloyd, Genevieve. 1984. The Man of Reason. Minneapolis: University of Minnesota Press.

Mead, Margaret. 1953. "A SR Panel Takes Aim at The Second Sex." Saturday Review of Literature 36, no. 8: 30–31.

Moi, Toril. 1994. The Making of an Intellectual Woman. Cambridge, Mass.: Basil Blackwell.

Sartre, Jean-Paul. 1969. Being and Nothingness. London: Routledge.

Seigfried, Charlene Haddock. 1984. "Gender-Specific Values." Philosophical Forum 15 (Summer): 425–42.

Simons, Margaret. 1983. "The Silencing of Simone de Beauvoir: Guess What's Missing From The Second Sex." Women's Studies International Forum 6, no. 5:559–64.

Walters, Margaret. 1977. "The Rights and Wrongs of Women: Mary Wollstonecraft, Harriet Martineau, Simone de Beauvoir." In The Rights and Wrongs of Women, edited by Juliet Mitchell and Ann Oakley, 304–78. Harmondsworth, Middlesex: Penguin.

Whitmarsh, Anne. 1981. Simone de Beauvoir and the Limits of Commitment. Cambridge: Cambridge University Press.

3

Simone de Beauvoir: Falling into (Ambiguous) Line

Michèle Le Doeuff
Translated by Margaret A. Simons

"And you, madame, are you an existentialist?" The scene takes place in 1943, in the Café de Flore, of course. Sartre has just introduced Simone de Beauvoir to Jean Grenier, then the two men launch into a discussion. "They spoke," and apparently out of the blue, Grenier asks Simone de Beauvoir if she is (meaning, if she is *also?*) an existentialist. She reports the anecdote in *The Prime of Life* (1960), noting, "I still recall my confusion. I had read Kierkegaard; one had long spoken of 'existential' philosophy in connection with Heidegger; but I didn't know the meaning of the word 'existentialist' which Gabriel Marcel had just coined" (626).

Retrospectively, one can and must understand such confusion. It's a bit much for someone to ask you if you are this or that, and (in this case) if you belong to a movement that you have never heard of!

Moreover, Grenier's question is formulated as though it was asking about membership in a party, the framework of which one would have sufficiently accepted to then define oneself by one's membership in it. After 1943, one was going to be able to be or not be an "existentialist," as in other happier and freer times, one had been able to be or not be a Gambettist, Communist, or Boulangist. Of course, among academics of that epoch, one was certainly free to discuss interminably whether an author from the past ought to be or ought not to be considered a nominalist, rationalist, and so on. But when a living person, who has not begun publishing a body of work, is interrogated in such a fashion, what one is in fact asking of him or her is a profession of faith, a pure and simple declaration of allegiance, not a carefully worked-out view, bearing *on some thing,* an object, a theory, a statement, a concept.

Grenier's question appears all the more absurd because a short time before this encounter, Simone de Beauvoir had been busy with an entirely different matter, one more commendable than a game of self-labeling or positioning, and one that the publication of her letters to Sartre allows us to know in more detail—provided, of course, that one brings a certain viewpoint to these letters. The unhappy correspondence contains, as one knows all too well, stories of love affairs that have titillated the public. But no one has lingered long enough to notice that the correspondence also comprises texts whose content is philosophic and highly discerning. Should we allow a few bedroom escapades to obscure what took place at the Bibliothèque Nationale? A group of letters actually retraces an intellectual drama of the first order, which was played out, for Beauvoir, at the library, and which merits at least as much attention as the multiple adventures of the couple.

July 1940: In the midst of the *débâcle* and national chaos, Simone de Beauvoir spends a good part of her days in the library reading Hegel, with the aid of a book by Jean Wahl and some English commentators. She does not doubt that "Soldier Sartre" is still alive, but for several weeks it's been a betting matter. So she reads; and then, after finally receiving a word from the prisoner, she immediately sends him letters on *The Phenomenology of the Spirit.* The first one, written evidently as soon as she received the address of Sartre's prison camp, announces Beauvoir's intention to produce for him, as quickly as possible, a vast exposé of Hegel's philosophy (Beauvoir 1990b, 2:153; 11 July 1940). The second letter repeats: "I'm thrilled while reading Hegel by the very thought of explaining it to you" (Beauvoir 1990b, 2:155; 11 July 1940).

That continues until she no longer has an address to write to him. The Hegelean epigraph of *She Came to Stay* ("every consciousness pursues the death of the other") will be found during that month.

But above all, in reading Hegel Beauvoir rediscovers, she says on two occasions, the need to do philosophy. In fact she rediscovers the taste for philosophical debate or for philosophy as debate. Doesn't she want to organize a confrontation [*sic*] between the ideas of Sartre and those of Hegel on nothingness, the in-itself, and the for-itself? Hegel "is horribly difficult," but she patiently works to decipher it. And, even if it is discouraging to see that the commentators, instead of explaining it, reveal at length that they don't understand a word of it, Simone de Beauvoir sticks to it, with the hope of discussing it with Sartre, if he returns from the war.

That may seem like nothing, and yet here we find a wealth of information. The need to do philosophy is the desire to discuss ideas or theses by organizing their confrontation, after having labored long and hard to understand them. But this project also implies that she is freeing herself a bit from her role as Sartre's admirer/lover. If he is warned that a course on Hegel awaits him at his liberation and that Beauvoir is going to bring his ideas into confrontation with someone else's, she is informing him, in short, of the existence of a rival. Perhaps Beauvoir was, by the way, vaguely aware of the fact that her "sweet little one" was not necessarily going to like that. "I dreamt of you . . . you wanted to strangle me," reported one letter (Beauvoir 1990b, 2:170, 13 July 1940). Everything proceeds as though Beauvoir's perception of a proximity and a contrast between Sartre's ideas and Hegel's theses ("there are many analogies but . . .") had made her rediscover a freedom of thought, indeed the necessity of thinking, by herself and about something—even at the price of a modification in her love life. Always the amorous lover, no doubt more passionate than ever, she had nevertheless rediscovered a wisp of intellectual autonomy.

Now, a few years later, while *She Came to Stay* is in press, with the Hegelian epigraph one knows so well, we have Grenier asking her to place herself in relation not to an idea but to a word that Gabriel Marcel has just coined. The temptation would be strong to say that the question addressed to her that day tended to make her pass from the sublime to the derisory, from the laborious to the ephemeral, from an acute, strong, and personal reading of Hegel to a casual preoccupation with the Left Bank. She says that this question was an assault at once on both her modesty and her pride. Because, if she didn't grant herself enough importance to imagine that she "merited a label" [sic], she wanted to believe that her ideas reflected "the truth and not an ideological position" (Beauvoir 1960, 626). If she had stuck to this immediate reaction, we would be able to consider her as radically outside the history of existentialism.

Only, after having rebelled, she gives in, or at least she looks for ways to align herself. She writes *Pyrrhus et Cinéas* in a few months, an "existentialist" text that she will extend and take up again in *The Ethics of Ambiguity*. And then the adhesion to existentialism, far from remaining a question for her, even less a disconcerting question, becomes like a matter of course. "If it appeared so natural to me to rally to the thought of Kierkegaard, to that of Sartre and become an 'existentialist,' it's because my entire history prepared me for it," she says in *The Prime of Life* (Beauvoir 1960, 629). It's natural, and moreover the result of an apparently determinant evolution. . . ?

I don't believe one word of it, and I have had on more than one occasion, even before *Hipparchia's Choice*, to recount the constant problem that reading the works of Simone de Beauvoir poses for me. I suspect her of rarely being fair to herself, and of putting her own efforts into categories that are scarcely suitable for them, and that, even worse, depreciate them. She and I were never able to settle our disagreement on this point, nor even to tackle it frankly, though it intrigued her that I constantly struggled with the discrepancy between her work, as I saw it, and certain judgments that she had herself proposed of it. Now I am rediscovering this discrepancy here. Natural, her rallying to existentialism? Really? If indeed there was a rallying, one must say at the very least that it was of an extraordinary ambiguity! Here's how she explains it in *The Prime of Life*: "I made a distinction between two aspects of freedom: it is the very modality of existence. . . . On the other hand, the concrete possibilities that open up to people are unequal. . . . I do not disapprove of my endeavour to furnish a material content to existentialist ethics" (Beauvoir 1960, 628).

She *does not disapprove* of her own endeavor? The double negation as the sole mode of self-affirmation is here tragic. Why in the devil did she have a guilty conscience about having endowed an ethics, whatever it might be, with a material content? Is it because the idea may have crossed her mind that this content is not at all suitable for an existentialist ethics? That it would make it come apart at the seams? To what strange trial is she summoning herself, she who is justifying herself in such a convoluted manner by saying that, in spite of all she said, thought, and did, she remained all the same in the line reputed to be good? Or, inversely, must one consider that she concedes (and just halfheartedly) to whom it may concern that freedom is the very modality of existence, but that her own thought commences when she asserts that, "on the other hand," there is a concrete inequality in the possibilities that people can propose to themselves? This "on the other hand" appears as a rhetorical balancing more than a theoretical articulation.

Perhaps the history of the thought of Simone de Beauvoir, from that time on, will be precariously balanced between that which she really seeks to think and the doctrinal line that she receives ready-made, a line defined in 1943 by Sartre, Grenier, and Gabriel Marcel, readers of Kierkegaard and Heidegger. And the image she leaves us is that of a woman entangled in these references imposed by the times, neither truly gypped nor truly destroyed, but trapped, at least halfway, obliging herself to embrace a doctrinal framework with which, finally, she had little to do, and abandoning what she had found in grappling with the arduous reading of Hegel.

No one, neither woman nor man, is an absolute beginning in thought. If only through critique or polemic, we all, men and women, need to fasten our problematic to an already constituted thought. Simone de Beauvoir was no exception. Since the publication of her letters, I think that her true restarting point was Hegel, even more than Sartre. Even the resumption of the interrupted writing of *She Came to Stay* can be credited to her reading of Hegel, as a letter and her *Journal de guerre* attest (Beauvoir 1990b, 2:173; 14 July 1940; and Beauvoir 1990a, 341; 7 July). Because, in order to write her work, she needed a philosophy of consciousness that opened directly and radically upon a problematic of the plurality of consciousnesses, in struggle with one another, thus existing in a reciprocal exteriority. Now no such idea is at work in Sartre's existentialism. At the very most it appears as a menacing horizon and as nonthematisable. To say that "hell is other people," thus that others are a hell, amounts to the recognition that the relation of several people to one another goes beyond the order of the thinkable. The existential philosophy of Sartre will remain fundamentally shaped by a kind of Robinson Crusoe complex even when he deals with being-for-others: "The new being which appears *for* other does not reside *in* the other. I am responsible for it" (Sartre 1943, 276). To Hegel, whose "genial intuition" is "to make me depend upon the other *in my being*, . . . it's necessary here and everywhere to oppose Kierkegaard," declares Sartre (1943, 293, 295), who will thus stick to the primacy "for-myself" of the consciousness that is mine. The vast exposé that Simone de Beauvoir had promised him was thus in the end to provide him with a little foil for Kierkegaard, and nothing more. But with a postulate such as that of the primacy of my consciousness for me, one cannot write *The Second Sex*, which today appears to me as a prolongation of the reading of Hegel already used as an epigraph to *She Came to Stay*. Between consciousnesses, struggle takes place; thus there can be defeat for some and loss of certainty of self.

One understands in any case that at the beginning of existentialism it was *either* Hegel *or* Kierkegaard, Husserl, and Heidegger reread by the French. Either the idea of a struggle between consciousnesses to transcend a reciprocal exteriority seen as a given or a theory centered on one consciousness and one alone; mine, defined at first for-itself, and by a "fissure within consciousness," in an *ipséité* [selfhood] to which comes to be added an "other" who constitutes me "on a new type of being that must support new qualifications" (Sartre 1943, 120, 276). While there is no monadism in Hegel's philosophy when he speaks of consciousnesses, nor any real risk of solipsism, the French existentialism of the 1940s seems to have taken shape as a subtle play with this risk, always brushed against, always a bit avoided, always basically caressed. When Sartre describes himself as "a desert island" (1983, 1:57), he reveals a sort of fundamental intuition that is his and that has nothing to do with the conflictual world of Simone de Beauvoir.

"Of all of my books, that is the one that today irritates me the most," she says in regards to *The Ethics of Ambiguity* (1963, 1:98–99). It rests with her male and female readers of today to say whether they subscribe to this judgment, which for me testifies finally to the taste of ashes left by a book written on the side or against the grain of that which one had begun to elaborate oneself. To say it straight out: Why did she have to get involved in this existentialism business, when, from July 1940, she held the thread that would lead her directly from *She Came to Stay* to *The Second Sex*? Moreover, the tone changes when she speaks of this last work. She at last leaves the mode of double negation ("I do not disapprove of my . . ."). At last, she does not ask herself if it irritates her more or less than another. At last, one can read: "All said and done, it is perhaps of all my books the one which has brought me the most solid satisfactions. If one asks me how I judge it today, I don't hesitate to reply: I'm for it" (1963, 1:267).

References

Beauvoir, Simone de. 1960. *La Force de l'âge* (Prime of life). Paris: Gallimard.
———. 1963. *La Force des choses* (Force of circumstances). 2 vols. Paris: Gallimard.
———. 1990a. *Journal de guerre: Septembre 1939–Janvier 1941.* Ed. Sylvie Le Bon de Beauvoir. Paris: Gallimard.
———. 1990b. *Lettres à Sartre.* Ed. Sylvie Le Bon de Beauvoir. 2 vols. Paris: Gallimard.
Sartre, Jean-Paul. 1943. *L'Etre et le néant* (Being and nothingness). Paris: Gallimard.
———. 1983. *Lettres au Castor et à quelques autres.* Ed. Simone de Beauvoir. 2 vols. Paris: Gallimard.

4

Can a Woman Be a Philosopher? Reflections of a Beauvoirian Housemaid

Eleanore Holveck

> The girl had taken the Ph.D. in philosophy and this left Mrs. Hopewell at a complete loss. You could say, "My daughter is a nurse," or "My daughter is a school teacher," or even, "My daughter is a chemical engineer." You could not say, "My daughter is a philosopher." That was something that had ended with the Greeks and Romans. . . .
>
> One day Mrs. Hopewell had picked up one of the books the girl had just put down and opening it at random, she read, "Science, on the other hand, has to assert its soberness and seriousness afresh and declare that it is concerned solely with what-is. Nothing—how can it be for science anything but a horror and a phantasm? . . . science wishes to know nothing of nothing." . . . These words had been underlined with a blue pencil and they worked on Mrs. Hopewell like some evil incantation in gibberish. She shut the book quickly and went out of the room as if she were having a chill.
>
> —Flannery O'Conner

Mrs. Hopewell, a character in the short story "Good Country People" by Flannery O'Conner ([1955] 1988, 268–69), surely expresses the thoughts of many a mother, even though no one has yet written a song entitled "Mamas, Don't Let Your Baby Daughters Grow Up To Be Philosophers." Mrs. Hopewell typifies the bourgeois Southern woman, impoverished by historical circumstances as well as the death of her husband, who naively envies and trusts the "good country people" who work for her. However, Mrs. Hopewell is not my mother.

My mother lives in an apartment building with other tenants who are all over seventy. Whenever she and I are together, she thinks nothing of announcing loudly to any of her neighbors who happen to be unfortunate enough, say, to be trapped on an elevator with us: "This is my daughter, the philosopher." For my mother, this phrase is one of simple identification. She calls me her daughter, the philosopher, in order to distinguish me from my sister Alex, her daughter, the mathematician. Why is my mother so different from Mrs. Hopewell?

In this chapter, I shall discuss whether or not daughters can be philosophers. I am particularly interested in the one woman of our time who had a major claim to the title of philosopher but who, time after time, rejected it: Simone de Beauvoir. Hence, I shall discuss what philosophy is, how women can be philosophers in general, how Beauvoir was a philosopher in particular, and how I personally became a philosopher.

It must be admitted that the initial relationship between philosophy and women was not promising. According to a legend related by Plato in the *Theaetetus* (174A), Thales of Miletus, traditionally considered to be the first philosopher of Western European culture, was looking up at the stars so intently one day that he fell into a well. A servant-woman laughed scornfully at him for this, wondering how he could claim to know anything about the sky, when he could not even see what was directly in front of his feet.

Martin Heidegger quotes this story from Plato with enthusiasm and, indeed, makes it the basis of a preliminary definition of philosophy: "Philosophy, then, is that thinking with which one can start nothing and about which housemaids necessarily laugh" (Heidegger [1936, 1962] 1967, 3). This Heideggerian position illuminates the situation of Mrs. Hopewell's daughter in Flannery O'Conner's short story; she was reading the wrong philosopher. Heidegger could not help Joy, or Hulga, as she preferred to be called, relate to the men that her mother thought suitable for her. A Heideggerian is quickly outwitted by "good country people."

Many of us today are trying to articulate the relation between women and philosophy. This search sometimes takes the form of finding the proper metaphor. Michèle Le Doeuff has written of oral examiners in Paris who could not accept a beautiful young woman for the *agrégation* in philosophy because she did not have a long beard. Le Doeuff herself claims that the figure of the fool in Shakespeare's plays was suited to her own view of philosophy [1989] 1991, 9).

Some feminists name the hysteric and the woman dancing the tarantella as ancestors. The crone is certainly one, claimed even by women like Arleen Dallery, who is far too beautiful to be called one. Luce Irigaray names the mother, the *mater*, the material, the sea. Iris Young, borrowing from Linda Singer, fancies herself the bandit who steals from whatever philosophical system she wants, agreeing with Hélène Cixous and Catherine Clément who play on the similar sounds of *La Genet* and *La Jeune Née* (Cixous and Clément, 1975).

I respect all of these positions, but I point out that the proper metaphor for women was given to us at the very beginning of philosophy. I am happy to claim as my ancestress the housemaid who laughed at Thales. And it was Simone de Beauvoir who sobered me up. I argue that Beauvoir would not admit to being a philosopher because the philosophy that she studied and taught spent too much time on nothing.

Beauvoir's View of Philosophy

I claim that Beauvoir mistakenly accepted the narrow view of philosophy held by the men who were her forerunners, teachers, and colleagues, and thus refused to call herself a philosopher. However, Beauvoir developed a view of philosophy that is expressed, even created, in literature; this view enabled her to write that pioneering work in feminism, *The Second Sex.*

There is evidence in her memoirs and interviews that Beauvoir considered philosophy to be an abstract reflection that attempts to explain all things from a universal point of view. For example, Beauvoir wrote that when she and her friend Zaza first studied philosophy as teenagers, from texts based on Saint Thomas Aquinas, she was attracted to the subject because it allowed her to pose ultimate questions about the universe. Philosophy, she thought then, aimed at an understanding of the totality of the real; instead of detailed facts and empirical laws, philosophy studied essential structures; it presented a necessary order, a sufficient reason. However, she continued ironically, from day to day, Zaza and she did not seem to apprehend any great thing (*grand-chose*) (Beauvoir [1958] 1959, [220] 158).

Beauvoir remarked frequently that she preferred literature to philosophy and that she had wanted to be a writer from the age of fifteen, in part because her father thought writers to be superior to philosophers, scholars, and academics ([1958] 1959, 141). In one illuminating passage in *The Prime of Life,* she wrote that Sartre believed that her understanding of philosophers, including that of Edmund Husserl, was better than his. She explained that this was because Sartre was so original that it was difficult for him to take up a point of view that differed from his own. She, being less original philosophically, was able to understand other philosophers better ([1960] 1962, 220).

She seemed serious, although the idea that one can be a good philosopher only by misunderstanding all the great philosophers who preceded one seems questionable at best, even if this explains Sartre's method. She continued in this passage to write that she was not passive in regard to philosophical texts. When she agreed with a theory, it changed her way of being in the world (*mon rapport au monde*); it colored her experience ([1960] 1962, [254] 220–21).

Beauvoir wrote that she did not see why she should continually be asked to justify the fact that she did not create an original philosophy as Sartre did; rather, "it is more necessary to account for how certain individuals are capable of conducting that mad performance [*délire concerté*] that is a [philosophical] system and whence comes the obstinacy that gives to their cursory glance [*aperçu*] an evidence to be used as a clue to the universal [*la valeur de clés universelles*]. I have said often that the situation of women does not incline us to this type of pigheadedness" (1960, 254–55, my translation).

Here is as sober and articulate a model for our scornful housemaid as we might wish. Beauvoir as much as argues that philosophers pretend to explain all things universally, but in fact these "universals" are based in the consciousness of some individual thinker who claims knowledge of the universal, a claim that must be justified. Beauvoir uses words here that are close to Edmund Husserl's in the French translation of the *Cartesian Meditations;* one of the main problems of epistemology is to account for how my own experience of an individual object, my own evidence, can claim universal validity (Husserl [1929] 1931, nos. 69–70). Cartesian epistemology begins with the questions: What can I know for certain? How good is the evidence for the knowledge that I claim to have?

The point is clarified further if one looks at the 1974 "Conversations with Jean-Paul Sartre" published with Beauvoir's *Adieux: A Farewell to Sartre* ([1981] 1984, 131–445). When Beauvoir asked Sartre whether he would rather be remembered for his literature or for his philosophy, he replied that literature is essentially above philosophy. Philosophy is a speculation on eternal truths that occurs in a specific historical context; philosophical truths will always be overtaken and left behind by future philosophers (Beauvoir [1974, 1981], 1984, 153). Literature, on the other hand, is, in a sense, timeless; Hamlet seems "to have been written only yesterday" (Beauvoir [1974, 1981] 1984, 153–54), according to Sartre. Beauvoir commented then that it is literature and not philosophy that has an absolute character.

I contend that Beauvoir turned to literature because she was not interested in abstract speculation that had little to do with her own everyday life. She was not exactly a sober housemaid herself but she kept both feet solidly on the ground.

Beauvoir's View of Literature: The Metaphysical Novel

This brings me to my second claim concerning Beauvoir as a philosopher. From her earliest work, Beauvoir wrote her philosophy in literature. In her short stories and novels, for example, she tested the claims of "universal insight" by applying abstract philosophical theories to the real world of her own experience and that of other women. She used this method as a way to study her own existence, because she believed that her own conscious experience was the only absolute, the only thing that really exists. This position owes much to the early existentialism of Jean-Paul Sartre.

In the 1940s as she was writing her early fiction, Beauvoir wrote an essay, "Littérature et métaphysique" for Les Temps Modernes (Beauvoir, [1946] 1963). In this work Beauvoir stated clearly that, as a young girl, her love was split between the concrete temporal world of fiction and the rigor of abstract philosophical systems. "Where is truth situated?" she asked, "on earth or in eternity?" (90). Philosophers present "an intellectual reconstruction of their immediate experience," whereas novelists "recreate on an imaginary level . . . that very experience itself, just as it presents itself before all elucidation" (91).

Beauvoir went on in the article to argue that, since existentialism is a philosophy that emphasizes the singularity and drama of real, lived experience, the metaphysical novel is its perfect expression. "One will repudiate the philosophical novel if one defines philosophy as a completely constituted and self-sufficient system. . . . [I]t is in the act of building a philosophical system that an adventure of the spirit will have been experienced. A [metaphysical] novel which undertakes to illustrate this adventure cannot do it without risk and without the honest inven-tion of rich features" (97).

Beauvoir argued here that in writing a metaphysical novel, the imagination of the writer runs away with her. The adventure of the spirit that she is engaged in presents her with "truths whose faces she will not have recognized in advance . . . and, it is with astonishment that, at the end of her creation, she will consider her completed work, because she herself will not be able to give it an abstract interpretation. Rather, in one single movement, the finished work will have produced its meaning itself simultaneously with its embodiment" (96, using "she" instead of Beauvoir's "he").

In short, the metaphysical novelist tries to articulate and create imaginatively the singular, lived metaphysical situation that grounds the abstract philosophical system. "Metaphysics is not primarily a system. . . . '[T]o do' metaphysics is 'to be' metaphysical. . . . This means to face the world, to throw oneself into the totality of the world with the totality of one's own being" (98–99).

I am claiming that Simone de Beauvoir wrote her metaphysics in her fiction. She was able to ground her abstract philosophical positions in the real world of lived experience, a lived experience she created imaginatively in ordinary language that was more concrete, more rich than any abstract philosophical language. The problem of intersubjectiv-ity for her was no abstract issue to be discussed behind closed doors of universities. Rather, in her first published novel, L'Invitée, Beauvoir created two women who have a Hegelian fight to the death for recogni-tion, because they hold two completely opposed views of reality: Xavière is a Kojèvian Hegelian and Françoise is a Kantian idealist.

To give another example, "Anne," an early short story of Beauvoir's, published in When Things of the Spirit Come First ([1979] 1982), criticized Jacques Maritain's claim in La Primauté du spirituel that obedience to the Catholic Church was the foundation of the greatest freedom of the spirit. In Beauvoir's short story, Mme. Vignon is urging her daughter Anne to perform her Christian duty as a woman by marrying the rich older man chosen by her parents. Anne, a character based on Zaza, becomes emotionally distraught, sickens, and dies when the young man she loves, a character based on Merleau-Ponty, will not stand up to her parents, as Sartre did for Beauvoir. Thus, early in her career, Beauvoir was taking abstract philosophical political theories and applying them to the real lives of women.

In a similar vein, the novel *The Blood of Others* (1945) is a concrete instantiation of problems of freedom and violence that Beauvoir articulated theoretically in *The Ethics of Ambiguity* (1947). In *The Mandarins* (1954) Beauvoir took the infamous Kantian example, the right to lie to the murderer who is asking us to tell him where his next victim is, and applied it to the time of the Resistance in France, when murderers came to French doors daily, demanding the whereabouts of innocent Jews.

Beauvoir's Phenomenological Method

Despite the influences of Heidegger and Sartre on Beauvoir, which are manifested in the discussion above, I believe that her ultimate philosophical position owes as much, if not more, to Edmund Husserl. In works such as *The Cartesian Meditations* ([1929] 1931) and *The Crisis* ([1934–37] 1954), Husserl described his method of phenomenological *epochē* whereby one brackets all metaphysical claims about what really exists and considers every and any object simply in relation to the consciousness that grounds it. By eidetic variation, one varies an individual object to get to its essential structure.

Beauvoir used this method extensively in *The Second Sex*. In book 1 of that work, Beauvoir attempted to study the concepts of as many sciences (in Husserl's sense of *Wissenschaften*) as she could: biology, psychology, sociology, economics, history, literature, religion, etc. In book 2, Beauvoir applied these "scientific" concepts and tested them in the concrete experiences of women, which she finds articulated in women's fiction and autobiography. Beauvoir went back and forth, from the conceptual frameworks of the sciences, to the concrete experiences of women described in ordinary language, trying to articulate her own experience in a manner as free from prejudice as possible.

Ordinary language harbors cultural preconceptions about women that are then taken over by the "sciences." Critical reflection on scientific claims must try to ferret out these prejudices. A woman must attempt to describe the singularity of her own experience, the taste of her own life, as Beauvoir so often wrote. The ideal, as Beauvoir stated in an interview celebrating the twenty-fifth anniversary of the writing of *The Second Sex*, (Gerassi, 1976, 84) would be to have many different women, from as many cultures as possible, articulate their own lived experiences. Thus, in dialogue, women could compare the prejudices of their own cultures in the light of different prejudices in other cultures.

Beauvoir's own collections of short stories on young women and those on aging women might be seen as studies of eidetic variations of individuals, as can, of course, the sections of *The Second Sex* entitled the young girl, the mother, the woman in love, etc. However, most of these seem to be variations of Beauvoir's own type: bourgeois French women of a certain century. It might be that there are no essences that transcend all cultures. On the other hand, there may be sufficient similarity between women's situations that at least some general types might exist across many cultures. We have to keep talking and writing and learning each other's languages. Complete freedom from prejudice is an ideal that will never be reached.

The Philosophy of a Beauvoirian Housemaid

Finally, I would like to tell you about how I personally became a philosopher and about how it was natural for me to end up as someone interested in Simone de Beauvoir. I hope that you will not think that I am arrogant to talk about myself. I am trying to illustrate how one can do philosophy in literature, in music, and, even, in journalism.

When I first went to college, I majored in journalism. My childhood hero was the newscaster Edward R. Murrow, whose TV programs *See It Now* and *Person to Person* were the forerunners of *60 Minutes*. One of his most famous broadcasts, "Harvest of Shame," is still shown from time to time on public television. On a Thanksgiving evening, when most Americans were in a stupor from having eaten too much turkey and pumpkin pie, Murrow showed the unspeakable working conditions of the migrant farmworkers who had picked much of the food that we had just eaten. Since all of my grandparents had been peasants in Poland before they had emigrated to the United States in the 1890s, I was particularly impressed with Murrow's integrity and sense of justice. In addition to journalism, I was interested in literature and music.

When I was a freshman at Duquesne University, I went to my first class in philosophy, logic. The professor, who was an interesting-looking young blond man with thick glasses, said that before we studied logic, we had to try to understand something about philosophy itself. He began to read a story about a young man on a park bench who was having an experience of being. The meaning of ordinary things like park bench, chestnut tree, blue sky, grass, etc., began to recede for this man, and he began to be aware of the contingency of the being of all things. I had no trouble understanding this person. I had often sat in a park near my home having similar kinds of thoughts.

Of course, this book was the novel *Nausea* by Jean-Paul Sartre. Incidentally, my first philosophy professor was Alphonso Lingis, and it is his fault that I have always approached logic with nausea. So, Al Lingis showed me that what I really loved about literature was what Simone de Beauvoir loved in it, namely, that literature can express one's lived metaphysical experience. Apparently all my life, although I had not "done" metaphysics, I had "lived" it. In college, I learned what to call it.

As we all know, in *Nausea*, Sartre expressed great admiration for a record he mistakenly called "jazz." Throughout the novel "Some of These Days" is played over and over. Sartre thought this to be a song written by a Jewish man for a Negress to sing, but we know that it was written by an African-American man, Shelton Brooks, even though several white women, including Blossom Seeley and Sophie Tucker, made it famous.

In any case, when I was about twelve, I had liked a young singer, Elvis Presley. You might say that I spent my adolescence in "Heartbreak Hotel." On the other side of that record was a song called "Hound Dog." Now, while my friends and I liked this song, the words did not make sense. Why would Elvis Presley be singing a song to someone in which he calls him? or her? a hound dog and complains that he? or she? had never caught a rabbit?

My friends and I soon found out that this was a variation on an old blues theme; we started listening to a radio station in Pittsburgh that featured this kind of music on "race" records (i.e., records by African-American artists made originally for African-American audiences). We found out that "Hound Dog" was sung by a woman who is complaining that the man in her life is not providing his share of their food and shelter. In some songs, women complained that men treated them like dogs; for example, they would complain, "you dogged me 'round." But here was a woman turning the tables and calling a man nothing but a hound dog.

Soon our favorite singer, who we learned had been killed in an automobile accident before we were born, was Bessie Smith. Bessie, it was said, had been a woman who "didn't take no shit from nobody," and we felt that this was a good attitude to emulate. We enjoyed threatening our boyfriends with "Devil's Gonna Get You" and "It Won't Be You," as well as encouraging them to be like Bessie's "Slow and Easy Man."

Bessie sang and/or wrote lyrics that expressed the condition of many women. Here are some of the lyrics to "Washwoman's Blues," written by Sippy Williams:

> All day long I'm slavin'
> All day I'm bustin' suds.
> Gee, my hands are tired
> Washing out these dirty duds.
>
> Sorry I do washin'
> Just to make my livelihood,
> 'Cause the washwoman's life
> It ain't a bit of good.
>
> D'rather be a scullion
> Lookin' in some white folks' yard.
> I could eat a plenty
> Wouldn't have to work so hard.

It is not far-fetched to link up Bessie Smith with the philosophy of Simone de Beauvoir. She probably listened to her records (see Beauvoir [1960] 1962, 139). I would argue that although Beauvoir sometimes approached African-American music with the attitude of the bourgeois woman going slumming, there is in her writings an admiration for the working woman who lives her body, who incarnates her being in the world in an authentic way that Beauvoir envied.

If one listens carefully to the lyrics of songs like "Spider Man Blues," by Bessie Smith, one might find an influence on Sartre's theory of intersubjectivity in Being and Nothingness. This song is about a woman who feels like a fly caught in a man's spider web. She complains:

> Early in the mornin'
> When it's dark and dreary out doors,
> Spider Man makes a web
> And hides while you sleep and snore.

'Never I try to sleep
Mean eyes watchin' day and night
Gets every fly
As fast as she can light.

That black man of mine
Sure has his spider web
Controllin' after me
All of my natural days.

It seems clear that Jean-Paul Sartre took more than one good look at Bessie Smith. Thus, my love of journalism, literature, philosophy, and popular music all led me to the same place.

I will end my paper with the image I claimed at the beginning. My grandmothers were farmers who cooked and cleaned, raised chickens and milked cows. I come from really good country people. I met some men, however, Alphonso Lingis and Jean-Paul Sartre, who invited me to be a guest at the master's banquet table. I sat at that symposium for a long time listening to Plato, Aristotle, Descartes, Leibniz, Hegel; my favorite dinner companions were Husserl and Kant.

I listened to speeches for a long, long time, until—and I hope that I am not offending anyone—I became very bored. So, I left the table and went around to the kitchen. None of the men at the banquet, including Al Lingis, if he will pardon my saying so, ever seemed to ask where the food for the banquet had come from. It is wonderful to have food for thought, but without real food, we would not have any thought; real men might not eat quiche, but they have to eat something.

When I got to the kitchen, I found a woman who had already been there. Catherine Clément has called Beauvoir "a storyteller who cooks culture"; she compares Beauvoir to "a peeler . . . [who has] the sense of the multiple skins that constitute us" (Clément [1979] in Marks 1987, 171). If Beauvoir is a story-telling cook who peels the layers of vegetables so that we might taste every distinct ingredient in the stew of our existence, I am a mere kitchen-maid who follows her around, trying to articulate her methods, so that others may more easily use her recipes.

I know that some women scorn kitchens and recipes; these nomads seek out new ingredients in forests and oceans, which they cook outdoors in celebrations of song and dance. Other women sometimes sit at the master's table, occasionally playing the fool. Yet other women have not been allowed even in the kitchen; they wash clothes in muddy rivers or cultivate crops in the hot sun. In memory of our great- great-, however many times great-, grandmother, that housemaid who laughed at Thales, let us always remember that, if we gaze at the stars, we must never ignore the ground beneath our feet.

References

Beauvoir, Simone de. [1946] 1948. "Littérature et métaphysique." In *L'Existentialisme et la sagesse des nations*. Paris: Nagel, 89–107. Barbara Klaw and Eleanore Holveck provided the translation for this chapter.

———. 1958. *Mémoires d'une jeune fille rangée*. Paris: Gallimard. Translated as *Memoirs of a Dutiful Daughter*, by James Kirkup. New York: Harper and Row, 1959.

———. 1960. *La Force de l'âge*. Paris: Gallimard. Translated as *The Prime of Life*, by Peter Green. New York: Penguin, 1962.

———. [1979] 1982. "Anne." In *When Things of the Spirit Come First: Five Early Tales* (Quand prime le spirituel). Translated by Patrick O'Brian. New York: Pantheon, 117–66.

———. [1981] 1984. *Adieux: A Farewell to Sartre* followed by *Conversations with Jean-Paul Sartre* (La Cérémonie des adieux suivi des Entretiens avec Jean-Paul Sartre Août-septembre 1974). Translated by Patrick O'Brian. New York: Pantheon, 1984.

Clemént, Catherine. [1979] 1987. "Peelings of the Real." *Magazine Littéraire* 145 (February): 25–27. In *Critical Essays on Simone de Beauvoir*, ed. and trans. Elaine Marks, 170–72. Boston: G. K. Hall.

Cixous, Hélène, and Clemént, Catherine. [1975] 1989. *The Newly Born Woman*. Translated by Betsy Wing. Minneapolis: University of Minnesota Press.

Gerassi, John. 1976. "Simone de Beauvoir: *The Second Sex*: 25 Years Later." *Society* 13 (January–February): 79–85.

Heidegger, Martin. [1936, 1962] 1967. *What is a Thing?* Translated by W. B. Barton, Jr., and Vera Deutsch. Chicago: Henry Regnery.

Husserl, Edmund. [1929] 1931. *Méditations cartésiennes*. Translated by Gabrielle Peiffer and Emmanuel Levinas. Paris: Armand Collin.

Le Doeuff, Michèle. [1989] 1991. *Hipparchia's Choice*. Translated by Betsy Wing. Minneapolis: University of Minnesota Press.

O'Conner, Flannery. [1955] 1988. "Good Country People." In *Collected Works*, 263–284. New York: Library of America.

5

Simone de Beauvoir:
Teaching Sartre About Freedom

Sonia Kruks

"Independent" professional women, Simone de Beauvoir observed, "are not tranquilly installed in their new realm: as yet they are only halfway there. . . . For when she begins her adult life [the independent woman] does not have behind her the same past as does a boy; she is not viewed by society in the same way; the universe presents itself to her in a different perspective."[1]

Later, Beauvoir explained that she had begun her monumental study of woman, *The Second Sex* (1949), at a time when she had wanted to write about herself. For although her own femininity did not seem to present any difficulties to her, she had—as Sartre pointed out—been raised very differently from a boy; thus, self-understanding called for an investigation of "the female condition."[2] But whatever her initial motivations for writing *The Second Sex*, in the completed work Beauvoir seems to stand aloof from her subject: it is other women she is discussing and not, it appears, herself. It is striking that nowhere in her volumes of autobiography does she offer any acknowledgment that she personally experienced her femininity as a handicap, or even that she recognized it as a source of inner conflict in herself.

Even so, we still must see an autobiographical element, however unintended, in Beauvoir's comments on the "halfway" and untranquil character of the life of the independent woman. A careful reading of Beauvoir's autobiography suggests that characteristically feminine patterns of otherness and subordination, such as she had described in *The Second Sex*, were present in her relations with Sartre and others. This becomes a matter of importance if one attempts to examine her *philosophic* relationship to Sartre and to evaluate her own contributions to philosophy.[3] Repeatedly, and until the last years of her life, Beauvoir insisted that she lacked originality and was merely Sartre's disciple in matters philosophical. She attributed originality in the field of literature to herself; but in the more hallowed field of philosophy she could not compete but only follow. "[On] the philosophical level," she insisted, "I adhered completely to *Being and Nothingness* and later to *Critique of Dialectical Reason*."[4]

Most scholars and commentators have taken Beauvoir at her word. While some have upbraided her for her intellectual dependence on Sartre,[5] few have asked whether her self-portrayal is justified. Most assume that, as one author has recently put it, she simply uses Sartre's concepts as "coat-hangers" on which to hang her own material, even to the point where it can be said that "Sartre's intellectual history becomes her own."[6] I shall argue in this article that such a view, even though it is asserted by Beauvoir herself, is inaccurate. Although Beauvoir is clearly not of the same stature qua philosopher as Sartre, she is far from philosophically derivative. On the contrary, the case can be made that at certain points in Sartre's development it is Beauvoir's intellectual history that becomes his. This is particularly so with regard to Sartre's struggle, for a decade beginning in the late 1940s, to develop a social philosophy. In this struggle—first evidenced in his abandoned *Cahiers pour une morale* and reaching a certain fruition in the first volume of the *Critique*—Sartre can be seen to modify the absolute and radically individualistic notion of freedom he had elaborated in *Being and Nothingness*. In time he replaced it with a more nuanced notion of freedom as relative and as socially mediated—a notion that, however, Beauvoir had already developed by the late 1940s.

Sartre himself, while stressing Beauvoir's importance to him as a critic of his work,[7] did not attribute to her a significant role in the transformation his thought underwent between *Being and Nothingness* and the *Critique*. Rather, it was to Merleau-Ponty that he attributed the role of mentor and intellectual inspiration. It was, he said, Merleau-Ponty's collection of essays *Humanism and Terror* (1947) that forced him, in the face of events, to go beyond his individualism and taught him about the collective aspects of human existence, about history, and about politics.[8] But Beauvoir, it must be pointed out, had grasped the implication of Merleau-Ponty's work earlier than Sartre, and perhaps better. It was she, and not Sartre, who in 1945 wrote an extensive review of Merleau-Ponty's *Phenomenology of Perception* for *Les Temps Modernes*. In the review she both discussed the social aspects of Merleau-Ponty's thought and highlighted his divergences from Sartre. Merleau-Ponty, she pointed out, denied Sartre's notion of an "absolute freedom," elaborating in its place a notion of the "incarnate subject"—a subject in which history is incarnated through the generality of the body:

> While Sartre, in *Being and Nothingness*, emphasizes above all the opposition of the for-itself and in-itself, the nihilating power of consciousness in the face of being and its absolute freedom, Merleau-Ponty on the contrary applies himself to describing the concrete character of the subject who is never, according to him, a pure for-itself. . . . [For Merleau-Ponty] history is incarnated in a body which possesses a certain generality, a relation to the world anterior to myself; and this is why the body is opaque to reflection, and why my consciousness discovers itself to be "engorged with the sensible." It [that is, consciousness] is not a pure for-itself, or, to use Hegel's phrase which Sartre has taken up, a "hole in being"; but rather "a hollow, a fold, which has been made and which can be un-made."[9]

In this passage Beauvoir perceptively puts her finger on the main divergences between the two philosophies. But what is striking is that she also refrains from making any judgment between them. Although not prepared to criticize Sartre, her "superior" in matters philosophical, it would seem that she was also unwilling, at this time, to defend him.

For, in fact, there is a notion of the subject, and of freedom, in her own work which is strikingly close to Merleau-Ponty's: a notion of the subject that is "never a pure for-itself" but an embodied consciousness, a socially situated and conditioned freedom.

Beauvoir's disagreement with Sartre over the notion of freedom predates the writing of *Being and Nothingness*. In the autobiographical volume *The Prime of Life*, published in 1960, Beauvoir describes a series of conversations she had with Sartre in the spring of 1940. Sartre, briefly in Paris on leave from the army, sketched out for her the main lines of the argument of what was to become *Being and Nothingness*. Their discussions, Beauvoir recalls, centered above all on the problem of "the relation of situation to freedom." On this point they disagreed:

> I maintained that, from the point of view of freedom, as Sartre defined it—not as a stoical resignation but as an active transcendence of the given—not every situation is equal: what transcendence is possible for a woman locked up in a harem? Even such a cloistered existence could be lived in several different ways, Sartre said. I clung to my opinion for a long time and then made only a token submission. Basically [she comments in 1960] I was right. But to have been able to defend my position, I would have had to abandon the terrain of individualist, thus idealist, morality, where we stood.[10]

The "submission" Beauvoir made to Sartre in 1940 was indeed "token." Although she was never willing to challenge Sartre's conception of freedom head-on, she was quietly to subvert it—both in her ethical essays *Pyrrhus et Cinéas* (1944) and *The Ethics of Ambiguity* (1947) and, above all, in *The Second Sex* (1949). In these works, while ostensibly beginning from the central Sartrean premises of *Being and Nothingness*, her tenacious pursuit of her own agenda led her—doubtless in spite of herself—to some most un-Sartrean conclusions. This is particularly the case concerning the question of freedom and the related question of oppression.

Already in 1940 Beauvoir had insisted against Sartre that "not every situation is equal" from the point of view of freedom. In *Pyrrhus et Cinéas*, begun while *Being and Nothingness* was in press,[11] and again in 1947, in *The Ethics of Ambiguity*, she suggested that there might be situations of oppression in which freedom, such as Sartre describes it in *Being and Nothingness,* ceases to be possible. Freedoms, she suggested, are *not* self-sufficient but *interdependent.* For "[only] the freedom of the other is able to give necessity to my being."[12] But if my freedom depends on that of others, then it is vulnerable to their attack: "It is this interdependence [of freedoms] which explains why oppression is possible and why it is hateful."[13] If the life of the oppressed is reduced—as it can be—to no more than physically "perpetuating itself," then, she asserted, "living is only not dying, and human existence is indistinguishable from an absurd vegetation."[14] However, it was only in *The Second Sex* (begun in 1946 and completed in 1949) that she attempted systematically to analyze oppression. The attempt proved to be impossible within the confines of Sartreanism.

Beauvoir begins *The Second Sex* on firmly Sartrean ground. "What is a woman?" she asks, and she answers initially that woman is defined as that which is not man—as other: "She is determined and differentiated with reference to man and not he with reference to her; she is the inessential as opposed to the essential. He is the subject, he is the Absolute: she is the Other."[15] However, very early in the book, Beauvoir introduces a nuance into the notion of otherness that is not found in *Being and Nothingness.* For Sartre, at least in his early work, my "being-for-others" arises on the ground of the other's attempt to destroy my freedom. But since my freedom is an indestructible power of nihilation, the other can never finally touch it. Instead, the other must attempt to nihilate the visible *exterior* of my freedom: my "being-in-situation." It is thus when he or she *looks* at me that the other steals my "being-in-situation" from me and incorporates it, objectlike, within his or her own situation. But although the other objectifies what we might call the external manifestations of my freedom, I always remain a freedom. I remain free to choose my own action in response to the other's transcendence; and I always retain the possibility of turning the tables on the other. Conversely, if I objectify his or her "being-in-situation," I will always fail to reach the other's core freedom, and the other will thus remain for me always a potential threat, an "explosive instrument."[16]

In this account, Sartre assumes the freedoms in conflict to be not only autonomous but also *equal.* For in relations of looking per se there is no reason to assume that human beings are anything but equal. When he describes the torture victim turning the tables on his torturer by *looking* at him,[17] Sartre is asserting that two equal freedoms confront each other, irrespective of the fact that the torturer has the power of physical domination over his victim. Similarly, Sartre argues that "the slave in chains is as free as his master."[18] For, given Sartre's notion of the indestructible freedom of the "for-itself," the question of material or political inequality between master and slave is simply irrelevant to their relation as *two freedoms*. In the same vein, Sartre is able to write—in 1943!—that the Jew remains free in the face of the anti-Semite because he can choose his own attitude toward his persecutor.

It is this assumption—that relations of otherness are conflictual relations between two *equal* freedoms—that Beauvoir quietly challenges. Her challenge, as we will see, implies an account of human freedom that is much closer to Merleau-Ponty's than to Sartre's: it implies that there are degrees, or gradations, of freedom—and that social situations modify freedom itself and not merely its facticity or exteriority. Let us return now to *The Second Sex*. Having begun from the Sartrean notion that woman is other, Beauvoir immediately proceeds to qualify or nuance that notion. We can, she argues, distinguish two significantly different kinds of relations of otherness: those between social *equals* and those that involve social *inequality*. Where the relation is one of equality, she suggests that otherness is "relativized" by a kind of "reciprocity": each recognizes that the other whom he or she objectifies is *also* an equal freedom.

Furthermore, for Beauvoir, such "reciprocity" is not essentially a relation of *looks*. It is expressed and mediated through *institutions*— institutions as diverse as war, trade, festivals. Where, however, otherness exists through relations of *inequality*, there "reciprocity" is to a greater or lesser extent abolished; relations of oppression and subjection (also mediated through institutions) take its place. When one of the two parties in a conflict is privileged, having some material or physical advantage, then "this one prevails over the other and undertakes to keep it in subjection."[19] In relations of subjection, or oppression, as we will see, Beauvoir argues that freedom *itself* undergoes modification. For Beauvoir, the slave is *not* "as free as his master," for the restrictions that operate on his situation come to operate *internally* on his freedom—so as to suppress *his very capacity to project*. In reply to her question of 1940, "What transcendence is possible for a woman locked up in a harem?" Beauvoir's answer is now, "sometimes none." It is not, then, woman's otherness per se but her subjection—the *non*reciprocal objectification of woman by man—that needs to be explained.

Woman is not only other; she is an unequal other. Why? Beauvoir begins by rejecting the most pervasive explanation: biological inferiority. There is no such thing as biological "destiny." In current feminist terms she is saying that the biological facts of sex do not determine gender; the latter is a social construct, to be explained in the realm of human social existence. Beauvoir here agrees with Sartre that only the realm of the "in-itself" is subject to causality. Thus we can never describe any human condition as inevitable, as inscribed in nature. What is often called the "eternal feminine"—what today we would call gender—is not natural.[20] Moreover, and most important, since it is humanly created it is trans-mutable.

However, Beauvoir goes on to point out that although the "eternal feminine" is humanly created, it is created by *man* through the situation *he* imposes on woman. Moreover, this situation is not constituted only by woman's relations with the particular men who treat her as an inferior. For, subtending such direct, personal relations, woman also encounters as fundamental to her situation what we might call a set of social *institutions*. It is these institutions that function analogously to natural forces in perpetuating her inequality. If all that took place between an individual man and woman was a Hegelian—or Sartrean—struggle of consciousness between two human beings, one of whom happened to be male and one female, then we could not anticipate in advance which of them would objectify the other. If, however, we examine the relations of a husband and a wife, then it is very different. For the institution of marriage in all its aspects—legal, economic, sexual, cultural, and so on—has formed *in advance* for the protagonists their own relation of inequality. As Beauvoir points out in a strikingly un-Sartrean passage, "it is not as single individuals that human beings are to be defined in the first place; men and women have never stood opposed to each other in single combat; the couple is an original *Mitsein;* and as such it always appears as a permanent element in a larger collectivity."[21] Furthermore, although Beauvoir insists that biology is not a "destiny," the social constructions placed on the female *body* are very central in defining woman not only as other but as inferior other. There is, she argues, "a constant relation" between sexuality and other social and economic structures of a "collectivity," and she cites Merleau-Ponty's remark that "the body is generality" as part of the explanation for the ubiquity of woman's oppression. For Beauvoir, as for Merleau-Ponty, it is the *incarnate* nature of consciousness that accounts for its inherence in a world "anterior" to itself,[22] a world that is, for women, *already* structured as one of immanence. Expanding on Merleau-Ponty's remark, she discusses the generality of human existence in the following most un-Sartrean manner:

> Across the separation of existents, existence is all one: it makes itself manifest in analogous organisms; therefore there will be constants in the relation of the ontological to the sexual. At a given epoch, the techniques, the economic and social structure, of a collectivity will reveal an identical world to all its members: there will also be a constant relation of sexuality to social forms; analogous individuals, placed in analogous conditions, will take from what is given analogous significations. This analogy does not establish a rigorous universality, but it does enable us to rediscover general types within individual histories.[23]

In *Being and Nothingness*, Sartre cannot account adequately for the existence of "collectivities," of "general types," or of such a generality as "woman's situation." There is in his work a radical individualism that amounts to a kind of solipsism: each of us construes the meaning of both past and present only from the perspective of our own project. "There is," Sartre insists, "no absolute viewpoint which one can adopt so as to compare different situations, each person realizes only one situation—*his own.*"[24] Since situations are each uniquely brought into being by an individual free project, we cannot, for Sartre, conceive of a *general* situation. Nor, of course, could we judge one situation to be more free than another. The central problem raised by Sartre's early work is what I will call the problem of *discontinuity*, and it is a problem with which he himself had to grapple as he became increasingly committed to a politics of radical social transformation in the 1940s. There is a discontinuity, a hiatus he could not bridge, between, on the one hand, discrete, individually constituted meanings and, on the other, the existence of social and historical wholes that appear to have a reality beyond that given to them by each unique individual project. How could one consistently participate in a collective struggle to create a different society unless one could show that there is social being and that individuals can freely act together to create and transform it? In the above passage, while eschewing an "absolute viewpoint," Beauvoir points a way beyond Sartre's dilemma.

For Beauvoir, there is a generality, a weight, to woman's situation—even, we could say, an objectivity. Thus, although her situation is humanly created, a woman may frequently experience it as a "destiny," an exterior conditioning. Moreover, such an experience is not necessarily a choice of "bad faith" on her part. For if a woman is oppressed to the point where transcendence is no longer possible, then her situation *is* effectively her "destiny"; it functions upon her analogously to a natural force. "Every subject," she writes,

> continually affirms himself through his projects as a transcendence; he realizes his freedom only through his continual transcendence toward other freedoms; there is no other justification for present existence than its expansion toward an endlessly open future. Each time that transcendence falls back into immanence there is a degradation of existence into the "in-itself," of freedom into facticity; this fall is a moral fault if the subject agrees to it; it takes the form of a frustration and an oppression if it is inflicted upon him.[25]

Woman is locked in immanence by the situation *man* inflicts upon her—and she is not necessarily responsible. A consistent Sartrean position would make woman responsible for herself, no matter how constrained her situation. But for Beauvoir, although there are some women who comply with their oppressors in "bad faith,"[26] they are not the primary source of the problem. For many there is no moral fault because there simply is no possibility of choice. In the notion that freedom can "fall back into the 'in-itself,'" that the "for-itself" can be turned, through the action of other (that is, male) freedoms, into its very opposite, Beauvoir has radically departed from the Sartrean notion of freedom. Not only does woman fail freely to choose her situation, she is in fact its product: "when . . . a group of individuals is kept in a situation of inferiority, the fact is they are inferior . . . yes, women on the whole *are* today inferior to men, which is to say that their situation gives them less possibilities."[27]

Beauvoir's notion of the falling back of "existence" into the "in-itself" is not to be dismissed as a mere metaphor. Yet, from a Sartrean perspective one could not take the statement as wholly literal either. Strictly speaking, within Sartre's usage of the terms, the "degradation of existence into the 'in-itself'" would have to mean that oppressed woman has actually ceased to be human—which is not at all what Beauvoir wants to say. For Sartre, there is no middle ground. Either the "for-itself," the uncaused upsurge of freedom, exists *whatever* the facticities of its situation, or else it does not exist. In the latter case, one is dealing with the realm of inert being.

Insofar as Beauvoir's account of woman's situation as one of immanence involves the claim that freedom, the "for-itself," can be penetrated and modified by the "in-itself," it implies another ontology than Sartre's. Beauvoir is trying to describe human existence as a synthesis of freedom and constraint, of consciousness and materiality, which, finally, is impossible within the framework of Sartrean ontology. It is, however, possible—and indeed clarified—within the framework of Merleau-Ponty's ontology. It is possible that Beauvoir herself realized this. For, as we saw, not only was she very familiar with Merleau-Ponty's work, but she also quite explicitly drew on his notion that "the body is generality" in trying to establish the generality of woman's situation of oppression.[28] But if she did realize how close her own positions were to his, she was not prepared to say so. Moreover, even when, in 1955, Beauvoir tried to rebut Merleau-Ponty's critique of Sartre, she did not do so by arguing that Merleau-Ponty's philosophy was flawed. Instead she reversed her analysis of 1945, now claiming that Sartre's philosophy was, after all, like Merleau-Ponty's, a philosophy of embodied subjectivity and intersubjectivity.[29] It is, paradoxically, a Sartre refracted through Merleau-Ponty's lenses whom Beauvoir defends against Merleau-Ponty.

But, to return to 1945, a brief examination of Merleau-Ponty's account of human freedom in his *Phenomenology* will show how profound are the similarities between his ideas and Beauvoir's. As Beauvoir had observed in her review, Merleau-Ponty develops, as against Sartre's notion of consciousness as an "*absolute* freedom," an account of *embodied* consciousness. He describes, as she says, a consciousness "engorged with the sensible," a consciousness that is not a "pure for-itself." There is, for Merleau-Ponty, unlike Sartre, an undifferentiated or "general" being, a "primordial layer at which both things and ideas come into being," which is "anterior to the ideas of subject and object"[30] and in which each of us participates as embodied existence. It is through this common participation that we escape the solipsism implied in the Cartesian *cogito*—a solipsism still lurking in *Being and Nothingness*. For our common inherence in being grants us, however ambiguously, an indubitable "primordial communication," an "interworld," an "intersubjectivity." For such an embodied and intersubjective consciousness, freedom "is not distinct from my insertion in the world."[31] Rather, as Merleau-Ponty puts it, it "thrusts roots into the world,"[32] and thus it admits of degree. We will be more free or less free depending on how far our situation enables us to engage in free *actions*. By free actions, Merleau-Ponty means those actions that open onto and shape a future. From this perspective, it is clear that situations—particularly social situations—may qualitatively transform and even suppress freedom.

What Beauvoir described as "immanence," as the falling back of existence into the "in-itself," no longer presents itself as a philosophical problem if, with Merleau-Ponty, we accept that existence is embodied and intersubjective through and through. Against Sartre's claim that we are in principle free at any moment to choose fundamentally to change our lives, Merleau-Ponty insists that *generality* and *probability* are "real phenomena."[33] They exist as the real weight of human history, of institution, of circumstance upon us. Although Merleau-Ponty agrees with Sartre that we are not causally determined, he does not go on to conclude with Sartre that freedom is absolute. Our freedom "gears" itself to our situation, and it does not overturn it in an instant of choice. If women, or other oppressed groups, have "geared" their freedom to an oppressive situation—one that effectively denies them the possibility of action that opens onto the future—then there is no problem involved for Merleau-Ponty in saying that freedom has been suppressed. Since freedom involves *action* that is open, it can cease to be possible. The slave for Merleau-Ponty (like Beauvoir's woman in the harem) is not "as free as his master," because action that would bring a different future is closed to him.[34]

Indeed, in describing the situation of oppressed workers who lack class consciousness, Merleau-Ponty describes in other terms what Beauvoir had called "immanence." If such workers evaluate their situation at all, says Merleau-Ponty, their evaluation "represents the thrust of *a freedom devoid of any project* against unknown obstacles; one cannot in any case talk about a choice."[35] For Sartre, a freedom "devoid of any project" is, of course, a contradiction in terms. Beauvoir *described* such a crippled freedom. But without a critique of the Sartrean notion of freedom and its ontological basis—a critique she did not fully develop—she was unable adequately to *explain* how it was possible. Merleau-Ponty, we can now see, offers us such an explanation.

Moreover, having recognized that situations of oppression may modify freedom itself, Beauvoir and Merleau-Ponty offer striking parallel accounts of what is required for oppression to be overcome: they both recognize—well before Sartre—that there can be no effective *individual* freedom in the face of oppression, that oppressive situations must be changed collectively for freedom to be possible. This insight, already present in *Pyrrhus et Cinéas,* is fleshed out in the discussion of the "independent woman" at the end of *The Second Sex.* Here, although Beauvoir applauds those who struggle in their individual lives against their oppression, she also points out that such a struggle is doomed to failure. For the "independent woman's" existence is shaped not only by her own project but by the practices, institutions, and values of the world into which she is born. Oppression is socially instituted, and to overcome it requires a social as well as an individual transformation.

Similarly, for Merleau-Ponty, an oppressive situation cannot be lived as a freely chosen individual project; nor can it be overcome by individual initiative alone. Freedom comes into being in slow, tortuous movements born of "the concatenation of less and more remote ends." It cannot emerge until the point is reached where individuals cease to experience themselves as the isolated victims of an anonymous oppressive "fate" and experience oppression as collective. Such a transition from immanence can take place only because "my" situation is not, strictly speaking "mine," but part of a more general situation that transcends my immediate experiences. As such it can return to me (as in an emerging revolutionary situation) transformed into an opening toward a new project of which I had not previously dreamed. Freedom is a two-way relation, and it is, we have seen, "not distinct from our insertion in the world." On the contrary, "freedom is always a meeting of the inner and the outer."[36]

In 1960, looking back to 1940, Beauvoir had commented: "To defend my position, I would have had to abandon the terrain of individualist, thus idealist, morality where we stood." By 1949, in *The Second Sex,* she had already tacitly abandoned that terrain. The new terrain she had moved to, we can now see, was one that was not contiguous with that occupied by Sartre in *Being and Nothingness.* It was the terrain Merleau-Ponty had mapped out more fully than she in the *Phenomenology.* But by the late 1940s Sartre was also beginning to shift his ground. When he did so, he was influenced philosophically not only (as he acknowledged) by Merleau-Ponty but also by Beauvoir.

Sartre's intellectual trajectory from *Being and Nothingness* to the *Critique* is complex. I sketch here only an outline of what I take to be his path, but the outline will allow us to see the ways in which his thought moved closer to Beauvoir's. What Sartre lacked in *Being and Nothingness* was a theory that would permit him simultaneously to encompass and link, on the one hand, individual subjectivity and freedom and, on the other, the general weight of institutions, social structures, and events—in short, of history—on individual existence. The radical disjuncture between being "in-itself" and "for-itself," central to his early ontology, precluded such a theory. It was not until the late 1950s, when he wrote the *Critique of Dialectical Reason,* that he fully came to grips with this problem. But already in his *Cahiers pour une morale,* written in the late 1940s but abandoned as a "failure,"[37] he can be seen struggling with it, albeit indecisively.

The material in the *Cahiers* was written in 1947 and 1948, a period in which Beauvoir wrote one of her own works on ethics, *The Ethics of Ambiguity,* and also worked on *The Second Sex.* A detailed comparison of the first of these with the *Cahiers* would certainly be worth undertaking. Here I can only observe that if one contrasts the *Cahiers* with Beauvoir's contemporary works, it is striking that Sartre, still clinging to his early philosophy, finds himself mired in difficulties that do not arise for Beauvoir. In *Being and Nothingness* he had written: "[The] meaning of the past is strictly dependent on my present project. . . . I alone can decide at each moment the bearing of the past."[38] In the *Cahiers* he still writes in a similar vein: "[The] nothingness which separates consciousness from each other makes each determination by these consciousness absolute. . . . Thus, in the midst of History, each historical being is at the same time an a-historical absolute."[39]

Yet, against such a radically individualistic and detotalized notion, we also see Sartre grappling in the *Cahiers* with the fact that History, with a capital *H,* appears to be a real and supraindividual process,[40] and suggesting that one can talk of the "human condition." Thus, he writes:

> A man is a totality and he is an absolute subject. But he cannot be totalized with *another* man. On the other hand the *human condition* is a totality but it does not totalize itself with the in-itself. This does not mean there is no other kind of truth: it is rather that there is a truth of external relation. Triple external relation: between men, between man and nature, between natural phenomena themselves.[41]

But the relation of "the human condition," as a nontotalizing totality, to individual freedom is not explained in this passage. Nor is it clear how the different kinds of "external relations" Sartre lists here—between human beings, between human beings and nature, and within nature— are related either to each other or to "men" as "absolute subjects." While such questions are posed in the interior monologue that constitutes the *Cahiers*, no sustained replies are offered. Later Sartre was able to clarify such issues, first in *Search for a Method* and the *Critique*, then (at a biographical level) in *The Words* and *The Family Idiot*. But in these works he finally abandons the notion of the "absolute subject" (and its absolute freedom) for a notion closer to the embodied and "impure" subject of Merleau-Ponty and Beauvoir.

Sartre's reformulation is perhaps most clearly seen in the *Critique*. For here Sartre's investigation begins from an account of the subject as embodied, as an agent of *praxis* who, in order to overcome organic need, transforms nature into those humanized forms of matter Sartre calls the *practico-inert*. Much of the work examines the dialectic through which forms of the practico-inert come to function as alienating forces against their human creators. Praxis might seem, at first glance, to be a new word Sartre has substituted, after his discovery of Marxism, for "being-for-itself." However, this is not the case. For, unlike "being-for-itself," praxis does not involve an absolute freedom. The practico-inert does not merely impose itself as a series of *external* constraints on praxis. It can, through the mediation of other men and in its most intensely alienating forms, effect a transformation of freedom itself. Sartre uses the term *destiny*—Beauvoir's term from *The Second Sex*—to describe such a praxis alienated from itself. Like Beauvoir, he now describes a "destiny" that is not natural but is the result of a human oppression so intense that no element of choice, no possibility of a freely chosen project, remains for its victims.

Moreover, Sartre's fullest discussion of "destiny" concerns, surely not by chance, a woman. His key example is of a low-paid woman worker on a production line in a shampoo factory. "Oppression," he now observes, "does not reach the oppressed in a particular sector of their life; *it constitutes this life in its totality.*"[42] It constitutes this life such that, in Beauvoir's phrase, "living is only not dying" and no free project is possible. "The role and attitude imposed on her by her work and consumption have never even been the object of an *intention*," Sartre says. Even her so-called inner life, her daydreams and fantasies, are subordinated to the rhythm of the machine at which she must work. While outside the factory her low wages preclude for her the "choice" of motherhood:

> [When] the woman in the Dop Shampoo factory has an abortion in order to avoid having a child she would be unable to feed, she makes a free decision in order to escape a destiny that is made for her; but this decision is itself completely manipulated by the objective situation: she *realizes* through herself what she *is already*; she carries out the sentence, which has already been passed on her, which deprives her of motherhood.[43]

Just as Beauvoir's woman, living her "destiny," is not guilty of "bad faith," so Sartre's woman is not responsible for what she does since she could not have done otherwise. There is no future she could choose other than the one past praxis has decreed. In such a "destiny," and in its moment of subjective comprehension (which Sartre calls *necessity*), praxis is reduced to making oneself the material force through which things happen. Insofar as it still involves a moment of comprehension, such a praxis remains a distinctly human force; but it no longer involves the moment of absolute freedom that is "being-for-itself." For, Sartre now concedes, socially mediated worked matter can limit freedom to the point where no effective choice is possible, only a passive recognition of what one has been made to do: "the man who looks at his work, who recognizes himself in it completely, and who also does not recognize himself at all; the man who can say both: 'This is not what I wanted' and 'I understand that this is what I have done and that I could not do anything else' . . . this man grasps, in an immediate dialectical movement, necessity as the *destiny in exteriority of freedom.*"[44] What Sartre is describing here is, finally, what Beauvoir had called "immanence" and Merleau-Ponty "a freedom devoid of any project."

As this brief sketch indicates, Sartre has here traveled a long way from his claims, in *Being and Nothingness*, regarding the absolute and indestructible freedom of the subject. Clearly many diverse elements— political, personal, philosophical—are present in the complex trajectory that took Sartre from *Being and Nothingness* to the *Critique*, from "absolute freedom" to "destiny." In her public statements Beauvoir consistently cast herself, at least in matters philosophical, as Sartre's disciple—even, one might suggest, as a mere other to Sartre's philosophical absolute. But we should cease accepting her too "feminine" self-deprecation at face value. For, her own assessment notwithstanding, we have seen that Beauvoir's philosophical ideas of the 1940s anticipate in important ways those of Sartre in the late 1950s. And thus her work can be considered one of the significant influences on Sartre's intellectual trajectory.

Notes

1. *The Second Sex*, trans. H. M. Parshley (New York, 1974), 758. French original, *Le Deuxième Sexe*, 2 vols. (Paris, 1949). Cited hereafter as *TSS*. Citations will be given to the English edition. However, translations will sometimes be altered, in which case this will be indicated and a French page reference given in parentheses.

2. "Wanting to talk about myself, I became aware that to do so I should first have to describe the condition of woman in general." *Force of Circumstance*, trans. Richard Howard (New York, 1964), 185. French original, *La force des choses* (Paris, 1963).

3. Beauvoir's relationship to Sartre has, of course, also been scrutinized on the biographical and psychological planes, but these are not my concerns here.

4. "Interférences," interview of Simone de Beauvoir and Jean-Paul Sartre by Michel Sicard, *Obliques*, nos. 18–19 (1979), 325. In Alice Schwarzer, *After "The Second Sex": Conversations with Simone de Beauvoir*, trans. M. Howarth (New York, 1984), 109, Beauvoir makes a similar point: "In philosophical terms, he was creative and I am not. . . . I always recognized his superiority in that area. So where Sartre's philosophy is concerned, it is fair to say that I took my cue from him because I also embraced existentialism myself." See also Jessica Benjamin and Margaret A. Simons, "Simone de Beauvoir: An Interview," *Feminist Studies* 5 (Summer 1979): 330–45.

5. See, for example, Michèle le Doeuff, "Simone de Beauvoir and Existentialism," *Feminist Studies* 6 (Summer 1980): 277–89; Mary Evans, *Simone de Beauvoir: A Feminist Mandarin* (London, 1985).

6. Judith Okely, *Simone de Beauvoir* (London, 1986), 122. This standard view of the relation of Sartre and Beauvoir has so far been most forcefully challenged by Margaret A. Simons. In her papers "Beauvoir and Sartre: The Question of Influence," *Eros* 8, no. 1 (1981): 25–42; and "Beauvoir and Sartre: The Philosophical Relationship," in *Simone de Beauvoir: Witness to a Century*, special issue of *Yale French Studies* 72 (1986): 165–79, Simons argues (via a somewhat different route from my own) that Beauvoir's work anticipates Sartre's at several important points.

7. "Interférences," 326.

8. "Merleau-Ponty," *Situations*, trans. B. Eisler (Greenwich, Conn., 1965), 174–76. Sartre's essay was originally published shortly after Merleau-Ponty's death as "Merleau-Ponty vivant," in a memorial issue of *Les Temps Modernes*, nos. 184–85 (October 1961).

9. "La Phénoménologie de la perception," *Les Temps Modernes*, no. 2 (November 1945): 366–67.

10. *The Prime of Life*, trans. Peter Green (Cleveland, 1962), 346. Translation altered. French original: *La force de l'âge* (Paris, 1960), 2:498.

11. See ibid., 433–35, for Beauvoir's account of the circumstances surrounding the writing of this essay and her evaluation of its relation to Sartre's philosophy.

12. *Pyrrhus et Cinéas* (Paris, 1944), 95–96.

13. *The Ethics of Ambiguity*, trans. B. Frechtman (New York, 1967), 82. French original, *Pour une morale de l'ambiguïté* (Paris, 1947).

14. Ibid., 82–83.

15. *TSS*, xix. Translation altered; French 1:15.

16. Jean-Paul Sartre, *Being and Nothingness*, trans. Hazel E. Barnes (New York, 1966), 364. French original, *L'Etre et le néant* (Paris, 1943). Cited hereafter as *BN*.

17. Ibid., 495ff.

18. Ibid., 673.

19. *TSS*, 69.

20. For an intriguing discussion of some of the implications of this separation of gender and sex, see Judith Butler, "Sex and Gender in Simone de Beauvoir's *Second Sex*," in *Simone de Beauvoir: Witness to a Century*, special issue of *Yale French Studies* 72 (1986): 35–49.

21. *TSS*, 39. Translation altered; French 1:74. Compare with Sartre: "The essence of relations between consciousness is not the *Mitsein*; it is conflict," *BN*, 525.

22. Maurice Merleau-Ponty, *Phenomenology of Perception*, trans. Colin Smith (London, 1962), 219. French original, *La Phénoménologie de la perception* (Paris, 1945). Cited hereafter as *PP*. Beauvoir refers to this notion in her 1945 review of the *Phenomenology*.

23. *TSS*, 52. Translation altered; French, 1:88.

24. *BN*, 673.

25. *TSS*, xxxiii. Translation altered; French, 1:31.

26. Ibid., 802.

27. Ibid., xxviii. Translation altered; French, 1:25.

28. See ibid., 52; also 7 and 33n.

29. "Merleau-Ponty et le pseudo-Sartrisme," in *Privilèges* (Paris, 1955). The occasion for Merleau-Ponty's critique of Sartre and Beauvoir's attempt to rebut it was a political disagreement over the revolutionary potential of Marxism. However, in the course of the argument the major philosophical divergences also surfaced very clearly.

30. *PP*, 219.

31. Ibid., 360.

32. Ibid., 456.

33. Ibid., 442.

34. Ibid., 436ff.

35. Ibid., 444; emphasis added.

36. Ibid., 454.

37. See, for example, interview with Sicard, *Obliques*, 9–29. See also his comments in Michel Contat and Alexandre Astruc, *Sartre by Himself* (New York, 1978), 77–78, 80–81. For my fuller evaluation of the *Cahiers*, see Sonia Kruks, "Sartre's *Cahiers pour une morale*: Failed Attempt or New Trajectory in Ethics?" *Social Text*, nos. 13–14 (Winter–Spring 1986): 184–94.

38. *BN*, 610.

39. Jean-Paul Sartre, *Cahiers pour une morale*, ed. A. Elkaïm-Sartre (Paris, 1983), 32. Cited hereafter as *CPM*.

40. See, for example, the discussions of feudalism and of technological change in ibid., 81–86, 86–89.

41. Ibid., 477.

42. *Critique of Dialectical Reason*, trans. Alan Sheridan-Smith, ed. Jonathan Rée (London, 1976), 232; emphasis added. French original, *Critique de la raison dialectique* (Paris, 1960).

43. Ibid., 235.

44. Ibid., 226–27.

6

Sartre's Secret Key

Kate Fullbrook and Edward Fullbrook

Biography, like science, tends to divide into two activities: one concerned primarily with gathering facts, and one focused on ordering and explaining those facts. Science calls the results of the latter activity "hypotheses" or "theories"; biography tends to label these "stories" or "histories" or "legends." Though there are many exceptions (and cases are rarely pure), individual biographers, like scientists, tend to specialize in one of the two kinds of activity. In writing *Simone de Beauvoir and Jean-Paul Sartre: The Remaking of a Twentieth-Century Legend* (Fullbrook and Fullbrook, 1994) our study of the Beauvoir–Sartre partnership, we worked exclusively on the narrative that previously had ordered and explained the known facts about the couple. The experience of writing the book resembled riding a historical-intellectual rollercoaster. Disorientation, loss of balance, even vertigo are probably appropriate words to describe our reactions to our findings. Like scientists faced with the need to jettison a long-standing theory because the traditional interpretation of the observed evidence no longer fits, we found ourselves in the position of needing seriously to revise the standard account of one of the most famous (and well-loved) intimate and intellectual partnerships of the century, and to entertain entirely new hypotheses regarding its nature.

The scientific analogy may seem strained when dealing with as literary and historical a genre as biography, with its attention to narrative coherence and documentary evidence. However, in many ways, the analogy is an exact one. The Sartre–Beauvoir story has been told many times, so many times that it has become part of the intellectual hagiography of the modern era. Since 1985, following the deaths first of Sartre in 1980 and then Beauvoir in 1986, it has attracted a particularly distinguished and hardworking group of biographers with Annie Cohen-Solal ([1985] 1987), Ronald Hayman (1986), John Gerassi (1989), Claude Francis and Fernande Gontier (1989), Deirdre Bair (1990a), and Margaret Crosland (1992) all providing substantial studies of the two philosophers. Each of these accounts has added something, and often a great deal, to the general understanding of the dynamics of Beauvoir and Sartre's partnership. The volumes of letters and diaries by Sartre and Beauvoir themselves that have also appeared since their deaths have, inevitably, revealed more (Beauvoir 1990a, 1990b; Sartre 1984, 1992). All these works, however, whatever their differences, have shared one overwhelming feature: They have all been composed (or in the case of the letters and diaries, introduced to the public) under a single governing theory about the nature of the relationship they recorded and interpreted. And that theory was provided, ironically enough, by the subjects themselves. No biographer of Sartre or Beauvoir can begin anywhere other than with the autobiographies that the pair themselves offered as the definitive guides to their lives and times. Beauvoir's four volumes of autobiography, *Memoirs of a Dutiful Daughter* (1958), *The Prime of Life* (1960), *Force of Circumstance* (1963), and *All Said and Done* (1972); her books on the deaths of her mother (*A Very Easy Death* [1964]), and of Sartre (*Adieux* [1981]); as well as Sartre's account of his childhood in *The Words* (1964) and his young manhood in the introduction to Paul Nizan's *Aden, Arabie* (1987), offer versions of the facts of their lives and interpretations of them that have been accorded an understandably great deal of credence.

As writers who were asked particularly to address the nature of the relationship between the pair, we, too, necessarily began our work under the aegis of the theory that our subjects themselves constructed. This general theory regarding the relationship is almost too well known to be retold. Its two basic features were (1) the idea of the pair's distinctive vow of lifelong fidelity that escaped the strictures of bourgeois marriage and built in allowances for masculine promiscuity (and rare bouts of helpless, deep love for the female Beauvoir, who had two serious lovers besides Sartre: Nelson Algren and Claude Lanzmann), and, (2) more significant, their perfect enactment of a classic paradigm of female intellectual subservience to the mind and career of one of the great men of his era. This theory excited, charmed, and generally rather pleased readers from the time that Beauvoir first purveyed it in *The Prime of Life* in 1960. Despite puzzled suspicions by some scholars and commentators that the theory might be slightly shaky, the couple (and, in particular, Beauvoir) remained faithful to her account of the pair's relationship to the end (Schwarzer 1984; Simons and Benjamin 1979).

As we noted above, the inevitable starting point for our biography was this account too. However, as our research progressed we became increasingly unsure it was tenable. Scientists working under the guiding principles of any given theory historically have tended to discover anomalies as time passes. When such anomalies arise they can be dealt with in a limited number of ways. They can be treated as singularities that run counter to, but do not invalidate the governing theory itself. They can be accommodated by devising ad hoc hypotheses that are incorporated, no matter how uneasily, into the governing theory. In the case of particularly glaring anomalies, scientists have two drastic choices: they can abandon the theory that fails to incorporate the anomalies which run counter to it, or, being human and fallible (and sometimes at a loss as to how to proceed otherwise under the circumstances) they may choose to ignore the anomalies and carry on as if the theory has not been challenged by the anomalies. The history of physics presents a clear case of this process. The revisions made within physics from the time of Democritus and Aristotle, through to those of Copernicus, to Galileo and Newton, through Einstein, and on to the struggles of the physicists of our own day to reconcile the theories of relativity and quantum mechanics provide what is perhaps the most famous example of this revisionary process of hypothecation, which responds to the appearance of anomalies that, in turn, refuse to be accommodated by a succession of otherwise very useful theories regarding the behavior of the physical universe.

When we began our work on Sartre and Beauvoir, no one seriously questioned the basic outlines of the account that Beauvoir had given of the partnership we were to examine. Yet anomalies of various kinds, which seemed to undermine at least parts of the theory, kept drawing our attention. One of the interesting features of the appearance of these anomalies was that they were generated by scholars with widely divergent interests in Sartre and Beauvoir, which meant they were rather trouble-some to bring together in ways that made sense.

The first striking anomaly was the definitive revelation, in her pub-lished letters, of Beauvoir's bisexuality, a feature of her behavior that she had taken pains to conceal during her lifetime. Of course, we were aware from the start that Beauvoir, for all her voluminous attempts to give the appearance of telling all about herself and her friends in her autobiographical works, had warned her readers that she, in fact, meant to do no such thing. Her disclaimer at the opening of *The Prime of Life* was candid and honest, but strategically placed to be forgotten in the welter of detail and self-revelation that followed. In her introduction to this second volume of her autobiography, Beauvoir explicitly issued a warning aimed at anyone demanding complete self-revelation from her. After acknowledging the general public's curiosity about the writing profession, after offering her opinion that such curiosity can best be satisfied by studying the details of individual historical examples of such lives, and, finally, after noting that her autobiography is intended to "help to eliminate certain misunderstandings such as always arise be-tween writers and their public, and which I have frequently experienced, to my personal annoyance," she nevertheless goes on to say to her readers that "at the same time I must warn them that I have no intention of telling them everything. . . . I have no intention of filling these pages with spiteful gossip about myself and my friends; I lack the instincts of the scandalmonger. There are many things which I firmly intend to leave in obscurity. . . . though I have suppressed certain facts, I have at no point set down deliberate falsehoods" (Beauvoir [1960] 1965, 8–9). Beauvoir's claim to have eschewed falsehood is not reliable. However, in the mass and detail of her reportage on her life many of the items that might now be regarded as misrepresentations were, indeed, omissions from the record. Other aspects of her autobiography that might be queried can be explained by the need to build a satisfying narrative out of the disordered stuff of memory. Still other questionable features derive from the very real truism that any account of any life (including one given by the subject in question) is necessarily an interpretation of that life. As Beauvoir herself noted, "A novel is a 'problematique.' The story of my life is itself a problematique." (Simons and Benjamin 1979, 332) The explicit linkage of fiction and autobiography by one of the most sophisticated novelists of her era is instructive. As we proceeded with our research it became ever more clear to us that the powerful structures that Beauvoir had built to fit her accounts of her life into a coherent frame featured not only omissions, selective interpretations, and incomplete meditations on experience that was still very much in progress, but the deliberate laying of false trails, and a thorough and purposeful commitment to skewing the accounts of some of the central features at the heart of her story.

All this whetted our curiosity. We were not so much interested in the fact that Beauvoir and Sartre had falsified the record, but in what this falsification meant. As Michael Holroyd, the biographer of Lytton Strachey and George Bernard Shaw, points out: "It is understandable, and right, that people should seek to protect themselves and others close to them during their lives. But if we have these necessary prevarications and sentimentalities as our only knowledge of how people lived, and as our examples of conduct, then we will mislead ourselves and make ourselves unhappy by accepting impossible standards. The lies we tell are part of the life we live and therefore part of the truth" (1988, 99–100). When we viewed the Beauvoir–Sartre legend in this light we were all the more concerned with discovering the truths of which the lies were part.

To their credit, both Sartre and Beauvoir (and particularly Beauvoir) left letters and diaries that have been published posthumously which contain the information to generate entirely new hypotheses regarding their relationship. Beauvoir published Sartre's portion of their correspondence in 1983, against the wishes of Sartre's adopted daughter and literary executor, Arlette El-Kaim Sartre. Beauvoir's own adopted daughter, Sylvie Le Bon de Beauvoir, published Beauvoir's half of the letters in 1990. Beauvoir publicly claimed, during her lifetime, that the letters were "lost," though she showed them to her biographer, Deirdre Bair, allowing her only restricted access to their contents. The publication of these letters opened great fissures in the Sartre–Beauvoir story that Beauvoir had taken such pains to defend during her life (and she held to her version even when Sartre had exasperated her almost beyond tolerance with his behavior in his last years). The letters, put together, revealed an overwhelming anomaly in Beauvoir's accounts of her and Sartre's intimate lives. Both were shown to be sexually rapacious, given to titillating each other with graphic descriptions of their lovers' bedroom antics, and full of sniggering disregard for the dignity of their sexual partners. Beauvoir's bisexuality was also documented. All in all, it was a difficult performance for defenders of the pair to take. In a rather sad article in *The Guardian*, Bair begged that the letters be read, not alone, but in the context of the pair's entire association. "Alone," she said, "they are a sorry way to remember one of this century's most influential couples" (1990b).

Sorry or not, the publication of the Sartre–Beauvoir correspondence opened up a significant area of variance in terms of Beauvoir's accounts of their lives. Another such anomaly appeared in the first volume of John Gerassi's fine biography *Jean-Paul Sartre: Hated Conscience of His Century* (1989). In it, he revealed that Sartre had not been Beauvoir's first lover (90). We found that Beauvoir's letters supported this claim. Like Bair and like Francis and Gontier, Gerassi dismantled certain keystones of Beauvoir's autobiographical edifice. Close examination of the letters and diaries revealed another anomaly. It became more and more obvious to us that Sartre and Beauvoir's famous pact regarding essential and nonessential lovers and their agreement never to marry was grounded in Beauvoir's insistence on such an arrangement rather than Sartre's, who more than once unsuccessfully proposed marriage to Beauvoir. In 1991, Gilbert Joseph's controversial (and later branded scurrilous) book, *Une si douce Occupation*, queried the pair's active roles in the French Resistance. Though we remained undisturbed by this attack (Beauvoir had made their ambivalence, incompetence, buffoonery, and plain failure as resistants very clear, and Sartre was uncharacteristically modest about his personal involvement with the movement), the couple's intimate and political legend seemed to be coming apart at the seams.

All these revisionary factors called for a radical rethinking of the nature of the partnership. We had an increasingly difficult time incorporating the proliferating anomalies into the familiar Sartre–Beauvoir legend. However, though we necessarily were intrigued by the stream of corrections to Beauvoir's accounts of the couple's lives together, we were still more interested in suggestions by a few philosophers regarding the relative intellectual balance between the two.

By the time we had absorbed the documentary evidence that demonstrated the need for a radical rethinking of the interpretation of Sartre's and Beauvoir's private lives, we were ready to entertain much more significant (it seemed to us) revisions in terms of Beauvoir's performance as a philosopher. Beauvoir had skewed significantly the story of the couple's intimate association: perhaps she had also skewed her story about her performance as a thinker. With this possibility we felt ourselves in almost uncharted territory. After all, hiding one's own and one's partner's unedifying sexual behavior and proclivities as fairly mean-minded gossips appeared more than understandable (most of us might do the same), but adamantly refusing credit for major philosophical ideas *and* working indefatigably throughout one's life to ascribe them to someone else struck us rather differently.

Linda Singer's "Interpretation and Retrieval: Rereading Beauvoir" (1985) and Margaret A. Simons's "Beauvoir and Sartre: The Philosophical Relationship" (1986) strongly suggested to us there was something amiss in Beauvoir's consistent denials of her capacity for generating philosophical ideas. These essays were comparable to empirical findings that falsify part of a major scientific theory. They showed that, contrary to the legend, Beauvoir had made momentous philosophical contributions in the postwar period, some of which were subsequently taken up by and credited to Sartre. Simons's article was especially subversive, as it documented the appearance of the concept of the Social Other in Beauvoir's work prior to Sartre's.

A word needs to be said here about our terminology. To alleviate a long-standing source of confusion, we have introduced the terms *Individual Other* and *Social Other* to distinguish between two related but distinct Beauvoirean theories or concepts, both of which are commonly labeled merely as the Other. The former (the Individual Other) refers to her theory of ontologically possible relations between individual consciousnesses and to her profoundly original solution to the classical philosophical problem of the existence of other consciousnesses. The Social Other is an extension of the concept of the Individual Other to collectivities or social categories based on dualities, such as men and women, white and nonwhite, colonialist and colonized. Thus, in her introduction to

The Second Sex Beauvoir writes: "She [woman] is defined and differentiated with reference to man and not he with reference to her; she is the
incidental. . . . He is the Subject . . .—she is the Other." By relating
such social relationships to her theory of the Individual Other, Beauvoir
generates a framework for psychologically deep and culturally critical
analyses of socialization. Moreover, central to her earlier theory was "the
reciprocity of subject and object." When this finding was introduced
into her new theory, the effect was "to deprive the concept [Social]
Other of its absolute sense and to make manifest its relativity." This
made it possible, argued Beauvoir, for oppressed groups to turn the social
tables by regarding "themselves as subjects" and thereby "transform"
their oppressors into "others" (Beauvoir 1972, 16, 17, 19). Beauvoir's
concept of the Social Other, therefore, besides providing an intrinsically
radical instrument of analysis, also mapped out a nonviolent means of
social and cultural insurrection.

In the face of the Singer and Simons discoveries, the thesis that Sartre
was the original philosopher and Beauvoir merely his disciple could still
be saved, but only by radical amendment. Moreover, when revised to
take account of the newly discovered facts, we found the old story
somewhat implausible. We easily could believe that a spectacularly
brilliant university philosophy student like Beauvoir had turned out to
be totally without originality. But it overtaxed our credulity to believe
that this ex-student had shown, in fifteen years of philosophical work,
zero originality and then suddenly, in the late 1940s, in *The Ethics of
Ambiguity* and *The Second Sex,* earthshaking amounts of it.

We began to look for evidence that Beauvoir had contributed to the
philosophical system found in Sartre's *Being and Nothingness* (1943).
Although this search steadily accumulated facts suggesting Beauvoir had
played a creative part in the making of Sartrean existentialism (and
Beauvoir's autobiographies are littered with accounts of the pair working
side by side, exchanging manuscripts, critiquing each other's work), for
more than two years hard facts confirming such a contribution remained
elusive. During this time we periodically suffered crises of faith. The
more we read and reread texts by and about Sartre and Beauvoir, the
more we were immersed in the legend that proclaimed the futility of our
pursuit. Furthermore, it seemed that the findings of Singer and Simons
had not been admitted fully to academic consciousness. We found
ourselves reading works by both Sartre and Beauvoir scholars that,
though written well after the appearance of Singer's and Simons's

articles, continued to portray Beauvoir as devoid of philosophical originality. From time to time, one or both of us would wonder if we were
deceiving ourselves. Had we really read that Simons article? Did it really
say what we remembered it said? One of us would dig it out of our
Beauvoir documents box. Yes, Simons's paper had been published in
1986 in the *Yale French Review*. Yes, it credited Beauvoir with the
concept of the Social Other. But had Margaret Simons really got it
right? For the third, fourth, fifth, or sixth time one of us would check
her arguments against the relevant texts, *The Ethics of Ambiguity*, *The
Second Sex*, and Sartre's *Anti-Semite and Jew*. Yes, of course, Simons's
argument was sound. With the pertinent texts in hand, Beauvoir's
philosophical originality was glaringly obvious. Reconvinced and reliber-
ated from the old legend, we would return to the hunt.

We were searching for empirical evidence of some significant, if
minor, contribution to the evolution of French postwar existentialism.
Like players in the map-game who cannot find a geographical label
because it is the largest item on the map, we were astonished (and
somewhat embarrassed) when we found Beauvoir's marker written
grandly across the entirety of the philosophical territory.

Detection of Beauvoir's true part in the making of twentieth-century
philosophy owed much to the method we employed in the latter
stages of our research. We chronologically tracked the development of
"Sartre's" philosophical system as it appeared in his writings, paying
particular attention to his diaries and letters. This enabled us to chart,
with increasing precision, a sort of calender of the construction of
"Sartrean existentialism," leading up to the publication of *Being and
Nothingness* (1943). We then used this "calender" to direct our scrutiny
of the Beauvoir texts. This process brought no definitive rewards. But
the "calender" led us to another and wholly unexpected dimension of
the puzzle. It showed that by mid-February 1940 Sartre still lacked most
of the ingredients of the philosophical system found in *Being and
Nothingness*. Furthermore, he appeared to continue to hold views fundamentally contrary to that system. Given that he submitted his manuscript of *Being and Nothingness* to Gallimard for publication in October
1942, this meant that in a period of 32 months he had a revolutionary
change of philosophical heart, invented an astonishing range of philosophical ideas, organized them with great logical cohesion into a monumental system, and then, after all that, still had time left over to write a
brilliant 700-page account of his new philosophy. Meanwhile, in those

same 32 months he also spent four months as a soldier, nine months as a prisoner of war, a year as a full-time lycée teacher, while on the side he wrote two plays and a novel and a half, dabbled at organizing a resistance movement and toured France on a bicycle. If all this was to be believed, Sartre was an even more remarkable man than we, his admirers, had imagined.

From studying his *War Diaries* it became clear that the great watershed in the development of his philosophical system had come at the end of February 1940, in the week and a half immediately following his return from an eleven-day army leave in Paris. Only the previous month he had written to Beauvoir about his abject failure to invent any philosophical ideas of his own, but after his time with her in Paris, original ideas seemed to spring to his mind faster than he could write them down. Beauvoir's diaries show that while on leave in Paris, Sartre spent a considerable amount of his precious time reading her manuscript of *She Came to Stay.* We were familiar with at least three readings of this novel, none of which treated it primarily as a philosophical text (as, for example, has long been standard practice among philosophers with Sartre's *Nausea*). At this point we still failed to go beyond the traditional readings of Beauvoir's novel. But an anomaly that we had uncovered regarding the story of the genesis of the novel caused us to keep it in mind as we considered the astounding, and increasingly unbelievable bout of creativity that Sartre had enjoyed following his Paris leave (Sartre 1984, 197–262).

In *The Prime of Life* Beauvoir wrote an extended account of the planning and writing of *She Came to Stay,* but at the end of her life she gave Deirdre Bair a radically different version of its origins. In her memoirs, she tells how she sent Brice Parain, Sartre's editor at Gallimard, "a typed version of the first hundred pages of my novel—that is, the section dealing with Françoise's childhood." On Parain's and Sartre's recommendation she decided, once her "mind had been set at rest" by Munich (30 September 1938) "to omit not only my heroine's past life, but also her meeting with Pierre and the eight years they spent together." She then tells how, following a suggestion made by Sartre, she decided that in "the first chapter" of her novel she would introduce "Gerbert, and let Françoise be tempted by his youth and charm, only to renounce them" (Beauvoir [1960] 1965, 337). On the nonphilosophical level, this is what happens in the first chapter of the published novel. Furthermore, Gallimard's publication in 1979 of the discarded chapters in *Les Ecrits de*

Simone de Beauvoir confirmed Beauvoir's earlier account of her false start on *She Came to Stay* (Francis and Gontier 1979, 275–316). These two chapters show that the scrapped material was as Beauvoir described it in her memoirs. Thus, the new beginning that Beauvoir made with *She Came to Stay* took place long before, sixteen months to be exact, Sartre's February 1940 reading of her manuscript.

More than thirty years later, Beauvoir told Bair a very different story of her writing of *She Came to Stay*. What stands out in her later account, even before one comes to understand its significance, is that it is focused on the question of how much of the novel existed for Sartre to read on his leave in February 1940. Bair, paraphrasing her interviews with Beauvoir writes: "Actually, by February 1940 she had written what would later amount to less than fifty pages of the printed text." And "The parts of the earliest draft of *L'Invitée* that Beauvoir wanted Sartre to read during his leave did not concern her main character, Françoise." And a page later, "By the time of Sartre's February leave, she was no further along with the novel than the initial conception and the development of the two woman characters" (Bair, 1990a, 228–29).

So which of these two stories, both told by Beauvoir at length, was one supposed to believe, and why had she concocted the false one? We found the definitive answer to the first half of the question in Beauvoir's *Lettres à Sartre* (1990b). These show (more than thirty of her letters prior to Sartre's leave refer to her progress with the novel) that her account in *The Prime of Life* of writing *She Came to Stay* is the truthful one and that by the time of Sartre's leave she had drafted at least five hundred pages in her compact handwriting.

The answer to the second half of the question is more speculative, but no less interesting. When at the end of the 1950s Beauvoir was writing *The Prime of Life*, virtually no one (except herself and Sartre) was predisposed to believe in the possibility of a woman creating one of the major philosophical systems of her century. There was, therefore, no need for her to take pains to hide their ultimate secret. The story she had told about her relationship to Sartre and philosophy merely confirmed the more general story that society invariably told about the relations that necessarily held among men, women, and ideas. But by the 1980s, among a small but growing minority, the climate of belief was changing. Beauvoir also had been made aware by her 1979 interviewers, Simons and Benjamin, that capable writers were about who were deeply suspicious of her claims not to have contributed to "Sartre's" philosophical system. These very real threats to her story were greatly amplified when, in 1983, Sartre's *War Diaries* were published against Beauvoir's wishes.

In her new biographical study of Beauvoir, Toril Moi restates the traditional ground rules for the reading of Beauvoir's fiction. Moi distinguishes between "*his* [Sartre's] terrain," which was "the repertoire of classical philosophy"; and "*her* [Beauvoir's] terrain," which was "the subject of women's . . . position in patriarchal society" (1994, 154). It was Sartre, ironically, who demonstrated that this is not always the best way to read women's fiction. After many readings of his diary entry of 17 February 1940, it dawned on us that he must have read Beauvoir's manuscript of *She Came to Stay* as Plato's dialogues or his own *Nausea* are read; that is, as a philosophical text. With this new theory as to what kind of a work Beauvoir's novel might be, we turned back to her text.

A well-known pattern in the history of science is that when a new theory is conjectured in response to the appearance of anomalies to an old one, there often follows an extremely rapid discovery of empirical phenomena that all along had been, so to speak, under scientists' noses. These discoveries take place because the new theory provides the key to a kind of decoding of the empirical world. When we applied Sartre's own secret key to *She Came to Stay*, philosophical arguments jumped from its pages. A full decoding of Beauvoir's philosophical masterpiece, however, will require the industry of many scholars. In *Simone de Beauvoir and Jean-Paul Sartre: The Remaking of a Twentieth-Century Legend* we deciphered most of its first chapter, nine pages, in which Beauvoir outlines *her* philosophical system, which Sartre adopted as *his* philosophical system in *Being and Nothingness*.

Thanks to Sartre, and in turn to his disciples, the basic ideas of Beauvoirean existentialism—although for the time being known under another name—are widely appreciated. But the heights of its achievement on the terrain of classical philosophy have, for a variety of reasons, tended to be greatly underestimated. Arthur Danto, a distinguished member of the opposing school of analytical philosophy, has tried to set the record straight on this historically important matter (1985). But an even more powerful corrective is to read, with Sartre's secret key, the text in which it all began. There, starting on page one of her novel, we see Beauvoir, intellectually ambitious almost beyond belief, tackling head-on what have been perhaps philosophy's two most central and intractable problems: the conceptual gap between appearance and reality, and the question of the existence of other people as conscious beings whose consciousnesses act on one another.

Our discoveries struck us, and still strike us, as extraordinary. Famously, one of the great theoretical crises in physics was provoked by Copernicus's realization that the earth orbited the sun, and not, as in the time-honored Ptolemaic view that the sun circled the earth. In this great historical battle for the establishment of the truth, more was at stake—in terms of religious beliefs, political control, and the philosophical positioning of humanity in the universe—than the movements of heavenly bodies. And, under either view, the sun continued to shine. In a perfect world, the revision of the relative philosophical contributions of Sartre and Beauvoir would make little difference. The existential ideas promulgated in their philosophy remain in place; the effects these ideas have had on others are unchanged. However, as in the revision of the theory of the mechanism of the solar system, things are not altogether like this. And some of the questions generated by the revisions of the story of Sartre's and Beauvoir's relative philosophical contributions are profound.

A few of these questions are obvious. Despite doubts regarding authority, origination, and the intellectual ownership of ideas, of which one cannot be unaware at the present time, it is clear that the ascription of the generation of ideas to individuals has powerful social and political effects. The history of philosophy normally is read as an unbroken chain of work done exclusively by men. The fact that a woman devised what has a claim to be considered as the central philosophical system of the twentieth century throws this model into disarray. Moreover, a simple name change from Sartrean existentialism to Beauvoirean existentialism alters the cast of that system and gives it a radically different trajectory. The morbidity and pessimism found in Sartre's interpretation of Beauvoir's philosophical system is completely lacking in the original. In particular, whereas in *Being and Nothingness* Sartre identified the object-subject as the only possible mode of human relations, Beauvoir from *She Came to Stay* onward also admitted the possibility of the subject-subject or "reciprocity" mode. The way now appears clear to offer a unified account of Beauvoir's theory of the Other, which would provide continuity between the theory of the Individual Other and the theory of the Social Other. Finally, whereas Sartrean existentialism leads to a rapprochement with Marxism, a dead movement, Beauvoirean existentialism leads to feminism, the most prominent and vital social movement of the foreseeable future.[1]

However, feminist philosophers, who, it might be anticipated, would welcome these revisions, are also confronted by certain problems. Two of the most intelligent recent studies of Beauvoir, Michèle Le Doeuff's *Hipparchia's Choice* (1991) and Toril Moi's *Simone de Beauvoir: The Making of an Intellectual Woman* (1994), are both constructed on an absolute sense of Beauvoir's separation from and rejection of branches of philosophy that address the universal human subject, while favoring thought grounded in nongeneralizable female experience. Indeed, most feminist philosophy and psychology of recent years has stressed gender difference as the heart of its arguments for building a separatist philosophical tradition. This grounding theory, too, now demands reconsideration. But then, the disruptions of legends are always startling events, given to generating new questions as much as providing answers to questions whose full significance is rarely known.

Note

1. We are exploring these issues in a work in progress, a book on Simone de Beauvoir for Polity Press in the *Key Contemporary Thinkers* series (scheduled to appear in 1996).

References

Bair, Deirdre. 1990a. *Simone de Beauvoir: A Biography*. London: Jonathan Cape.
———. 1990b. "Simone's Scarlet Letters." *The Guardian*, 15 March.
Beauvoir, Simone de. 1948. *The Ethics of Ambiguity*. Translated by Bernard Frechtman. New York: Citadel.
———. 1958. *Memoirs of a Dutiful Daughter*. Translated by James Kirkup. Harmondsworth, Middlesex: Penguin.
———. [1960] 1965. *The Prime of Life*. Translated by Peter Green. Harmondsworth, Middlesex: Penguin.
———. 1968. *Force of Circumstance*. Translated by Richard Howard. Harmondsworth, Middlesex: Penguin.
———. 1969. *A Very Easy Death*. Translated by Patrick O'Brian. Harmondsworth, Middlesex: Penguin.
———. 1972. *The Second Sex*. Translated by H. M. Parshley. Harmondsworth, Middlesex: Penguin.
———. 1977. *All Said and Done*. Translated by Patrick O'Brian. Harmondsworth, Middlesex: Penguin.
———. 1979. *Les Escrits de Simone de Beauvoir*. Edited by Claude Francis and Fernande Gontier. Paris: Gallimard.

———. 1984. *She Came to Stay*. Translated by Yvonne Moyse and Roger Senhouse. London: Flamingo.

———. 1985. *Adieux: A Farewell to Sartre*. Translated by Patrick O'Brian. Harmondsworth, Middlesex: Penguin.

———. 1990a. *Journal de Guerre: Septembre 1939–Janvier 1941*. Edited by Sylvie Le Bon de Beauvoir. Paris: Gallimard.

———. 1990b. *Lettres à Sartre*. Vol. 1, *1930–1939*; Vol. II, *1940–1963*. Edited and annotated by Sylvie Le Bon de Beauvoir. Paris: Gallimard.

Cohen-Solal, Annie. [1985] 1987. *Sartre: A Life*. London: Heinemann.

Crosland, Margaret. 1992. *Simone de Beauvoir: The Woman and Her Work*. London: Heinemann.

Danto, Arthur C. 1985. *Sartre*. London: Fontana.

Francis, Claude, and Fernande Gontier. 1989. *Simone de Beauvoir*. Translated by Lisa Nesselson. London: Mandarin.

Fullbrook, Kate, and Edward Fullbrook. 1993. *Simone de Beauvoir and Jean-Paul Sartre: The Remaking of a Twentieth-Century Legend*. Hemel Hempstead: Harvester Wheatsheaf; New York: Basic Books, 1994.

Gerassi, John. 1989. *Jean-Paul Sartre: Hated Conscience of His Century*. Vol. 1, *Protestant or Protester*. Chicago: University of Chicago Press.

Hayman, Ronald. 1986. *Writing Against: A Biography of Sartre*. London: Weidenfeld and Nicolson.

Holroyd, Michael. 1988. "How I Fell into Biography." In *The Troubled Face of Biography*, edited by Eric Homberger and John Charmley. London: Macmillan.

Joseph, Gilbert. 1991. *Une si douce occupation . . . : Simone de Beauvoir et Jean-Paul Sartre, 1940–1944*. Paris: Albin Michel.

Le Doeuff, Michèle. 1991. *Hipparchia's Choice: An Essay Concerning Women, Philosophy, etc.* Translated by Trista Selous. Oxford: Basil Blackwell.

Moi, Toril. 1994. *Simone de Beauvoir: The Making of an Intellectual Woman*. Oxford: Basil Blackwell.

Sartre, Jean-Paul. 1956. *Being and Nothingness: An Essay on Phenomenological Ontology*. Translated by Hazel E. Barnes. New York: Philosophical Library.

———. 1964. *The Words*. Translated by Bernard Frechtman. New York: George Braziller.

———. 1965. *Anti-Semite and Jew*. Translated by George J. Becker. New York: Schocken.

———. 1984. *War Diaries: Notebooks from a Phoney War, November 1939–March 1940*. Translated by Quintin Hoare. London: Verso.

———. 1987. Forward to *Aden, Arabie* by Paul Nizan, and translated by Joan Pinkham, 9–56. New York: Columbia University Press.

———. 1992. *Witness to My Life: The Letters of Jean-Paul Sartre to Simone de Beauvoir, 1926–1939*. Edited by Simone de Beauvoir. Translated by Lee Fahnestock and Norman McAfee. New York: Scribner.

Schwarzer, Alice. 1984. *Simone de Beauvoir Today: Conversations, 1972–1982*. Translated by Marianne Howarth. London: Chatto and Windus/Hogarth Press.

Simons, Margaret A. 1986. "Beauvoir and Sartre: The Philosophical Relationship." In *Simone de Beauvoir: Witness to a Century*. Special issue of *Yale French Studies* 72:165–79.

———, and Jessica Benjamin. 1979. "Simone de Beauvoir: An Interview." *Feminist Studies* 5, no. 2 (Summer): 330–45.

Singer, Linda. 1985. "Interpretation and Retrieval: Rereading Beauvoir." *Women's Studies International Forum* 8, no. 3:231–38.

7

a response to a letter from Peg Simons, December 1993

Jeffner Allen

and today I open a letter from Peg Simons, who asks, ". . .
    with the posthumously published material, how has your perspective
on Simone de Beauvoir and existentialism changed?"

Notebooks and letters, a fragment of which are now edited by Sylvie
Le Bon de Beauvoir (Beauvoir 1990a, 1990b), each shift the manifold of
possible readings of a lifetime of published work, as well as the readings
of Beauvoir's life. Here Beauvoir is silent, offering us after her death, 14
April 1986, nothing to accompany these leavings. The letters are
discovered, moreover, in Beauvoir's small apartment in Paris, as Le Bon
tells us in her preface: "I did find them. One gloomy day in November

1986, while rummaging aimlessly in the depths of a cupboard at her place, I unearthed a massive packet: letters upon letters in her hand, most of them still folded in their envelopes. Addressed to 'Monsieur Sartre.'" Letters, as Le Bon reminds us (Beauvoir 1990b, 9), concerning which Beauvoir had said, March 1984, in reply to questions from a Canadian feminist magazine:

"After the appearance of *Lettres au Castor* many people wondered why you hadn't published your replies. We feel the lack of them. Do you intend to do that?"

"No. In the first place, my letters have mostly been lost, because they weren't in my possession but in Sartre's. And since there was a bomb attack at his place, lots of his papers were lost. Secondly, I don't feel that I ought to publish letters of my own during my lifetime. When I'm dead they might perhaps be published, if they can be found."

I wonder if what I have read of the letters and notebooks
will change my ideas about the writings Beauvoir chose to publish
during her lifetime, or my ideas about existentialism—or if it
changes something else?

As soon as a single myth is touched, all
myths are in danger.
—Simone de Beauvoir, *Brigitte Bardot
and the Lolita Syndrome*

In "Myth and Reality," chapter 11 of book 1, "Facts and Myths," of *The Second Sex*, following studies of dreams, fears, idols, and the myth of woman in five authors, Beauvoir describes myth as the universalization and projection by a society of those institutions and values to which it adheres. Unlike significance, which is immanent in an object and understood through lived experience, myth is a transcendent idea that reifies belief and defies experience. Myth would rob individuals of transcendence, namely, their self-defined projects and goals, and would confine individuals to immanence, that is, to inert being. Yet myth, despite its power, is not destined to an eternal life; to name a myth is already to begin its destruction.

Beauvoir's analysis of myth as institution reflects her existential ethic, which takes as its point of departure the understanding that humans are free. The life task of each individual is to assume that freedom, and not to flee it. Freedom is assumed by a constructive moment, by undertaking projects that serve as a mode of transcendence, that is, acting such that one's freedom is achieved by reaching out toward the freedom of others. In *The Ethics of Ambiguity*, transcendence that falls into immanence, or stagnation, is termed by Beauvoir an "absolute evil" that "spells frustration and oppression" if it is inflicted upon an individual and that "represents a moral fault" if an individual consents to it (1948b, 156). Freedom also is assumed by a negative movement that rejects oppression for oneself and others.

Common to both movements for taking up one's freedom is Dostoevsky's maxim, which is quoted by Beauvoir in the opening lines of *The Blood of Others* (1948a): "each of us is responsible for everything and to every human being." Such an ethics is individualistic, for it gives to the individual an absolute value and recognizes in the individual alone the power to lay the foundations for its existence. Beauvoir writes in *The Ethics of Ambiguity*, "If each man did what he must, existence would be saved in each one without there being any need for dreaming of a paradise where all would be reconciled in death" (1948b, 156). Yet Beauvoir's existential ethic is not solipsistic. In *L'Existentialisme et la sagesse des nations* (1945, 35), she describes how each individual is defined only by relationship to the world and to other individuals. The separation of consciousnesses can be overcome by friendship, love, and the many emotions, none of which is given in advance, and each of which is to be made.

To touch a myth, then, is for Beauvoir to assume the freedom that one is, to take on responsibility for everything and everyone, to realize those emotions through which the separation of consciousnesses can be overcome.

Named by Beauvoir are the myth of man, that is, abstract man spoken in the name of all, the myth of old age, the bourgeois myths of affluence. Named also are all myths related to motherhood, including the idea of a maternal instinct, the feminine vocation and marriage, which, she contends, enslave women to the home, to housekeeping and to husbands, and the myth of woman. Beauvoir asserts in *The Second Sex*, "few myths have been more advantageous to the ruling caste than the myth of woman: it justifies all privileges and even authorizes their abuse" (1953, 288).

With the posthumous publication of the notebooks and Beauvoir's letters to Sartre, however, it is clear that Beauvoir's understanding of myth extended far beyond the naming of individual myths, indeed, a courageous naming of multitudinous overlapping myths, to include myth-making activities of her own, notably, a series of myths about herself. Her configuration of these myths historicize not only herself but, more precisely, the lives, writings, times and values of herself and of those around her, and the myths of Plato regarding poetics, truth and the polis might well be compared to those of Beauvoir. Beauvoir was silent about this myth-making. She vigorously and, it appears, quite convincingly, denied such activities when asked and enforced a corresponding silence in those who knew her. Given the spontaneous acceptance of Beauvoir's myths by the public of her day, and the further elaboration and embellishment of her myths by a great many journalists, writers, historians and filmmakers, it may be said that Beauvoir's myth-making was a success. One can observe the complexity of the myths by sorting through her differing accounts of them as found in her letters to Sartre, her notebooks, and her autobiographical, fictional and theoretical writing.

She who touches a myth may also be myth-making; if there is a danger in this, where does that danger lie? That Beauvoir's sexual relationships were with men exclusively, that her first and primary relationship was with Jean-Paul Sartre, that Beauvoir was safely heterosexual—although critical of motherhood, marriage, and man (in the generic)—is established vividly and undeniably as myth by the posthumously published works. Margaret A. Simons's "Lesbian Connections: Simone de Beauvoir and Feminism" (1992) contains insightful discussion of Beauvoir's sexual and intimate relationships with women, including Sylvie Le Bon, who Beauvoir for legal reasons made her adoptive daughter, and with men, including her relationship with Jacques-Laurent Bost, which Beauvoir came to consider more primary than her relationship with Sartre. Perhaps the only aspect of this myth that remains to be questioned is that the men Beauvoir had sexual relations with were safely heterosexual too.

And, despite Beauvoir's assertions to the contrary, it is no longer fact that Beauvoir was not a philosopher or that she had no philosophical influence on Sartre or that her field was exclusively that of literature.

Beauvoir's work was not derivative of Sartre's, but rather, the reverse. Beauvoir's letters to Sartre, especially when read in conjunction with Sartre's letters to Beauvoir, make apparent that Sartre had read *She Came to Stay* by the first week of February 1940, significantly prior to his completion of *Being and Nothingness* in 1943. Sartre's theoretical impasse at combining his belief in absolute freedom with collectivity was not broken until after *The Second Sex*, which was published initially in *Les Temps modernes*, 1948 and 1949. Sartre did not ever acknowledge publicly his unattributed use of Beauvoir's philosophy, that is, his act of appropriation: 'appropriation', also a key term in existentialism, which relates 'appropriation' positively to the constitution of 'autonomy' through grasping as one's own what one finds to be 'proper' to one's 'self'. In "The True Philosopher and the Man with the Black Gloves," chapter 5 of *Simone de Beauvoir and Jean-Paul Sartre: The Remaking of a Twentieth-Century Legend* (1994), Kate Fullbrook and Edward Fullbrook pursue in a ground-breaking manner Sartre's intellectual and philosophical debt to Beauvoir.

To these two endangered myths of Beauvoir's life, I would add at least two more. These four endangered myths have shaped a strong public sense of the myriad constellation that most often comprises that which is designated 'Beauvoir', namely, Beauvoir's writings, those published during her life and those published posthumously, accounts by Beauvoir and by those who are not Beauvoir of Beauvoir's writings and life, Beauvoir's interviews and films, etc., all in some nonspecific but, somehow, seemingly clear relationship to each other.

Beauvoir, or perhaps more plausibly 'Beauvoir', may no longer be said to have grown up living the bourgeois life so familiar to many of the French writers of her time. Her statement 17 September 1985 to Claude Francis and Fernande Gontier, that no one ever mentioned the bankruptcy of her father and that the Beauvoirs had lived a very comfortable economic and social life, scarcely coincides with her comments of 20 May 1985 to Francis and Gontier that "We never had any children's parties. We lived a very thrifty life, my father was totally ruined" (Francis and Gontier 1987, 371). Indeed, Beauvoir escaped marriage and became a student in part because her family could not afford the marriage dowry that was expected to be provided by provincial bourgeois families of the early twentieth century. Although Francis and Gontier, in *Simone de Beauvoir: A Life . . . a Love Story* (1987; first published in French, 1985), attempt to disband the myth of Beauvoir's bourgeois girlhood, further material for such a demythologizing is found in the notebooks.

Finally, Beauvoir's claim, abundant in her interviews and her autobiographical, fictional and theoretical writing, that she was never discriminated against as a woman, comes to a long overdue end with the posthumously published works.

Beauvoir, an astute observer of the mechanisms of myth, describes Brigitte Bardot (1960, 5–7) as being against "official prudery" and as extremely aware of how she was viewed. Beauvoir relates that she had found in the French public a "very peculiar hostility to Brigitte Bardot" and that she had come to attribute that hostility to the fact that Bardot's body "rarely settles into a state of immobility" (1960, 20):

> (I reread this note. How is it that
> I first have written Brigitte Beauvoir . . . "in
> the French public a 'very peculiar hostility to
> Brigitte Beauvoir' "?)

. . . dislike of mobility, at least, in a woman. The myths that Beauvoir made and enforced of her own life establish a publicly proclaimed zone of mobility, a space already too public and too spacious for the dominant French society of her time. The zone, maintained with extreme difficulty, is immobilized at the edges, immobilized all around: dissimilation/dissimulation—to become unlike/to hide under false appearance. Edges at the edges of which, and beyond which, are zones of mobility that she publicly proclaims not to know or to enter. The zone is the locus where Beauvoir asserts her mobility, her autonomy, where she assumes responsibility and freedom.

Beauvoir didn't just write about myth, destroy myths or create myths; she openly left her notebooks, and she left her letters, a massive packet, in the depths of the cupboard, one gloomy day in November to be found by Sylvie Le Bon, whose life Beauvoir describes as so closely interwoven with her own.

By drawing on the significance, or lived experience of Beauvoir, as it appears in the notebooks and letters, the facts of Beauvoir are shown to be myth. Dilute and multitudinous bits of significance relevant to Beauvoir have become myth, and out of the pages of notebooks and letters, myths of Beauvoir have become significance, moments of lived experience.

Since any reasons that may have justified cuts in 1983 no longer exist, I have made almost none. Is it not, by now, preferable to tell all in order to tell the truth? Through the indisputable power of direct testimony, to set aside clichés, myths, images—all those lies—so that the real person, as she really was, may appear? Simone de Beauvoir used to say that one of her most enduring fantasies involved the conviction that her singular existence, with all its frivolous incidents and the incomparable taste of mortal instants—her entire existence— was recorded somewhere on a giant tape-recorder. These letters, in their own way, form part of that dream of a complete recording.

—Sylvie Le Bon de Beauvoir, in her preface to
Beauvoir's *Letters to Sartre* (1990b, 10)

Was Beauvoir, by leaving her letters and notebooks, "dreaming of a paradise where all would be reconciled in death"? I think not. Consider the "giant tape-recorder" that plays several tapes at once, at different speeds, starting and stopping, tangling up, playing forward, backward— scarcely a harmonizing process. Or the "giant tape-recorder" multi-tracking and overdubbing that "entire existence." Or the "giant tape-recorder" with delay processing, randomly or nonrandomly processing its memory in a reverberant interactive environment.

Offering us nothing to accompany these leavings, assuredly Beauvoir is a participant in the interaction, changing, expanding, modifying that "entire existence." No risk that she might leave some definitive final words that we could read, debate, and then count her out. Not (limited to) the apparition of her "real person" (another zone of immobility within which she then would need to make space for her freedom), Beauvoir is a traveler on these journeys. For the development of narrative perspective(s) her skills are hard to surpass. And as she, she and she travel, one may wonder if there can be a giant tape-recording of a *single* "entire existence."

Beauvoir, in the myths of her life, represents herself as free. Herself free, in an exceptional historical moment she touches the myths that limit those who are not free. Free-flowing lived experience edged by representations of inertia and myth, she can touch myths, touch the other because she is not constituted by the situation that shapes the other who is to be freed.

Yet Beauvoir was there all along, living her daily experiences while writing her letters, writing her notebooks. Perhaps that is not/has never been her only account?

". . . her hands keep the desire to embrace smooth skin," she writes in the transitional paragraph to "The Lesbian," chapter 4 of book 2, "Lived Experience," of *The Second Sex* (1953, 450). Her hands keep the desire to embrace smooth skin, that is, to embrace 'her' smooth skin, but she does not touch the skin she perceives as smooth, so smooth, and therefore she can touch the myth. If she had touched the smooth, smooth skin, she could not, with credibility (credibility to whom? and why did that matter?) have touched the myth. But, to say, "I touched her smooth skin," or "She and I, we touched"—does not that simple assertion touch several myths at once? After the delay of a lifetime, Beauvoir's letters and notebooks initiate multiple journeys into these memories and questions.

Why did not Beauvoir begin with the "power of direct testimony," instead of with "all those lies"? Can the journey of a biographical tourism, which would document precisely all events as lived and told by Beauvoir, resolve this matter? "All those lies" truly are recounted by Beauvoir herself. The "lies" and the "direct testimony" are 'authentic' Beauvoir; they are 'true'. This matter, which appears to be one of truthfulness and intent, or could it be one of fraudulent authorship and spurious texts—which 'Beauvoir' is genuinely the author? and which are her 'real' writings?—is difficult, and perhaps cannot be ascertained.

Beauvoir's notebooks and letters exercise an awesome power over the four endangered myths. However, just because what Beauvoir said was/is not true and also was/is true, and this is publicly known, does that mean that the truth of those "frivolous incidents and the incomparable taste of mortal instants" can be found?

In "The True Philosopher and the Man with the Black Gloves," the Fullbrooks ask, "Why would Beauvoir, of all people, want a woman's central contribution to the stock of philosophical ideas credited to a man" (1994, 98)? That question, too, is on my mind. However, I am not sure that, as the Fullbrooks assert, "It is now possible to answer that question. Two sets of documents, which Beauvoir left to be discovered after her death, reveal facts which provide a solution to the mystery" (1994, 98).

The assignment of truth and intent is a risky undertaking. Where myth, significance and reality lie may tell us as much about ourselves as narrators and readers as it does about Beauvoir. While Beauvoir's life may appear to be unique, exceptional, solitary, a "singular existence," her life may also appear not to be, and never to have been, a "singular existence," either to Beauvoir, to those close to her, or to her readers.

Peg, perhaps it is this confusion, or not a confusion, but an ambiguity, regarding the 'singularity' of Beauvoir's 'existence' that elicits in she, she and she a desire to respond to your letter.

My Simone de Beauvoir notebook: three scratch pads on which I write, little bits of paper with a few notations, the cover flap of an airmail envelope from an eagerly awaited letter, the back of two grocery receipts—when returning from the grocery store I had a thought here and there, some ideas 'in the air', all scattered out in, or hovering about, this space in the trees and the sunshine that Lauren has so generously offered me for writing. Although I still feel convinced of my earlier critique of existentialism, "An Introduction to Patriarchal Existentialism" (1982), which I wrote fifteen years ago, and which I have revised twice since then, now, along with Beauvoir's letters and notebooks, there is so much to consider.

The notes on scratch pads and elsewhere can be lost, found, assembled, reassembled, torn up, folded, safeguarded in a special place. They are not (yet) pages stitched together to make a book.

The Married Woman

Her attitude toward her home is dictated by the same dialectic that defines her situation in general: she takes by becoming prey, she finds freedom by giving it up; by renouncing the world she aims to conquer a world. . . . Thanks to the velvets and silks and porcelains with which she surrounds herself, woman can in some degree satisfy that tactile sensuality which her erotic life can seldom assuage. . . . The battle against dust and dirt is never won. Washing, ironing, sweeping, ferreting out rolls of lint from under wardrobes—all this halting of decay is also the denial of life; for time simultaneously creates and destroys, and only its negative aspect concerns the housekeeper. . . . She shuts out the sunlight, for along with that come insects, germs, and dust, and besides, the sun ruins silk hangings and fades upholstery; she scatters naphthalene, which scents the air. She becomes bitter and disagreeable and hostile to all that lives: the end is sometimes murder. . . . A continual renunciation is required of the woman whose operations are completed only in their destruction. . . . However respected she may be, she is subordinate, secondary, parasitic. . . . As a rule, the husband takes pleasure in this role of mentor and guide. . . . In spite of new opinions she has acquired, in spite of principles she echoes like a parrot, she retains her own peculiar view of things. . . . In certain privileged cases the wife may succeed in becoming her husband's true companion, discussing his projects, giving him counsel, collaborating in his works. But she is lulled in illusion if she expects in this way to accomplish work she can call her own, for he remains alone the free and responsible agent. . . . Only independent work of her own can assure woman's genuine independence. . . . Sometimes a *True* collaboration exists between a man and a woman. . . . But then the woman, as competent as the man, steps out of her role as wife; their relation is no longer of the conjugal type. . . . There are also women who make use of a man to attain their personal ends; they, too, are outside the situation of the married woman. (Beauvoir 1953, 502–32)

Beauvoir by choice and by conviction did not engage in marriage. Yet, her situation in relation to writing is not without parallel to that of the married woman Beauvoir pictures in *The Second Sex*. The passages above, excerpted from a sequence of thirty pages in "The Married Woman," chapter 16 of book 2, "Lived Experience," of *The Second Sex*, seem not alien to moments in Beauvoir's relationships with individual men, especially Sartre, with a movement defined by men, namely, existentialism, and antecedent to existentialism, with a lineage of white European-born male philosophers.

She casts in all directions, spraying vigilently and diffusely, also, flinging about heedlessly, she scatters—naphthalene. The naphthalenic gesture, which Beauvoir reveals when she leaves her notebooks and letters to be published, has lingered, still lingers, and just as it seems to settle it does not settle, it hovers. "Her singular existence, with all its frivolous incidents and the incomparable taste of mortal instants"—spots and streaks of naphthalene run, drip across. The tongues, a long tongue, a short tongue, a long narrow flame-tongue, a proboscis, the long spirally rolled tongue of a butterfly, tongue-flowered orchids, a tonguefish— attempt that space of suspense, the space of Beauvoir's naphthalenic gesture now evident.

Taking liberties with Beauvoir's life? And did not Beauvoir take liberties with her life and with us, her readers? If she who touches a myth may also be myth making, when there are still so many dreams, fears, idols, and at times, so little frivolity, how not to replicate the restricted zone of mobility, and how not to render the zone more narrow still?

While a life and a writing need not correspond, there is with Beauvoir's posthumously published writing a greater openness, as you call it, Lois, while we talk on the telephone, a permission to read without such a stern forbiddingness, without disciplinary script. The zone, itself a space that is changing, acts on and is acted upon by the transformations, modulations, reverberations of the tongues' readerly and narrative styles.

Yet, perhaps she who has asked some of the questions that are confirmed by the posthumously published journals and letters may find that confirmation unsettling. Even though angered that Beauvoir had manipulated her and withheld the truth, she may wish to displace the import of the events now known, as well as the virtual space of reading that they portend. As if to preserve Beauvoir she states, "Do as She said, Not as She Did," as does Deirdre Bair, author of *Simone de Beauvoir: A Biography*, in her 18 November 1990 letter to the *New York Times Magazine*.

Beauvoir: she who exists for the sake of her need to believe that what Beauvoir once had said still is true. Here Beauvoir and the feminist both are rimmed by the heavy burden of Beauvoir–Sartre as model couple. By her disregard for the life that it now is apparent Beauvoir lived, for Beauvoir's posthumously published narrative of that life, and for the impact of that narrative on readings of Beauvoir, the 'daughter' sets out to realize the 'truth' that, according to the 'daughter', the 'mother' once wrote but failed to live. Is this not a deradicalization of Beauvoir, including Beauvoir as presented by Beauvoir in her writing published during her lifetime—with the publication of *The Second Sex* Beauvoir was hounded out of cafés and seriously harassed, Beauvoir long before that had given up the role of dutiful daughter. In this context, Beauvoir's concern that motherhood, at this time and condition in history, is a trap for women, assumes new significance.

But there are many stories to be told and retold, tales that cross the paths of tales sometimes interrupted, sometimes rearranged. Consider first: a woman has ideas that are taken by a person she says she trusts. The ideas are the basis of her connection with this person. She never says that her ideas were taken, although she knows that they were, and she has written letters and a journal to that effect. She observes that the taken ideas seem, at second glance, and more and more so, gradually, not to resemble her own. Sometimes they are confused. Sometimes they are in disagreement. To get the ideas back on track she sometimes explains them more clearly than does he who took them. And so she continues to write—describing, clarifying, criticizing, expressing the ideas more or less obliquely. In time she observes many men and books that relate to those ideas that no longer quite resemble her own, and over time, a movement: existentialism.

Consider second, a science student in a lab with her mentor, or a student or writer active in feminist or lesbian or gay or multicultural studies, who finds her/himself in the presence of a culture vulture. The mentor picks up bits and pieces here and there and then writes as if he/she has discovered them for the first time. His/her descriptions are often mistaken and miss their mark, but the taker is called brilliant, gets a job, receives grants, is published.

The Fullbrooks, in "The True Philosopher," give still another account of Beauvoir's situation in this regard, an account that is carefully based on the spirit and the letter of Beauvoir's writing, including that which has been published posthumously. They observe that Beauvoir learned from the rejection by Gallimard (who had published Sartre's *Nausea*) of her short story collection in 1937, later published as *When Things of the Spirit Come First,* that "she could write an entire book on what a woman thought about philosophy if she disguised its content" (Fullbrook and Fullbrook 1994, 123). In the light of Gallimard's rejection, which Beauvoir subsequently found was based on the subject matter of the book—women and what women think—she continued her writing and she also began to place some of her ideas in the mouth of Sartre, who never acknowledged her contribution, so that those ideas could make their way into the public world of print. Through detailed comparison of the letters of Sartre to Beauvoir and the letters of Beauvoir to Sartre, Beauvoir emerges as founder and "matriarch" of existentialism.

The Fullbrooks portray Beauvoir throughout this process as a person of great originality of thought, and as a woman who consciously exercised a will to control, bringing her, after the appearance of her posthumously published works, if not during her life, to ultimately get the upper hand in an untoward situation. Such emphasis on rationality, freedom, and choice in her decisions concerning writing and concerning her work with Sartre is consonant with Beauvoir's self-descriptions. Emphasis on these traits, or values, is conspicuously absent in either of the tales above.

We do not know whether the individuals whose ideas are taken in the second tale possess such qualities. They do not claim to have these qualities; indeed, they tell us little about themselves. Or, perhaps they did speak up and were disregarded, or fired, or disappeared. Nor does the narrator of the second tale assign such qualities, for any of a wide variety of possible reasons. In the first tale, she who watches Sartre and existentialism take her ideas appears, also, without mention of the rationality, freedom, and choice that Beauvoir tends to attribute to herself. Surely she is not Beauvoir?

Are not freedom, choice and rationality the very stuff of which the myths of Beauvoir have been made? Are not these the tools, highly esteemed by western philosophy, that have made of Beauvoir, if belatedly, a sort of existential hero(ine)? A rereading of the Beauvoir myths would seem to necessitate a rereading of those virtues. This is not to say that Beauvoir may not have had more ideas and originality, etc., than Sartre—the evidence fully supports the claim that she did. It may also be revelatory, however, to consider Beauvoir as she who was without many of these tools, even while she claimed to have them. She had, after all, observed them and could describe them as if they were her own.

Is it not a belief in these tools that made the Beauvoir myths come true, for Beauvoir and for her readers? No longer defended, the tools that have shaped the myths are found to be myth.

I am not sure that Beauvoir would agree.

We walk along the beach at sunset, Melyssa Jo, and you say that your picture of Beauvoir remains constant. You see Beauvoir so well equipped for happiness, belaboring so stubbornly to achieve it, in her writing catching a glimpse of pleasure and happiness and concentrating on nothing else.

Why should it be hard to imagine that Beauvoir wrote for herself?

This morning I, Jef, find myself considering my favorite readings of Beauvoir. I have always been moved most by *Memoirs of a Dutiful Daughter* and *A Very Easy Death*, which Beauvoir wrote upon the death of her mother. I have been greatly affected by *The Second Sex*, which Margaret Simons, in "Lesbian Connections" (1992), has shown owes its genesis to Beauvoir's relation with her mother, her sister, and Zaza, Beauvoir's companion when she was a girl.

Beauvoir's relation to a male lineage need not be, is not always, paramount. She dedicated many of her books to women—*All Said and Done* to Sylvie, *She Came to Stay* to Olga, *The Blood of Others* to Nathalie Sorokine, and *The Ethics of Ambiguity* to Bianca. She thought of her writing as a step toward social change, as leading necessarily to activism. Beauvoir participated in the French feminist campaign for free abortion. She publicly testified for Djamila Boupacha, a young Algerian woman illegally imprisoned by the French military forces and tortured in 1960. In France, she worked to secure housing for poor women and for old women. In 1972 she named herself a militant feminist and joined the women's movement.

Although Beauvoir's role with the journal *questions féministes*, published in Paris, 1977–1980, was, I find, extraordinarily lesbophobic, she has been inspirational to many feminist writers, including Ti-Grace Atkinson, Shulamith Firestone and Awa Thiam, the author of *Black Sisters, Speak Out: Feminism and Oppression in Black Africa* (1986; first published in French, 1978). She had much impact on the feminist "underground," including the Redstockings, in the u.s.a. in the late 1960s and early 1970s. I remember myself sitting in intense "consciousness raising" groups and discussing Beauvoir.

And Beauvoir's letters and notebooks? Perhaps they are a response to the gaze of Zaza, with whom, Beauvoir recounts in *Memoirs*, she had fought together against the revolting fate that had lain ahead of both of them as young women. As I, Jef, sort through my memories and questions, I want to say, a response not to the gaze of a Zaza whom Beauvoir once had construed as reproachful and of whom Beauvoir says in *Memoirs*, "I believed that I had paid for my own freedom with her death," but to the gaze of a Zaza still present. This morning I see also, as one among many figures fluttering in and out of the naphthalenic mist, a woman about whom Beauvoir, just when she had wanted to continue her study of philosophy, read an article in an illustrated magazine. In those days, Beauvoir remarks in *Memoirs*, the women who had a degree or a doctorate in philosophy could be counted on the fingers of one hand. Beauvoir wanted, at that time, to become like her, Mademoiselle Zanta: "she had obtained her doctorate; she had been photographed in a grave and thoughtful posture, sitting at her desk; she lived with a young niece whom she had adopted" (1959, 255–56).

The posthumously published letters and notebooks open a further space for considerations around and about Beauvoir, but is it the letters and notebooks that make the difference in how the Beauvoir myths are considered?

That Beauvoir's writing was the work of a philosopher, for instance, was recognized even by *Paris Match*. The cover of *Paris Match*, August 1949, the year in which *The Second Sex* first was published and met with immediate success, featured a photograph of Beauvoir and, in French, the caption, "First woman philosopher in the history of man." During the past decade some feminist philosophers already have carried out significant textual and interpretive studies demonstrating that Beauvoir's ideas were not the same as Sartre's, that her existentialism, as it were, was more ample, connective, grounded in history and aware of the experience of oppression, more far-reaching, than that of Sartre. Beauvoir's skill with languages and her scholarly expertise, for instance, with the German philosophers Hegel and Heidegger, already has been shown to far have surpassed that of Sartre.

That Beauvoir had lived erotic relationships with women and with men might have been surmised from the pages of her work published during her lifetime. Elaine Marks, in "Transgressing the (In)cont(in)ent Boundaries: The Body in Decline" (1992), offers an extremely moving interpretation of some of these relationships. I also remember a conversation at a feminist conference, somewhat over a decade ago. Beauvoir had arisen as a topic of conversation, and the director of an archive happened to mention that in the archive was a series of love letters between Beauvoir and a writer of the history of ideas in the u.s.a., who was herself a lesbian, and whom the archivist identified by name. Two of us asked some questions and then fell silent, puzzled that no one else in the group seemed interested in whether or how the letters could be studied. After the archivist left the group, conversation turned to whether the archivist could possibly be credible. Once a consensus, generally in the negative, was reached, the matter was dropped.

In "The Phenomenon who could not be Judged," chapter 2 of *Simone de Beauvoir and Jean-Paul Sartre*, the Fullbrooks propose, in regard to Beauvoir's account in *Memoirs* of her relation with her girlhood friend Zaza, or Elisabeth Le Coin,

> Whether this literary treatment of Elisabeth fits the reality of the situation scarcely matters. It is safer to read Zaza as an allegorical device than as a faithful portrait of a real young woman. . . . When she [Beauvoir] was 19 and her need for Zaza's love and approval had, to a large degree, passed, Beauvoir revealed to her friend her former passion for her. Zaza seems to have been amazed by the revelation. (1994, 44)

As further support for this reading the Fullbrooks refer to Beauvoir's sister, Hélène de Beauvoir, who in an interview in Bair's *Simone de Beauvoir*, had expressed astonishment at the importance accorded to Zaza in her sister's memoirs and said,

> "I had not realized ZaZa meant so much to her, or that my sister continued to think of ZaZa for so many years after her death. We knew she was upset at the time, but we all assumed it was due to her exaggerated fear of death and not specifically of the death of ZaZa." (1994, 44)

If one pauses to consider lesbian relationships between young women, and the plethora of misinterpretations that those relationships undergo in lesbophobic societies, to each of the suggestions and conjectures drawn above one can find at least as plausible an abundance of alternative readings. In marked contrast, in the subsequent discussion of Beauvoir's relationship with Jacques Champigneulle, the Fullbrooks do not propose that it is safer to read Jacques as allegorical device, but directly identify Jacques as "Beauvoir's first male romantic object."

Interestingly, Beauvoir's letters and notebooks, whether published or not published, do not seem to be the key factor, or at least, not the sole key factor, in the undoing of the Beauvoir myths.

She has a hard time getting to her subject matter. It takes her and us a long time to get to it, and that is the subject matter: the journey. As we talk, you say this to me, Faye, on your first telephone call after you have moved halfway across the Pacific, just to get a job.

Her attitude toward her home, her attitude toward her writing, her attitude toward her work—I return to Beauvoir's observation in "The Married Woman"—"is dictated by the same dialectic that defines her situation in general."

And this dialectic?

Peg, you may hear me asking, even without telephone, without mail, without electronic mail, without voice mail, but asking so persistently that you hear me when you are 2,000 miles away. Why am I reading Beauvoir? Beauvoir is so boring! But today it seems that this boringness, the tedium, comes not from Beauvoir, but from the tiresome monotony of this dialectic in its infinite modulations. The boredom, too, may be a screen for the fear, anxiety, dread, terror, anger, grief, as well as the pleasure, joy and sensuous delight, that sweep through the dialectic.

The dialectic, for Beauvoir, is an instance of the dynamic Hegelian sense of the verb 'to be', that is, a 'to have become' in which the question is, should that state of affairs continue. Given that Beauvoir left her notebooks to be published after her death and her letters to be found, with no directives not to publish them, perhaps she had decided, or had come to feel, that 'Beauvoir', that state of affairs she had become, should not continue.

These journeys, the naphthalenic tales, reflect, however, not only a decision, or a feeling, but a process—the dialectic, Beauvoir's statement of which opens book 2 of *The Second Sex*, my favorite line in all of her writing: "One is not born a woman, one becomes a woman."

I tend more in the direction of Monique Wittig's, "One is not born a Woman," which began to circulate in 1980 and which was published recently in Wittig's *The Straight Mind* (1992). Wittig starts with "one is not born a woman," but proceeds immediately to therefore she and all females are not women. That is, she begins by breaking off the heterosexual contract by which females become women. Wittig refuses the name 'woman'. I have the deepest conviction and experience that, in regard to the dialectic—shall I say it?—Wittig is right. Yet, so strong is the power of patriarchy that, day by day, I also find myself experiencing the dialectic as articulated by Beauvoir. For the Beauvoir of *The Second Sex*, too, just as woman is not determined by biology, psychology, or economic fate, sexuality is in no way determined by anatomical or psychological disposition. There is no natural or necessary linkage between biological features, gender, and sexuality, between women or men or heterosexuality or homosexuality or femininity or masculinity. It is for us to take up our freedom and to give shape to these and myriad possibilities through our being in the world.

The dialectic of woman is not the sole oppression, according to Beauvoir, and in view of the multiplicity of overlapping oppressions, the dialectic—on some days a tiresome spectacle—becomes ever more complex, as is life.

For the tongues, as she, she and she travel in/through/near this dialectic, the process of not being, yet of becoming, and of refusing to become, may at times be neither pleasant or easy. There is, I find, scant little in the male lineage of western philosophy that offers nourishment as we witness this dialectic and as we heal within it and from it. The alternatives of objectification and distancing, or else of appropriation, yield an itinerary that may in safety render touristic assessments, but that offers nothing vital for this process of transformation.

"At first I did not agree with my colleagues, but then I read your paper on existentialism.

"You must see a psychiatrist. You are completely mistaken to write this way. Existentialism is not against woman. Existentialism is humanism. Sartre was not a phallocrat, neither was Camus, and Merleau-Ponty very much liked woman, he was quite attached to his mother. As for Beauvoir, she was an angry woman, also in need of a psychiatrist. It was Freud, and F.J.J. Buytendijk, especially, in his *De Vrouw, haar natuur, verschijning, en bestaan; een existentieel-psychologische studie,* who really understood what is woman.

"I am not against the liberation of woman. But just as man needs woman, woman needs man. I tell you this for your own good, as your friend."

—Comment from a colleague who wished to
explain to her why she did not get tenure
U.S.A. 1982

"While it is undeniable that I have been away in Europe during your time here, my colleagues have explained to me your work. A strong cup of tea. I want to tell you myself that I have changed my vote from abstain to against, making the decision in this matter unanimous."

—Comment by another colleague in philosophy
U.S.A. 1982

What does she think as she reads Beauvoir again and again, and she finds that she does not yet know what she really thinks of Beauvoir. As she reads Beauvoir again and again is it surprising that in 1993 she and she may still wait, notes in drawers, notes on computer files . . . or perhaps she and she decide not to wait, but to write, to publish, to speak. What will be the economics of her decision and of her decision and of her decision?

What account to give of Beauvoir's relation to existentialism?

In "The True Philosopher," the Fullbrooks state that Beauvoir had already produced "a full statement of 'Sartrean' existentialism" by 1940 (1994, 102). I find this exciting, and the Fullbrooks show convincingly that an unraveling of Sartre's texts does lead to Beauvoir, or to a Beauvoir of sorts. Yet in the theft of Beauvoir's ideas, which Sartre ripped off and took the life out of, her ideas often are changed almost beyond recognition. Those ideas that Sartre could not take over are denigrated frequently, as in his *Being and Nothingness*, in which women's sexuality and nature become "holes and slime." The task of extracting Beauvoir from Sartre's texts and therein making more precise her relation to existentialism seems difficult, though not implausible, given obstacles such as these. Perhaps one might at the same time, or instead, liberate Beauvoir from her intellectual marriage to Sartre—Beauvoir in her writings liberates herself from Sartre quite often—and pursue her relationship to some of the many facets of the existential movement.

Imagine finding an account of Beauvoir's work in the history of western philosophy, leading to her formulation of aspects of her existentialism. Such an account is routine for (male) philosophers in encyclopedias, histories, anthologies, etc., of philosophy:

. . . she read widely the work of her contemporaries and developed aspects of her existentialism out of that dialogue. Beauvoir found fruitful Lévi-Strauss's conception of the mark of otherness, which arises in the exchange of women by men, among men, in marriage. Scheler's account of *ressentiment* she characterized as very weak and Lévinas's account of the feminine as the full flower of otherness, absolutely other and in meaning opposite to consciousness, she termed an assertion of masculine privilege. Of particular interest is her thematization of the Husserlian reduction in *The Ethics of Ambiguity*. There she compares Husserl's reduction to an existential turning of the will. . . .

Imagine, too, a time when an account such as the following might be understood as history, rather than as mere opinion:

Through an oversight of patriarchal discourse, Sartre, Camus and Merleau-Ponty, that is, French existentialism, came to be referred to as having its immediate roots in the work of the German philosophers, Hegel, Husserl and Heidegger, rather than, more directly, in the groundbreaking work of Beauvoir. . . . In the place of Beauvoir's joy in nature and among humanity existentialism substituted Sartre's nausea in the presence of the root of a tree. . . . Were it not for Beauvoir's strong impact on aspects of the women's liberation movement, by the early 1990s existentialism would have dropped entirely out of view.

Or, one could as readily venture with Beauvoir in the direction of accounts that do not marry her to existentialism. For instance:

Recognition of Beauvoir's work, prompted by the posthumous publication of some of her notebooks and letters to Sartre, broke the calm of those who had been surprised at the rise of the women's liberation movement in Western Europe, the United States and Canada in the late '60s and early '70s, but who had reassured themselves that, apart from a few borrowings from Sartre and Marx, that movement had nothing radical or philosophical about it.

It would be accurate to rewrite the history of French existentialism, with Beauvoir at its origin. But what would it mean to attribute to existentialism a history in the light of which, it seems, no member of that movement would recognize him/herself? Is not a movement based, to some degree, on the self-recognition of its members and on an interaction with a public world that reflects, in some way, that self-recognition? Indeed, existentialism appears as a movement that was based on the nonrecognition, for whatever reasons, of one of its members. Merleau-Ponty and Camus, like Sartre, worked with Beauvoir at length but attribute to her no intellectual influence. If Beauvoir's notebooks and letters evidence a matriarchal origin to existentialism, they do so only because they simultaneously show existentialism to be more abysmally patriarchal than before.

To posit a revised order of influence in existentialism would challenge resistance to the idea of "a great woman thinker," and I agree with the Fullbrooks that it is important to make that challenge. However, contemporaneous with Beauvoir, may not there have been numerous "women thinkers," Gertrude Stein, Simone Weil, Violette Le Duc, as well as "women thinkers" of the period who remain unpublished and unknown, but whose books, diaries, letters, words remain to be recorded? When will the letters to and from Beauvoir and the women who were her close friends be edited and published? If writings such as these do not sometimes, or do not ever, connect well with existentialism, or with other established movements in the history of ideas, will they be considered not intellectually relevant? "Writing with a woman in mind," Kim, as you remind me, challenges all of our assumptions of relevance. It is time to give up artificial distinctions between 'thinker' and 'literary writer', especially in the case of Beauvoir, whose writing is at once philosophical-literary-psychological-political-sociological-historical and it is time to abandon the drawing of disciplinary lines that effects the conversion of assorted individuals from a movement into a canon.

In *Memoirs of a Dutiful Daughter*, Beauvoir shows how experience, for her, was always ambiguous. As a child she desired to express neutral tints and muted shades; she felt that there might be a gap between word and object; she was wary of the assumption, encouraged by adults, that the definition of a thing expresses its 'substance': "Whatever I beheld with my own eyes and every real experience had to be fitted somehow or other into a rigid category: the myths and the stereotyped ideas prevailed" (1959, 17). The virtual space of reading that is opened by Beauvoir's posthumously published notebooks and letters need not be exclusively, or primarily, a space of citation, demonstration and proof. At least as important to an understanding of Beauvoir is reflection on multiple narratives, situations and relations. The glowing wheels of myth, reality and significance, in their interrelations and their dissolution, induce in that virtual space of reading journeys in which she, she and she may, may not, may sometimes, change the dialectic—one is not born a woman.

spin, tumble, somersault, stand, leap, squat   a canon, a rule, a
model or standard, authoritative, authentic, for the most part unchanging
        shining stone, sparkling stones, black stone with stripes, green
grey red stones, clay stones, moss agate, ribbon agate, porcelain stones,
dirt stones, glass stones, mottled stones, star agate   to cane, to
    discipline, to beat or to flog *she, she and she, rarely settling into*
a state of immobility   cannon, from the Italian "cannone,"

augmentative form of "cana," reed, tube or cane, a large tube, an
artillery piece   *into the marbles, click, goes the taw, large*
and fancy stone tap tap
        click

                            .   in music, a canon: a contrapuntal
musical composition in two or more voices, parts in which the melody is
imitated exactly and completely by the successive voices, though not always
        at the same pitch   integrated, assimilated, into a canon, can she
        and she still speak? voices imitating the melody exactly and completely,
though sometimes at a different pitch, how can she and she listen to her
and to her?   *between the marbles, among the marbles, she*
        stands on three marbles, no lines of restraint. she takes two
marbles out of her mouth and gives one marble to her friend

to cane—from a dense thicket of reed cane, green, moist, pliant,
    strong, to take cane and cane a chair, to repair by caneing parts of a
chair   of glass cane—each color and strand inside a marble, to spin
        bundles of glass cane in patterns inside a marble, to add glass
    cane to molten glass, and then more heat, stretching, twisting
into a marble, into marbles and more marbles   *no sound, a favorite*
marble cracks clusters of marbles *she, she and she* spin tumble
    somersault stand leap

Dear Peg,

    With reference to Beauvoir and existentialism, I might suggest, a
woman without a movement is like a fish without a bicycle.

                                        See you soon,
                                        Jef

References

Allen, Jeffner. 1982. "An Introduction to Patriarchal Existentialism: Accompanied by a Proposal for a Way out of Existential Patriarchy." *Philosophy and Social Criticism* 9:450–65.

———. 1989. "An Introduction to Patriarchal Existentialism: A Proposal for a Way out of Existential Patriarchy." In *The Thinking Muse: Feminism and Recent French Thought*, edited by Jeffner Allen and Iris Young, 71–84. Bloomington: Indiana University Press.

———. 1995. "An Introduction to Patriarchal Existentialism: A Proposal for a Way out of Existential Patriarchy." In *SINUOSITIES // Lesbian Poetic Politics*. Bloomington: Indiana University Press, 1995.

Bair, Deirdre. 1990. *Simone de Beauvoir: A Biography*. New York: Summit.

Beauvoir, Simone de. 1945. *L'Existentialisme et la sagesse des nations*. Paris: Nagel.

———. 1948a. *The Blood of Others*. Translated by Roger Senhouse and Yvonne Moyse. New York: Knopf.

———. 1948b. *The Ethics of Ambiguity*. Translated by Bernard Frechtman. Secaucus, N.J.: Citadel.

———. 1953. *The Second Sex*. Translated by H. M. Parshley. New York: Knopf. (My translation used for this chapter)

———. 1959. *Memoirs of a Dutiful Daughter*. Translated by James Kirkup. New York: Harper and Row.

———. 1960. *Brigitte Bardot and the Lolita Syndrome*. Translated by Bernard Frechtman. New York: Reynal.

———. 1990a. *Journal de guerre: Septembre 1939–Janvier 1941*. Edited by Sylvie Le Bon Beauvoir. Paris: Gallimard.

———. 1990b. *Lettres à Sartre: 1940–1963*. 2 vols. Edited by Sylvie Le Bon Beauvoir. Paris: Gallimard.

Fullbrook, Kate, and Edward Fullbrook. 1994. *Simone de Beauvoir and Jean-Paul Sartre: The Remaking of a Twentieth-Century Legend*. New York: Basic Books.

Francis, Claude, and Fernande Gontier. 1987. *Simone de Beauvoir: A Life . . . A Love Story*. Translated by Lisa Nesselson. New York: St. Martin's.

Simons, Margaret A. 1992. "Lesbian Connections: Simone de Beauvoir and Feminism." *Signs: Journal of Women in Culture and Society* 18, no. 1:136–61.

Thiam, Awa. 1986. *Black Sisters, Speak Out: Feminism and Oppression in Black Africa*. Translated by Dorothy S. Blair. Dover, N.H.: Pluto.

Wittig, Monique. 1992. *The Straight Mind and Other Essays*. Boston: Beacon.

8

Beauvoir's Woman: Eunuch or Male?

Céline T. Léon

Under the pretext of taking a closer look at Simone de Beauvoir, I shall address here the question "What is woman?" a question that until recently, has been conspicuously absent from the discourse of philosophy. We know ever since Heidegger, one of the greatest influences on Sartre and Beauvoir, that the essence of man is in the form of a question. Beauvoir's leading thought, the thought that guides her from *Le Deuxième Sexe* to *Tout compte fait* and beyond, is that "one is not born a woman, one becomes a woman" (Beauvoir 1949, 2:13; 1972, 614). Men, at least those who read and understood him, discovered Heidegger in fear and trembling. Women read de Beauvoir with a sense of liberation. What came as a freeing revelation to woman came as a shock to man: She hated the essence; he hated the question.

My purpose here is to examine, with and through Beauvoir, what is the essence of this essence traditionally attributed to woman. Is woman different from man? Is there such a thing as an essence of the sexual difference? Is this difference natural or artificial? Should it be gotten rid of or cultivated? By what can it be replaced? Will the ersatz (re)inscribe itself in the context of some other essence, some further essence of the sexual difference or will it, lying beyond feminine/masculine, displace sexual opposition altogether?

If there are gropings in my essay, they may be attributed—partially at least—to the evolution of Beauvoir's thought between 1949 and 1986, the year of her death, as much as to the fact that Beauvoir, although she did not go far enough for the neo-feminists, if I dare say so, came too early for women in general. Beauvoir raised more questions than she answered. So did and so will, it is hoped, those whom she inspired. The whole gender question has just begun to be asked; its concepts need elucidation. The quest may be frustrating; it has, however, the exhilarating savor of beginnings. As for the reality of coming to terms with gender differences, it may not be in sight for a long time—if ever.

The Female Eunuch

In the traditional scheme, woman finds herself debased and despised by man, who wields for sole credentials the truth of his phallus. This system, criticized by Beauvoir, privileges, universalizes the male experience and, from its lofty perspective, looks down on woman whom it, in turn, compels to perceive herself as an incomplete being, a male *manqué*, a eunuch. "What?" asks Freud, "does the little girl (woman?) want?" She simply *wants*. The Phallus—notwithstanding its status as potentially absent—comes to stand in for the missing object of desire. Around the age of five, the little girl discovers the anatomical differences between the sexes, and reacts to her lack of a penis by a castration complex: She considers herself to have been mutilated, and consequently suffers. The castration complex ends the boy's Oedipus complex (his love for his mother) and inaugurates for the girl the one that is specifically hers: She transfers her object love to her father who does seem to have the Phallus and identifies with her mother who, to the girl's disappointment, does not. For those who, like Beauvoir, oppose Freud, the concept of the castration complex is derogatory to women and Freud's theory is phallocentric insofar as, arguing that girls envy the Phallus, it takes man as the norm and woman as different from the norm. Since all thought of mutilation implies comparison and valorization of one economy—the masculine one, in this case—over the other, woman finds herself, by virtue of such a scheme, divided, and forced either to virilize herself in order to recover her autonomy or, renouncing all manly pretenses, to fulfill herself in amorous submission. Such is the deadlock in which Western civilization has placed its "second sex": It forced more than half its population either to renounce its humanity in order to accept its femininity, or to deny its femininity in order to accept its humanity.

In a thesis that is purely her own, and that she never revoked, Beauvoir advances that "one is not born; one becomes a woman" (1949, 2:13). Anatomy is not destiny; one is no more born a woman than, say, a Jew, a slave, or a male. There is no given feminine nature, but only a feminine situation imposed upon woman. "It is civilization as a whole that produces this creature, intermediate between male and eunuch, which is described as feminine" (1949, 2:13). The difference between men and women is purely cultural. Woman's Otherness is fabricated, imposed by culture, not by biology. There is no such thing as a woman, as the "eternal womanly," no truth in itself of woman in itself (1972, 623). Nor is there a maternal instinct and this cultural fiction, this myth, this mystification must therefore be destroyed. (1949, 2:178).

Woman's tragedy lies in the fact that, in a world where man has always considered himself as the essential, the Self, the Absolute, and woman as the Other, she is torn asunder "between the fundamental claim of any subject which posits itself as the essential and the demands of a situation which constitutes her into an inessential" (1949, 1:xxxi; also 1:xv). Since she is constantly forced to choose between affirming her transcendence and denying it, her desire is equivocal, made of attraction and of repulsion. Heidegger threatened man, for he (man) aspires to be nothing but a man; Beauvoir brought comfort to woman, for she (woman), considering what man has made her into, would rather be anything but a woman.

The question now before us is to see how this female eunuch, defined by an absence—the absence of a part—will ever overcome the humiliating revelation that has been inflicted upon her, if she is to become, like the male, a "complete human being" (Schwarzer, 1972, 49). What does Beauvoir envision when she enjoins women to become similar to men? Does she advocate equality with a difference, variations on a common base of humanity? Does she propound instead a radical transformation for both sexes, something like the development of a new essence based on a cultivation of their difference? Or does she have in mind the emulation of one sex by the other; that is, the abolition of the difference?

Feminine Difference and Essence

Down with the Difference!

Beauvoir undeniably opposes the notion of equality with a difference which, she feels, implies inferiority (1949, 1:xxiv, 24; 1972, 620). She envisions a woman who, far from experiencing her femininity as a mutilation, would not envy man his penis. Such an individual would realize herself through work, economic and social independence: a producer, active, she would re(dis)cover values of transcendence and, through projects, assert herself concretely as a subject.

Since women cannot achieve this ideal alone, Beauvoir urges them to imagine simultaneously a general change in structures of education, training, reproduction, and a real liberation of sexuality; that is to say, a transformation of each through her body and the Other's body. This, Beauvoir felt at the time of *The Second Sex*, could not be done without political transformation, for only a radical restructuring of laws and institutions would ensure the equality of the sexes.

Her feminism radicalized itself as, in time, she began to feel that women had only themselves to count on. Progressively she came to realize that, although there remained a necessary bond between social-ism, class struggle, on the one hand, and feminism, on the other, the bond was no longer sufficient (de Barsy, 1968, 12; see also Schwarzer, 1984b, 27–51; Beauvoir 1972, 622–24).[1] Her militancy, in time, say, around 1970, ceased being theoretical, political, and the affair of both sexes, to take on a practical, economic, radical feminist bend, which, she felt, would in turn necessitate a remolding of sociocultural structures.

Down with the Essence!

Beauvoir's desire, based on the rejection of most assumed differences between masculine and feminine, could be taken at first as a displacement of the sexual difference, a challenge to categories, with the result that gender would be altogether overcome. Although Beauvoir fails to specify whether or not men will also have to be the best of both sexes, she is aware of the difficulty—impossibility perhaps—for the "other sex" to ensure its liberation alone. She clearly feels that "to change the mentality of women one would also need to change that of men, so as to create a person in whom is combined the best of man and the best of woman" (Moorehead 1974, 9).

To Rimbaud who wrote his friend Demeny that women, these re-creations of men, would, once freed from the masculine hold, generate original poetic deliriums, undreamed of in man's wildest imaginings, Beauvoir objects: "It is far from sure that woman's world of ideas will ever be different from men's because it is only through integration (*s'assimilant avec eux*) that she will free herself" (2:559). Women's equality will entail the development of no specific feminine values (see Schwarzer 1977, 16). Feeling that all notion of specific feminine values implies the belief, monstrous in her eyes, in a feminine essence, she rejects firsthand the possibility for woman to transcend her sex. Although the liberated woman will be as creative as man, Beauvoir argues that she will bring about no new values and that to think otherwise would be to re-establish the belief in the existence of a feminine nature, a concept she has from the start sought to eradicate (Schwarzer 1972, 53). That all her life Beauvoir remained opposed to such a conceit is sufficiently proven by these lines from *Tout compte fait*: "I don't believe that there are qualities, values, ways of life specifically feminine; this would amount to admitting the existence of a feminine nature, i.e., adhering to a myth men have invented to lock women in their condition of oppression" (508; also Schwarzer 1972, 53).

Let us not have woman perpetrate against herself the manipulations and crimes that man has perpetrated against her! Yet, knowing what woman should not be in terms of "her" essence still leaves unanswered the question of devising the avatars that will enable the eunuch she has been made into to become a "complete human being." Since the essence traditionally assigned to her will not do, since no new essence spreads on the horizon, her only road to freedom may consist of glancing down at Adam's endowment and, like the frog of the fable, making herself commensurable.

Vive la différence!

Not so, says Beauvoir. Actually, aware as early as 1949 of the misunder-standings her *Second Sex* would bring, she stresses in her introduction a healthy sense of alterity and denounces the women who, denying their femininity, assert themselves qua men and who, wishing for a penis, no more become men than cease being women (1:xiii). Her answer to the skeptics who object that women, by discarding their femininity in order to become the equals of men, will neither become men, nor achieve equality, but rather will only succeed in becoming monsters, is that equality is not synonymous with identity. Woman, she argues, must not be a copy of man anymore than man must be a copy of woman (1967).

Becoming increasingly aware that she had become a "class collabora-tionist" and that her privileges "were the result of my having abdicated, in some crucial respects at least my womanhood," Beauvoir in time came to refuse to be a token woman, a "male d'honneur," an accomplice in the mystification of woman (Gerassi 1976, 79–80; Schwarzer 1984, 101). From 1970–71 on, she felt that the moment a woman gets power, she ends up adopting masculine standards and loses track of the solidarity that ought to link her to other women. Women who seek to reach positions of importance tend to take on the same faults as men. Like them, they become vain, imbued with their own authority and ruthless in their ambition (see Bair 1984, 27). Definitely aware of the physiologi-cal differences that separate the sexes, Beauvoir unconditionally refuses to erect them into caste differences. In other words, woman is woman and it is pointless to say otherwise. No one will ever be foolish enough to deny that there are women existing as different entities from men: "Actually all one has to do is keep one's eyes open to notice that humanity is divided into two categories of individuals whose clothes, faces, bodies, smiles, demeanors, interests, occupations are obviously different: although it could be that these differences are merely superficial . . . it is nevertheless certain that they exist with flagrant evidence" (1949, 1:xiii).

Even where she is personally concerned, Beauvoir refuses to dissociate her being as a woman from her sense of self. Unthrilled by her father's early pronouncements: "Simone has a man's brain; she thinks like a man; she *is* a man" (1959, 121; also, 179), she chooses to declare her identity as a woman: "If one says to me, 'Oh, you, you are not a woman, you are a man,' it's wrong because actually I am a woman and definitely experience myself as such" (Jeanson 1966, 264). It must be borne in mind that, rather than brushing aside the question: "In what ways am I typically 'feminine' and in what ways not?" she set about to do the research that eventually led to the writing of *The Second Sex* (see 1963, 1:136). Anticipating the reproach of misogyny that would be addressed to her twenty years later, she insists: "If I want to define myself, I am first obliged to declare: 'I am a woman,' this truth constitutes the background against which will be erected all other assertions" (1949, 1:14; see also Leighton 1975; Stassinopoulos 1975; Leclerc 1974; and Lilar 1969).

Essence and Difference

The Essence of (the) Difference

It is difficult not to feel that Beauvoir was and remained something of a puritan, whose characters and alter egos would be better off without a body. She, who tells us in *La Force de l'âge*, her second volume of memoirs, dedicated to Sartre, of their early fondness for games, for all that which un-realizes life, shows a Christian, middle-class hostility to the flesh and to the senses (1960, 25). Her pretense at scientific rigor is drowned by cascading images of limp clamminess generated by masculine disgust and repugnance. Hers is indeed a male, and far from healthy, way of looking at women and sexuality. Breasts and buttocks are fleshy proliferations that, in the fullness of their gratuitous immanence, dread mirrors and caresses. While she equates sex with an animal function of brutal reality, she defines female physiology in terms of inertia, passivity, abandon, all negative terms that act as a foil to the omnipotent Phallus and the "purity" of masculine desire (see 1949, 2:141).

Furthermore, the French writer unquestioningly embraces the polarities of atheistic existentialist jargon—a jargon that, one must confess, does little more than rehash and intensify perennial phallocratic bromides. Her point of view, as she readily concedes, is that of existentialist humanism as defined by Heidegger, Merleau-Ponty, and mostly Sartre (see 1949, 1:31, 39–40, 73; also, Schwarzer 1984, 114; and Sicard 1979, 325). Masculine delirium, mostly in the case of Sartre, knows no bounds when it addresses the issue of the feminine—that part of himself against which man can do nothing, for it belongs to the inexorable cycle of his biological *fatum*—desire, disease and death.[2] In these horrifying passages, which inform more on the neuroses of their author than on a presumed feminine essence, nature is identified with woman who is, in turn, identified with the disgust generated by her sexual organs.

Like a giant, the sex of woman, this spiraling vortex softly, slimily, in "sickly-sweet feminine revenge," sucks in the soul and sex of man. Women's sickeningly sweet, sugarly, clinging flesh gapes "obscenely," like an all-absorbing sponge, or a carnivorous shellfish (see Sartre 1969, 613; 1964, 59). That Sartre should insist upon drying up the humid vitality, the "sliminess" he identifies with feminine anatomy, fine; but how on earth could an intelligent woman be so beguiled as to let herself be contaminated by a man's—be he her companion—irrational fear of the Other, a fear he seeks to exorcize by calling it names? How can one help reading this surrender on the part of the very woman who was calling attention to the lures of masculine manipulation as an interesting and parodic commentary on the topsy-turvy situation in which women have been traditionally placed by occidental man's discourse?[3] The following passage—one of many—speaks for itself:

> The sex organ of man is clean and simple as a finger; it exhibits itself with innocence and often boys have shown it to their comrades with pride and challenge; the feminine sex is mysterious even to the woman herself, concealed, troubled, mucous, moist; it bleeds every month, it is often soiled with secretions, it has a secret and hazardous life. . . . Whereas a man gets a "hard-on," a woman becomes "wet"; in the word itself are memories of bedwetting, of guilty and involuntary yielding to the need of urinating. . . . When the flesh oozes—as does an old wall or a corpse—it seems not to project a liquid but to liquefy: it is a terrifying process of decomposition. Feminine sexual desire is the soft palpitation of a shellfish; whereas man is impetuous, woman is only impatient . . . man dives on his prey like the eagle and the falcon; she waits like a carnivorous plant, a swamp in which

insects and children are engulfed [s'enlisent]; she is suction, suction cup, humus, pitch, and glue, the lure of passivity [appel immobile], insinuating and viscous . . . after her first coition, a woman very often rebels more than ever before against her sexual destiny. (Beauvoir, 1949, 2:147–48)

Who in her right mind would contest that, notwithstanding their claim to be normative as well as informative, Beauvoir's facts—including her facts of biology—are more often than not fictions: fictions of pollution, mutilation, humiliation, defilement, and wounded shame patterned after an insalubrious masculine design? (see 1949, 1:35–77). Woman's existence consists of a series of alienations (1949, 1:62). The victim of the species, the "dirty receptacle" of man's desire (1949, 2:149), she is "violated" by the male at the moment of penetration (1949, 1:57–58; 2:145–46). Although Beauvoir, feeling later on that she had gone too far, tempered somewhat her position (see 1972, 627), it is nonetheless true that she began by describing intercourse as an act which woman, ridden like an animal, only engages in at the risk of losing her mind, and fertilization, as the time when, almost possessed, "she is both herself and another, another than herself" (1949, 1:58; see also 2:144–45). Also woman, like man, is her body but, whereas he coincides with his, she does not correspond to hers: She always experiences it the way an alien would the foreign soil of a planet on which she or he has just landed. In fear and trembling. Who could ever believe that Beauvoir is actually describing things as they are, and not through the befogged lens of an inoperative, vindictive, sado-masochistic male— the self-proclaimed "masturbator, rather than lover (coïteur) of women" evoked in the Cérémonie des adieux? (1981, 385). What kind of reality is she alluding to? A reality of "situation," or of nature? An unhappy concourse of circumstances, or an ineluctable state of affairs? How is one to respond to statements like the following: "[The young girl] is from the beginning much more opaque in her own eyes, more profoundly invested by the obscure mystery of life than the male?" (1949, 2:25). Here, as elsewhere, subjective terms creep through the claimed scientific rigor of the essay ("opaque," "obscure") and its castrating/ed delusion of virility, whereas the expression "from the beginning," pointing to the natural, rather than the cultural, does little to dispel the ambivalence.

Not only does Beauvoir take her cues directly from Sartre's nauseous distaste of a world whose grasp eludes him, but she indirectly accepts as given the binarities of Oedipal culture—man/woman, activity/passivity, culture/nature. Notwithstanding all protestations to the contrary, her desire remains based on a lack, a stasis, and she never moves away from the cultural stereotypes she attacks. She validates transcendence, traditionally considered as the masculine principle of freedom and aptness to create, over and against the immanence, contingence, in It-selfness of the traditionally feminine. In spite of her belated interest in some type of feminist psychoanalysis, the model of freedom she offers women cannot be distinguished from the one proffered hitherto by the masculine gender.[4] Her woman is a Penthesilea who rushes to conquer her fate, invigorated by the wind of adventure and braced by "the strength of a virile soul" (1949, 1:172). It is difficult not to smile at the thought of this female eunuch whose phallus, inflated at the pump of existential morality, swells under the flimsy cover of promised liberation.

Beauvoir's perspective borrows obviously from Sartre's analysis of an aggressively defensive *pour autrui*, but also from Marx's and Engels's dialectical materialism, and all the way back to Hegel's imperialism of consciousness. In spite of many rather spontaneous intimations to the contrary (1960, 1:34), her preferences thus stem indirectly from Hegel's "master and slave" (actually "servant") dialectic where the subject can be posed only in being opposed, where each consciousness seeks the death of the other and where active and informative productivity is favored over unproductive and feminine passivity (Hegel's analysis of the passivity of clitoral pleasure is well known). Even when Beauvoir decides to give materialistic, rather than idealist, bases to such oppositions, even when she decides to replace the antagonism of consciousnesses by the economic basis of scarcity, she still puts everything in terms of conflict, alienation, rejection, and systematic oppression of one sex by the other (1972, 614; see also 1963).

In fact, Beauvoir goes as far as to advance that there is a specific feminine experience that will always elude the grasp of men. Woman's situation has made her different from man, which works both to her advantage and her disadvantage. In other words, by the very fact of her oppressed status, woman "has not only developed in her certain flaws, but also certain qualities which differ from men's" (1975, 20). In a world that has continually oppressed them, women, like all colonized people, have developed some negative characteristics—lack of aggressiveness, daring, self-confidence—but also some marvelous qualities. Beauvoir feels that women, in contradistinction to men, are better able to retain a sense of humor, to maintain a certain distance between themselves and the established hierarchies. Also, they tend to be kind, tender, generous, giving, understanding, compassionate, and altruistic; in brief, to have less self than men. As a rule they do not relish the thought of squelching competitors. Closer to everyday life, they possess irony, detachment, humor, patience, a sense of the concrete, and they do not take themselves so seriously as men do. Whereas men wallow in self-complacency, manifest a self-destructive taste for power and role-playing, women experience much less "the necessity of always wearing masks, of always playing a role;" they do not evince "this hollow, vacuous side, which often accompanies man's taste for generalizations, pompous sentences and abstractions" (1975, 26). Beauvoir does not hesitate to assume that woman's essence—that essence she had set out ferociously to eradicate—predisposes her to homosexuality! (Schwarzer 1984, 119). (I am not at all reacting to the attraction of homosexuality, but to the arbitrariness of the pronouncement, as well to the criteria upon which it is based).

Asked by Dorothy Kaufmann McCall why she hardly ever praises women for their positive differences, Beauvoir attributes her reticence to the necessity for woman 'to exercise extreme caution in these matters. With essence, as with charity, to give (in) a little is to end up giving all: "If one insists too much on difference, even positive differences, one risks imprisoning woman again in a feminine nature. And yet if we want to think clearly and look at things in their totality, without either fear or complacency, we have to admit that there are also feminine qualities" (Kaufmann McCall 1986, 130).

Therefore, never does Beauvoir mention such characteristics without carefully insisting on the cultural, rather than physiological, origin of the dissimilarity (see Beauvoir 1976). For, in a relationship where there exists no reciprocity, "we are shown women solicited by two modes of alienation: it is quite evident that playing at being a man will lead her to failure; but playing at being a woman will also be a mystification; being a woman, would mean being the object, the Other" (1949, 1:94; see also 2:146). Each time woman behaves as a human being and claims her freedom, she is told that she imitates the male. Each time she accepts what is offered to her, she becomes an Object, a thing, the Other—a eunuch. The essential is therefore to deny the significance of this difference: "I am radically feminist, in that I radically discount the difference as a given having a significance by itself" (Jeanson 1966, 258).

The Difference as Essence

That to give all, to give in/to the essence, could be a new direction for woman, Beauvoir never suspects; or if she does, it is only to discard the possibility as crazed and utopian. Her embarrassment with regard to woman's biological difference, her timid recognition of woman's psychoethical superiority are a far cry from the glorification of the Feminine that one finds in the writings of, say, Hélène Cixous, Julia Kristeva, and Luce Irigaray. These women, who paradoxically tend to consider themselves nonfeminists, draw their inspiration from Lacanian and Derridian epistemologies and emphasize the difference for the sake of the difference. Their ambition is to displace the rule of the Phallus and to replace it by that of the feminine difference. Opposing women's bodily experience to the phallocentric/symbolic patterns of Western thought, they feel that women must write with what they have, and not with what they lack. For Irigaray and Cixous at least, women must begin with their sexuality, that is, with their bodies, with their uterus, with their genital and libidinal difference from men. Once masculine values have been rejected, a new universe, degree-zero, comes into being, where the positions of man and woman are destabilized and interchangeable. Such an *Umdrehung* consists not only of reversing the hierarchy of the two worlds of the masculine and the feminine, but of establishing a new hierarchy with its new order of priorities. Beyond the double negation of classical/traditional feminism and antifeminism, the neofeminists reach to woman recognized and affirmed as a Dionysiac power. They insist on *jouissance*, the experience of the physical pleasures of infancy and of later sexuality where the unconscious, the maternal body—generous/genital/nurturing/spending/plural/fluid—overflows and floods the graphemes and morphemes of phallic discourse.

Cixous, for one, feels that language, because it was forged by men, has been made into an instrument of women's oppression which, if it is to reflect feminine specificity, desperately needs an injection of lifeblood and an im/explosion of structures in the direction of the maternal, the matrical, the matriarchal etc. Woman must write woman with her body, with her milk, with her breasts, with her uterus: Woman becomes a metaphor for everything that eludes man's grasp and her voice must not just challenge but displace the sterile echo of Western man's monologue. Like her difference, woman's language must in turn become universal.[5]

Beauvoir's Woman Is a Male:
Phallus Redux

For such a "transsexual" movement—a meeting of androgynes—Beauvoir has nothing but contempt, insofar as it amounts to "taking the place of men to fall back on the same faults as they" (Viansson-Ponté 1978a, 2). She takes no more seriously a transcategorical cultivation or exacerbation of the feminine difference than she tolerates the notion of equality with a difference. In her eyes, it is antifeminist to declare that there is a feminine nature whose expression differs from that of man. By perceiving difference as a source of potential liberation and by emphasizing woman's traditionally praised ability to love, to feel, to intuit, to live the life of the unconscious, etc. these writers, Beauvoir feels, validate again feminine stereotypes. In her opinion, the idea of a return to the concept of a "feminine nature," implied in the statements of the neo-feminists "hinders, rather than promotes, the emancipation of women" (Schwarzer 1984, 108).

For one thing, linking one's *Weltanschauung* to the female body amounts to giving oneself irrationally and mythically a "counter-penis" (Beauvoir 1976, 20; Schwarzer 1972, 16). For another, deplores the French existentialist, the stance does little more than oppose, rather than assimilate, woman to man. Beauvoir criticizes harshly the notion of a feminine alterity or superiority, declaring it an absurdity that does little more than allow women to take a giant step backward (Schwarzer 1984, 19, 84, 85). For yet another, she, who never ceased to consider the maternal, the matrical, the *ewige Weibliche*, even as metaphor, as the essential trap of Judeo-Christian civilization, pronounces herself against what she deems to be a dangerous, albeit more sophisticated, rebirth of the eternal feminine. Particularly insufferable to her are statements like Cixous's: "We are not going to refuse, if it should happen to strike our fancy, the unsurpassed pleasures of pregnancy" (Marks and Courtivron 1980, 261). To Beauvoir, such a concept, notwithstanding the flattering wrapping of its latest avatar(s), is nothing but a lie and a mystification. Finally, there always lurks the danger of sameness within one set of opposing terms/propositions. Although Cixous claims that there is "no general woman, no one typical woman," she expatiates on what women have *in common* (her emphasis) (Beauvoir 1975, 39–54, or Marks and Courtivron, 1980, 245). As Ann Rosalind Jones has pointed out: "One libidinal voice, however nonphallocentrically defined," speaking for all women, "flattens out the lived differences among women" (Showalter 1985, 371).

More essentially perhaps, although Beauvoir would not disagree that for millennia women have written like men, she explicitly and repeatedly rejects the practicality, even the desirability of a specifically feminine discourse. Over and against the neo-feminists' attempts at getting rid of phallologocentrism and at creating a new writing style, she denounces as a contradiction this imprisonment of women in a ghetto of difference/singularity: "I consider it almost antifeminist to say that there is a feminine nature which expresses itself differently, that a woman speaks her body more than a man" (Jardine 1979, 230). Even though men have invested a universal language with a "viriloid" content, women will never be able to invent, within a universal language, a code that would be all their own (David 1979b; cf. Zéphir 1982, 109, 162). Language and logic are universal values that women can neither make up, nor make over. The existentialist deems feminine writing far too self-conscious for the unmediated libidinal discourse it claims to create and objects to its hermeticism and elitism. Such a conceit will end up, she fears, endangering the cause of women, because its major interest lies in satisfying an author's narcissism rather than in establishing any real bond of communication between a writer and her audience. To Alice Jardine who questioned her concerning Cixous's attempt at a new feminine writing, Beauvoir quipped, "I'm of an older generation. I can't read her, understand her. And I think it's wrong to write in a totally esoteric language. . . . There is something false in this search for a purely feminine writing style" (Jardine 1979, 229). Reflecting on the cultivation of difference for the sake of difference, she told Catherine David: "It's hard to imagine that women can invent within the universal language a code that would be all their own. As it happens they are doing no such thing. They are using men's words, even if they do twist the sense of them" (David 1979b, 295).[6]

Like Prometheus, woman will have to steal the divine fire, the sacred tool from the mouths and hands of men for "to refuse masculine models is nonsense" (Beauvoir 1972, 628). Rather than formulating a new discourse, women will have to persist in challenging the discourses that stand, to work at changing the instrument and at introducing their own values. Women, rather than being iconoclasts, must sort out, select, and reappropriate the tools, concepts, and values that men have made available to them. They need to make use of the only available building materials: the genres, conventions—stereotypes even—that surround them, for these are the only stories at their disposal. Men's world is theirs for the taking, if not for the asking (Schwarzer 1972, 53; and 1984, 122). Just like the bourgeois who, in order to free the proletariat, keeps on using the ideologies of his class, woman in search of a liberation must proceed with the language that is familiar to her. She must annex the value man has traditionally placed on the logos. Refusing the double standard, Beauvoir accepts one—man's—for both men and women alike; she assimilates masculine values with the purpose of utilizing them to feminine ends. Here again, all difference must disappear.

Yet, in this case as in many others, Beauvoir keeps one foot in both camps, for, no sooner has she discounted the hydra of feminine specific- ity than she allows it to grow another head. "Don't worry," she almost says, for woman's difference always has a way of inscribing itself in the interstices, the silences of man's speech. The female writer, say, a Colette or a Virginia Woolf, will keep on writing differently from her male counterpart. She will mark the world with her femaleness, not only because she is a woman, but also because, when one writes, one writes with one's entire being. Her way of looking at the world is different from that of man, as the perspective of the historically oppressed varies from that of the oppressor. Like national origin, the linguistic "difference" of a being more attuned to the sensations of nature (woman) will survive in spite of all attempts made at eradicating it: "If the writer is a woman, feminist or not, it will give the language something that it would not have [had] if it had been used by a man" (Jardine 1979, 230).

The only road available to woman, short of the antifeminism that Beauvoir denounced all along, is therefore, as was first suspected, that of an emulation of the masculine by the feminine. Equality for women can only be obtained through the grafting of a phallus. Even when the French existentialist understands being as being human rather than being sexual, even when she subsumes sexuality under ontology; that is, sees in sex just another activity similar to, say, work or play, her analyses are elaborated on the basis of a masculine pattern that she enjoins women to reproduce. Short of saying with Elizabeth Hardwick that "there is hardly a thing I would want to say contrary to her thesis that Simone de Beauvoir has not said herself" (Hardwick 1953, 322), one can only identify the existentialist's glorification of transcendence with the type of feminism that Luce Irigaray denounces in *Ce Sexe qui n'en est pas un:* "Woman simply equal to men would be like them and therefore not women" (1977, 150). There is, however, a twist the second time around, that of effecting the shift via a move from the particular to the general, rather than from one gender to the other. Insofar as male experience with the value it has traditionally placed on transcendence has [ph]allaciously universalized itself as the whole human experience, the "ideal" woman can only reach the universal through an analogous transformation: "I banked," said Beauvoir in the course of a *Vogue* interview, "on values that could be called masculine—although in my eyes they are universal" (David 1979b, 295). Has man not particularized the universal? Has he not imposed his particular language as universal language; that is, universalized the particular of his own difference? It is hard indeed to call universal, values from whose elaboration more than one half of the population has been excluded (See Zéphir 1982, 109, 162). Let us not forget, however, the existential philosopher's admiration for the "feminists [who] refuse to be the equals of men, [and to share with them] the idea of competition, of masculine glory, and of celebrity" (Patterson 1979, 746). Women, she suggests, will have to work at realizing the difficult balancing act of reconciling the singular and the universal. Theirs will be a difficult dialectic between, as Beauvoir told Alice Jardine, "accepting power and refusing it, accepting certain masculine values and wanting to transform them" (Jardine 1979, 228, 235).

As is plain to see, the French existentialist does not speak with a single voice. Either she wishes to have it both ways, or she takes with one hand that which she gives with the other. On the one hand, she [re]assures [!] her audience that "boys will always be boys and girls will always be girls"; on the other, she grafts a mystifying member upon her unduly castrated female. On the one hand, she denies the existence of feminine qualities and values (Beauvoir 1972, 628); on the other, she ends up, with her back to the wall, forced to recognize the existence of a feminine specificity. What kind of specificity? Biological? Historical? Positive? Negative? Willed? Tolerated? Mixed? One never knows for sure. She hesitates, goes this way and that, and, when cornered, runs to the masculine camp. When all is said and done, even the residual/ infinitesimal difference she has allowed to subsist between men and women, she is willing to sacrifice. Beauvoir finds herself trapped in phallocentrism and her feminism is nothing but the operation of a woman who aspires to be like a man and whose voice is that of the ventriloquist's dummy. Beauvoir's women, in truth, are men, and men not altogether healthy. To the spur/ious character of the endeavor could be applied these words of Derrida:

> And in truth they too are men, those women feminists . . . Feminism is nothing but the operation of a woman who aspires to be like a man. And in order to resemble the masculine dogmatic philosopher this woman lays claim—just as much as he—to truth, scientific and objective in all their castrated delusions of virility. Feminism too seeks to castrate. It wants a castrated woman (1979, 65)

Back to Back

Actually Beauvoir and neo-feminism are not so far apart as may have appeared at first. Although both tendencies proceed from inverted patterns, they eventually and by virtue of their symmetry realize the economy of the "difference" by forgetting [all about] it. In the beginning, says classical feminism, there was man, both *homo* and *vir;* in the beginning, echoes neo-feminism, there was woman, both *homo* and *mulier.* Then came the great split of *homo* into *vir* and *mulier,* man and woman. Therefore all one has to do now is to get rid of the sexual difference: Cancel out the sexual determination of that which used to be called "man," or "woman," and the difference, the sex, will disappear, restoring *homo* to his/her sovereign, original indifference. But, whether the liberation of women asserts itself in the cultivated difference of the neo-feminists, or the negated one of existential feminism, it "equally" results in a neutralization, an indifference *(indifférend),* with the consequence that whether it be masculine or feminine matters little. In that sense, Suzanne Lilar appears to be correct when she argues that Beauvoir's "obsession" amounts to "cancelling out" the difference, to "desexualizing" woman and to "neutralizing" her problem (Lilar 1969, 19). To Beauvoir's universal maleness with a tolerated difference corresponds the neo-feminists' pattern of global femininity with no variance. The rule of the uterus displaces that of the Phallus; yet, not much is really changed.

Those who indulge the coercive glorification of motherhood segregate and ostracize the dissidents just as much as do those who tell women to renounce all desire of bearing children. Between those who tell women that the feminine difference must become everything and those who tell them that it must be abolished, it is never a question of giving women a choice. Indeed, as Derrida has well shown, not only is castration the operation that each sex perpetrates against the other; it is the operation of woman against woman. When all is said and done, in neither instance is there a genuine questioning of the existence of some sort of essence or of the linking of gender with sex: The sexual organs—vagina or penis—remain the model. Is not woman, just like man, a mixture of transcendence and frailties? Just like antifeminists, feminists à la Beauvoir and neo-feminists hang the Feminine—either in its immanent (negative), or in its transexual (positive) principle—upon the female sex identified with passivity, receptivity, intuition, empathy, and immanence and the Masculine upon the male sex, equated with activity, aggressiveness, rationality, solipsism, and transcendence. It matters little that these writers do so by favoring history over biology or by extending the physiological to the psychological: although they appear to speak different languages, they actually say the same thing.[7] Neo-feminism reverses the values assigned to each side of the polarity, but it remains bound up through symmetrical opposition with the very ideological system it set about to destroy: In its very attempt at eluding the snares of the male/female dichotomy, it succumbs all the more surely to them. Beauvoir's, meanwhile (but how differently?), is a movement that, like the one that guides the players on the field, merely allows them to trade places with the opposing team. The very moment the sexual difference is determined as an opposition, each term becomes inverted in/to the other, all difference(s) must disappear and nothing really changes. Choosing between the Feminine and the Masculine amounts to reinforcing their antagonism, to confirming the traditional segregation. In the (infinitely) reversible mechanism of contradiction, subject and predicate mirror each other in the copula with the consequence that any new proposition becomes reflected out of existence.

The problem with difference is that it is either too essential to be accidental, or too accidental to provide a basis for an essential distinction. If Beauvoir does know how to handle the obstinate resurfacing of (the) "difference" in the form of an arbitrarily acknowledged "destiny"—"anatomic" or "sexual"—the others fail to give a satisfactory account of the reason why such importance ought to be placed upon the biological and the sexual. Could it be rather that sex is nothing but a back-formation of gender, and gender itself the constricting result of a dualistic, Manichaean tendency to slice the world into arbitrary and antagonistic categories? Why this prolongation of the fictitious concept that the species divides itself neatly into two halves? As Beauvoir herself recognizes very early on in *The Second Sex,* "the division of the species into two sexes is not always clear-cut" (1949, 1:36). Why restrict oneself to a binary system of gender definition? Why, rather than observe in the individual man and woman an infinite variety of combinations between opposing impulses, systematically divide human beings into masculine and feminine? Isn't the notion of opposite sexes, elaborated by centuries of Western civilization, as dangerous a myth as that of woman's essence?[8] Some of us are plural, or even indifferent. As Cixous cautiously emphasizes, one must be careful to avoid the confusion man/masculine, woman/feminine for "there are men who do not repress their femininity, women who more or less inscribe their masculinity" (from "Sorties" in Cixous 1975). Some of the best "masculine" writing has been done by women (George Eliot, Marguerite Yourcenar, Doris Lessing, etc.); some of the best "feminine" writing by men (Flaubert, Proust, Tennessee Williams, etc.). Can we allow ourselves to dream of a scenario à la Deleuze or à la Guattari, of an economy which, transcending the male/female, phallus/uterus opposition, would exalt the individual beyond all sexual differentiation? Meanwhile, let us not forget that some of us still write with a pen—rather than with our bodies—*jouissants,* or not.

Conclusion

In many respects, Beauvoir's contradictory statements—and perhaps also the others'—reproduce the power structure by which Western civilization has been shaped. Like most of us, these female writers did not escape the schizophrenia in which occidental man has placed women and himself. Even as Beauvoir rejects the concept of a feminine essence, there sprout, through the crevices that riddle Western man's discourse, the very seedlings she has trampled underfoot.

Yet let us not cry anathema too soon. For all this Beauvoir remains a model, or at least an inspiration. Writing *The Second Sex* might have been the only means a postwar woman had at her disposal to correct a man-made illusion. It can also be that, as Beauvoir herself felt as late as

1979, the situation of women has not greatly improved: There is still much household tedium, much enslavement to men, marriage, and motherhood, much occultation of the values traditionally linked to the Feminine, much intensification of speed, technology, competitiveness, values from which women have been kept for centuries, much unfairness where their careers are concerned, compounded by the recent challenge of reconciling domestic and professional responsibilities—a combination that, unfortunately, often ends up crushing, rather than liberating the "second sex" (David 1979b, 266, 268, 294, 295, 296, 297). In the words that Colette Audry, a onetime colleague of Simone de Beauvoir, wrote in her preface to Michelle Coquillat's *La Poétique du mâle*, "the reign of patriarchy is far from over," for in our society, "the female sex remains a second sex, subordinate in the facts and in the heads" (Coquillat 1982, xviii–xix). Even as staunch a detractor of *The Second Sex* as Hardwick has mollified her stance, admitting that "it's a wonderful, remarkable book. Nothing that has come since on the matter of women compares to it" (Hardwick 1989, 218).

Man has created this illusion: Woman. As Prospero well knew, one fights one illusion with another. Then, the time comes to discard the second illusion, to break one's staff and drown one's book. Beauvoir would have agreed with Shakespeare's magician, she who said, "I think that *The Second Sex* will seem an old, dated book, after a while. But nonetheless . . . a book which will have made its contribution" (Jardine 1979, 236). She also knew that her work was better at describing problems than at solving them, better at denouncing costly illusions than at bringing specific answers; "even if I have not brought solutions to each particular trouble, I have at least helped my contemporaries to become aware of themselves and of their situation" (1963, 109–110). Her spiritual heiresses wish to move farther. Like so many Electras, they wish to murder their sexist mother. At least, there has begun a dialogue where there used to be a monologue—that of man with himself. Let us remember the words of Virginia Woolf: "The garrulous sex, against common repute, is not the female but the male; in all the libraries of the world the man is to be heard talking to himself and for the most part about himself (1979, 65)."

And let us make sure the dialogue that has recently begun ends neither in verbiage nor in soliloquy.

Notes

1. This translation and all other translations from the French are mine.
2. See the chapter "Quality as a Revelation of Being," in Sartre (1969), 600–615.

3. For more on the sexism of Sartrean philosophy, see Collins and Pierce (1976), 112–27.
4. Beauvoir told Alice Schwarzer in this respect that "I would not take Freud as my starting point but go right back to the basics and from a feminist perspective, from a feminine, rather than a masculine viewpoint" (Schwarzer 1984, 89, 94).
5. For a further study of this point, see Marks and Courtivron (1980), 147.
6. In order to study further what Beauvoir thinks of feminine writing such as, say, Cixous practices it, see Beauvoir's preface to a study of La Femme rompue in A. Orphir (1976), 15. See also David (1979), 84; and Wenzel (1986), 11.
7. To emphasize, as Lilar does, the necessity of a male/female dialectic within each sexually bipolar subject is hardly worth it, since the Teilhardian lays the accent upon the difference and its cultivation—a difference hooked on neither history nor biology—posits the existence of a maternal instinct, celebrates peace, love, happiness, and maternity as typically feminine values (Lilar 1969, 121), and concludes her Misunderstandings of The Second Sex by opposing "critical negativity" and "virile rigor" to the "acquiescence of woman to the natural order" (266).
8. For the explosion of such polarity, see Foucault (1979; 1980).

References

Bair, Deirdre. 1984. "Women's Rights in Today's World: An Interview with Simone de Beauvoir." 1984 Britannica Book of the Year. Chicago: Encyclopedia Britannica, 27–28.

Barsy, M. de. 1968. "Un Grand Entretien par Martine de Barsy." Pénéla, Connaître et comprendre (September): 10–17.

Beauvoir, Simone de. 1949. Le Deuxième Sexe. 2 vols. Paris: Gallimard.

———. 1959. Memoirs of a Dutiful Daughter. Cleveland: World Publishing.

———. 1960. La Force de l'âge. Paris: Gallimard.

———. 1963. La Force des choses. 2 vols. Paris: Gallimard.

———. 1967. "The Philosopher of the Other Sex in Cairo." Al Ahram, 27 February.

———. 1972. Tout compte fait. Paris: Gallimard.

———. 1975. "Simone de Beauvoir et la lutte des femmes: Simone de Beauvoir interroge Jean-Paul Sartre." L'Arc 61:3–12. (This interview is available in English under the title "Simone de Beauvoir questions J.-P. Sartre," New Left Review 97 [May 1976]: 71–80.)

———. 1976. "Simone de Beauvoir: Le Deuxième Sexe trente ans après." Marie-Claire, no. 209 (October): 15–20.

———. 1981. La Cérémonie des adieux suivi de Entretiens avec Simone de Beauvoir, août-septembre 1974. Paris: Gallimard.

Cixous, Hélène, and Catherine Clément. 1975. La Jeune Née. Paris: Union générale d'Editions.

———. 1976. "The Laugh of Medusa." Signs: Journal of Women in Culture and Society 1:875–99.

Collins, Marjorie, and Christine Pierce. 1976. "Holes and Slime: Sexism in Sartre's Psychoanalysis." In Women and Philosophy: Toward a Theory of Liberation, edited by C. Gould and M. Wartofsky, 112–27. New York: Putnam.

Coquillat, Michelle. 1982. La Poétique du mâle. Paris: Gallimard.

David, Catherine. 1979a. "Beauvoir elle-même. Propos recueillis par Catherine David. Le Nouvel Observateur, 22–29 January.

———. 1979b. "Becoming Yourself." Vogue (May): 226–97.

Deleuze, G., and F. Guattari. 1976. Anti-Oedipus. New York: Viking.

Derrida, Jacques. 1979. *Spurs/Eperons*. Chicago: University of Chicago Press.

Foucault, Michel. 1979. *The History of Sexuality*. Vol. 1. New York: Bantam.

———. 1980. Introduction to *Herculine Barbin: Being the Recently Discovered Memoirs of a Nineteenth-Century French Hermaphrodite*. Translated by Richard McDougall. New York: Pantheon.

Francis, Claude, and Fernande Gonthier. 1979. *Les Ecrits de Simone de Beauvoir*. Paris: Gallimard.

Gerassi, John. 1976. "Simone de Beauvoir: *The Second Sex* 25 Years Later." *Society* 13, no. 2 (January–February): 79–85.

Hardwick, Elizabeth. 1953. "The Subjection of Women." *Partisan Review* 20, no. 3 (May–June): 321–31.

———. 1985. "The Art of Fiction LXXXVII." *The Paris Review* 96, 20–51.

———. 1989 (reprint). "Elizabeth Hardwick." In *Women Writers At Work: The Paris Review Interviews*, edited by George Plimpton, 201–24. Introduction by Margaret Atwood. New York: Penguin.

Irigaray, Luce. 1974. *Speculum de l'autre femme*. Paris: Editions de Minuit.

———. 1977. *Ce Sexe qui n'en est pas un*. Paris: Editions de Minuit.

Jardine, Alice. 1979. "Interview with Simone de Beauvoir." *Signs: Journal of Women in Culture and Society* 5:224–35.

Jeanson, F. 1966. "Deux entretiens de Simone de Beauvoir avec Francis Jeanson." In his *Simone de Beauvoir ou l'entreprise de vivre*, 251–56. Paris: Seuil.

Jones, Ann Rosalind. 1985. "Writing the Body: Toward an Understanding of L'Ecriture Feminine." In *The New Feminist Criticism: Essays on Women, Literature and Theory*, edited by Elaine Showalter, 361–77. New York: Pantheon.

Kaufmann McCall, Dorothy. 1986. "Simone de Beauvoir: Questions of Difference and Generation." In *Simone de Beauvoir: Witness to a Century*. Special issue of *Yale French Studies* 72:209–23.

Leclerc, Annie. 1974. *Parole de femme*. Paris: Grasset.

Leighton, Jean. 1975. *Simone de Beauvoir on Women*. Rutherford, N.J.: Fairleigh Dickinson University Press.

Lilar, Suzanne. 1969. *Le Malentendu du Deuxième Sexe*. Paris: Presses Universitaires de France.

Marks, Elaine, and Isabelle de Courtivron, eds. 1980. *New French Feminisms*. Amherst: University of Massachusetts Press.

Morehead, Caroline. 1974. "Simone de Beauvoir: Marriage is a very dangerous institution. A talk with Simone de Beauvoir." *Times* (London), 15 May.

Orphir, A. 1976. *Regards féminins. Condition féminine et création littéraire*. Preface by Simone de Beauvoir, 15–17. Paris: Denoël and Gonthier.

Patterson, Yolanda A. 1979. "Entretien avec Simone de Beauvoir." *French Review* 52, no. 5 (April): 745–54.

Sartre, Jean-Paul. 1964. *Nausea*. New York: New Directions.

———. 1969. *Being and Nothingness*. London: Methuen.

Schwarzer, Alice. 1972. "Radicalization of Simone de Beauvoir." *Ms. Magazine* (July): 60–63, 134.

———. 1977. "Talking to a Friend—An Interview with Simone de Beauvoir." *Ms. Magazine* (July): 12–13, 15–16.

———. 1984. *Simone de Beauvoir aujourd'hui. Six entretiens*. Translated, in parts, from the German by Léa Marcou. Paris: Mercure de France.

Sicard, M. 1979. "Interférences. Entretien avec Simone de Beauvoir et Jean-Paul Sartre." *Obliques* 18–19: 325–29.

Stassinopoulos, A. 1975. *La Femme femme*. Paris: Lafont.

Viansson-Ponté, P. 1978a. "Entretiens avec Simone de Beauvoir I." *Le Monde,* no. 10247, 10 January.

————. 1978b. "Entretiens avec Simone de Beauvoir II. Le Féminisme maintenant est une force." *Le Monde,* no. 10248, 11 January.

Wenzel, Hélène. 1986. "Interview with Simone de Beauvoir." In *Simone de Beauvoir: Witness to a Century,* 5–32. Special issue of *Yale French Studies* 72:11.

Woolf, Virginia. 1979. *Women and Writing.* Edited and with an introduction by Michèle Barrett. Orlando: Harcourt Brace Jovanovich.

Zéphir, Jacques. 1982. *Le Néo-féminisme de Simone de Beauvoir.* Paris: Denoël and Gonthier.

9

Beauvoir's Concept of Bodily Alienation

Kristana Arp

Commentators have often remarked that Simone de Beauvoir takes a decidedly negative view of the female body in *The Second Sex*. And they have certainly found it easy enough to support this observation with excerpts from the text. In the first chapter and elsewhere in the first volume of the work Beauvoir does offer a rather harsh description of female biological functions. But she also goes out of her way to deny that biological facts determine the way that one experiences one's body. "It is not so much as a body, but as a body subject to taboos, to laws, that a subject is conscious of itself and fulfills itself," she says among other things (1:75).[1] In the second volume of the work, "Lived Experience," Beauvoir describes in detail *how* a woman experiences her body as a body subject to "taboos and laws," subject in sum to the complex web of social forces dominating women's lives in patriarchal culture.

As Julie Ward's paper in this volume attests, there has long been a debate among feminists over how to interpret Beauvoir's comments about female biology. In these pages I want to trace the incisive account that Beauvoir offers in *The Second Sex* of how female bodily experience is constructed through social and ideological means. I contend that we should acknowledge the power of Beauvoir's analysis here while mainly discounting her remarks on female biology, as she in fact almost invites us to do. Female biological functions such as pregnancy, lactation, menstruation, etc. of course have an undeniable significance for female bodily experience. It is just that this significance is never experienced at the biological level alone. To begin to uncover the social significance these functions have come to have we must turn to Beauvoir's account of the social construction of female bodily experience in the second volume.

Beauvoir's greatest contribution to an analysis of the social construction of female bodily experience is her concept of bodily alienation. In the chapter on biology and elsewhere Beauvoir offers ample testimony that women do experience their bodies in a highly negative fashion, as alien, curiously inert things. She initially describes woman's alienation from her body in biological terms. But in the second volume she details how the young girl comes to look upon her body as something alien to herself as the result of intensive social conditioning. Following Beauvoir's approach in the second volume I interpret bodily alienation as a social and cultural phenomenon and not as a purely biological one. I myself do not see how there is anything intrinsically alienating (at least alienating in a negative sense) in the experiences of pregnancy, lactation, and menstruation.

Beauvoir's View of the Body

Some critics have complained that Beauvoir presents too harsh a portrayal of women's condition in general (Leighton 1975; Crosland 1992). But feminist critics are concerned with Beauvoir's depiction of female biology specifically. Many charge that Beauvoir expresses a hardly disguised disgust with female bodily functions or a revulsion toward human physicality in general (Whitmarsh 1981; Ascher 1981; Okely 1986). Inevitably some trace her squeamishness about the female body back to Sartre's personal and intellectual influence over her (McCall 1979; Lloyd 1984; Okely 1986). Others claim only that she and Sartre shared the same outlook toward the female body, perhaps due to their similarly puritanical upbringings (Whitmarsh 1981; Asher 1981). Critics also complain that Beauvoir has stacked the deck against women by associating transcendence or the full expression of human freedom with male physical characteristics and immanence or the lack of freedom with female biological functions (Lloyd 1984; Okely 1986).

On the other side on this issue are writers like Ward, who argues that Beauvoir's remarks about female biology have been misinterpreted, and Judith Butler, who ignores Beauvoir's remarks about biology, stressing instead how Beauvoir sees gender to be socially constructed (Butler 1986). The problem with denying outright that Beauvoir held a negative view of female biological functions is that Beauvoir makes many state-ments in the chapter on biology and elsewhere in the first volume that do express a gloomy view of the female's biological destiny. In biological terms, the male "seems infinitely favored," she concludes (1:69). In intercourse the female is "taken" by the male (1:56). In pregnancy she is "inhabited by another" and in lactation still connected to it (1:58). In menstruation she feels her body to be "an obscure, alien thing" (1:66).

Perhaps the most problematic aspect of Beauvoir's characterization of the female body in these places is the almost complete passivity she ascribes to it. This passivity cannot help having great significance within Beauvoir's ontological scheme. In this scheme, which she did not so much borrow from Sartre as share and even help form (Schwarzer 1984; Simons 1986; Bair 1990), passivity is equated with immanence, which is the death of freedom or transcendence:

> The perspective that we are adopting is that of existentialist ethics. Each subject situates itself concretely as a transcendence through its projects; it only accomplishes itself as freedom through going beyond itself towards other freedoms; there is no other justification for its present existence than its expansion towards an indefinitely open future. Each time that transcen-dence falls back into immanence, there is a degradation of existence into the "en-soi," of freedom into facticity. (1:31)

Beauvoir's depiction of the female body as passive and inert in its biological role gives credence to those critics who charge that Beauvoir has associated female physical characteristics with immanence. The problem is that this identification leaves the implication that women have to somehow rise above their bodies to achieve transcendence and thus fulfillment as a truly human existence.

No one can (or does) deny that Beauvoir makes these statements in the opening chapter and elsewhere. Instead of trying to explain these statements away, we might consider, as some critics have, why she was led to make them. Perhaps Beauvoir herself, as well as many of the women of her time and place, did experience her body in this way. Beauvoir's ambivalence toward the body comes through in many of her works.[2] The detailed description of how women experience the different stages of their lives in the second volume was rooted in her own experiences and those of her acquaintances. The attitudes toward the body depicted there are hardly positive.

Of course in this second volume she is describing the experience of the female body as a body subject to laws and taboos—the socialized body. In the first chapter she is discussing the female body from the perspective of biology alone. Or is she? In my view the female body described in the opening chapter on biology is the socialized body as well. The tip-off here is precisely the passivity she ascribes to the female body at the biological level. How can immanence and transcendence, which in Beauvoir's thinking are ontological attributes, be manifested in biological structures? The passivity of the female body, I shall argue, is a social construction. It is a result of a process of alienation that unfolds at the social level. I think that in her portrayal of female biological functions Beauvoir has slipped in, unbeknownst to herself, an account of female bodily experience in patriarchal society.

Beauvoir's Account of Bodily Alienation

In any case, I belong to the second camp, which does not take Beauvoir's statements about female biology at face value. Biology alone cannot determine how a woman experiences her body. For Beauvoir to assert otherwise would contradict the philosophical basis of her thought. Beauvoir explicitly identifies herself as an existentialist in *The Second*

Sex and in her other work, and for an existentialist biology is certainly not destiny. As Beauvoir puts it: "a society is not a species: in a society the species realizes itself as existence; it transcends itself towards the world and the future: its mores cannot be deduced from biology; individuals are never abandoned to their nature, they answer to that second nature which is custom into which their basic ontological attitude is carried over" (1:75).[3] Human existence, which is social existence, incorporates but surpasses biological existence. Humans' basic ontological stance is more decisive in shaping their lives than are biological drives and characteristics.

Today, I think feminists regard Beauvoir's existentialist pedigree as somewhat of an embarrassment. But as the French feminist critic Michèle Le Doeuff points out, it was Beauvoir's existentialist stance that allowed her to reject any explanation of women's position that tied it to woman's nature, leaving her free to conceptualize it as a social construct instead (Le Doeuff 1980).[4] And in keeping with her existentialist roots, Beauvoir always rejected any form of essentialism, even a feminist essentialism, which exalts feminine qualities (Simons and Benjamin 1979). There is no "specifically female nature" (Beauvoir 1974:458).[5]

Generally, though, much less has been made of Beauvoir's roots in the phenomenological movement than of her existentialist background. Yet Beauvoir explicitly testifies to how her attitude toward the body has its origins in phenomenological schools of thought: "However, one will say, in the perspective I am adopting—that of Heidegger, Sartre and Merleau-Ponty—if the body is not a *thing*, it is a situation; it is our grasp upon the world and the sketch of our projects" (1:72). Of these three, Merleau-Ponty, with his concept of the *corps vécu* or lived body, seems to have had the most influence on Beauvoir's understanding of the body.[6] She says, mirroring the central thesis of his *Phenomenology of Perception,* "it is not the body object described by the experts that exists concretely, but the body lived by the subject" (1:77).[7] And the language of Merleau-Ponty is also echoed in the French title of the second volume of the work: "L'Expérience Vécu" or lived experience. Merleau-Ponty's concept of the embodied subject, elaborated at length in his *Phenomenology of Perception,* transcends the remaining traces of dualism found in Sartre's account of the body in *Being and Nothingness.*

Because she shares Merleau-Ponty's perspective on the body, Beauvoir mostly manages to escape the taint of dualism as well. I cannot go along with those critics who claim that Beauvoir falls back on a mind/body split to escape from the fact of female biological inferiority (Ascher 1981). What her chapter on biology shows, at the very least, is that the body plays a tremendously important role in human experience. Even Freud got this right according to Beauvoir: "The value of Freudianism derives from the fact that the existent is a body: the way in which it experiences itself as a body confronted by other bodies expresses its existential situation concretely" (1:104).

But Beauvoir does not accept Merleau-Ponty's analysis of bodily experience completely. At one point in referring to the *Phenomenology of Perception* she makes a most provocative statement: "Woman, like man, *is* her body; but her body is something other than her" (1:66). This statement is an implicit critique of Merleau-Ponty: his thesis holds true, strictly speaking, only for men, not for women. A woman in being her body is something other than herself.

What does it mean to be other than oneself? The quest for self-identity concerned Beauvoir throughout her life, surfacing in different guises in various places in her work. In an early philosophical work, *The Ethics of Ambiguity*, she searches for a way one can manage to "coincide exactly" with oneself (1991, 13, 23). This search is rendered in personal terms in her novel *The Mandarins* when one of the central characters thinks to herself: "It's easy of course to say 'I am I.' But who am I? where find myself?" (1956, 43). And in her memoirs Beauvoir muses over the mystery that lurks behind the "necessary coincidence of the subject and his history: "Why am I myself?" she asks (1974, 1).

However, in *The Second Sex* this theme surfaces in a rather different form. Here the problem of self-identity is a more concrete one and is considered mainly in terms of a woman's experience of her own body. Furthermore, in *The Second Sex* a woman's lack of identity with her own body is conceptualized in terms of Beauvoir's philosophical concept of alienation. To say that a woman is something other than her body means that she is alienated in her body. She experiences her body as an "obscure, alien thing," a thing separated from herself in some way. This is a diminishment of her humanity because, as the phenomenological tradition points out, a human *is* her body. That Beauvoir sees a woman's alienation from her body ás problematic shows that she shares this central premise as articulated by Merleau-Ponty. To see one's body as a thing separate from oneself might be considered as normal by a mind/body dualist.

The point in the book where Beauvoir makes this emendation to

Merleau-Ponty's views about the body is in the initial chapter on biology that feminist critics have found so problematic. In undergoing the biological functions of menstruation, pregnancy, and lactation, she asserts, the human female is alienated in her body. Beauvoir's character-ization of these normal female functions as alienating of course gives support to those critics who charge that Beauvoir regards the biological functions of the female body as an obstacle to realizing full human potential. However, this is not the only place in the book where Beauvoir discusses female bodily alienation. In the chapters on "Child-hood," "The Young Girl," and "Sexual Initiation" in the second volume she describes how the young woman comes to look on her body as something alien to her as a result of her socialization. Beauvoir's comment in response to Merleau-Ponty that "Woman, like man, is her body, but her body is something other than her" is certainly applicable in this context. Indeed, as I have maintained, bodily alienation can be and should be seen to originate at the sociocultural level and not at the biological level alone.

That Beauvoir ultimately conceives bodily alienation and the dimin-ishment of human potential that it entails to result from social forces can be seen from the implication she leaves that this process of bodily alienation can be resisted to some extent. Though Beauvoir sometimes chooses to see alienation in a positive light,[8] for the female at least alienation is seen as resulting when "the anguish of liberty leads the subject to search for itself in things, which is a way of fleeing itself" (1:88). In these moments Beauvoir is obviously conceiving alienation along the lines of Sartre's concept of bad faith.[9] Beauvoir's presentation of alienation in these terms has led some feminist critics to complain that Beauvoir depicts women as giving in to this process out of personal weakness. But Beauvoir herself realizes that due to the configuration of sex roles often the only choice open to women is between different types of alienation: "Woman is shown to us to be incited to two modes of alienation; it is evident that to play at being a man would be a source of defeat for her; but to play at being a woman is also a trap: to be a woman is to be an object, the Other" (1:92–93).

It is a woman's acceding to "play at being a woman" that leads to bodily alienation. But a woman does not accede to being female—to having a female's biological functions and not a male's. At the time Beauvoir wrote The Second Sex at least, a woman had no choice about this. Of course the development of technology has radically changed the impact that biology has on human life, if not human biology itself. But these changes have unfolded at a social and historical level, not the personal level of existential choice. When Beauvoir implies that individual women might resist the process of bodily alienation in some fashion, that means that it is not originally a biological phenomenon. And if bodily alienation is culturally induced, then having (or rather being) a female body presents no obstacles at the biological level to achieving the existentialist ideal of transcendence.

This interpretation of the concept of bodily alienation renders it a powerful tool for explaining how women's experience of their bodies, seemingly so private and personal, can be deeply affected by social forces. The process whereby a woman comes to look on her body as something alien to her is sensitively described in the second volume of *The Second Sex*. The tendency toward alienation manifests itself early, she hypothesizes, in both genders. But soon different expectations are placed on girls than are on boys. Around the same time that the little boy finds his alter ego in his penis, according to Beauvoir, the girl comes to see herself in her doll. Harmless enough in itself, or even a positive sign, this experience comes to have a distinct significance in light of the girl's subsequent social development: "The big difference is that, on the one hand, the doll represents the whole body, and, on the other, it is a passive thing. On this account, the little girl will be encouraged to alienate herself in her whole person and to regard this as an inert given object" (2:25). This identification with passivity is imposed by society not biology, Beauvoir asserts: "it is a destiny that is imposed on her by her educators and by society" (2:26). The girl's relationship with her doll is just part of a larger drama in which she is dressed, talked to, and fussed over like a live doll and overall taught that to please: "she must make herself object" (2:27).

Puberty, however, is the time that the female body fully assumes its status as an object in the eyes of others and in the young woman's own eyes. The changes that the body goes through draw male attention to it and only increase her feelings of alienation from it. This is one of the times that physiological events cannot but have an effect on one's state of mind. But the same is true for males at puberty. Here again Beauvoir asserts that it is the young woman's general situation, not biology per se that limits her bodily capacities.[10] Many female complaints are psychosomatic: "It is in great part the anxiety of being a woman that consumes the feminine body" (2:85). At the same time the young woman's erotic feelings are channeled in such a way by society that she comes to look upon her body as a sexual object for others, and for herself.

This tendency to see oneself as a sexual object, which is inculcated by society, gives rise to the desire for an "affectionate possession" of oneself that can culminate in the full-blown narcissism that Beauvoir details in a later chapter. Beauvoir conceives female narcissism somewhat differently than other writers have done and it is easy to misunderstand the role it plays in her analysis in *The Second Sex*. Sandra Bartky, for one, does not distinguish narcissism, or the having of erotic feelings toward one's own body, from the general alienation a woman feels from her body that Beauvoir describes (Bartky 1982). Yet certainly one can experience one's body as a thing and not be in love with it. The anorexic, for instance, experiences her body as an object, but as a loathsome object.

Beauvoir explicitly conceives narcissism along more narrow lines than she does bodily alienation in general, although she does stress that women are predisposed toward narcissism by bodily alienation.[11] The peculiar thing is that for Beauvoir true narcissism represents a triumph of sorts for a woman. That is why she put the chapter on narcissism, along with chapters on female mystics and the woman in love, in a section entitled "Justifications." The narcissist attempts to achieve her individual salvation by realizing her transcendence in the immanence to which she has been condemned by her upbringing and culture. Narcissism is the attempt to realize the union with one's own body—one's own self—that has been denied through the process of bodily alienation: "Being made object, lo, she becomes an idol in which she recognizes herself with pride," Beauvoir says of the narcissist (2:106). This reassimilation of oneself, being as it is at the same time a revenge of sorts, might account for the pleasure deriving from female narcissism that Bartky and others point to as its most problematic aspect (Bartky 1982).

The pleasures that narcissists take in their own bodies is problematic for feminists because it makes it seem that women's tendency to objectify their own bodies comes from other sources than their oppression by men. Beauvoir seems to leave a similar implication when she ascribes women's becoming alienated in their bodies to their desire as subjects to flee from their own freedom: "to prefer a estranged image to the spontaneous movement of one's own existence" (1:92). This is the problem that many feminist critics have with Beauvoir's account, as I mentioned earlier. They object that Beauvoir makes it sound too much like women have colluded in their own oppression (Kaufmann McCall

1979; Felstiner 1980; Le Doeuff 1980; Whitmarsh 1981; Lloyd 1984). It is possible to make several different responses to this charge on Beauvoir's behalf.

Some critics, for instance, see Beauvoir's acknowledgment of women's complicity in their own subservience as a strength rather than a weakness (Ascher 1981). Within an existentialist framework it is not paradoxical to say that women have expressed their freedom through the ways they have chosen submission. Thus, although oppressed, women are not completely powerless in the face of social forces. And it is this agency that women continue to possess that renders feminist social transformation possible. For this reason Beauvoir's analysis of how the body is socially constructed leaves room for what Judith Butler calls "emancipatory potential" (Butler 1986, 41) to a much greater extent than Michel Foucault's treatment of the same theme does, I think.

Beauvoir points out that some women have managed to resist the process of bodily alienation that is imposed on them by their culture. For instance in her chapter "The Lesbian" Beauvoir describes one form such a refusal can take: "A large number of athletic women are homosexual; this body which is muscle, movement, expansion, dash they do not grasp as passive flesh; it does not magically call for caresses, it is a grasp on the world, not a thing of the world" (2:177). She goes on to describe how even some heterosexual women come to achieve this type of attitude toward their bodies and their sexuality. Indeed, she asserts that the majority of women would take this attitude "if the equality of the sexes were to be realized concretely" (2:177).

The key to answering those critics who charge that Beauvoir sees women to have connived in their own defeat is to stress that women do not live under conditions of equality. They did not in 1949 and they do not now. Even Beauvoir herself recognized that she was absurdly optimistic when she declared in her introduction regarding women: "by and large we have won the game" (1:29) (Beauvoir 1974; Schwarzer 1984). In the meaning given freedom in existentialism a woman always remains free to give her own meaning to her existence. Yet Beauvoir realized, more than did Sartre at this juncture in their development, that a person's choices are gravely limited by social and historical circumstances (Beauvoir 1962; Schwarzer 1984). A woman is always presented with certain limited concrete options. In terms of her relation with her body a woman is always presented with one compelling option, the "normal" feminine phenomenon of bodily alienation.

In the account of bodily alienation sketched earlier, a woman comes to identify herself with her body, not the body "lived by the subject," but rather the female body as an inert passive thing. Under the most unforgiving interpretation of alienation Beauvoir gives, the woman succumbs to this process out of the anxiety that living as a free conscious subject induces in her. But even under this interpretation one should ask how the woman, or rather the young girl is presented with this choice in the first place. The young girl, the pubescent woman does not make her body into a thing on her own account. It is with *surprise* that the young girl discovers that her body is this strange curious object, as Beauvoir stresses in an evocative passage: "She becomes an object, and she sees herself as object; it is with surprise that she discovers this new aspect of her being: it seems to her that she has been doubled; instead of coinciding exactly with herself, she now begins to exist *outside*" (2:90). A living body can become a thing only under the gaze of another. And it is to this gaze that the young woman at puberty now relentlessly is subjected. Without this step, the initial objectification of the body by others, the process of alienation the young woman undergoes, whether consented to at some level or other, could never occur. The temptation to flee from freedom into this sort of immanence would never arise.

However, to say that the young woman's body is objectified under the gaze of others, as I have here, is to give too Sartrean a cast to it, though there are many specific incidents in women's lives when this does occur. Beauvoir does not appeal to what has come to be known as Sartre's account of the Look (Sartre 1956), except in passing, to explain women's oppression.[12] Instead she offers an alternative theory as to how one subject or group of subjects comes to diminish the subjectivity of another: by forcing them into the category of the Other or the inessential, a category set up by and indeed defining the original subject as the essential, the absolute, the One. It is not only the female who has been defined as the Other over the course of human history, but she has always been so defined and she has never been able to set up herself as the essential in turn.

This concept of the Other plays a key role in the explanation of women's oppression Beauvoir gives. Not enough attention has been paid to it, I think, in the debates that have arisen among feminists over how to interpret Beauvoir's thought. With regard to the debate over what role biology plays in women's oppression, one can point to Beauvoir's own statement: "Biology does not suffice to give us an answer to the question we are concerned with: why is woman the *Other?*" (1:76). Furthermore, in response to those who charge that Beauvoir sees women as somehow responsible for their own oppression, it can be pointed out that women do not choose to become the Other. This is not a status one can choose for oneself; it must be imposed by someone else.

What is not made quite explicit in Beauvoir's theory, though, is the role played by the female body in the categorization of woman as the Other. However, the role of the body can be extrapolated by looking deeper into the means resorted to by men to make woman into the Other. According to Beauvoir woman has been regarded as the Other since the beginning of human culture. But what is woman, as Beauvoir asks at the beginning of her introduction? Beauvoir asserts in accord with her existentialist perspective that there is no such thing as a feminine essence or feminine nature. The female body, however, is a real material presence. The female body thus becomes the point of contact where social forces take hold: it is what is subjected to classifica-tion as the Other. Through its foothold in the body this classification process takes hold of woman's existence, for a human *is* her body, as Merleau-Ponty asserts.

The way that the female body is taken hold of and conceptualized as the Other by men is abundantly suggested in Beauvoir's long chapter detailing the many myths that have been created involving women over the ages. As she shows, the female has been associated with a dizzying variety of phenomena in myths, some of them conflicting, some even opposed: nature, artifice, life, death, animality, maternity, sexuality, the flesh, youth, old age, etc. What these phenomena have in common is that they are related more or less directly to the body. These are myths about the female body—its functions and significance. In these myths culture constructs the female body as immanence or passivity. It is the passivity of the female body that makes it other than man, for the male body is active: "The Other can be incarnated in the sea, the mountain, as perfectly as in woman; they oppose to man the same passive and unforeseen resistance that enables him to fulfill himself" (1:255–56).

Beauvoir approaches the phenomenon of female bodily alienation from more than one perspective in *The Second Sex.* I have contended that it is best interpreted as a cultural phenomenon brought about through ideological means and not something originating in women's experience of biological functions such as pregnancy, lactation, and menstruation.

Furthermore, women cannot chose the society they are acculturated within. So, although women are not powerless in the face of social forces, the options they are presented with are limited. In historical times at least their culture has always been patriarchal. In widely different cultures woman has been relegated to the status of the Other by, among other means, the objectification of her body. A woman is only liable to become alienated in her body because it has been alienated from her by this culture. The process could not occur without the mediation of culture. As Beauvoir says further down in that famous passage that begins "One is not born, but rather becomes a woman":

> Only the mediation of someone else can establish an individual as an *Other*. In so far as it exists for itself, the child would not know to understand itself as sexuality differentiated. With girls as with boys the body is first of all the radiation of a subjectivity, the instrument that makes possible the comprehension of a world: it is through the eyes, the hands, that children apprehend the universe, and not through the sexual parts. (2:13)

It is female socialization, she goes on to demonstrate in this second part of the work, that effects the transition from experiencing one's body as the radiation of a subjectivity to experiencing it as an "inert given object" (1:25), not biology. Of course a woman has certain choices within this framework. Beauvoir details some of these choices in her chapters on narcissism and lesbian experience. But a woman never has the choice to break free from her socialization altogether.

Beauvoir's description of the way this process of bodily alienation forms the woman's experience of her body and the world is very important not least because this phenomenon still deeply affects women's lives at the present moment. Some of the aspects of female experience that Beauvoir describes—the young woman's sexual ignorance, her horror of menstruation—are no longer so prevalent in Western culture today, but this is not true of bodily alienation generally. Indeed, one could even argue that alienation of women's bodies through cultural means has intensified in the years since *The Second Sex* was first published. Today everywhere one looks one is confronted by images of the female body. They are used to sell every product imaginable. Any person living in a modernized society is deluged with them.

I am reminded, for instance, of a billboard a few years back that presented a young blond woman in a bikini with the name and trademark of a brand of gin traced out in pale skin against the suntan of her belly. The use of the female body in this advertisement is a metaphor for the way the female body is used by popular culture as a whole. Cultural associations, cultural identifications have come to be inscribed into our very skin. Is it any wonder that young women growing up in Western industrialized societies manifest a great deal of anxiety about their bodies? This anxiety is reflected in the record-high incidence of eating disorders among adolescent females and is fed on and exploited by advertising in turn. Indeed, the point has even been reached where the male body is beginning to be appropriated by popular culture as a means to sell things. This hardly seems a step forward.

What I am speaking of here is something like the "fashion-beauty complex" that Sandra Bartky sees behind the perpetration of female narcissism: "Like the "military-industrial complex," the fashion-beauty complex is a major articulation of capitalist patriarchy" (Bartky 1982, 135). As my musings suggest, I think that Beauvoir's concept of bodily alienation is one that could be fruitfully extended in a more materialist or Marxist-inspired analysis of the continuation of patriarchy. Such an analysis might be able to account for some of the ways the social construction of the female body has changed in the almost fifty years since *The Second Sex* was written. (For instance, the taboo against menstruation has greatly weakened now that it has created a market for products—products now advertised on the TV evening news.)

Beauvoir herself regretted later in her life not having provided a more economically based analysis in *The Second Sex* (Beauvoir 1964 and 1974). But as she has also said, this would not have modified the basic argument of the book: "that all male ideologies are directed at justifying the oppression of women, and the women are so conditioned by society that they consent to this oppression" (Beauvoir 1974, 449). One of the primary ways, if not the primary way that women are conditioned to accept their oppression is through bodily alienation. And the alienation of women in their bodies and from their bodies has been effected through male ideology. For these reasons, Beauvoir's concept of bodily alienation is a major contribution to feminist thought.[13]

Notes

1. All page numbers for *The Second Sex* are from Beauvoir (1949). For the most part the translations are my own, although in places I have retained or incorporated the Parshley translation.

2. See, for instance, her account of her mother's death (Beauvoir 1965).

3. This passage is one of the many passages in the original that are mangled in the English translation. Parshley replaces the phrase "attitude ontologique" with the phrase "essential nature," which renders the passage contradictory. (Beauvoir 1980, 36; see Simons 1983).

4. It was Mary Wollstonecraft of course, who, influenced by empiricism, first explored how women's personalities are shaped by social conditioning (Wollstonecraft 1975).

5. In this last volume of memoirs she also reiterates that femininity is a cultural formation, not a natural datum and categorizes biology as "suspect" because it is male-dominated (Beauvoir 1974, 459).

6. The affinity between Beauvoir's and Merleau-Ponty's views on the body is attested to in her review of his *Phenomenology of Perception* in one of the fledgling issues of *Les Temps Modernes*. Here she completely endorses Merleau-Ponty's thesis about the central role of the lived body in all experience, while acknowledging the way Merleau-Ponty's conception of intentionality diverges from Sartre's (Beauvoir 1945).

7. Parshley translates this as "the body lived in by the subject," which obliterates the resonances with Merleau-Ponty's thought and makes Beauvoir sound more dualistic than she is (Beauvoir 1980, 38).

8. Problematic for feminist readings of Beauvoir is that alienation tends to be presented as a positive phenomenon precisely when it is indulged in by men. For instance, the establishment of private property is a result of man's desire to alienate himself in the material world, but here alienation is described almost as a form of transcendence: "the existent only succeeds in grasping itself in alienating itself," she says (1:100). (Of course this remark is somewhat at odds with Beauvoir's general attitude toward private property.) Similarly, when the young boy projects himself into his penis making it his alter ego, this is described as the incarnation of his transcendence (1:89, 24).

9. Interestingly, a new book on Beauvoir's and Sartre's philosophical relationship suggests that Sartre originally found the idea for his notion of bad faith, or at least his most vivid example of this concept, in a draft of Beauvoir's novel *She Came to Stay*, which he read during the war (Fullbrook and Fullbrook 1994). In any case, in formulating her concept of alienation, Beauvoir perhaps was influenced more deeply by Hegel's *Phenomenology of Spirit*, which she pored over during the German occupation, than by Sartre's thought.

10. "One sees that if the biological situation of woman constitutes a handicap for her, it is due to the perspective from which it is grasped" (2:85).

11. "If she can thus offer *herself* to her own desires, it is because since infancy she has appeared to herself as an object. Her education has influenced her to alienate herself in her whole body, puberty revealed this body to her as passive and desirable" (2:460).

12. The Fullbrooks also claim that Sartre's concept of the Look owes much to "Beauvoir's concept of the Look," which was implicitly developed in her novel *She Came to Stay* (Fullbrook and Fullbrook 1994, 111).

13. I completed this work with the support of the Release Time Committee of Long Island University, Brooklyn. I also thank the editor of this volume, Margaret A. Simons, for her direction and feedback.

References

Ascher, Carol. 1981. *Simone de Beauvoir: A Life of Freedom*. Boston: Beacon.

Bair, Deirdre. 1990. *Simone de Beauvoir: A Biography*. New York: Simon & Schuster.

Bartky, Sandra L. 1982. "Narcissism, Femininity and Alienation." *Social Theory and Practice* 8:127–43.

Beauvoir, Simone de. 1945. "La Phénoménologie de la Perception de Maurice Merleau-Ponty." *Les Temps Modernes* 1:363–67.

———. 1949. *Le Deuxième Sexe.* Paris: Gallimard.

———. 1956. *The Mandarins.* Translated by L. M. Freidman. Cleveland: World Publishing.

———. 1962. *The Prime of Life.* Translated by P. Green. Cleveland: World Publishing.

———. 1964. *The Force of Circumstance.* Translated by R. Howard. New York: Putnam.

———. 1965. *A Very Easy Death.* Translated by Patrick O'Brian. New York: Warner Books.

———. 1974. *All Said and Done.* Translated by Patrick O'Brian. New York: Putnam.

———. 1980. *The Second Sex.* Translated by H. M. Parshley. New York: Vintage. (Original edition, 1949)

———. 1991. *The Ethics of Ambiguity.* Translated by B. Frechtman. New York: Carol Publishing. (Original edition, 1948).

Butler, Judith. 1986. "Sex and Gender in Simone de Beauvoir's *Second Sex.*" *Yale French Studies* 72:35–49.

———. 1989. "Gendering the Body: Beauvoir's Philosophical Contribution." In *Women, Knowledge and Reality,* edited by A. Garry and M. Pearsall, 253–62. Boston: Unwin Hyman.

Crosland, Margaret. 1992. *Simone de Beauvoir: The Woman and her Work.* London: Heinemann.

Felstiner, Mary F. 1980. "Seeing *The Second Sex* through the Second Wave." *Feminist Studies* 6:247–76.

Firestone, Shulamith. 1970. *The Dialectic of Sex.* New York: William Morrow.

Fullbrook, Kate, and Fullbrook, Edward. 1994. *Simone de Beauvoir and Jean-Paul Sartre.* New York: Basic Books.

Hardwick, Elizabeth. [1953] 1987. "The Subjection of Women." *Critical Essays on Simone de Beauvoir,* ed. Elaine Marks, 49–58. Boston: G. K. Hall.

Irigaray, Luce. 1985. *This Sex Which Is Not One.* Translated by C. Porter. Ithaca: Cornell University Press.

Kaufmann McCall, Dorothy. 1979. "Simone de Beauvoir, *The Second Sex,* and Jean-Paul Sartre." *Signs: Journal of Women in Culture and Society* 5:209–23.

Le Doeuff, Michèle. 1980. "Simone de Beauvoir and Existentialism." *Feminist Studies* 6:277–89.

Leighton, Jean. 1975. *Simone de Beauvoir on Women.* Rutherford, N.J.: Fairleigh Dickinson University Press.

Lloyd, Genevieve. 1984. *The Man of Reason.* Minneapolis: University of Minnesota Press.

Merleau-Ponty, Maurice. 1962. *Phenomenology of Perception.* Translated by C. Smith. New York: Humanities Press.

Moi, Toril. 1986. "Existentialism and Feminism: The Rhetoric of Biology in *The Second Sex.*" *Oxford Literary Review* 8:88–95.

———. 1990. *Feminist Theory and Simone de Beauvoir.* Oxford: Basil Blackwell.

Okely, Judith. 1986. *Simone de Beauvoir.* New York: Virago/Pantheon Pioneers.

Pilardi, Jo-Ann. 1989. "Female Eroticism in the Works of Simone de Beauvoir." In *The Thinking Muse,* edited by Jeffner Allen and Iris M. Young, 18–34. Bloomington: Indiana University Press.

Sartre, Jean-Paul. 1956. *Being and Nothingness.* Translated by H. Barnes. New York: Philosophical Library.

Schwarzer, A. 1984. *After The Second Sex.* Translated by M. Howarth. New York: Pantheon Books.

Simons, Margaret A. 1983. "The Silencing of Simone de Beauvoir: Guess What's Missing From *The Second Sex.*" *Women's Studies International Forum* 6:559–64.

———. 1986. "Beauvoir and Sartre: The Philosophical Relationship." In *Simone de Beauvoir: Witness to a Century*. Special Issue of *Yale French Studies* 72:165–79.

———, and Jessica Benjamin. 1979. "Simone de Beauvoir: An Interview." *Feminist Studies* 5:330–45.

Whitmarsh, Anne. 1981. *Simone de Beauvoir and the Limits of Commitment*. Cambridge: Cambridge University Press.

Wollstonecraft, Mary. 1975. *A Vindication of the Rights of Woman*. New York: Norton. (Original edition, 1792)

10

Out from Under: Beauvoir's Philosophy of the Erotic

Debra B. Bergoffen

Simone Beauvoir disclaimed her philosophical proclivities. Sartre, not she, was the theoretician. She would write philosophy sparingly and always under Sartre's umbrella—at least that is what she said. Shall we take her at her word? I think not. Sparse as they may be, Beauvoir's philosophical works, *The Ethics of Ambiguity* (1948), *The Second Sex* (1974), and "Must We Burn Sade?" (1966), move out from under Sartre's cover. They explore the desires of intentionality in ways that challenge the dynamics of autonomous subjects caught in the struggles of the look and the dodges of bad faith. Beauvoir did not, however, announce her challenge to Sartre. (Whether she would not or could not I leave to her biographers to decide.) Claiming to be Sartre's echo, she called in other keys, the keys of the erotic. She left us with the challenge to assume the risks of subjectivity; the lure to reach the other through the flesh; and the question, Can there be an ethic of the erotic?

My essay stakes out the territories of Beauvoir's challenge, lure, and question. I read *The Second Sex* within the context of the earlier *Ethics of Ambiguity* and the later "Must We Burn Sade?" to argue that the discussion of *The Second Sex* is not limited to the question, How did it happen that one sex became the permanent and inessential other? Drawing from *The Ethics of Ambiguity*'s discussions of intentionality, the situation, and childhood, and opening toward the Sade essay's analysis of the ethical risks and implications of the erotic, I suggest that *The Second Sex*'s analyses of women's situations be read in the context of the question, What are the communicative possibilities of the human situation?

The Ethics of Ambiguity

Beauvoir opens the *Ethics of Ambiguity* by situating herself within the ontological categories of *Being and Nothingness*. In phrases reminiscent of "The Look" she describes the ambiguity of the human condition as that of being a "unique subject amidst a universe of objects . . . [and] . . . in turn an object for others" (1948, 7; all page references in this section are to this work). Continuing in the vein of *Being and Nothingness* she accuses us all of bad faith, saying that all "felt this tragic ambiguity of their condition but as long as there have been philosophers and they have thought, most of them have tried to mask it" (7). Calling upon the only virtues recognized in *Being and Nothingness*, honesty, truthfulness, and confrontation, she asks us, "to look the truth in the face . . . [and] to assume our fundamental ambiguity" (9). Well before calling on Sartre by name she invokes his categories, making it clear that what she calls an existentialist ethic is intended to be a Sartrean ethic.

The issues confronting Beauvoir are Sartre's issues: Is everything permissible in a world without God? (15) Can we define human beings as fissured, as freedoms who cannot be who they are, and still hold them accountable for what they are? Beauvoir's answer to the first question is no. Her answer to the second is yes. Sounding like Sartre in his essay "Existentialism is a Humanism" (1946), Beauvoir claims that focusing on the freedom that grounds the ambiguity of our condition allows us to escape the relativism, subjectivism, and solipsism that threaten any ethical position. Freedom, she says, provides the criteria of an ethic. It is not a condition of license but one of limit. The tautology that all choices are free is empirically vacuous and morally misleading. The moral choice recognizes the meanings of freedom. The immoral choice violates them.

Key to this philosophical project is the account of freedom, and it is here, at the crucial point of departure, that Beauvoir moves away from Sartre. It comes early in the text where she writes:

> It is not in vain that man nullifies being. Thanks to him being is disclosed and he desires this disclosure. There is an original type of attachment to being which is not the relationship "wanting to be" but rather the relationship "wanting to disclose being." Now there is not failure but success. . . . I take delight in this every effort toward an impossible possession. . . . This means that man, in his vain attempt to *be* God makes himself exist *as* man. . . . It is not possible for him to exist without tending toward this being which he will never be. But it is possible for him to want this tension even with the failure it involves. (12–13)

It is, I think, important to stay with this passage for a few moments; for as I read it, it is crucial for understanding the differences between Sartre and Beauvoir and crucial for the argument of the *Second Sex*. Like Sartre and within the parameters of the phenomenological tradition, Beauvoir defines consciousness as intentionality. But where Sartre almost immediately ensnares the intentionality of consciousness in the bad faith project of the desire to be God, Beauvoir pauses to distinguish between two moments of intentionality, the moment of disclosure and the moment of the object disclosed. Both moments are permeated by desire. Consciousness is the desire for disclosure that desires to be that which it discloses. We are familiar with this second moment of desire, the desire to be the disclosed object. We have a name for it: bad faith.

One of the reasons, I think, that Sartre's arguments for the pervasiveness of bad faith are so compelling is that he establishes an essential relationship between the experience of freedom and the experience of anxiety. Though *Being and Nothingness* gives reasons for abandoning bad faith, desire, never being impressed with reasons, prefers the path of repression. The reasons to be honest are overwhelmed by the desire to elude anxiety and the desire to be. Bad faith prevails. Beauvoir recognizes the relationship between freedom and anxiety. She refers to it as a tension. But she also identifies another relationship between freedom and desire: delight and joy. The issue of bad faith here is not a question of whether the power of anxiety can be persuaded by the demands of honesty but rather whether the anxieties that empower the desire to be the disclosed object must prevail over the delight of the desire to exist as the becoming that signifies itself by disclosing objects of its desire.

Desire cannot be severed from its disclosed object. It can, however, want this object differently. That is, instead of wanting to *be* it, it can, in recognition of its desire to be a disclosing of meaning, want to *relate* to the object/meaning it discloses. In this expression of its desire, consciousness forgoes the bad faith project of forgetting that it reveals the objects it desires. It recalls its delight in disclosing the object of its desire. In order to live the complexity of its desire, it desires the tensions bad faith would escape.

In wanting to relate to its object of desire rather than to be it, consciousness restrains its desire to be for the sake of the delight of disclosure. Instead of allowing its desire to be to nihilate its desire to disclose, instead of closing itself off from the place of disclosure in the act of identification, desire keeps the place of disclosure open so that the desire of disclosure and the desire of the object may both express themselves and intersect each other.

The Sartrean constellation of intentionality, freedom, anxiety, and bad faith is refigured. Beauvoir's constellation, by introducing the delight of disclosure, opens a new path. The route to bad faith remains open and heavily traveled, but it is also challenged. We are left with the same structures of consciousness. It remains freedom, fissured and the sole ground of meaning, but the mood and meaning of these structures is altered.

With this new meaning a new question arises. If there is a delight and joy in disclosing meaning, why would we fall into bad faith at all? Is bad faith a mirage? Beauvoir may be moving away from Sartre, but not that far. Bad faith is for Beauvoir what it was for Sartre, a permanent threat to the possibility of a humanist ethic. Anxiety still characterizes freedom. But unlike Sartre who links anxiety and freedom ontologically, Beauvoir links them historically. Bad faith is one of the ways we express our nostalgia for the securities of childhood.

Beauvoir remembers what so many philosophers forget (and what psychoanalysis warns we forget at great risk), the adult was first a child;

and the child, Beauvoir tells us, is unaware of its subjectivity. It is, "the naive victim of the mirage of the for-others, he believes in the *being* of his parents and teachers" (35). The child does not know the desire or delight of disclosure. It only experiences the desire to be. It experiences values and meanings as already given, and itself as being something (36–37).

As we all begin as children, the original condition of our existence is one of domination by our situation. We come to know ourselves as free in the existential sense only through the crisis of adolescence. Prior to that the only freedom we know is the freedom to be the already given meanings of the world. Adolescence marks a turning. Now the individual must assume its subjectivity (39). The joy of childhood gives way to the joy of liberation but this joy is ambiguous. It carries with it the anguish, tension, and confusion of existential freedom (40). The decision of adolescence is not ahistorical. The joy of being liberated from the world of the other, the delight of discovering the power of disclosure is contested by another mood: nostalgia (40). Here is the source of bad faith. Not the anxiety of freedom per se, but the nostalgia for the original condition of our being where neither the anxieties nor the joys of freedom are known; where the joys of the desire to be dominate experience and experience themselves as fulfilled.

In referring us to childhood and nostalgia Beauvoir empowers the situation in ways foreign to the analyses of *Being and Nothingness*. Not only does she identify the child as innocent, that is, as not being in bad faith, she also identifies others, "the negro slave of the 18th century" and "the Mohammedan woman enclosed in a harem" (38) who exist in situations that preclude their knowing their freedom and whose submission to the authority of the other cannot be counted as an act of bad faith. Those who are ignorant and mystified cannot be accused of evading their freedom (98).

Freedom, consciousness, then is permeated by desire and embedded in its situation. How does it stand with the other? Does the Look tell the full story? Referring to Hegel's consciousnesses who seek each other's death rather than to Sartre's pour-soi's whose looks steal each other's freedom, Beauvoir claims that the desire to dominate the other struggles against itself (71). This struggle takes two directions. The first involves consciousness recognizing that its disclosures are always grounded in a world that is already there and that the already given meanings it confronts are the meanings of other freedoms.

The human past is not a brute fact. It is radically different from the natural past in that it is humanly signified. It is the work of other freedoms. We may rebel against the past, but Beauvoir warns us not to do so lightly. Though hardly an advocate of preserving the past out of a sense of reverence, Beauvoir links the transcendence of freedom and the power of disclosure to an ability to recognize the paths opened up to us by our ancestors (92–93).

Rebellion against the freedom of the other is not then the essential mark of transcendence. Transcendence, the meaning giving moment of consciousness is linked to a relationship to the past and a recognition of the past other. Were there no already given world of the other there would be no world for my freedom to engage. No adolescence without childhood (71). The second direction of the struggle against the desire to dominate the other is grounded in the recognition that the other challenges the domination of the desire to be. However it may stand with the indigenous tensions between the desire to disclose and the desire to be, without the other to challenge the meanings of my freedom, I risk forgetting the subjective sources of my values. I risk believing that the object disclosed by me is independent of me and that I can be its being. "Only the freedom of others," Beauvoir writes, "keeps each one of us from hardening into the absurdity of facticity" (71).

Following Husserl's Fifth Cartesian Meditation, Beauvoir grounds her ethic in an analysis of the intentionality of consciousness that links it to the other as fundamentally as it links it to the world. "The me-others relationship," she writes "is as indissoluble as the subject-object relationship" (72). Given this equal primordiality of the world and the other, Beauvoir will argue that I am as responsible for disclosing the freedom of the other as I am for revealing the meaning of the world. This responsibility takes two forms. First, it requires that none of my projects assert my freedom without simultaneously affirming the freedom of others. Second, it requires me to liberate those whose freedom is negated. The first form of responsibility is grounded in the desire of disclosure. The second is derived from the judgment that submission to authority is not always a sign of bad faith (85).

As we pull this ethic together, we discover that though it is indebted to the analyses of *Being and Nothingness*, it is not submissive to them. Beauvoir's project is marked by embedding desire in the intentionalities of consciousness. We are not condemned to be free; we take delight in our freedom. Further, my freedom marks a primordial confirming relationship between myself and the other. Hell is not necessarily other people. The look and bad faith are recognized but reassessed. It is not always the case that my submission to the look is an act of bad faith. It is not the case that the look is the ground of human relationships. The notion of autonomy is also rethought. The individual is still accorded absolute value and still recognized as the foundation of its own existence (156) but it is also situated among others who sustain it. Autonomy may be the ground of the value of the I, but it also directs us to the value of the other and requires that the I be responsive to demands of the we. Finally this ethic is permeated by a mood foreign to Sartre's writings: joy. As Beauvoir sees it, the anxieties of freedom are, in the ethical moment, overridden by the joys of freedom (135).

As I see it, *The Second Sex* develops, in the sense of making concrete, the themes of *The Ethics of Ambiguity*. Specifically, I see *The Second Sex* developing the themes of desire, delight, and joy into a thematic of the erotic. Also, I see it moving the analyses of subjectivity and relationship toward an exploration of the body and the gift. This making concrete is more than a filling in. It also becomes a challenge to the idea of autonomy. With its provocative suggestion that free relationships might best be understood as gift relationships, *The Second Sex* sets *The Ethics of Ambiguity* in new directions.

"Must We Burn Sade?"

Though it was written after *The Second Sex* I would like to reflect on the Sade essay before turning toward *The Second Sex* as a way of preparing for some of its surprises. Reading the Sade essay makes it clear that Beauvoir saw *The Ethics of Ambiguity* as developing a set of principles that could be used to understand the existential meaning of the concrete. Here the concrete is a particular man, the Marquis de Sade. In *The Second Sex* it is more diffuse, the particular circumstances of women. In both cases, however, the move to the concrete crystallizes the meaning of ambiguity and reveals the complexity of desire. In both cases, the move to the concrete moves the question of subjectivity to the question of the erotic.

Relying on the analysis of consciousness that grounds her ethic, Beauvoir begins her analysis of Sade by claiming that his obsession with cruelty is an expression of his desire to disclose the meanings of existence. She makes sense of the debauched despot's refusal to become a political tyrant by distinguishing (and claiming that he distinguished) between the project of tyranny and the sadist project. The project of tyranny is the project of the look: to assert one's freedom by objectifying and thereby negating the freedom of the other. The project of sadism is the project of cruelty: "to reveal . . . particular individuals and [one's] own existence as on the one hand consciousness and on the other as flesh" (1966, 15; all page references in this section are to this work). Where the tyrant's projects oppose the demands of disclosure, the sadist's do not. Where the tyrant dehumanizes the other, the sadist valorizes the humanity of the victim (16).

It is not, however, the case that the sadist and tyrant have nothing in common. They share a common blind spot: the inability to see the essential connectedness of individual consciousness. The tyrant's blindness may be traced to his project of objectification. Sade's is traced to the ultimate failure of his project of disclosure. This blindness is not accidental. It reflects a refusal of the risks of subjectivity (59). The subject who recognizes itself as ambiguous and as related to others, recognizes that this relationship can be dangerous. The tyrant who recognizes no other subjects, and the sadist who recognizes the other only as the subject of cruelty deny the possibility of subjective exchange. In refusing to recognize their communicability with the other, they refuse to disclose their vulnerability to the other. The tyrant and the sadist are cowards.

What interests Beauvoir about Sade is the way he transforms his sexuality from a given into an ethic. What interests me about Beauvoir's reading of Sade is the way she understands the meaning of this ethic and the way she uses this understanding to pursue The Second Sex's ethical affirmations of the erotic. The Sade essay is also of interest on another level. It shows us the tension between the Beauvoir who claims to be Sartre's shadow and the Beauvoir who moves out on her own. The essay speaks in two voices. The first voice affirms the Sartrean affirmation of the value of autonomy. The second undermines this affirmation. It speaks against the dominations of lucidity and develops a sense of subjectivity at odds with the values of autonomy.

We can either accept or assume our sexuality. To accept it is to submit to it as a private biological function. To assume it is to transform a condition of facticity into a concrete expression of the ethical. According to Beauvoir, Sade assumes his sexuality. Instead of allowing others to define him as aberrant, he defines himself and he does so publicly. He writes. In his writing he establishes himself as a standard. Sexuality is not something that happens to him; it is something he assumes responsibility for and something he declares to be justifiable (6). His writing and his living are in defiance of the other. The other has the power to imprison him. The other does not, however, have the power to determine him. Sade, whatever the judgment or the power of the other may be, makes eroticism the meaning of his existence (19). In insisting on his right to define himself, in defying the definition of the other and in refusing to see himself as determined by the demands of his sexuality, Sade expresses his transcendence. This is what makes him moral.

In identifying Sade's sexuality as moral, Beauvoir does not intend to endorse it. The judgment "this is moral" is not equivalent to the judgment "this is ethical." The moral person recognizes the power of freedom; the ethical person correctly assumes the responsibilities of this power. The moral person refuses bad faith. The ethical person refuses the look. Sade is moral. He knows that he is the source of the meaning of his life and he accepts this responsibility of autonomy. He is not ethical. In revealing the relationships between sexuality and cruelty (20), torturer and victim (60), crime and rebellion (58), he conceals the bonds of mutuality and recognition. Attached as he is to the concrete (6), he is deaf to the meaning of the concrete cries of his victims. He cannot hear their indictment of his morality. His acts of rebellion, his crimes, are justifiable insofar as they challenge the injustices of the given. They cease to be justifiable when they stop short of disclosing the freedom of the other; that is, when they rebel against one situation of alienation in the name of another (58).

Beauvoir identifies Sade as someone who understood but never experienced the ambiguity of the human condition. He is fascinated by the conflicts between consciousness and the flesh (29). He is aware of the ambiguous unity of the inwardness of consciousness and the opacity of the flesh (31), but he never seems to have experienced emotional intoxication, that state of being where consciousness gives up its lucidity and intersects with the body to become flesh (21).

Unable to experience his own ambiguity, Sade is unable to experience the ambiguity of his relationship with the other. It is from the erotic intoxicated experience of ourselves as simultaneously subject and object that we are able to experience the other as simultaneously subject and object with us. But Sade cannot escape his lucidity. He is always only the subject. His sadism, according to Beauvoir, is a compensation for this inability. She writes: "The state of emotional intoxication allows one to grasp existence in one's self and in the other as both subjectivity and passivity. The two partners merge in this ambiguous unity; each one is freed of his own presence and achieves immediate communication with the other" (22).

Sade is correct. The erotic is the mode of subjective communication. His error lies in his understanding of the erotic. He misses the meaning of sexuality: that we escape our consciousness in our flesh and understand another's consciousness through their flesh (22). Or, more precisely, it is because Sade recognized the consciousness of the other that he refused political tyranny; but it is because he could not escape his consciousness in his flesh that he turned to erotic cruelty. Thus, though I become aware of myself through conscious activity and assume responsibility for myself by affirming the power of lucidity, I can only experience the other by experiencing the passivity, the flesh that is also me. I become aware of the human reality of the other that I act upon by experiencing myself as a reality that can be acted upon. I can retreat before this experience. I can refuse to allow it to take hold of me. I can move to negate the other's subjectivity: the look. Or, I can open myself to this experience by opening myself to the erotic. Fully open I experience the intoxications of touching the other through myself and of being touched by an otherness that is me. Afraid of this risk but sensitive to the erotic I turn to sadism.

As I listen to Beauvoir reading Sade, I hear her criticizing him for not understanding the limits of autonomy. His political refusal to submit to the demands of the collective is grounded in his affirmation of his individuality. As a consciousness subject he will define himself, assume responsibility for this definition, and live out this meaning of his existence. So far, so good. But how will we live among others? Only in defiance? For Beauvoir this is not adequate. An ethic that limits itself to affirming the individual misses the full meanings of freedom. My freedom is engaged with the freedom of the other. Sade revealed the point of this engagement, the erotic; but by figuring the erotic according to the dictates of autonomy and pleasure he misses the engagement itself. "Pleasure," according to Beauvoir, "requires neither exchange, giving, nor gratuitous generosity. Its tyranny is that of avarice, which chooses to destroy that which it cannot assimilate" (26).

Beauvoir's *Second Sex* shows how to engage the erotic and escape the tyranny of pleasure. It shows that though pleasure does not require exchange, giving, or generosity, it is not at odds with exchange, giving, or generosity. *The Second Sex* situates Sade's ethic of the erotic against another erotic ethic, a feminist one. This ethic is grounded in the courage to accept the risks of subjectivity, is open to erotic intoxication, and is motivated by the desires of intentionality and communication. The cruelties of sadism reflect the failures of an eroticism submissive to the tyrannies of pleasure. The feminist ethic of *The Second Sex* sets the erotic in a direction guided by the desires of disclosure and relation. The avarice of pleasure gives way to the pleasures of gifting and the intoxica-tions of the flesh.

The Second Sex

The Second Sex draws on the analysis of *The Ethics of Ambiguity* to work through the more radical implications of Husserl's ideas of intentionality. The bodied subject is a sexually gendered subject. Its spatial temporal point of view is perceptual, epistemic, and erotic. It desires to be that which it discloses as being and its desires are coded patriarchially. There are places, however, where the challenges to Sartre are pushed further than those of the *Ethics;* places where *The Second Sex* breaks new ground. The Sade essay shows that these breaks are more than Freudian slips. The surprise appeal to the erotic as the site of a transcendence that embraces the otherness of the other cannot be marginalized once we see Beauvoir focusing on these themes several years later.

Much of *The Second Sex* seems to ascribe to the ontology of the Look: our fundamental relation to the other is hostile. In looking for the sources of woman's domination Beauvoir heads straight to the ontology of violence calling man "a being of transcendence and ambition" (1974, 63; all page references in this section are to this work), describing "the imperialism of human consciousness, seeking always to exercise its sovereignty in objective fashion" (64) and speaking of "an original aspiration to dominate the other" (64). In trying to understand woman's complicity with her domination, however, Beauvoir uncovers a different ontological dimension of our being, the desire for reciprocity and the value of the bond. She writes: "woman may fail to lay claim to the status of subject . . . because she feels the necessary bond that ties her to man regardless of reciprocity" (xxiv–xxv). Where man forfeits the requirements of reciprocity in the exercise of his transcendence, woman forfeits the requirements of reciprocity in the name of the bond. Beauvoir does not approve of either forfeiture. She condemns both women and men for allowing it to occur. But in searching for an ontology of transcendence without domination, she indicates that something more complex than Sartrean bad faith is at work in the woman's relinquishing her claim to subjectivity. This value of the bond needs to be recovered. Can there be a bond without bondage? Beauvoir offers a tentative yes in her analysis of erotic love. For Beauvoir erotic love is a privileged human relationship where "in the midst of carnal fever . . . [men and women] live out in their several fashions the strange ambiguity of existence made body" (810). This ambiguity can be lived out according to the structure of the look as the prevalence of sadism and masochism in patriarchy makes clear, or it can be lived out as "a consenting voluntary gift" (810). In gift-giving, transcendence expresses the value of the freely accepted bond. As lovers we give ourselves to each other as embodied subjects. We become flesh for the taking. We allow ourselves to be overtaken by erotic passions. We make ourselves vulnerable to our lover. We risk being violated as subjects. In this mutual gift-giving, risk-taking, we accept each other's worth and vulnerability. In Beauvoir's words, we recognize that "in both sexes is played out the same drama of the flesh and the spirit, of finitude and transcendence; both are gnawed away by time and laid in wait for by death, they have the same essential need for one another" (810).

This drama of essential need is not a drama that obliterates otherness. Lovers do not lose themselves in each other. They do not become one. Their giving to and receiving of each other is a concrete and carnal act of mutual risk and recognition (448). Again Beauvoir writes: "The dimension of the relation of the *other* still exists; but the fact is that alterity has no longer a hostile implication" (448).

Amidst all the discussions of violence, domination, conquest, and war that delineate the ways in which humanity *has* articulated the living of bodily risk-taking that expresses the transcendence of the human subject, the few pages dedicated to the analysis of erotic love reveal that of all the risk-taking activities invented by humanity this is the most dangerous and the most indicative of our human condition. In erotic love we must each assume our carnal condition as we ask to be received as free subjects. Given the current situation woman, who has been taught to see herself as flesh must regain her dignity as a subject, and man, "an easy dupe of the deceptive privileges accorded to him by his aggressive role and by the lonely satisfaction of the orgasm" (450) must learn to accept/experience himself as flesh. This enterprise, "fraught with difficulty and danger . . . often fails" (449–50). When it succeeds, however, "The erotic experience is one that most poignantly discloses to human beings the ambiguity of their condition; in it they are aware of themselves as flesh and as spirit, as the other and as the subject" (449).

This analysis of erotic love breaks new ground. Here the ambiguity of the body is embraced by the subject. Instead of experiencing its flesh as the alienation of immanence, the subject is aware of its flesh as the other it becomes for its lover. That is, flesh is not that which objectifies me, but that through which I express myself as gift. Put differently, I cannot offer you the gift of my body if I do not experience it as mine for the giving, that is, as informed by my project. Here my flesh is offered as flesh. My body is not the tool of domination, but the passivity of my subjectivity. The idea that my body as immanence is a threat to my subjectivity is undermined by the idea that my body may become a threat to subjectivity only if I experience immanence as objectification. It is not the otherness of the body that is alienating, but the way I live this otherness that determines its relationship to subjectivity.

In exploring the meanings of erotic love, Beauvoir challenges the equation: subjectivity = transcendence. She proposes a new understanding of the subject: subjectivity = the ambiguity of the body. In this equation, transcendence is moved from the defining characteristic of the subject to a dimension of subjectivity. The subject is also immanence, a being who may become a gift. Finally the transcendence-immanence distinction escapes its sexual bipolarization and collapses into the ambiguous fluidity of all embodied subjects. This body could become the ground of a new social order.

In pointing to this possibility, Beauvoir suggests that the dynamics of domination-exploitation are not original ontological categories of being, but socially encoded expressions of the subject's transcendent desires. These desires and codes, however, do not tell the full story of the subject. The imperialist subject is also erotic. It desires the other as it desires to be desired by the other. Here its desires can only be pursued if it aligns the demands of transcendence with the requirements of reciprocity, the gift and the bond.

The Second Sex examines the relationship between subjectivity and embodiment by insisting on the significance of sexuality, society, and history. It examines the ways patriarchy coagulates sexual differences into systems of otherness that hide the human being's fundamental ambiguity. It suggests that there is an alliance between sex and gender that is exploited by the dynamics of bad faith. Against this codification of bad faith, Beauvoir discovers the erotic body. She retrieves the subject's ambiguity from its patriarchal splitting and points to ways that the erotically ambiguous subject's mode of transcendence—gifting—may become the ground of an ethic that draws upon the value of the bond without submitting to the alienations of bondage.

References

Beauvoir, Simone de. 1948. *The Ethics of Ambiguity.* Translated by Bernard Frechtman. New York: Philosophical Library.

———. 1966. "Must We Burn Sade?" In *The Marquis de Sade,* translated by Annette Michelson, 3–64. New York: Grove.

———. 1974. *The Second Sex.* Translated by H. M. Parshley. New York: Vintage.

Sartre, Jean-Paul. 1956. *Being and Nothingness.* Translated by Hazel Barnes. New York: Philosophical Library.

———. 1973. *Existentialism is a Humanism.* Translated by P. Mairet. London: Methuen.

11

Sexuality in Beauvoir's *Les Mandarins*

Barbara Klaw

In this essay I respond to critics who fault Simone de Beauvoir for perpetuating patriarchal stereotypes of female sexuality throughout her life. I argue that her fourth novel, *Les Mandarins*, honestly portrays the originality of her eroticism in fictional guise. In a 1978 interview Beauvoir underlined the importance of sexuality in her works by commenting that if she were to rewrite her memoirs, she would give a frank and balanced account of her own sexuality, which she saw as not only a personal matter but also a political one (Schwarzer 1984, 84–85). Although her memoirs do not overtly explore her sexual experiences, in *Les Mandarins* Beauvoir suggests that female sexuality is active, considers bisexuality as a real possibility, and stresses that each woman has numerous erogenous zones that constitute her erotic pleasure.

Yet, many critics interested in her treatment of sexuality often dismiss her for simply repeating patriarchal traditions in her life, her essays, and her novels. Jo-Ann Pilardi (1989) examines her novels, *Le Deuxième Sexe (The Second Sex)*, and her later essays to conclude that Beauvoir fails to go beyond cultural stereotypes describing women's experience as passive, repelling, and primarily vaginal, and men's experience as active (19, 25–26). Liza Potvin and Brenda Sully (1991) have accused Beauvoir of manifesting self-loathing and disgust for the flesh in all of her works. Ronald Hayman (1992, 13) postulates that she derived more enjoyment from telling Sartre about her sexual encounters than from having them! Others have suggested that Beauvoir's intimate relationships with women were simple acts of tyranny in which she could enjoy power in a stereotypically male and exploitative manner.[1]

Although showing elements definitely present in Beauvoir's works, these rather disdainful studies omit another significant constituent in her writings, and most specifically in *Les Mandarins*, which expresses a love for the body and a violation of the dominant cultural codes concerning sexual relations. Beauvoir's interviews help us understand why her works contain both manifestations of distaste and love for bodily pleasures. In discussing men who demonstrated for legalized abortion she implies the impossibility of totally divorcing oneself from the ideology in power: "This doesn't mean that they were not sexist; to uproot what has been anchored in one's behavior pattern and value system from the earliest days of childhood takes years, decades. But these were men who were . . . conscious of that sexism in society and took a political stand against it" (Gerassi 1976, 82). Her defense of men might be applied to her own difficulty in completely escaping the values of her upbringing. Like these men, she takes a political stance against cultural stereotypes of women's sexuality and even successfully challenges them, but Beauvoir cannot divorce her entire being from the influence of her sexist education. Furthermore, had she written a novel totally void of patriarchal discourse, she would have betrayed the goal, which she clearly stated in a 1957 interview, of portraying the complexity and ambiguity of human experience, "In a novel, in contrast [to an essay], one strives to show. One must render life and people in their ambiguity. The novel must not conclude. It is constructed to give an account of these uncertainties and this experimentation" (Chapsal 1984, 64).[2]

Some scholars comment rather on the contradictions between Beauvoir's affective and sexual life and her writings. Reviewing Beauvoir's journal, letters, and interviews in conjunction with *Le Deuxième Sexe,* Hazel Barnes (1991) agrees that Beauvoir sometimes displays disturbing patriarchal behavior in her relationships, "All of the women, as we knew already from *Lettres au Castor,* were constantly lied to and manipulated as Sartre and Beauvoir tried to keep them in the dark with regard to the couple's own meetings and Sartre's commitments to other mistresses" (24), but she subsequently defends her by stressing her positive actions, "whatever our judgment of what Beauvoir was then, we have to recognize that she had not yet become the Simone de Beauvoir that we have known and admired," whose "first efforts to help other women through her writing took the form of demanding for all of them the privilege of making a life as satisfying as she had found hers to be" (26). A recent biographer, Margaret Crosland (1992), stresses the importance of sexuality to Beauvoir's life and works, but remarks in reference to *Le Deuxième Sexe,* "As in Sartre's novels, there is not much sign of 'the Joy of Sex' " (370).

Still other critics applaud Beauvoir for exceeding patriarchal boundaries in a variety of areas. After reviewing what had been written about Beauvoir and her works up to the early 1980s, Elaine Marks (1986) points out that all seem to accuse Beauvoir of excessiveness and argues that Beauvoir's very originality is precisely the act of trespassing: by not obeying the discursive taboos established by the patriarchy, both her discourses and silences concerning the body, sexuality, aging, and God tend to shock or offend. Yet, Marks ignores Beauvoir's novels and focuses on the writings of Beauvoir that deal with old age such as *Une Mort très douce (A Very Easy Death)* and *La Cérémonie des Adieux (Adieux: A Farewell to Sartre)* to support her thesis. Judith Butler (1989) interprets Beauvoir's view of the body as equally important, but stresses rather the variety of choices of each biological sex. In *Le Deuxième Sexe* Beauvoir claims that the body is not a natural fact but a historical idea and that one is not born, but rather becomes a woman. In so doing, Beauvoir violates predominant cultural codes, for she implies that gender is no longer causally dependent upon biological sex and that each sex permits a number of different genders that blend the current meanings of masculine and feminine (Butler 254–55, 260–61). Linda Singer (1990) adds the idea of freedom and responsibility to those of transgression and choice, stressed by Marks and Butler. Singer compares the ideas on freedom and responsibility presented by Beauvoir in *Le Deuxième Sexe* and *Pour une morale de l'ambiguïtè (Ethics of Ambiguity)* with those posited by Sartre in his works to conclude that "Beauvoir's writing ruptures or disrupts the structure of the very phallocentric language and speech which claims to speak for and include the position marked as *other*" (324). Beauvoir rewrites the discourse of freedom from the position of the oppressed feminine and thereby, unlike the traditional [patriarchal] existentialist account "gives freedom a foundation, a context, a history, and something to do" (332).

Similarly, Beatrice Slama (1987) theorizes that Beauvoir innovatively transgresses socially acceptable discursive codes. Slama insightfully as-serts that *Les Mandarins* depicts the fundamental ambiguity of sexuality for a woman, who is simultaneously a delighted subject and a defiled object as she discovers pleasure with another person (226). In reflecting on *Les Mandarins*, Slama remarks, "A woman writer had never before laid bare, as Simone de Beauvoir does in the face of shame and taboos, sexual relations between a man and a woman, experienced in this manner from the inside, from the viewpoint of a woman" (226). Yet, Slama's analysis needs to be expanded. Not having access to Beauvoir's letters to Sartre or to other biographical materials, Slama views this novel as testimony only to the feelings of other women or to those Beauvoir had toward Sartre. Furthermore, whereas Slama asks if Beau-voir's eroticism still appeals to women (226), a more revealing question might be, Why and how do women still enjoy this novel? Slama implies that Beauvoir's innovation is to depict the paradoxical nature of female sexuality but she does not explain how, in depicting the conflictual feelings of women and men, Beauvoir criticizes existing social practices and points to a solution.

Using the analyses of these critics as background, my essay posits that in *Les Mandarins*, Beauvoir presents sexuality from the view of a biologically female adult trying to express her desires within the con-straints of a culturally repressive world. Although many have called this novel a *roman à clef*, which Beauvoir has vehemently denied (FC 1:366), none has yet specifically analyzed *Les Mandarins* as representative of Beauvoir's myriad experiences through the early 50s.[3] Even Slama cites comparatively few quotes from *Les Mandarins* relying instead on *Le Deuxième Sexe*. Beauvoir's portrayals provide a fictional universe, within which she could comfortably hide an honest account of her own intimate experiences, address female attitudes toward sexual feelings, and describe sexual activities so openly for the 1950s that she often offended her readers.

The indications that Beauvoir broke sexual taboos may help explain why she was unwilling to discuss her sexuality as frankly in her memoirs. By 1956, *Les Mandarins* had been placed on the index of prohibited books by the Catholic Church (Bair 1990, 456). The 1956 English translation evidently also judged the novel as too sexually explicit: as I shall later show, the two scenes evoking oral sex are neatly omitted in the English text and several passages are changed either to attenuate the boldness of the sexual imagery or to strengthen the criticism of women who act upon their desires. Beauvoir recalls in her memoirs, "He [my American editor] was happy with the translation of *The Mandarins* but he apologized for having had to cut some lines here and there: 'In our country, one can talk about sexuality in a book,' he explained to me, 'not about perversion' (FC 2:99).

Although patriarchal institutions attempted to modify or even to forbid the supposed perversions recounted by Beauvoir, the force of her creation could not be sabotaged. In writing this novel, Beauvoir uses much more than merely suggestive words as subversion. Plot, textual structure, derisive allusions to Freud, compromising situations for males as well as females, mockery of myths and stereotypes, the objectification of the male body and the subjectification of the female—all violate patriarchal stereotypes as the following arguments will show. Each chapter either defends the right of men and women to control their own sexuality and to choose their sexual partners or discusses one of the characters' actual or potential lovemaking. Beauvoir's creative method even points to the primacy of eroticism: in conceiving this novel, she first wrote many of the scenes depicting love relationships (Bair 1990, 425).

The plot itself focuses particularly on sexual relationships and cultural expectations. Anne, a psychoanalyst approaching the age of 40, struggles in postwar France to recapture the same zest for life that she enjoyed before the Second World War. Her rebellious and sexually active teenage daughter Nadine, her aging and no longer sexually interested husband Robert, the mental breakdown of her best female friend Paule, and a passionate affair with the American writer Lewis Brogan cause her to take stock of her emotional and sexual feelings. She contemplates her earlier sexual experiences with Robert and argues with Nadine about love and physical intimacy. Challenged by Nadine's theories, she indulges in a one-night stand with Scriassine, a famous Russian-born author, whom she had met through Robert and Henri, her husband's best friend.

Eventually, when she rediscovers her eroticism in America, she will be torn between choosing unrivaled sexual pleasure or an emotionally and intellectually meaningful but sexless existence with her husband, her family, and her job. Like Anne, Henri, a journalist and fiction writer, experiences difficulties in readapting to life as an intellectual and a man of passion in a debilitated France. No longer in love with Paule, his female companion of ten years, he explores ways to end their relationship while still trying to satisfy himself and Paule emotionally and physically. Having viewed Robert as his best friend and mentor for many years, he begins to perceive him as a dominating and manipulative enemy. Anne implies that she and Henri could easily have a physically intimate adventure which they both avoid for inexplicable reasons, but he ends up in a sexual relationship first with her daughter Nadine, then with the actress Josette, before definitively breaking up with Paule and subsequently marrying Nadine.

I propose that Beauvoir exploits textual structures such as the placement and importance of male and female characters in Les Mandarins to depict her disagreement with Freud's theories and societal rules concerning eroticism. Elizabeth Fallaize (1988) similarly implies the significance of structures in Les Mandarins by analyzing the lengths and types of narrations, but her conclusion that "neither of the characters through whom the narrative is focused is entrusted with an authoritative interpretation of events which the reader is invited to accept" (90), does not go far enough. It is through the sex and placement of the characters who view the events related in this novel that Beauvoir depicts her internal struggle to understand the proper conditions for sexual relations and, in so doing, sabotages Freud's theories concerning penis envy. Violating his discourse, she problematizes sexuality, constructing it as both feminine and masculine for both sexes, and she revalorizes the female sex.

If one imagines the text as an independent body created by a woman and thus representative of her ideals, the bisexuality of this body/text immediately evidences itself. The masculine, as represented by Henri, and the feminine, as symbolized by Anne, alternately focalize or perceive events with neither sex having a significant priority overall. For example, Henri views and experiences 52 percent of the text and his viewpoint opens the novel. Although focalizing and narrating only 48 percent of the total novel, Anne examines and recounts 61 percent of it in the second volume and has the last word by closing the story.[4] Thus, in creating this text, Beauvoir symbolically subverts Freud. His psychoanalytic equation posits the female and thus the feminine as lack because the male possesses the only visible and active sex organ. As in Freud's theories, the male sex forming this body shows itself prominently at first. Yet, Beauvoir accentuates that if one continues to study the body, as represented by her text, its femaleness takes precedence and remains the parting image.

Thematically too, *Les Mandarins* manifests a celebration of the body and an antipathy toward domination in lovemaking. It struggles against societal mores promoting love relationships based on female bodily shame and male authority and transgresses the contemporary heterosexual norm. These two factors ultimately imply the need of sexual partners to be both intellectually and sensually satiated for a totally gratifying relationship. Theoretical discourse about sexuality, descriptions of erotic scenes, and the trajectory of intimate relationships foreground these major themes as the following discussion will show.

Just as Beauvoir structures her novel to contradict Freud by showing the female body as a lasting presence, so too she exploits themes for the same ends. To mock Freud's conclusions more effectively, Beauvoir makes Anne a psychoanalyst who ridicules his theories, "I didn't see how that [an analysis] would have helped me . . . my feelings are not illnesses" (2:355), and even loses faith in curing people through such treatments, "My job, what a joke! How would I dare to keep a woman from crying or obligate a man to sleep" (2:495). As the locus for the feminine part of the text, Anne thus triply undermines Freud. She not only receives greater textual time as the novel unfolds but also participates in more sexually explicit scenes than her male counterpart. Her scenes with Scriassine and Lewis focus on her pleasure. The literally masculine side of the text, that lived and seen by Henri, is much less sexually suggestive and centers either on his female companion or his lack of pleasure during the sex act. Once again belying Freud's experience or conclusions, the female body obscures the male.

Having claimed that she based the characters of Anne, Henri, and even Robert on herself, Beauvoir is and is not all of them.[5] Their sexuality and sexual problems thus mirror some facet, if only minimally, of her own life. She apparently envisions her own sexuality, and by analogy, that of other women and men as masculine and feminine. In *Le Deuxième Sexe* she writes that women seek many of the same sensual joys as men,

> like man, woman is enchanted with the warm softness of the sand dunes so often compared to breasts, with the touch of silk,

with the downiness of eiderdown, with the velvety-smoothness of a flower or a fruit. . . . it is maternal flesh that she, like her brothers, first caressed and cherished; in her narcissism, in her diffuse or precise homosexual experiences, she was posing herself as a subject and was seeking the possession of a female body. (2:153–54)

In Butler's terminology, one might say that *Les Mandarins* depicts in more culturally acceptable guises the various genders permitted by Beauvoir's biological sex. Or in other words, Beauvoir disguises certain of her own experiences as those of Henri because the status quo would reject a woman who had such experiences or dared to relate her feelings about them without the sanction of a man.

Nadine and Paule, although initially meant to mock unlikeable traits in Beauvoir's female companions and intended as objects of scorn, soon became examples of how society destroys healthy women. Beauvoir states,

> In the beginning, I was planning to use Nadine to avenge myself on certain characteristics in Lise [Beauvoir's fictional name for Nathalie Sorokine, her former student and eventual friend and lover] and in many of my younger sisters which had annoyed me, among other things, a sexual brutality which unpleasantly revealed their frigidity. Bit by bit, I began to see excuses in the circumstances which explained her disgraceful behavior; Nadine appeared to me to be more a victim than one worthy of blame. (*FC* 1:364)

Because patriarchal culture does not freely accept the myriad possibilities of becoming that each biological sex affords, women's frustrations evince themselves in self-destruction. Their behavioral problems indict the teachings of culture instead of offering inherent patterns of female behavior.

Yet, Beauvoir's letters describing her experiences with her female lovers also bring to mind this frigidity that she belittles, "we went upstairs to my place and we petted each other a bit, as much as possible, when all is said and done, but I was as cold as ice. Besides, it seems to me that I am totally frigid, that's also a way to be blocked (*barrée*)"

(1990b, 1:131). *Le Deuxième Sexe* provides a fuller explanation of the functioning of this barrier to sexual fulfillment,

> The young girl considers herself guilty for giving herself to another and she punishes herself for it by voluntarily doubling her humiliation and servitude. . . . Frigidity itself has already appeared to us as a punishment that woman imposes as much on herself as on her partner: wounded in her vanity, she harbors feelings of rancor against him and herself and she forbids herself pleasure. (2:187)

By showing Nadine's anger against her sexual partners and the status quo, and by subsequently linking this rage to Nadine's frigidity, perhaps Beauvoir was attempting to analyze some of her own feelings as well.

Likewise, Beauvoir experienced conflictual emotions in constructing Paule. She wished simultaneously to evoke women who give up their own goals to devote their lives to male artists or writers and women who exhaust themselves trying not to change the brilliance and beauty they had in their youth. She sees Paule as a woman, who, grasping tradition-ally feminine values, which are insufficient for coping, becomes "torn apart to the point of madness" (FC 1:365). In depicting this type of woman, Beauvoir is also portraying a facet of herself and thereby reminding herself of her own difficulty in letting go of traditional values of femininity. In *La Force de l'âge (The Prime of Life)*, she comments in reference to her first novel *L'Invitée (She Came to Stay)*,

> In my dealings with Sartre, as previously with Zaza, I reproached myself for failing to hold on to the truth about our relationship and for thereby risking the alienation of my own freedom. It seemed to me that I would cleanse myself of this error and even that I would make amends for it if I succeeded in transposing it in a novel. (118)

The truth about which Beauvoir speaks is the knowledge that one must be responsible for one's own existence and decisions. It is only in depending too much on another individual that one can alienate one's freedom. Due to her passion first for Zaza and later, Sartre, Beauvoir was tempted to live for and through their goals and desires and, in so doing, almost forgot her own.

Similarly, Beauvoir's relationship with the Chicago author Nelson Algren, which formed the basis for much of *Les Mandarins*, reflects how easily she could be drawn to giving up, at least momentarily, her nontraditional beliefs and behavior. Apparently, during Algren's visit to her in New York, not only did she drop all her New York friends and, catering to his needs just like all the American women she had previously mocked, devote herself entirely to him, but she also supposedly enjoyed this subservient behavior (Bair 1990, 340). These reminders of Beauvoir's struggles with ideology along with the associations between feminine values, self-destruction, and madness, which she uses to describe Paule, also point to statements explaining how social conditioning puts woman in a double bind, "Raised with respect for the superiority of the male, it may be that she still considers that it is man's right to occupy first place . . . torn between the desire to affirm herself and that of erasing herself, she is divided, torn apart" (1949, 2:616).[6]

In addition, the male-female couples in *Les Mandarins* strongly suggest a parallel between Henri's love affairs and Beauvoir's intimate experiences with women. Henri's inability to tell Paule of his loss of love for her coupled with his distaste for their sexual encounters reflect Beauvoir's difficulty in breaking with Louise Védrine (identified by Deirdre Bair as Bianca Bienenfeld, 634), a former student with whom she and eventually Sartre had love affairs. Henri's thoughts reveal his discomfort, "Never again would he find her as he had ten years earlier when he so desired her. . . . Didn't she realize that they were no longer the same couple?" (13–14). Just as Henri finds Paule's sexual overtures to him distasteful once he no longer loves her, so Beauvoir dislikes Védrine's attention to her:

> All evening she did not stop her half smiles, fluttering eyelashes, and tender hand caresses, it makes me sick [1990b, 2:53]. Védrine came to work by my side . . . with the worst comical expressions of sidelong glances, discreet and mysterious smiles, hesitations, etc., all that in order to ask me passionately on the quay of the metro if I still loved her as much. . . . Does she imagine that I can answer "no" between two stops? . . . I thus said yes without too much warmth and she squeezed my hands with reverence. (1990b, 2:113)

In various ways Beauvoir points to Henri's guilt. Robert both implicitly criticizes Henri's insincere behavior with Paule, "What bad luck for

Paule! It is a catastrophe for a woman to be loved by a man of letters. She believed everything that Perron [Henri] told her about herself" (59). Henri describes his own treatment of Paule as blackmail, "I'm blackmailing her, that's what I'm doing. . . . It's rather ignoble" (136). Henri admits that it would be best for Paule if he were to tell her that he no longer loves her, "Besides, it would be a lot better for Paule's sake if he explained things to her before leaving instead of letting her hang on to false hopes during their separation" (129). Similarly, like Henri, Beauvoir regrets her treatment of the woman whom she no longer loves, "But I reproached us, myself as well as you, in the past, in the future, in the absolute, for our way of treating people; that we managed to make her [Védrine] suffer in this way seems unacceptable to me" (1990b, 2:105). Yet Beauvoir defends him and perhaps herself by describing his decision to tell or not to tell Paule that he no longer loves her as that of either a bastard or a martyr, "I don't want to behave like a bastard, but I'm not cut out to be a martyr" (318). Evoking the ambiguity of the situation simultaneously allows Beauvoir to expiate and to deny her mistake. Similarly, Henri's hesitancy over making love to Josette unless she has true tenderness for him recalls Beauvoir's own hesitation in entering into physical intimacy with Nathalie Sorokine, one of her former students who eventually became her friend and lover, "So I told her that, as for me, I very much desired a more complete relationship but that I didn't want to do anything that would displease her" (1990b, 2:18). By giving her own feelings to a male character whom none of the critics found too feminine, Beauvoir erodes the myth that the sexual behavior or needs of males and females must radically differ. Given identical circumstances, both men and women experience similar emotions. By giving these feelings to Henri, however, instead of to a female character, Beauvoir implicitly underlines that societal expectations rule the acceptance of sexual behaviors.

According to the theory implied in *Les Mandarins*, ultimately satisfying lovemaking requires two individuals who mutually attract each other mentally and physically and who could potentially become close friends. Though as a young girl, Beauvoir experienced overwhelming sexual urges unconnected to a specific person, in her adult life, she claims that sexuality always went "hand in hand with love" (Schwarzer 1984, 85). Yet, in making this statement about her childhood and even her adult life, perhaps Beauvoir was still hiding her own eroticism or romanticizing her existence. Margaret Simons finds evidence of Beauvoir's erotic passion for Zaza in one of her unpublished journals from 1928–29 (143). In a 1983 interview with Bair (1990) Beauvoir states, "I had a 'couple flings' [sic] in New York in 1947" (340). Her letters to Sartre indicate that she even yearned for casual sexual contact with anyone when feeling adrift: "I was in such a state, that, although God knows he disgusts me, I believe that I would have gone to bed with this guy that night if he had wanted; I would have really regretted it in the morning, because in the morning in spite of everything, I feel very solidly anchored in my life; but often at night I would do anything in order to kill time" (1990b, 1:96).

It is most likely, however, that in linking sex to love in her interviews, she was speaking of her ideal for sexual relations. This ideal creates tension throughout Les Mandarins for although not denying the value and pleasure of the pure carnal desire that Anne experiences with Scriassine ("He took me in his arms. I felt on my mouth a violent and gay mouth. Yes, it was possible, it was easy; something was happening to me: something new" [LM 1:118]), the text repeatedly points to the problem inherent in Robert's and Nadine's stance that it is perfectly acceptable to have intimate relations with anyone whenever they want, ("it seemed normal to Robert to pick up a pretty whore in a bar and to spend an hour with her" [LM 1:115]), "Nadine maintained that she was as indifferent about getting into bed as sitting down to eat" [LM 1:117]).[7] Sex, the novel implies, too often yields little sensual pleasure to women who use it only to barter. Nadine, for example, admits that she only engages in sexual activity because it is a prerequisite to going out with boys, "How do you expect me to have relationships with guys if I don't fuck? Women are a damned nuisance, I only have fun with boys; but if I want to go out with them, I have to sleep with them; I don't have a choice" (2:96).[8] Similarly, her physical intimacy gives her little carnal pleasure, "Oh you know, women who like to get laid, I'm sure there isn't more than one in a hundred; it's an air they put on out of snobbishness" (1:155). But, as Le Deuxième Sexe indicates, woman often likes sex only when she is freely choosing sexual intimacy or her own pleasure, "woman can transcend caresses, sensual turmoil, and penetration toward her own pleasure, thereby maintaining the affirmation of her subjectivity; she can also seek union with the lover, and give herself to him, which signifies a surpassing and not an abdication of oneself" (2:186). Nadine is therefore frigid because she is neither seeking physical ecstasy nor giving herself to anyone. She wants only to trick men into spending time with her.

Nadine's attitude does not, however, indicate that Beauvoir dislikes the flesh. On the contrary, this character's perspective implies that Beauvoir deplores the fact that society has taught women to exchange their bodies as material goods in return for fleeting attention. Singer's (1990) interpretation of Beauvoir helps to understand this Beauvoirian fictionalization of the female body, pleasure, and power. Although Beauvoir herself indulged in fleeting sexual relationships, her philosophy criticizes them. If as Singer argues, Beauvoir sees genuine human contact as possible only through the concerted effort we make with others to bring it about (331), then perhaps what Beauvoir really dislikes is the preconceived decision not to work out a meaningful and complete relationship with the potential partner. Furthermore, her journals and letters support this conclusion. Even if one agrees with Simons that her behavior with her female lovers during the 1930s and 1940s is "best characterized as deceptive and manipulative" (1992, 151), it is nevertheless true that Beauvoir built deep and lasting relationships with these women and continued to support them monetarily and emotionally throughout most of her life.

Furthermore, Nadine's boldness in talking about her sexual exploits serves a specific subversive intent. Not only does she praise or criticize her current beau to Anne as society traditionally perceives women do, but she also transgresses the boundaries of acceptable discourse by announcing her sexual promiscuity, "In case you want to know, I slept with him yesterday and it had no effect on me whatsoever" (1:97); discussing the methods of different lovers, "Only, there are some who do it more or less often, for more or less time. With Lambert it's all the time and it never ends" (2:96); and explaining her method of birth control, "On top of everything else, if I weren't careful, he'd knock me up every time. . . . But it's not very much fun having to put in a plug each time you fuck" (2:95).[9] Anne's distaste for such discourse, "I looked away, I didn't really want to know" (1:97), "Nadine was spying on me out of the corner of her eye; she knew very well that I hated this type of confession" (2:95), mirrors the standard prejudice against women who speak plainly. If, as Irigaray asserts, the female expression of "feminine pleasure signifies the greatest threat to masculine discourse," then Nadine's description of sexual practices that horrifies her mother implies one way of attempting to free women from the silence of their mothers (Irigaray 1985, 157).[10] As Beauvoir clearly indicates in *Mémoires d'une jeune fille rangée*, nice girls must not look at their bodies (81) or acknowledge their personal desires (58), and must certainly never talk about sex and especially not with their mothers,

> Suddenly, following a walk in the woods, the heroine, who wasn't married, found herself pregnant. My heart began to pound: don't let Mom read this book! For then she would know that I knew. . . . Maybe she would feel obligated to have a talk with me: this prospect horrified me because, from the silence that she had always maintained on these problems, I assessed her disgust in approaching them. (154)

In order to underline the hypocrisy involved in this custom, *Les Mandarins* stresses that although freely accepting that Nadine makes love, Anne shudders at the thought of hearing about it. Likewise, she recounts her sexual experiences to Robert, perhaps as a way of asserting her equality with him, but hides them from her adult daughter. A similar inconsistency exists in Beauvoir's writings. Her letters and her war journal reveal that Beauvoir recounted a great many of her sexual experiences to Sartre whereas in her autobiographical works and *Le Deuxième Sexe*, all works addressed primarily to women, she included relatively few stories concerning her own sexuality. Even in the ones mentioned, she omitted the intimate details recounted in her letters. Beauvoir's fictionalization of her own behavior seemingly questions her reasons for not overtly providing a frank and balanced account of her erotic experiences to her figurative sisters and daughters.

Possible answers to this inferred question might be found in this novel's presentation of male myths and discourses that stymie women. During Beauvoir's lifetime, the mere publication of her research on women, *Le Deuxième Sexe*, earned her such epithets as unsatisfied, frigid, nymphomaniac, lesbian, abortionist, and clandestine mother (FC 1:260). The opening chapter of *Les Mandarins* carefully specifies certain details of Anne's past as she reviews her life. She had a very pious upbringing (68). Although, even as a young woman, she considered bourgeois principles a lie, Robert mocks her for holding onto bourgeois dreams (69). In short, Anne has been heavily influenced by values that, despite her efforts, she cannot totally disregard. Because of having internalized patriarchal ideas about women during her childhood, Anne cannot openly acknowledge her right to pursue her physical desires without thinking ill of herself, "Why am I acting like a woman in heat?" (*LM* 2:23).[11] Henri, on the contrary, exploits the myth that posits man as naturally active, free, and promiscuous to explain his loss of love for Paule, "For a woman it is perhaps different, but for a man, it is impossible to desire infinitely the same body" (1:473). Beauvoir's fiction thus illustrates what she explicitly states in *Le Deuxième Sexe:*

> Patriarchal civilization has doomed woman to chastity: one recognizes more or less openly the male's right to satisfy his sexual desires whereas woman is confined to marriage: for her, the carnal act, if it is not sanctified by the code . . . is a fault, a downfall, a defeat, a weakness: she owes it to herself to defend her virtue, her honor; if she *cedes,* if she *falls,* she incites scorn; whereas even in the blame inflicted upon her vanquisher, there is admiration. (2:150)

By juxtaposing two such portraits of human sexual behavior, Beauvoir asserts that no positive myth exists to give a woman the right to act upon her desires, that even the most philosophically liberated of females feels affected by this lack, and implicitly explains why she does not openly discuss her own erotic relationships.

The text provides two separate situations in which men denigrate women who freely act out their desires. This indicates that it is male-dominated society that rejects females who attempt to express their own sexuality. Using Singer's terminology, one could say that in *Le Deuxième Sexe*, Beauvoir explains at least one culturally acceptable way for a biological female to assume gender, "If woman offers herself too boldly, man slips away: he insists upon conquering. Woman can therefore only take by acting as a prey: she must become a passive thing, a promise of submission" (*DS* 2:609–10). In *Les Mandarins*, Beauvoir illustrates the impossibility of this position for women. As if to stress the machismo of males (such as Mauriac, Camus, Boisdeffre, and Nimier, to name only a few) that she herself encountered once she began to talk about female sexuality, Beauvoir first provides an episode in which Henri and Anne jointly defend woman's right to control her own body and to choose her own sexual partners. Louis, the imperious seducer who tries to dominate Marie-Ange, offers the usual arguments males use against women who do not hide their sexuality but who then refuse their sexual favors to some. Because Marie-Ange has had a variety of sexual partners, wears makeup, shows off her legs, pads her bra, and even gets excitingly close to men, Louis maintains that she has no right to refuse her body to anyone. For him, she is nothing but an unthinking, unfeeling object (2:126). Marie-Ange's seductive dress and behavior implies her attempt to be a subject, to give herself the possibility of *taking* someone, of selecting and rejecting sex partners. Louis, on the other hand, represents the traditionally male position as the conqueror who wants to deny any subjectivity to his prey. Beauvoir defends herself and her sisters against such men through the mouths of Anne and Henri who ridicule Louis for his behavior, "Would you look at this guy who thinks that he's Nietzsche because he's yelling at a woman," calling him rude, and a boor (2:126). In the second instance, a liberal young man excuses his own sexual adventures as perfectly acceptable but irrationally denigrates Paule's, "A truly charming woman, Paule Mareuil; only she is too fond of peckers" (2:374). Like Marie-Ange, Paule has trespassed into traditionally male domains by asserting herself as a desiring subject. Perhaps Irigaray best expresses what Beauvoir attempts to fictionalize, "What remains the most completely prohibited to woman, of course, is that she should express something of her own sexual pleasure. This latter is supposed to remain a 'realm' of discourse, produced by men" (Irigaray 1985, 157). In order to be approved by the status quo, she must therefore cloak her supposedly masculine initiative in the feminine garb of passivity.

Slama (1987) comments that by showing "the violence of social discourse on woman" in *Les Mandarins*, Beauvoir wanted to illustrate that man's desire dictates when and if a woman feels sexually alluring or interested in making love (227). But it has not been noted that Beauvoir also shows through Anne's self-analysis that women disagree with societal opinion concerning their attractiveness and sexual activity. Unconsciously desiring to be approved by the moral order, Anne stifles her own sexual impulses, which still vibrantly exist. Despite the survival of her desire, she adopts the societal opinion that a forty-year-old woman has lost her physical attractiveness, "Under my wilting flesh, I affirm the survival of a young woman with her demands still intact, a rebel against all concessions, and disdainful of those sad forty-year-old hags; but she doesn't exist anymore, that young woman; she'll never be born again, even under Lewis's kisses" (2:375).

It is because female efforts, like Paule's, to maintain a healthy sex life earn male criticism, that Anne would rather give up her sexuality altogether than be similarly denounced, "If I ever lose Lewis, when I lose Lewis, I'll immediately and forever give up the belief that I'm still a woman. I don't want to be like them. . . . [I]t hurts me that Paule manages to get herself talked about like that" (2:373–75). To show that culture forces women to deny their sexuality, the text provides Anne's self-analysis, which acknowledges that she is only giving up her sexuality because she doesn't want it to be taken from her,

> I wanted to be different from these overripe ogresses: in all honesty, I had other ruses which were worth no more than theirs. I hurry to say: I'm finished, I'm old; like that I cancel out these 30 or 40 years that I'll live old and finished, regretting the lost past; one cannot deprive me of anything because I have already given it up. (2:375)

It is important to consider the probable identity of the "one" who might deprive Anne of her sexuality. It cannot be women for it is with them that she identifies in this passage. Nor does she explicitly blame time or nature. The motivating force for her thought is Julien's comment about Paule. If, as Singer suggests, Beauvoir rewrites the discourse of freedom in her essays from the position of the oppressed feminine, then one might add that in *Les Mandarins*, she also stresses from that same position the way in which patriarchal discourse impinges on woman's freedom.

In spite of Anne's willingness to accept the patriarchal notion that female desirability fades at a very young age, which mirrors Beauvoir's feelings about her own premature physical demise, Anne rejects the status quo, which considers lesbian love a pathology (Downing 1991, 9).[12] Perhaps Beauvoir was hinting at her own bisexuality when she included the scene in which Anne realizes that Marie-Ange is trying to seduce her and analyzes her feelings about it, thus indicating that she considered bisexual relations a real possibility.[13] It is unclear whether or not Anne actually likes same-sex love relationships, but her discourse clearly states that they neither scare nor shock her. She is not worried about appearing unnatural but rejects the implicit invitation because Marie-Ange's reasons for pursuing her are too predictable, "I would have rather liked having dinner with her, but I knew too well how things would turn out: she was afraid of men, she acted like a little girl, she would have quickly offered me her heart and her frail little body . . . it's not that the situation frightened me but I foresaw it with too much fatality to enjoy it" (1:308–9).

To undermine the dominant order's notions concerning sexuality even further, Beauvoir compares sex without love to physical violation. She fictionalizes what Dale Spender explicitly states years later, that the terms used to describe intercourse, such as foreplay and penetration, derive only from the viewpoint of the male subject (Spender 1980, 178). Although both Henri and Lewis hurry to penetrate their sexual partners supposedly to satisfy them more quickly, the text questions the ecstasy and stresses the female disappointment in the lack of what is normally termed foreplay. Despite Henri's physical excitement and pleasure in bedding Paule, once he loses his love for her, "Paule appeared in the doorway, solemn and nude, her hair tumbling over her shoulders; she was almost as perfect as in the past, but to Henri all this beauty no longer meant anything" (36), their lovemaking horrifies him and even evokes images of rape in his mind, "She uttered a long credulous moan; He embraced her violently, smothered her mouth with his lips, and to get it over with as quickly as possible immediately penetrated her. . . . He was horrified by her and himself. . . . It seemed that he had raped a dead or crazy woman and yet he couldn't keep himself from enjoying it" (37).[14] Although he has no doubts about Paule's satisfaction with his performance, the absence of her point of view coupled with the presence of her first words after the lovemaking, "Are you happy?" (37), suggest not sensual satiation but only her delight in pleasing him. As if to stress that such an encounter is equally dissatisfying to both parties, the text reproduces the same scene between Lewis and Anne from a female point of view. Far from feeling grateful to Lewis for serving her needs, Anne hates him for treating her like an object with no feeling:

> Suddenly he was laying on top of me, he penetrated me and had me without a word, without a kiss. It all happened so quickly that I remained bewildered. . . . A desperate rage seized me by the throat. "He has no right," I murmured. Not for one instant had he given me his presence. He had treated me like a pleasure machine. Even if he didn't love me anymore, he wasn't supposed to do that! (2:393)

By contrasting Anne's only sexual encounter with Scriassine to her initial intimacy with Lewis, Les Mandarins most fully illustrates the necessity for women and men to feel spiritually united in both body and soul with their partners in order to achieve full physical satisfaction. Beauvoir's letters to Sartre similarly indicate the importance of this phenomenon to her personal life. In a letter dated 14 January 1940, Beauvoir writes,

> I found Sorokine reproachfully waiting for me, planted in front of my door. . . . We went in, we sat down side by side and after ten minutes of conversation we had progressed to kissing; after a quarter of an hour of kisses, we were in bed. . . . [T]his seems to me a little like an *initiation* and it would bother me if I wasn't completely taken up in the moment by this totally charming little person. . . . [I]t's violent tenderness because I find her of such perfection and such charm. . . . [I]t is certainly not what it was with Kos. [Olga Kosakievitch, a former student and lover who remained Beauvoir's friend], but I have a very strong taste for her body and I find these moments and especially her faces which are completely moving, and her totally confident but unabandoned tender affection extremely pleasant. (1990b, 2:41–42)

Full unity between sexual partners, Beauvoir stresses in *Les Mandarins*, precludes the male attempt to control female pleasure. For instance, Anne cannot attain orgasm with Scriassine because he insists upon governing her experience. Already in *Le Deuxième Sexe*, Beauvoir had stated that woman often closes her eyes during lovemaking so as to abolish any barriers between herself and her lover (2:183). *Les Mandarins* offers concrete examples of the barriers that woman has to destroy. It is to escape man's domination, his judgment, and his games that she closes her eyes. Scriassine clarifies that, in his mind, she is playing the part of "the ravished maiden." He commands her to open her eyes, caress him upon demand, and faults her for not showing more liking for his penis (118–21).[15] Each time that she begins to immerse herself in tactile delight, his voice jolts her back to reality, demanding that she ignore her own secret joy and participate in his games: "I closed my eyes. I entered into a dream as heavy as reality and from which I would awaken at dawn, lighthearted. Then I heard his voice. . . . These words which were not addressed to me woke me harshly. I had not come here to play the ravished maiden nor any other game" (118). With Lewis, on the contrary, her delectation is immeasurable primarily due to his total acceptance of her in his bed as herself instead of his fantasized version of woman, "He was naked, I was naked, and I felt no embarrassment; his gaze could not harm me; he wasn't judging me, he preferred nothing to me" (2:39). Lewis too benefits from his embracing of her as herself; unlike Scriassine, he does not have nightmares after making love with Anne and never needs to reassure himself that she achieved orgasm.

Although, by the theory it proposes, *Les Mandarins* weakens the attractiveness of viewing sexual activity as a way to manifest or to gain power over anyone, this textual imperative does not imply a dislike for sensuality. On the contrary, the descriptions of lovemaking show a clear devotion to the gratification of the bodily appetites through the repeated reference to the senses and a lyrical enumeration of the body parts embraced during the sexual act. In *Le Deuxième Sexe*, Beauvoir explains that in the erotic experience, one discovers the ambiguity of the human condition, that of being simultaneously body and mind, subject and other. Because woman already sees herself as an object, she must work at finding dignity as a transcending subject while acknowledging her physicality. Man, in contrast, dupes himself that he is primarily an acting subject, thus hesitating to see himself as other, as body, and thus ignoring half of his existence (2:190–91). Due to this situation, Beauvoir concludes, "Woman has a more authentic experience of herself" (2:191). Through the concrete examples of the awareness of all senses, the poetic description of the body, the use of voice, and reference to creation myths, *Les Mandarins* suggests the myriad ways in which woman, as opposed to man, has a more authentic experience of the self in lovemaking.[16] Anne responds strongly to odors and temperature. During her various episodes of lovemaking with Lewis, his bodily scent and warmth intoxicate her, "his odor, his warmth were making me drunk" (2:55). The perfume of his body also reassures her when she doubts his love, "He was there, that's all that mattered. I had his legs entangled in mine, his breath, his scent, his eager hands on my body" (2:274). Upon Lewis's avowal that he no longer loves her, she first blames his loss of desire on her new expensive perfume masking her true odor, "It's because of this bizarre smell" (2:383).

Purely tactile sensations similarly engulf her with waves of ecstasy. Scriassine awakens her desire by the feel of his hands and skin, "Again I gathered my thoughts together under his hands. I reassembled the silence. I clung to his skin and I devoured his warmth through all my pores: my bones, my muscles were melting from this fire and peace wrapped itself around me in silky spirals" (1:119). With Lewis, Anne more actively seeks the pleasures of touch as she kisses his eyes, his lips, the length of his chest, his navel, and finally his penis, which is lovingly described as having a faintly beating heart of its own, "I kissed his eyes, his lips, My mouth moved down the length of his chest; it lightly caressed his childish navel, his animal fur, his genitals where a heart was striking tiny beats" (2:55).[17] Significantly, this detailing of Lewis's anatomy also stresses the equality between males and females. Regardless of man's beliefs that he remains the transcendent subject during sexual activity, just like woman, he becomes body and other in the arms of his lover.

Both sound and sight also play integral roles in sexual fulfillment and thus nuance the claims made by Beauvoir in *Le Deuxième Sexe* about the female's liking for total darkness during lovemaking. It is the nature of each relationship that dictates the woman's need to close her eyes in order to achieve unity with her lover. Anne first suspects that Lewis no longer loves her when he refrains from pronouncing her name and darkens the room so that she cannot see him before he penetrates her, "Last night before entering inside me, Lewis had turned off the light, he hadn't given me his smile, he hadn't pronounced my name: why?" (2:380).

In her study of Beauvoir's works, Pilardi (1989) finds it disappointing that Beauvoir characterizes a woman's erotic experience as primarily vaginal and "never acknowledges, to any extent, the other erotic areas of a woman's body" (25). Yet, a close reading of *Le Deuxième Sexe* and *Les Mandarins* calls Pilardi's conclusion into question. Already in *Le Deuxième Sexe* on a purely theoretical level, Beauvoir linked sexuality, even for a virgin, to a sensuality that includes taste, smell, and touch, "In her [the virgin], the aggressive eroticism of childhood survives . . . the prey that she covets, she wishes it to be endowed with qualities which through taste, smell, and touch are revealed to her as values because sexuality is not an isolated domain, it prolongs the dreams and joys of sensuality" (2:153). In *Les Mandarins*, Beauvoir concretizes and expands the tenets of *Le Deuxième Sexe* to suggest that woman is able to live her sexuality through all of her senses, through much of the surface area of her body, detailed for the reader as her eyes, mouth, breasts, belly, genitals, and legs. Good sex for women means rejoicing in their own fragrance and nourishment, feeling at one with the earth, "His desire transformed me. Me, who for such a long time had no longer any taste or any form, I again possessed breasts, a belly, genitals, flesh; I was as nourishing as bread, as fragrant as the earth. It was so miraculous that I didn't think of measuring my time nor my pleasure" (2:39). It is perhaps also this feeling of communion with the earth, with nature that makes her experience more genuine.

Moreover, Beauvoir glorifies woman's erotic experience as other than merely vaginal by stressing the importance of a variety of individual characteristics such as voice, gaze, and skin. Feminist critics often equate voice and gaze with the power to act independently and to influence others. Claudine Herrmann (1989) argues that both Western and Eastern cultures have demanded that woman silence or camouflage her voice in order to make herself socially acceptable in a male-dominant culture (19–31). E. Ann Kaplan (1983) postulates that the gaze can carry with it "the power of action and possession" (311). The French word for skin, *peau*, figuratively connotes both the exterior appearance and the personality of an individual in frequently used expressions such as "être dans la peau de quelqu'un" (literally, "to be in a person's skin," but equivalent to the English expression, "to be in someone else's shoes") or "être bien ou mal dans sa peau" (literally, "to be feeling well or poorly in one's skin," but closer to the English expressions "to feel great or awful" [physically] or "to feel at ease or ill-at-ease"). Thus, as if to show the primacy of the flesh, the text shows Anne exultant over the knowledge that Lewis loves her whole, healthy, and powerful potential self as signified by her voice, her gaze, and her skin, the figurative loci of strength and independence in an individual: "I who am always interrogating myself suspiciously about the feelings I inspire, I never asked myself who Lewis loved in me. I was sure that it was me. He knew neither my language nor my friends nor my worries: nothing but my voice, my eyes, my skin; but I didn't have any other truth than this skin, this voice, these eyes" (2:56).

The trajectory of intimate relationships further indicates the supremacy of the female body on a subconscious and symbolic level. After one of Anne's major quarrels with Lewis at Murray's house, she seeks solace in the lake, thus symbolically returning to the womb, "I suddenly desired the coolness of the water. . . . It was very mild out. I closed my eyes under the stars and the purring of the water lulled me to sleep" (2:284). This escape back to the female origin simultaneously transforms into a rebirth of both Anne and the world as she awakens on the fourth day of creation just after the birth of the sun (2:284). In one ultimate subversive move, Beauvoir thus rewrites the mythology of creation. The male God conveniently disappears through use of the passive voice, "the suffering of beasts and men had not yet been invented" (2:284). Some unnamed figure now invents the world. Not only is a woman, Anne, the first creature to appear in this universe void of any male figures but she is also weightless and totally at one with her femaleness as depicted by her unity with, in the original French, "la mer," which phonically yields both the sea, its literal meaning and by association, the mother *(la mère)*, "I blended myself with the sea (mother); lying on my back, I floated with my eyes full of sky and no longer weighed anything" (2:284).[18] Anne symbolically succeeds in reaffirming her sex by reuniting with the mother and thus derives her strength and will to survive from the female body.

Paule and Anne similarly immerse themselves in other liquids, also stereotypically female attributes, at the end of their respective liaisons with Henri and Lewis, which brought them such pleasure. Both cry and drink profusely. Although excessive drinking is most often considered to be a male stereotype, *Les Mandarins* focuses rather on the ability of liquor to create the mirage of transcendence while actually exaggerating the stereotypical femininity of the body. Anne likes the way liquor throws her off balance and momentarily separates her from the reality of her flesh, "A body, it's so tight, it's even too cramped, you feel like bursting through the seams. They never do burst but in some instances you give yourself the illusion that you are going to jump out of your skin" (2:355). But her description of Paule drinking evokes a mindless female animal in the most exaggerated female state, that of pregnancy, "I didn't know this fat woman, with the sweat-soaked face and the bovine eyes who was swigging down whisky beside me" (2:353). Associating Paule's eyes, which are traditionally the windows of the soul, with those of cattle suggests that she is even closer to nature, more intensely body and not mind than before: cow eyes blindly adore those who feed them for slaughter. Added to this animalistic image, both her corpulence and the moistness of her face, the body part that most often mirrors the spirit according to the Platonic tradition, stress her position as the overblown female unable to control the discharge of her bodily fluids. Unlike Anne's earlier images of the sea, alcohol does not produce a pleasing view of the female body.

An equally unpleasant image is produced when both Anne and Paule contemplate ending their lives with a liquefied poison. This return to the body is too solitary; instead of rediscovering the value of their sex, they work to destroy themselves and the authenticity of their experiences as women. Figuratively, Beauvoir thus indicates that it is not the femaleness in itself but what one makes of it that gives it value. Anne, for example, ratifies the female more positively in the end by rejecting death in order to be with her daughter and granddaughter. It is her daughter who reminds her that she does not have the right to make femaleness into something so unattractive and self-destructive. Or in the earlier mentioned vocabulary of Butler and Singer, Anne should not opt to express her gender in such an irresponsible and uncaring fashion:

> Nadine said very loudly in an irritated voice: "Mom should not have left Maria all alone." . . . Suddenly there was a faint echo in me, a tiny gnawing noise. "Did something happen?" Maria alone on the lawn: a cat could scratch her, a dog bite her. No: They were laughing in the garden; but the silence didn't close in again. . . . And I imagined Nadine's voice powerful and indignant: "You shouldn't have done it. You had no right to do it!" The blood rushed to my face and something full of life burned my heart. . . . The burning awakened me. (2:498–99)

These few examples thus indicate that Beauvoir neither proved her own self-hatred, nor loathing for the flesh, nor her will to dominate others in writing *Les Mandarins*. Literally and symbolically she glorifies lovemaking and revalorizes the female body. Yet, this is not to suggest that her exaltation of sensuality and femaleness contradicts her arguments of *Le Deuxième Sexe* by representing woman as essence. She also claims masculine and feminine traits for all individuals. Women should be able to control their bodies and have stereotypically masculine careers. Men too should be able to envision physical passion without intellectual unity as rape. Her consistent theoretical and illustrative arguments against dominating love partners also deny that *Les Mandarins* is an anti–*Deuxième Sexe* as Jean Rabaud, Charles Moeller, and Robert Poulet have claimed. Rabaud of *La Revue socialiste* argues that although asserting her contempt for the feminine mystique and declaring in *Le Deuxième Sexe* that this mystique will disappear due to ethical and sociological progress, Beauvoir negates this position via her female characters in *Les Mandarins*. Similarly, Moeller of *La Revue nouvelle* views her novel as proof that she accepts that a woman in love should be dominated by the man she loves. Poulet of *Rivarol* contends that *Les Mandarins* reveals that Beauvoir is not a strong individual, but a rather weak, hesitant, and nostalgic being, whose life should not serve as an example (Larsson 1988, 130–34).

Teresa de Lauretis (1984) comments that narratives traditionally seduce a female into believing that her biological destiny is to fulfill the social contract, the biological and affective destiny, and most important, the desire of her male counterpart (133). According to this definition, Beauvoir's prize-winning novel transcends the traditional because none of her women characters ultimately acquiesce to male desires. Nevertheless, Beauvoir still struggles with defining the future of women who can successfully merge the pleasures of the body and the mind. None of her female characters finds both. Women cannot, Beauvoir stresses, happily survive on sensuality alone. Although Anne finds true physical satisfaction with Lewis, she refuses to give up her life, her country, her worries, her job, or her family to be with him full-time even if it means losing him. Choosing to remain with Robert rather than fulfilling her sexual desires is her decision: as portrayed by the text, Robert remains ambivalent about her departure. Having opted for marriage and motherhood, Nadine remains restless and unfulfilled. Her husband and child fulfill her affective and sensuous needs, but, mentally, she still seeks a career identity and wonders what she can do with all her spare time. Josette, having invested all in becoming famous even during her relationship with Henri, achieves her goal as a celebrated actress: the text mentions only her career not her romantic attachments. The only female character to be portrayed unattractively in the end, Paule devotes more energy to seeking the new man of her dreams in bed than to launching her recently desired writing career.

In ending her novel with problems, Beauvoir challenges the reader to solve the riddle that continues to plague society: Is it possible for woman to have the right to control her sexuality and have a successful career of her own choice just as man does? Perhaps because Beauvoir feared the impossibility of such rights in her own society, she persisted in portraying herself as a paragon of feminist virtues to the public and disguised the primacy of her sensual pleasures and numerous love affairs. *Les Mandarins*, however, reveals the ambiguities involved for her in continually becoming a gender that fuses stereotypically masculine and feminine traits and actions within the confines of male-authored social laws that favor males and offer only unsatisfactory culturally acceptable possibilities to females. Her novel thus transgresses patriarchal codes both by describing what woman should not become and by asking continually why.

We thus return to the question: How and why does Les Mandarins still appeal to women? As this study demonstrates, it is through Les Mandarins that Beauvoir shows numerous infractions of the discourses that impede woman from becoming a self-esteeming individual. Beauvoir challenges Freud's notion of the female body as lack and suggests the similarities in behavior between men and women in parallel situations. Showing that women do experience physical pleasure from fleeting sexual encounters, she foregrounds the greater intensity of their delectation in situations involving commitment from the head and heart of both parties. She illustrates how patriarchal commonplaces and myths discourage woman from maximizing her erotic joys and implies ways to subvert these detrimental discourses through the thoughts of Anne. Anticipating what would become some of the most heated issues of the early 1990s, she depicts bisexual relationships as an acceptable possibility and redefines rape as an act that can occur within the confines of a couple. She suggests that female eroticism goes far beyond the purely vaginal. Via Anne's consciousness, which reveals her as body and mind, Beauvoir revalorizes the female sexual experience, glorifies the female body, and poeticizes the male as a physical object. In short, a truly sensual, sexual, authentically desiring woman, who evokes Beauvoir's adventures in becoming a gender, emanates from the pages of this novel. In writing Les Mandarins, Beauvoir not only testifies to a woman's quest to develop a satisfying possibility of gender for herself; she also breaks the taboo dictating that woman must not speak of her own desire. Providing a bisexual body that shows the inherent equality between the male and the female, she encourages awareness on the part of both men and women of all times of the necessity for both sexes to blend intellectual challenges and sexual ecstasy in their own lives.[19]

Notes

1. At the 1991 conference entitled "The Legacy of Simone de Beauvoir and Jean-Paul Sartre," much discussion concerned Beauvoir's behavior with other women; see also Barnes (1991), 23–26.

2. This and all other translations of French texts are my own unless otherwise indicated. The page numbers given in the text refer to the original French.

3. Page references for *La Force des choses* (The force of circumstances) will be indicated as *FC* in the text.

4. These percentages were derived by counting the number of pages each character focalizes and/or narrates in each of the two Folio edition volumes.

5. In an interview with Bair, Beauvoir insists that she put parts of herself into each of the two male characters, especially Henri (Bair 1990, 662). Similarly, in *La Force des choses*, she indicates that both Anne and Henri were based on herself (1:367).

6. Page references for *Le Deuxième Sexe* will be indicated as *DS* in the text.

7. The translation by Leonard M. Friedman renders "a pretty whore" (une jolie putain) as "a good-looking girl" (79). Page references for *Les Mandarins* will be indicated as *LM* in the text.

8. Friedman's translation considerably weakens the vulgarity and overall impact of Nadine's discourse by translating "If I don't fuck" (si je ne baise pas) as "If I don't go to bed with them"; and "les femmes m'emmerdant," which is closer to "women are a damned nuisance," as "women annoy me" (373).

9. Nadine's impudence and the boldness of the sexual imagery is again destroyed by Friedman's translation: "But it's not very much fun having to put in a plug each time you fuck" (Mais ce n'est pas très marrant d'avoir à se mettre un bouchon chaque fois qu'on baise) is given as "But it isn't much fun having to be all protected every time you so much as kiss" (373).

10. Beauvoir implies her interest in psychoanalysis and her agreement with much of Irigaray's work in a 1977 interview with Alice Jardine: "I would certainly like to see some young women take up psychoanalysis seriously and reconstruct it from an absolutely new viewpoint. . . . Irigaray . . . is trying to do something. She hasn't gone far enough in my opinion. But she is trying to construct a psychoanalysis which would be feminist" (228).

11. Friedman translates "Why am I acting like a woman in heat?" (Qu'est-ce que ces moeurs d'une femme en chaleur?) as somewhat baser than the original French, "What about those morals of a bitch in heat?" (332).

12. In her memoirs, correspondence, and conversations with friends from January to July 1952, at the young age of 44, Beauvoir repeatedly referred to herself as aging or simply old (Bair 442, 664).

13. Beauvoir's *Journal* (1990a) and *Lettres à Sartre* (1990b) clarify that she had love affairs with at least three other women, Olga Kosakievitch, Louise Védrine, and Nathalie Sorokine (*Journal* 139, 185, 233; *Lettres* 1930, 294; *Lettres* 1940, 23, 36, 41).

14. Friedman's translation ignores the ambiguity of Paule's pleasure. He translates "She uttered a long credulous moan" (Elle eut un long râle crédule) as "She uttered a long moan of satisfaction" (30).

15. Friedman's translation of this scene gives Anne a less active role than the original French. The lines "avec autorité il mit son sexe dans ma main; je le flattai sans enthousiasme" (He authoritatively put his sex organ in my hand; I caressed it without enthusiasm) becomes in translation, "Decisively he put his sex in my hand; I held it without enthusiasm" (82).

16. These elements in *Les Mandarins* strongly evoke Colette's works. In my forthcoming "The Rewriting of Sexual Identity from Colette's *Chéri* to Beauvoir's *L'Invitée*," I discuss Beauvoir's indebtedness to Colette in depicting relationships between men and women and sexuality.

17. In Friedman's translation, Anne's activities below the chest and her poetic thoughts about Lewis's penis disappear. Friedman translates, "J'embrassai ses yeux, ses lèvres, ma bouche descendit le long de sa poitrine; elle effleura le nombril enfantin, la fourrure animale, le sexe ou un coeur battait à petits coups" as "I kissed his eyes, his lips; my mouth went down along his chest" (350). Similarly, the other reference to oral sex disappears in the translation.

With Scriassine, the original French reads, "Sa bouche taquina mes seins, rampa sur mon ventre, et descendit vers mons sexe" (119) (His mouth teased my breasts, slithered across my stomach, and descended toward my genitals). Friedman's translation reads only, "His mouth teased my breasts" (82).

18. Friedman's translation obliterates the image of unity with the mother. He translates the same passage, "Je me suis mélangée à la mer; couchée sur le dos, je flottais les yeux pleins de ciel et je ne pesais plus rien" as "I plunged into the ocean and floated on my back; my body lost all its weight and my eyes were full of sky" (483).

19. Faludi (1991) provides a thorough overview of the way the government and media in America have worked hard to revoke women's rights over the past decade and to convince them that they cannot successfully marry intellectual and bodily pleasures. I would like to thank Katherine Kurk and Margaret Simons for the insightful comments made on earlier versions of this essay.

References

Bair, Deirdre. 1990. *Simone de Beauvoir: A Biography.* New York: Summit.

Barnes, Hazel E. 1991. "Simone de Beauvoir's Journal and Letters: A Poisoned Gift?" *Simone de Beauvoir Studies: The Legacy of Simone de Beauvoir and Jean-Paul Sartre* 8:13–29.

Beauvoir, Simone de. 1949. *Le Deuxième Sexe.* 2 vols. Paris: Gallimard.

———. 1954. *Les Mandarins.* 2 vols. Paris: Gallimard.

———. 1956. *The Mandarins.* Translated by Leonard M. Friedman. Cleveland: World Publishing.

———. 1958. *Mémoires d'une jeune fille rangée.* Paris: Gallimard.

———. *La Force de l'âge.* 1960. Paris: Gallimard.

———. *La Force des choses.* 1963. 2 vols. Paris: Gallimard.

———. 1990a. *Journal de guerre: Septembre 1939–Janvier 1941.* Edited by Sylvie Le Bon de Beauvoir. Paris: Gallimard.

———. 1990b. *Lettres à Sartre.* 2 vols. Edited by Sylvie Le Bon de Beauvoir. Paris: Gallimard.

Butler, Judith, 1989. "Gendering the Body: Beauvoir's Philosophical Contribution." In *Women, Knowledge, and Reality: Explorations in Feminist Philosophy,* edited by Ann Garry and Marilyn Pearsall, 253–62. Boston: Unwin Hyman.

Chapsal, Madeleine. 1984. "Simone de Beauvoir." In *Envoyez la petite musique,* 50–66. Paris: Grasset.

Crosland, Margaret. 1992. *Simone de Beauvoir: The Woman and Her Work.* London: Heinemann.

Downing, Christine. 1991. *Myths and Mysteries of Same-Sex Love.* New York: Continuum.

Fallaize, Elizabeth. 1988. *The Novels of Simone de Beauvoir.* London: Routledge.

Faludi, Susan. 1991. *Backlash: The Undeclared War Against American Women.* New York: Crown.

Freud, Sigmund. 1977. "Woman as Castrated Man." In *History of Ideas on Woman: A Source Book,* edited by Rosemary Agonito, 299–322. New York: Putnam.

Gerassi, John. 1976. "Simone de Beauvoir: The Second Sex 25 Years Later." Interview. *Society* 13, no. 2 (January–February): 79–85.

Hayman, Ronald. 1992. "Having Wonderful Sex, Wish You Were Here." *New York Times Book Review,* 19 July:13–14.

Herrmann, Claudine. 1989. *The Tongue Snatchers.* Translated by Nancy Kline. Lincoln: University of Nebraska Press.

Irigaray, Luce. 1985. *This Sex Which is Not One.* Translated by Catherine Porter. Ithaca: Cornell University Press.

Jardine, Alice. 1977. "Interview with Simone de Beauvoir." Translated by Ellen Evans. *Signs: Journal of Women in Culture and Society* 5, no. 2 (Winter 1979): 224–36.

Kaplan, E. Ann. 1983. "Is the Gaze Male?" In *Powers of Desire: The Politics of Sexuality*, edited by Ann Snitow, Christine Stansell, and Sharon Thompson, 309–27. New York: Monthly Review, 1983.

Klaw, Barbara. Forthcoming. "The Rewriting of Sexual Identity from Colette's *Chéri* to Beauvoir's *L'Invitée.*" In *The Metaphysical Novel*, edited by Eleanore Holveck and Barbara Klaw.

Larsson, Björn. 1988. *La Réception des Mandarins: Le Roman de Simone de Beauvoir face à la critique littéraire en France.* Lund, Sweden: Lund University Press.

Lauretis, Teresa de. 1984. "Desire in Narrative." In her *Alice Doesn't: Feminism, Semiotics, Cinema*, 103–57. Bloomington: Indiana University Press.

Marks, Elaine. 1986. "Transgressing the (In)cont(in)ent Boundaries; The Body in Decline." In *Simone de Beauvoir: Witness to a Century.* Special issue of *Yale French Studies* 72:181–200.

Pilardi, Jo-Ann. 1989. "Female Eroticism in the Works of Simone de Beauvoir." In *The Thinking Muse: Feminism and Modern French Philosophy*, edited by Jeffner Allen and Iris Marion Young, 18–34. Bloomington: Indiana University Press.

Potvin, Liza, and Brenda Sully. 1991. "Memory and 'Otherness' in M. F. K. Fisher and Simone de Beauvoir." M. F. K. Fisher's Gastronomical Selves. MLA Convention, San Francisco, 29 December.

Schwarzer, Alice. 1984. "Women have less far to fall." Interview. In *Simone de Beauvoir Today: Conversations 1972–1982*, translated by Marianne Howarth, 85–93. London: Chatto and Windus; Hogarth Press.

Simons, Margaret. 1992. "Lesbian Connections: Simone de Beauvoir and Feminism." *Signs: Journal of Women in Culture and Society* 18, no. 1 (Autumn): 136–61.

Singer, Linda. 1990. "Interpretation and Retrieval." In *Hypatia Reborn: Essays in Feminist Philosophy*, edited by Azizah Y. al-Hibri and Margaret A. Simons, 323–35. Bloomington: Indiana University Press.

Slama, Beatrice. 1987. "Simone de Beauvoir: Feminine Sexuality and Liberation." In *Critical Essays on Simone de Beauvoir*, edited by Elaine Marks, 218–34. Boston: G. K. Hall.

Spender, Dale. 1980. *Man Made Language.* London: Routledge and Kegan Paul.

12

Beauvoir's Two Senses of "Body" in *The Second Sex*

Julie K. Ward

It was Beauvoir's dictum that one *becomes* but is not *born* a woman and her broad analysis of the reality behind that statement that charted the course for most contemporary currents in modern Western feminism and for which she has been hailed in the past as an emancipator.[1] Yet in the wake of a gynocentric wave in feminist thinking, Beauvoir's work has increasingly come under scholarly scrutiny, with the result that Beauvoir, far from being hailed as a liberator, is reviled as a turncoat. Some of the more trenchant criticism centers on Beauvoir's discussion of woman's body and related subjects such as sexual intercourse, pregnancy, and maternity (O'Brien 1981, Seigfried 1984, Evans 1987, Léon 1988). Almost uniformly, these critics have found her analysis of these areas to reflect a negative attitude about the female body, and so her view has been labeled "masculinist" and essentialist.[2] In a sense, the evidence for their claims is not difficult to find: Beauvoir's descriptions of females as more enslaved to the species than males, of women as less transcendent than men and as alienated from their bodies in the course of normal processes such as menstruation, pregnancy, and childbirth seem tailored to fit the critics' charges. And so, some have gone on to conclude that Beauvoir, perhaps unknowingly, has adopted a hostile, "masculine" stance toward women, and toward the female body in particular (Seig-fried 1985, 221). Others have maintained that Beauvoir assumes that female characteristics are fixed by nature so as to doom her to inferiority. Judith Okely, for example, finds that Beauvoir's account is deterministic: "Despite Beauvoir's formal rejection of biological determinism, when the details of her arguments are closely examined it can be seen that she contradicts any claim that biological factors are irrelevant or arbitrary. Again and again she slips into biological reductionism to explain the primary cause of women's subordination" (1986, 90). First, it should be pointed out that, as far as the critics' charges are concerned, biological determinism does not coincide with biological reductionism: the latter is a weaker view than the former in the sense that it reduces human abilities like thinking to biological properties, but it does not entail the further view that these capacities are subject to deterministic biological laws. However, in spite of Okely's contrary implication—since the two positions are not logically equivalent—for the purposes of this essay, I shall offer arguments against both sorts of objections to Beauvoir's account of women's oppression and of the body. So, while one cannot deny that readers of *The Second Sex* encounter a host of negative remarks about woman's biology, the question to address is whether these claims constitute biological reductionism or determinism. I contend that they do not, and that Beauvoir clearly rejects both these positions. It would, in fact, be surprising for Beauvoir to embrace any incompatibilist position that would preclude the possibility for individual choice and responsibility, as does biological determinism. In order to make this case, I argue that one has to take seriously Beauvoir's claim[3] that it is her intention to consider the body not as a *thing*, but as a *situation* (34), about which more will be said in the following section. Briefly, if we follow her suggestion, we see in her theoretical analysis of woman's body at least two different perspectives from which the discussion about the body is conducted, so that we must put her comments in their proper context by noting the perspective from which she makes them. By differentiating between these levels, I contend that neither the charge of biological determinism (or reductionism), nor that of "masculinism" has a firm foundation. The charge of "masculinism" will be displaced by showing that Beauvoir is not committed to the negative views about woman's body that she mentions—which is why she distinguishes the "biological" treatment of the body from her own way of accounting for it.

As a general observation, the method of philosophical analysis Beauvoir employs in *The Second Sex* is fundamentally nonreductionist in the sense that it depends on a synthesis of social, economic, and historical factors to one perspective she sometimes calls the "existential" perspective, which is her preferred stance in comprehending the full reality of woman's oppression (60). Once the theoretical complexity of Beauvoir's perspective is acknowledged, two obvious objections to the reductionist interpretation of Beauvoir emerge. First, the possibility that we could reduce the intrinsically heterogeneous analyses of female experience—psychological, biological, economic, etc.—to a single kind of analysis looks to be slight. Second, even supposing that we could achieve this reduction, why should we be inclined to think that for her the biological explanations, rather than historical ones, say, are the most fundamental? These two basic objections warrant against the reductionist program.

But, so her critics would maintain, even though Beauvoir's overall analysis of woman is multifaceted, her account of woman's body is seriously flawed: Beauvoir herself succumbs to some of the well-worn, patriarchal myths about the female body. I reject this criticism, finding that Beauvoir's distinction between the two senses of the body, and of the physical generally, has been overlooked or not addressed adequately by her critics. Briefly, my interpretation of Beauvoir's position is this: she appears to make neutral statements about females and biology in chapter 1, and so looks to be making essentialist statements about women's bodies; in fact, this is not true. For, as Beauvoir points out, one cannot make neutral, aperspectival claims about female biology since the physical capacities of either sex gain meaning only when placed in a cultural and historical context—this, I argue, is what Beauvoir means by saying that the body is to be seen as a *situation*. In the rest of this essay, I shall contend that if Beauvoir takes seriously the notion that the body is itself a situation, as I believe she does, she must reject the idea of the body as a purely biological mechanism, contrary to her critics' charge. For these same reasons, I shall also find that Beauvoir is not fundamentally opposed to typically female functions, such as maternity. Instead of

being cast as holding some form of biological reductionism or determinism, she should be seen as developing a social-constructivist view of the
body. In this vein, I generally agree with Judith Butler's view of Beauvoir
(1986, 1989). In the last section, I shall argue that Beauvoir's claim
about the body as situation may be taken as rejecting the notion of a
natural, sexed body. So interpreted, we may comprehend Beauvoir's
dictum that one only *becomes* a woman to imply not only that gender,
but the body itself, is socially constructed.

Putting Biology in Context

"the body is not a thing, it is a situation"

In coming to general conclusions about Beauvoir's view of woman's
body, I have followed two heuristic principles. The first is that when
confronted with apparent contradictions among an author's claims, one
needs to look deeper for some means of reconciling them. The second
principle consists in taking the structure of the work as central to its
interpretation. On this latter point, it is useful to note that the initial
three chapters of the work, on biology, psychoanalysis, and historical
materialism, preface the chapters on history and myths about women.
Together these chapters constitute the volume entitled "Les Faits et Les
Mythes" (Facts and myths), which precedes the second volume entitled
"L'Expérience Vécu" (Lived experience). By naming them thus, the two
halves of the work suggest distinct yet interrelated levels of analysis, the
first half emphasizing abstract constructs with which male thinkers have
theorized about woman, the second what woman's experience under
patriarchy has been like. This order, then, suggests a "top-down"
approach to her discussion: a mode of analysis such that the current
myths and theories detailed in her first volume are to be regarded as part
of the conceptual apparatus presupposed in the lived histories of women
in the second volume. Since the theories and myths detailed in volume
1 constitute part of the theoretical framework of patriarchy, it would be
naive to think that that which is said about women and their experience
is necessarily affirmed by Beauvoir herself. For example, in chapter 1,
Beauvoir asserts that the theoretical justification in biology of the male
as the sole creator of the offspring coincides with the advent of patriarchy

(8). Additionally, Beauvoir ends each of the three initial chapters with critical comments detailing the inadequacies of each theoretical approach. We must infer, then, that Beauvoir is open to rejecting either part or all of the conceptual analyses of women given in volume 1. In this regard, we may note that she rejects psychoanalysis for its partiality and ahistoricity, specifically faulting the theory for its failure to explain, rather than merely assert, the supremacy of male as against female power as it is reflected in the sovereignty of the phallus (49). Beauvoir's comment that "representation of the world, like the world itself, is the work of men . . . which they confuse with absolute truth" (143) is instructive here: she clearly acknowledges the dominant myths and ideologies that men have created about women, but she by no means thereby subscribes to them.[4] This said, it is highly improbable to think—as her critics maintain—that the traditional view of woman merely as a reproductive vessel, such as is expressed in the opening lines of chapter 1, can be identified with Beauvoir's own view: "Woman? very simple, say the fanciers of simple formulas: she is a womb, an ovary, she is a female—this word is sufficient to define her" (3). While even her critics may acknowledge that such a line does not express Beauvoir's position it seems to me that the critics have charged her with holding views as improbable as this one—largely by overlooking the fact that since much of the theoretical discussion in volume 1 is the product of male theorizing about women, it will inevitably be subject to some criticism by Beauvoir. If true, it follows that when we encounter various apparently essentialist statements about woman's body in the chapter on biology, we cannot thereby conclude that Beauvoir is uncritically accepting them. In general, any reductive account of woman, such as what Beauvoir calls the "sexual monism" of Freud or the "economic monism" of Engels (60), clearly runs contrary to her own foundations since the whole thrust of Beauvoir's analysis of woman is to appreciate the complexity of being feminine. For the same reasons, one can imagine Beauvoir calling the simplistic view that woman is merely "a womb, an ovary"[5] as a kind of "biological monism" and dispensing with it.

Although Beauvoir has been faulted (Seigfried 1985, 219–20) for opening her work with a chapter on biology, in fact the chapter involves a complex task. It aims to set out a nonreductive, nondualistic account of human beings.[6] So, while Beauvoir rejects the notion that woman can be reduced to her reproductive organs, she wishes to mark the importance of the physical by emphasizing the central role that the body plays in human experience. She reflects a strongly anti-Cartesian, or antidualist, perspective in her general conception of human beings, claiming: "the body [is] the instrument of our grasp upon the world" (32).[7] She then goes on to claim that women and men do not "grasp" the world in the same terms, for differences in body entail differences in experience. Now, when she summarizes the differences between the sexes, she says that the two biological traits that characterize woman are that her grasp upon the world is less "extended" than man's ("sa prise est moins étendue que celle de l'homme"), and that she is more narrowly enslaved to the species ("elle est plus étroitement asservie a l'espèce," 95). Presumably, what Beauvoir has in mind here are various physiological differences she details in chapter 1, for example, the relatively smaller musculature of women to men, and the possession of fewer red blood corpuscles so that the gross muscular effort is lower (34).

Do these and related comments entail she is being "masculinist" in her view of the female body as her critics charge? I think not, although it is easy enough to see in her descriptions of woman as having "a less extended grasp," and as being "enslaved to the species" the basis for the criticism that she is mixing biological facts with value judgments. However, Beauvoir is in fact not unaware that "factual" descriptions are insignificant in themselves and acquire meaning by being placed in a cultural context. As she notes at the opening of chapter 3: "these facts [above-mentioned] take on different values according to the economic and social context. In human history, grasp upon the world has never been defined by the naked body . . . on the contrary, technique may annul the muscular inequality of man and woman" (53). Consequently, although she acknowledges physical differences such as the relatively greater musculature of men over women, she correctly points out that this difference in itself signifies nothing. In fact, as she here argues, the large part of human history has been concerned with the improvement of technology, the historical effect of which has been to negate all the advantages of brute strength. Thus, she is arguing precisely contrary to what she ought to be if she were in fact holding some form of biological determinism. Again, in a related passage, Beauvoir astutely comments that the notion of "weakness" one presupposes depends upon both one's instruments and one's goals; in any case, bodily force alone is hardly the sole criterion for determining what power is (34). Even if one sums up all the physical differences between men and women, including the apparent inequalities, one cannot infer any truths about female experience from this "data." For, as Beauvoir is quick to note, the so-called biological facts do not set an inevitable destiny for woman, contrary to the Freudian estimation.[8] Rather, she maintains that woman's physical and physiological characteristics are themselves the effect, or result, of woman's social and material conditions, and so, they are inadequate to explain her subordinate social status.[9] So, while Beauvoir asserts that woman's biological characteristics place a kind of constraint on her experience, it does not follow that these characteristics stand as the explanatory determinants of her experience, for they are themselves accounted for in terms of social, economic, and cultural conditions, at the level which Beauvoir refers to as *situation*.

Before looking more closely at the significance of Beauvoir's term *situation* and how it relates to her view of the body, one needs to make mention of two fundamental threads of her analysis of woman. She subscribes, first, to the existentialist notion of humans as conscious beings able to shape themselves through freely chosen projects, and second, to some form of historical materialism. Both of these commitments are evident in chapter 3, "The Point of View of Historical Materialism," where she embraces the notion of humans as subject to historical material conditions, yet maintains that the Marxist theory itself is inadequate to explain the concrete situation for human beings: "to comprehend that situation we must look beyond the historical materialism that perceives in man and woman no more than economic units" (60). One may conclude that Beauvoir thinks that humans as conscious beings have the ability to transform their environment, yet as social beings they should be considered primarily in relation to the historical and economic conditions that to some extent determine them.

Although it may appear to some that existentialism and historical materialism are opposed on the issue of the extent to which human beings may choose their actions—with the former emphasizing individual freedom and the latter determination by material conditions—yet in both views there exists a combination of indeterminacy or freedom, and determinacy in the sense of being subject to certain unchosen conditions. Thus, Beauvoir's attempt to synthesize the two views should not be viewed as prima facie implausible. But leaving aside the larger issue of whether one can strike a precise balance between the existentialist and historical materialist conceptions of human beings, I find that Beauvoir tries to combine these two views in her general notion of situation. The task may appear less daunting to us once we note that

Beauvoir embraces a form of existentialism that does not insist on the radical and fundamental freedom of human beings to the exclusion of deterministic factors like race, class, or gender; she finds, instead that humans are only partly free because they are partly determined by various internal and external factors. In her introduction, Beauvoir actually points out several kinds of limiting factors on human freedom: here she insists on the seriousness of gender discrimination, likening it to forms of racial and ethnic discrimination. In her words: "whether it is a race, a caste, a class, or a sex that is reduced to a position of inferiority, the methods of justification are the same" (xxvii). Especially striking evidence of the latter in her analysis of women is the analogy Beauvoir draws between racial and gender discrimination: "there are deep similarities between the situation of woman and that of the Negro. Both are being emancipated today from a like paternalism, and the former master class wishes to 'keep them in their place'—that is, the place chosen for them" (xxvii). So, it may be said that in her analysis of women, Beauvoir eschews the radical freedom sometimes attributed to existentialists. Yet having stated this one cannot conclude thereby that woman for Beauvoir is not also responsible for her actions due to oppressive institutions and customs. On the contrary, it is precisely because she is free to some extent that Beauvoir criticizes the middle-class woman for her complicity in various patriarchal and sexist institutions which she can use to her advantage (xxi–xxxiii).

We may conclude that, on the one hand, Beauvoir claims that women as human beings are transcendent—able to choose their own projects—and yet, on the other hand, are often caught up in social and economic forces beyond their control, forced into *immanence*. So we see Beauvoir attempting to correct the extreme voluntarist form of existentialism with her insistence that we take a broader, historical view of human beings, as exemplified here in a passage from chapter 3: "The theory of historical materialism has brought to light some important truths. Humanity is not an animal species; it is a historical reality. Human society is an *antiphysis*—in a sense, it is against nature; it does not submit to the presence of nature but rather takes over the control of nature on its own behalf. This arrogation is not an inward, subjective operation; it is accomplished objectively in practical action" (53). We may draw a parallel, then, between Beauvoir's view of the position of human beings and of woman's situation in particular: both are culturally and historically bound, yet are not wholly subject to the social and economic constraints placed upon them. It is fitting, then, for Beauvoir to deny that any one set of given conditions, in this case, biological characteristics, could ever be fully determinative of feminine experience. Thus, she demurs in giving undue importance to physical or sexual properties in her explanation of woman: "Thus, woman could not be considered simply as a sexual organism, for among the biological traits, only those have importance that take on concrete value in action. Woman's awareness of herself is not defined exclusively by her sexuality; it reflects a *situation* that depends upon the economic organization of society, which in turn indicates what stage of technical evolution mankind has attained" (53). Beauvoir's point here is that biological characteristics are not themselves explanatory of feminine experience; rather, women's status and self-identity is constituted by the set of external, social conditions in which women find themselves. But if woman's self-awareness cannot be said to be determined by a natural, sexual identity, then it becomes untenable to claim Beauvoir subscribes to some form of biological reductionism.

We may now turn to our examination of Beauvoir's term "situation," a word that appears often in *The Second Sex* and one that has special significance in her analysis of the body. In general, Beauvoir uses "situation" to signify the specific historical and social contexts in which women find themselves to be *Other*, that is, relegated to a subordinate status relative to men. In these occurrences, the word clearly signifies the set of social, economic, and in general, material conditions that give rise to the psychological, subjective condition of being a woman. Significantly, she also chooses to analyze the concept of the body in terms of situation, the effect of which is to reconceive the body as a social construction, as opposed to a physical thing. In fact, we find both senses of "body" alluded to in the chapter on biology where Beauvoir asserts her preference for the constructivist conception of the body, in spite of her long discussion of the "alienating" aspects of female biological functions. Notwithstanding such comments, she employs the notion of situation to explain the sense in which the biological statements about "body" are to be considered. She distinguishes between two conceptions of "body": in one sense, it may be said to signify the body conceived of as inert matter or stuff, "a thing," as she terms it; in another sense, it signifies how the physical body is experienced, given the social and economic conditions, and here her term is situation.[10] Now the body conceived of in the first sense is roughly equivalent to the

Cartesian *res extensa*, extended matter lacking all thought, whereas in the second sense the notion presupposes thought and consciousness, and so, is anti-Cartesian. And it is just this latter sense of body that Beauvoir embraces in chapter 1, rejecting the Cartesian notion.[11]

It should be clear that seen from the perspective of situation, what "body" signifies is not an entity with certain invariant characteristics, but an entity whose features can change since the nature and value of bodies depends upon the social, historical, and economic context within which embodied individuals exist. In surprising fashion, Beauvoir then weaves the existentialist notion of human beings as incomplete in their nature with the Marxist view of human beings as subject to historical variants into the notion of the human situation:

> As Merleau-Ponty very justly puts it, man is not a natural species, he is an historical idea. Woman is not a completed reality, but rather a becoming, and it is in her becoming that she should be compared with man; that is to say, her *possibilities* should be defined. What gives rise to much of the debate is the tendency to reduce her to what she has been, to what she is today, in raising the question of her capabilities; for the fact is that capabilities are clearly manifested only when they have been realized—but the fact is also that when we have to do with a being whose nature is transcendent action, we can never close the books. (34)

The passage illuminates Beauvoir's existentialist notion of humans as dynamic beings, in her term, "transcendent," that create themselves through their activities.[12] Yet more striking is her insistence upon marrying this view with historicism in considering the meaning of woman's physical attributes. Thus, in spite of the fact that she claims woman's body to be weaker, less muscular, less stable, and to possess less lung capacity than a man's, she also argues that when interpreting the female body on the "basis of existence," such weakness is incomplete, without meaning. For, it is only within the context of certain social norms and values that differences in lung capacity and muscular mass have any significance. As Beauvoir rightly observes:

> "weakness" is revealed as such only in the light of the ends that man proposes, the instruments he has available, and the laws he

establishes. . . . In brief, the concept of *weakness* can be defined only with reference to existentialist, economic, and moral considerations. . . . Thus, while it is true that in the higher animals the individual existence is asserted more imperiously by the male than by the female, in the human species individual "possibilities" depend upon the economic and social situation. (34–35)

The direction of Beauvoir's analysis of woman's body, then, is toward subjecting the biological statements concerning the body to further historical and material analysis. For, as she consistently points out in the first three chapters, human biology is incomplete: biological "facts" about human beings cannot be interpreted in isolation from the relevant social and economic conditions in relation to which they take on value. She argues, for example, "these facts [biological facts] take on different values according to the economic and social context. In human history, grasp upon the world has never been defined by the naked body" (53).[13] Rather, "the value of muscular strength, of the phallus, of the tool can be defined only in a world of values" (60). So, at the close of the chapter on biology, she notes, "we must view the facts of biology in the light of an ontological, economic, social, and psychological context" (36).

Beauvoir thus sets forth a standard for assessing biological claims. But does she herself follow it? At first glance, it would appear that she does not carry out the promised broad analysis of biology in terms of social, economic, and existential factors. As previously noted, chapter 1 contains a number of statements that appear to be ahistorical and essentialist, such as that in intercourse, as in fertilization, woman experiences a "profound alienation," and that since the embryo requires the woman to become "other than herself," she becomes alienated from her body (22, 29, 32). Or, again, we find that in morning sickness we see "the revolt of the organism against the invading species" (30). I suggest, however, that it is unnecessary to read these claims as essentialist and masculinist. After all, it is only if we expect Beauvoir to be making ahistorical claims that we find this is the only possible interpretation. If, on the other hand, we acknowledge that she is not limited to describing the body as a *thing*, there is no need to read these statements as essentialist. Instead, as Arp (Chapter 10, this volume) demonstrates, Beauvoir's claim that the female is alienated from her body has to be interpreted as a description about the body as "situation," not about the body as a thing.[14] I suggest that once we acknowledge the legitimacy of analyzing the body as situation, we need not find her comments about woman's body as essentialistic and misogynistic. Instead of reading enslavement to the species, for example, as a description of the female body outside of social and historical context, I suggest that we consider it as a description of the female body under various patriarchal periods. Under this interpretation, the above-mentioned objections leveled against her discussion of the body are perhaps understandable, if unjustified. For it may be admitted that when Beauvoir makes these essentialist-sounding comments, she is not always careful to explain at which level she is speaking, and so sometimes invites confusion. As a consequence, some of what Beauvoir says about the female body appears to have escaped her critical lens and so, her work has achieved the reputation of evincing an aversion to "femininity" and specifically, to the female body.

Situating Maternity

"the close bond between mother and child will be for her a source of dignity or indignity according to the value placed upon the child—which is highly variable"

Of all the female experiences Beauvoir critically observes, perhaps her most controversial account is that of pregnancy and maternity. Mary O'Brien (1981), for example, finds that Beauvoir's account of motherhood simply repeats the traditional view that women are doomed by their biology: since maternity prevents women from participating in social, public life, women should refrain from becoming mothers, according to Beauvoir. Where Beauvoir errs, as O'Brien sees it, is in the initial assumption that female reproduction and birth is alienating; according to O'Brien, it is men who, in lacking the continuity between sexual intercourse and birth, are alienated from sexual reproduction (O'Brien 1981, 52–62). And so, O'Brien argues, since Beauvoir begins with the wrong premise about women's reproductive experience, she necessarily comes to the wrong conclusion about maternity. This criticism raises the question whether Beauvoir is, in fact, taking the position that women's biology necessarily entraps them so as to prevent their attaining equal status in society.

There is, as noted above, the appearance of a conflict in the text insofar as one interprets Beauvoir's comments ahistorically. So, for example, much has been made of the fact that Beauvoir describes the female reproductive capacity as making the woman the "prey to the species" (32), and that she seems to denigrate the usual functions of motherhood. But when Beauvoir speaks of the female's subordination to the species she is usually thinking of the host of unfavorable conditions under which women, lacking adequate food, health care, and contraceptive control, become pregnant and bear many children to the detriment of their well-being (30). In addition, she points out that regarding children as an universal panacea for one's happiness can be naive and harmful (521).

But having said this, we are not compelled to think that Beauvoir finds maternity always to have negative value for women. Beauvoir clearly wants to argue that the value of maternity, like pregnancy, depends upon the *situation* of the woman: the attitude she takes toward these experiences, her social and economic condition, and whether they are freely chosen acts or states imposed upon her.[15] Depending on the external conditions, as well as the psychological attitude of the mother, the experience of birth is variable among women, Beauvoir finds. Some women, she notes, find birth an enriching experience, one that gives them "a sense of creative power; [that] they have accomplished a voluntary and productive task," while for others the experience of birth makes them feel like passive instruments (506). So, too, with the experience of child-rearing: Beauvoir argues that the mother's relations to her child are not univocal, but vary according to the "situation." Some women feel alone and empty following birth, others welcome and find delight in the child, as Colette's description of her own feelings toward her daughter in *L'Etoile Vesper* which Beauvoir quotes: "I marvelled at the assemblage of prodigies that is the newborn child: her fingernails transparent as the pink shrimp's convex shell, the soles of her feet, which had come to us without touching the ground. The feathery lightness of her eyelashes, lowered on her cheeks or interposed between the scenery of the earth and the pale-blue dream in her eyes" (508). Beauvoir, in choosing to quote this and many other positive passages about motherhood, indicates her openness to the rewards of maternity. As she claims in her chapter on the mother, "the fact remains that unless the circumstances are positively unfavorable the mother will find her life enriched by her child" (511).

Beauvoir's general point in the discussion of motherhood has been overlooked by her critics in the presence of certain negative remarks. In this chapter, her theoretical objective is to restore the plurality of women's experience. By bringing together all kinds of accounts of motherhood, both literary and "scientific," Beauvoir effectively demonstrates: first that it is of necessity a heterogeneous experience, and second that since the former is true, there is no such thing as "maternal instinct." It is true that she thereby seeks to dispel a familiar assumption, namely, the notion that maternity is an univocal experience for women and one that in some way is a guarantee of their happiness, but for women living without contraception and adequate wealth, this would hardly seem to be controversial. So it is that Beauvoir dares to question whether one can say that human beings possess a maternal instinct, concluding that "the mother's attitude [toward the child] depends upon her total situation and her reaction to it. . . [which] . . . is highly variable" (511). So, although Beauvoir is hardly averse to pointing out the problems and pitfalls of maternity, neither is she blind to its potential as a source of positive experience. Rather, her point is to reveal two basic misconceptions about maternity: first, that it is not sufficient in itself to ensure woman's happiness; and second, that a child is not certain to be happy in its mother's arms (521, 523). Not only is her discussion adequate to this goal, but Beauvoir is surely right in arguing for these two premises. For the related notions that women are necessarily fulfilled by motherhood and that they are naturally good mothers ignores the role that negative conditions such as poverty, ignorance, and general deprivation play in the experience of mothers and children. Beauvoir is highly sensitive to these external conditions that may definitively color the experience of motherhood for women. So, while some feminists charge Beauvoir with classism (Spelman 1988), it is instead the feminists who insist on the primary place and value of motherhood who may themselves be guilty of a classist assumption, one that assumes that all women are able to undertake pregnancy voluntarily, in comfortable economic situations and supportive surroundings, enjoying good health care throughout. Of course, as Beauvoir admits, under favorable conditions, children are bound to be highly positive experiences for the woman, but society can hardly choose to disdain women as human beings, give them no economic support for being mothers, exclude them from public life and then expect them to find motherhood rewarding.

Nor do children raised under the conditions of inequality mentioned flourish, as the myth maintains. Instead, as Beauvoir notes, the social contempt for women is often played out in the relations among the family members, with the result that children suffer. Since there is nothing "natural" about maternal love, according to Beauvoir, there is the possibility that there be bad mothers (523), a point illustrated in her fiction with dramatic examples of mothers like Madame Blomart in *The Blood of Others* (1945) who is at once the passive, submissive martyr and a mother who causes both guilt and resentment in her son.[16] Yet Beauvoir's criticism of such mothers does not lie, as some think, with the relation itself, but rather with its present expression in society. Beauvoir's recommendation in the *Second Sex* is that society come to care for its children and help its mothers by furthering them in careers. She is right, I believe, in rejecting talk about the "sacred rights of the mother" and its attendant notion that through motherhood in the abstract woman somehow attains the social and political equality of men (525). However, having said this, she also holds that there is no essential conflict between woman's transcendence and maternity: "In a properly organized society where children would be largely taken in charge by the community and the mother cared for and helped, maternity would not be wholly incompatible with careers for women. . . . The woman who enjoys the richest individual life will have the most to give to her children and will demand the least from them; she who acquires in effort and struggle a sense of true human values will be best able to bring them up properly" (525). The emphasis in this discussion, then, lies in the social and economic context surrounding maternity, not in the institution in itself. Thus, the objection that Beauvoir deprecates motherhood misses the mark in failing to appreciate the historicized stance she adopts toward maternity. O'Brien's criticism that Beauvoir errs in neglecting the role of motherhood in the path toward woman's emancipation is thus flawed since Beauvoir eschews taking an ahistorical perspective in her analysis of maternity.[17] Furthermore, it appears that O'Brien confuses two senses of alienation that are at work in Beauvoir's discussion, one biological, one social, so that even if O'Brien is correct to dispute the idea sometimes suggested by Beauvoir that woman is biologically alienated in reproduction, she has not thereby disproved Beauvoir's other contention that woman is socially alienated in reproduction (Lazaro 1986). But as I have noted, even Beauvoir in her more careful moments rejects biological determinism as untenable, preferring to analyze woman's biological capacities in light of what she calls "the total situation."[18]

Constructing the Body

"it is not the body-object described by biologists that actually
exists, but the body as lived by the subject"

As Judith Butler (1986, 1989) has pointed out, Beauvoir's insight that
one *becomes* a woman ought to be interpreted as related to another, less
familiar idea, that there is no "natural" body. The argument for this
conclusion would be that just as for Beauvoir there is no gender identity
that one is born with, so, too, there is no sexual identity that one is
born with. Thus, the body itself should, on Beauvoir's grounds, come to
be seen as a cultural and historical idea, not as a natural fact. Yet the
notion of the physical body as a social artifact may strike some as
implausible; they would argue that the biological body is simply something natural or given. Yet it is precisely this notion with which Beauvoir
has tried to take issue in her distinction between the two senses of
"body," arguing that the relevant sense for understanding woman's
oppression is the sense in which the body is experienced by the subject,
and this body, surely, is a product of social and cultural meanings. Then
it becomes comprehensible how one must set aside the idea of a "natural
body"; that is, a body whose features are capable of being "neutrally" or
"scientifically" described, in order to understand how the body can be
socially constructed. If we approach Beauvoir's statement in volume 2
that one is not born but becomes a woman with her idea that the body
should be conceived of as a situation, we would not be led into thinking
that she intends that a "natural" body comes to take on a gendered
identity, or equally, that a genderless subject pre-exists the acquisition
of gender. As Butler (1989, 255) points out, it is incorrect to think that
Beauvoir's dictum implies either that some mysterious "I" exists apart
from the gendered subject or that an ungendered subject exists prior to
becoming female, since Beauvoir never assumes the existence of a
natural, ahistorical body.

As I have argued, Beauvoir's biological discussion needs to be
interpreted in relation to the historical comments with which she flags
such discussion. So, for example, when she claims that woman of all
mammals is the one most alienated by her biology (1989, 32), that her
body dooms her to immanence, she should be read as intending to say
that because woman's social and economic status throughout history has
been subordinate to men's, as a consequence her body has been despised
and derogated to the level of something shameful. Consequently, Beau-

voir's descriptions of women's biology should be interpreted in light of her further analysis of the roots of women's oppression, noting well that for her these roots are historical and cultural. So conceived, the claim that, for example, woman is "alienated" from her body should be taken as asserting a true proposition about women's bodies as conceived within patriarchal societies; biology thus repeats culture.[19]

On the interpretation I have proposed of how to read her claims about the female body and its biological capacities, Beauvoir is far from thinking that biology determines destiny in any straightforward sense. By the same reasoning, Beauvoir is not committed to maintaining that gender acquisition, that is, coming to be feminine or masculine, is a wholly deterministic process, although it may be limited by the social, historical, and economic conditions that place constraints on what counts as femininity and masculinity. Thus, if one were to place Beauvoir's position on the spectrum of determinist and indeterminist views, one would have to locate it on the end conventionally termed "indeterminist" since she maintains the reality of choice, although I do not find her holding that we possess the kind of contra-causal freedom characteristic of the libertarian position. In contrast to my reading of Beauvoir, Butler (1989, 1990) places more emphasis on the indeterminacy of gender and thereby upon the freedom that the individual has in attaining some gender identity. Butler even suggests that we may conceive of a wide spectrum of genders, expanding Beauvoir's insight that gender is culturally constructed so as to provide for a multiply gendered society. That is, Butler takes Beauvoir's fundamental insight that one becomes a woman to suggest that gender is, or should be, a fluid category. So, Butler reads Beauvoir as saying that although there is cultural constraint as to the general "shape" of gender that one becomes, one is nevertheless free to realize it in various ways. Concerning the relation of gender to body, one may say that the body becomes the stage, as it were, upon which one acts out one's gender identity. In this respect, gender is not a process that happens to the mute, static body—like poaching an egg—but it is an activity consciously engaged in by the subject, and one over which the subject herself can exert considerable control. Butler makes the point that "gender is a corporeal style, a way of acting the body, a way of wearing one's own flesh as a cultural sign," such that to become a woman means "to execute, institute, produce, reproduce, wear, flaunt, hide, and always stylize [one's womanhood] in one way or another" (Butler 1989, 256). If one can interpret the descriptions such as "acting the body" and "wearing one's own flesh" as nondualistic metaphors for the agency implicit in gender expression, I concur. Furthermore, the idea that gender is nondeterministic, or fluid, in the sense that it is historically and culturally contingent strikes me as both true and liberating, rather than defeatist or "masculinist." Beauvoir's account of how an apparently nonsocial thing, the human body, is in fact itself the product of profound social and historical forces is highly original, no feminist before Beauvoir thinking to analyze our very ideas about the body in this way. Furthermore, her account concerning the social and historical roots of the ideas about woman's body yields both a description of the malady and the suggestion for a cure. Insofar as she pinpoints certain prevalent Western cultural myths and assumptions about the female body that affect our present reasoning about women's bodies, she correctly diagnoses the problem, and insofar as she expresses the need for universal dignity and self-creation, she indicates the direction for social change to allow women to participate fully in the human arena.

Notes

1. Leaving aside the issue of whether one finds Beauvoir exemplifying what Iris Young (1985, 173) has called "humanist feminism" typical of the first wave of feminism, or as characterized more by radical feminism as Simons (this volume) maintains.

2. Similarly, current French feminists such as Irigaray and Cixous have found Beauvoir's thought to be "phallic feminism": see Kaufman McCall (1987) and Dallery (1985).

3. The page references to Beauvoir's *Le Deuxième Sexe* are to the English translation by H. M. Parshley, 1989 edition, from which the textual translations are also derived. On the issue of the adequacy of the Parshley translation, see Simons (1983).

4. Beauvoir is said to have composed the chapters of her work in the order in which she became conscious of the subject: see Felstiner (1987).

5. See Beauvoir (1989, 3), where Beauvoir is mentioning the reductionist view of woman defined solely in terms of her reproductive organs; in this account, woman is said to have but one ovary, not the actual two.

6. For example, "it nevertheless remains true that both a mind without a body and an immortal man are strictly inconceivable, whereas we can imagine a parthenogenetic or hermaphroditic society" (Beauvoir 1989, 7).

7. Beauvoir finds a similar virtue in Freudianism: it assumes the fundamental value of the body, which she takes to be the core of her own existentialist perspective: "what he [the subject] experiences as a body confronted by other bodies expresses his existential situation exactly" (Beauvoir 1989, 60).

8. As Beauvoir notes, "I deny that they [the biological facts] establish for her a fixed and inevitable destiny. They are insufficient for setting up a hierarchy of the sexes; they fail to explain why woman is the Other; they do not condemn her to remain in this subordinate role forever" (1989, 32–33). On the formulations offered by Freud, see Freud (1925, 1931, 1933).

9. See Beauvoir (1989), 697: "This does not mean that their ills [women's physical ills] are imaginary: they are as real and destructive as the situation to which they give expression. But the situation does not depend upon the body; the reverse is true. Thus, woman's health will not affect her work unfavorably when the woman worker comes to have the place she should." See also Beauvoir (1989), 32–33.

10. As she puts it, "it will be said that if the body is not a *thing*, it is a situation [si le corps n'est pas une chose, il est une situation (1949, 72)], as viewed in the perspective I am adopting—that of Heidegger, Sartre, and Merleau-Ponty; it is the instrument of our grasp upon the world, a limiting factor for our projects" (1989, 34).

11. See also Sartre's rejection of disembodied thought in his insistence that *transcendence* is embodied: "it would be best to say, using "exist" as a transitive verb, that consciousness *exists* its body" (Sartre 1947).

12. The correlative terms Beauvoir uses to describe the two modes of being are *transcendent* and *immanent*: the former signifies the way in which conscious beings exist (the pour-soi); the latter, the way in which nonconscious beings, i.e., static objects, exist (the en-soi: see Beauvoir 1989, xl–xli). Significantly, Beauvoir's analysis of woman's situation is that she, a transcendent being, is constrained (at least in part) to immanence: "every time transcendence falls back into immanence, stagnation, there is a degradation of existence into the *en-soi*—the brutish life of subjection to given conditions—and of liberty into constraint and contingence. This downfall represents a moral fault if the subject consents to it; if it is inflicted upon him, it spells frustration and oppression. In both cases, it is an absolute evil" (1989, xli).

13. On the same point, see Beauvoir (1989), 9, 14, 32–37, 38, 45, 49–50, 53–54. As I have previously suggested, Beauvoir's general point about the relation of biology as a science to economy suggests a Marxist interpretation of the relation of ideology, or superstructure, to the material base.

14. Beauvoir's account of how this alienation comes about is unfolded to us in subsequent chapters of her work, one part of the account being given through the analysis of the literary and mythic depictions of woman as body in volume 1 (chaps. 9–11), the other part given through the analysis of lived experience in volume 2.

15. See, for example, Beauvoir (1989), 54: "for the burdens of maternity, . . . are crushing if the woman is obliged to undergo frequent pregnancies and if she is compelled to nurse and raise children without assistance; but if she procreates voluntarily and if society comes to her aid during pregnancy and is concerned with child welfare, the burdens of maternity are light." See also Beauvoir (1989), 35.

16. See also Lucie Belhomme in *The Mandarins* (1954), Murielle in "Monologue," *The Woman Destroyed* (1967), her own mother in *A Very Easy Death* (1964). On Beauvoir and maternity, see Yolanda A. Patterson (1987).

17. See Mary O'Brien (1981), 74–75, for this criticism of Beauvoir's account of maternity. From O'Brien's use of *Second Sex*, it does not appear that she made use of the chapter on motherhood but relies instead on material in the first chapter on biology.

18. See, for example, Beauvoir (1989), 511: "the mother's attitude depends on her total situation and her reaction to it"; cf. Beauvoir (1989), 34.

19. Ruth Bleier (1984), herself a biologist, also holds that the historical reality of woman's biology, i.e., her reproductive capacity, is culturally constructed.

References

Beauvoir, Simone de. 1949. *Le Deuxième Sexe*. Paris: Gallimard.
———. 1954. *The Mandarins*. Paris: Gallimard.

————. 1964. *A Very Easy Death*. Paris: Gallimard.

————. 1967. *The Woman Destroyed*. Paris: Gallimard.

————. [1952] 1989. *The Second Sex*. Translated by H. M. Parshley. New York: Vintage.

Bleier, Ruth. 1984. *Science and Gender: A Critique of Gender and Its Theories on Women*. New York: Pergamon.

Butler, Judith. 1986. "Sex and Gender in Beauvoir's *Second Sex*." In *Simone de Beauvoir: Witness to a Century*. Special issue of *Yale French Studies* 72:35–49.

————. 1989. "Beauvoir's Philosophical Contribution." In *Women, Knowledge and Reality*, edited by Ann Garry and Marilyn Pearsall, 253–62. Boston: Unwin Hyman.

————. 1990. *Gender Trouble*. New York: Routledge.

Dallery, Arleen B. 1985. "Sexual Embodiment: Beauvoir and French Feminism." *Women's Studies International Forum* 8, no. 3:197–208.

Evans, Mary. 1987. "Views of Women and Men in the Work of Simone de Beauvoir." In *Critical Essays on Simone de Beauvoir*, edited by Elaine Marks, 172–84. Boston: G. K. Hall.

Felstiner, Mary. 1987. "Seeing *The Second Sex* through the Second Wave." *Feminist Studies* 6, no. 2:247–76.

Freud, Sigmund. 1925. "Some Psychical Consequences of the Anatomical Distinction between the Sexes." In *Complete Psychological Works of Sigmund Freud*, 19:241–60. London: Hogarth, 1961.

————. 1931. "Female Sexuality." In *Complete Psychological Works of Sigmund Freud*. 21:225–43. London: Hogarth, 1961.

————. 1933. "Femininity." In *Complete Psychological Works of Sigmund Freud*, 22:112–35. London: Hogarth, 1961.

Kaufman McCall, Dorothy. 1987. "Simone de Beauvoir: Questions of Difference and Generation." In *Simone de Beauvoir: Witness to a Century*. Special issue of *Yale French Studies* 72:121–31.

Lazaro, Reyes. 1986. "Feminism and Motherhood: O'Brien vs. Beauvoir." *Hypatia* 1, no. 2:87–102.

Léon, Céline T. 1988. "Simone de Beauvoir's Woman: Eunuch or Male?" *Ultimate Reality of Meaning* 11:196–211.

O'Brien, Mary. 1981. *The Politics of Reproduction*. London: Routledge and Kegan Paul.

Okely, Judith. 1986. *Simone de Beauvoir*. New York: Pantheon.

Patterson, Yolanda A. 1987. "Simone de Beauvoir and the Demystification of Motherhood." In *Simone de Beauvoir: Witness to a Century*. Special issue of *Yale French Studies* 72:87–105.

Sartre, Jean-Paul. 1947. *Being and Nothingness*. Translated by Hazel Barnes. New York: Philosophical Library.

Seigfried, Charlene H. 1984. "Gender-Specific Values." *Philosophical Forum* 15, no. 4:425–42.

————. 1985. "*Second Sex*: Second Thoughts." *Women's Studies International Forum* 8, no. 3:219–29.

Simons, Margaret A. 1983. "The Silencing of Simone de Beauvoir: Guess What's Missing From *The Second Sex*." *Women's Studies International Forum* 6:559–64.

Spelman, Elizabeth V. 1988. *Inessential Woman: Problems of Exclusion in Feminist Thought*. Boston: Beacon.

Young, Iris. 1985. "Humanism, Gynocentrism and Feminist Politics." *Women's Studies International Forum* 8, no. 3:173–83.

13

The Second Sex:
From Marxism to Radical Feminism

Margaret A. Simons

Despite the acknowledgment by radical feminist theorists of the women's liberation movement in the 1960s that Simone de Beauvoir provided a model for their theorizing,[1] *The Second Sex* (1949) has yet to find a secure place in the history of political philosophy.[2] The feminist philosopher Alison Jaggar, for example, whose pioneering work defined the categories of feminist political philosophy (i.e., liberal, socialist, and

A longer version of this paper was published as: "Beauvoir and the Roots of Radical Feminism," in *Selected Studies in Phenomenology and Existential Philosophy*, edited by Stephen Watson and Lenore Langsdorf (Albany: State University of New York Press, 1994). I gratefully acknowledge the helpful critical comments of Pamela Decoteau, Alison Jaggar, and members of the following organizations where earlier versions of this paper were presented: Midwest Division of the Society for Women in Philosophy, Philosophy and Women's Studies Colloquium at Loyola University, and the Society for Phenomenology and Existential Philosophy.

radical feminism), does not include a discussion of *The Second Sex* in her definitive text, *Feminist Politics and Human Nature*, despite her recognition of the "historical significance" of *The Second Sex* as "a forerunner of the contemporary women's liberation movement" (Jaggar 1983, 10).

Jaggar omits "religious and existentialist conceptions of women's liberation" (including Beauvoir's) because they fall "outside the mainstream of contemporary feminist theorizing" and she finds them "implausible" from her socialist feminist perspective (Jaggar 1983, 10). But I shall argue in this paper that far from being outside the mainstream of feminist philosophy, Beauvoir provides the very foundation for radical feminism in *The Second Sex*, where the historical importance of radical feminism to both socialist and radical black theorizing of racial oppression is apparent.

Demonstrating the foundational relationship of *The Second Sex* to radical feminism addresses one of Jaggar's fundamental criticisms of radical feminism: that it lacks a "comprehensive theoretical framework" and in particular any psychological explanation of male behavior. Ignoring Beauvoir's work in *The Second Sex*, Jaggar traces the roots of radical feminism to a "contradictory heritage" in "the basically liberal civil rights movement and in the Marxist-inspired left" (Jaggar 1983, 10–11). Liberal feminism and socialist feminism, in contrast, have strong foundations in the philosophies of Mill and Marx, respectively. But a recovery of Beauvoir's philosophy in *The Second Sex* can both reveal the philosophical foundation for radical feminism, and challenge the conception of the civil rights movement as "basically liberal," since Beauvoir drew upon the challenge to Marxist reductionism in radical black theorizing of racial oppression in formulating her theory. Her work thus challenges the definition of the feminist "mainstream" by affirming the interconnections of different forms of oppression while challenging the reductionism of identity politics.

In the discussion that follows I draw upon the definition of radical feminism provided by the feminist historian, Alice Echols (1989), author of *Daring To Be Bad: Radical Feminism in America, 1967–1975*, the first comprehensive historical study of the radical feminist movement. Echols, unlike Jaggar, makes a helpful distinction between radical feminism and "cultural feminism," the movement that followed it in the 1970s. Jaggar charges radical feminism with falling back on biological determinism for an explanation of men's behavior, defining women's oppression under patriarchy as seamless and absolute with women as absolute victims, and focusing on the construction of a womanculture as the sole political strategy. But Echols differentiates these "cultural feminist" positions from earlier radical feminism, which was "a political movement dedicated to eliminating the sex-class system." According to Echols, radical feminists were both "typically social constructionists who wanted to render gender irrelevant," and at least "implicitly" "anti-capitalists" who "believed that feminism entailed an expansion of the left analysis." Cultural feminists, in contrast, "conceived of feminism as an antidote to the left," "dismissed economic class struggle as 'male' and, therefore, irrelevant to women," and sought to establish a womanculture where " 'male values' would be exorcized and 'female values' nurtured" (Echols 1989, 6, 7, 5).

In Echols's view Jaggar's analysis of radical feminism reflects a misreading of the movement common to socialists: "Most leftist and socialist-feminists mistakenly characterized radical feminism as apolitical. To them radical feminism involved changing the 'cultural super-structure' and developing alternative life-styles, rather than effecting serious economic and political change. . . . So when radical feminism began to give way to cultural feminism, socialist feminists simply did not notice" (Echols 1989, 7). Echols can provide convincing evidence for the existence of a radical feminist movement that was social-constructionist and leftist in its critique of racism and economic class oppression. But her focus on American movement history prevents her from identifying Beauvoir's contribution to radical feminism in writing *The Second Sex* in France some twenty years earlier. To do that, it is most useful to adopt a methodology more akin to Jaggar's own philosophical analysis.

Echols's history of the movement reminds us that radical feminism was born out of dissatisfaction with both liberal feminism and socialism, and inspired by the transformation of the liberal civil rights struggle into the radical black power movement, a development that Jaggar does not acknowledge. In obvious parallels with radical black criticisms of the civil rights movement, radical feminists criticized liberal feminists for pursuing "formal equality within a racist, class stratified system, and for refusing to acknowledge that women's equality in the public domain was related to their subordination in the family" (Echols 1989, 3). Much like the radical black theorists who defended the specificity of the African-American experience against Marxist reductionism, radical feminists also differed from socialists "who attributed women's oppression to capitalism, whose primary loyalty was to the left, and who longed for the imprimatur of the 'invisible audience' of male leftists." For radical feminists "male supremacy was not a mere epiphenomenon" (Echols 1989, 3).

In *The Second Sex* Beauvoir rejects liberalism and its legalistic model of society as a public sphere governed by a social contract, and accepts instead a Marxist model of history as shaped by material factors and class struggle. Beauvoir recognized in 1949 the importance of the hard-fought battle for legal equality but saw it as insufficient. "Abstract rights . . . have never sufficed to assure woman a concrete hold on the world" (*DS* 1:223). Women have yet to attain "the union of abstract rights and concrete opportunities" without which "freedom is only a mystification" (*DS* 1:222). Even with many legal rights won, "the institutions and the values of patriarchal civilization have largely survived" (*DS* 1:223). Liberal individualism is no solution: "The success of a few privileged women can neither compensate for nor excuse the systematic degrada-tion on the collective level" (*DS* 1:222). The analysis of the causes of women's oppression would have to go much deeper.

In an important theoretical step toward radical feminism—one paral-leled by the radical African-American writer Richard Wright, whose work Beauvoir read and published in the 1940s—Beauvoir begins with a Marxist historical-materialist analysis of oppression and class struggle. In *The Second Sex* she argues that economic and technological develop-ments provided the conditions for a women's liberation struggle. The industrial revolution "transformed women's lot in the nineteenth century and . . . opened a new era for her" by enabling her "to escape from the home and take a new part in production in the factory," thus "winning again an economic importance lost to her since the prehistoric era" (*DS* 1:191). Developments in technology made this possible by "annulling the difference in physical strength between male and female workers in a large number of cases" (*DS* 1:191).

New methods of birth control "permitted the dissociation of two formerly inseparable functions: the sexual function and the reproductive function" (*DS* 1:199). Reproductive technology will provide the material conditions for further gains by women: "By artificial insemination the evolution will be achieved which will permit humanity to master the reproductive function. . . . [Woman] can reduce the number of her pregnancies, and integrate them rationally into her life instead of being a slave to them. . . . It is by the convergence of these two factors: participation in production and emancipation from the slavery of reproduction that the evolution of woman's condition is to be explained" (*DS* 1:203).

When economic developments in advanced capitalist societies freed bourgeois women from dependence on their families, the material conditions were laid for the collective struggle by women, across economic classes, for their liberation. Beauvoir's feminism is activist: the only recourse for women is the collective struggle for their own liberation. "Freedom remains abstract and empty in woman, and can be authentically assumed only in revolt. . . . There is no other issue for woman than to work for her liberation. This liberation can only be collective, and it demands before all else that the economic evolution of the feminine condition be achieved" (*DS* 2:455).

An analogy with racism was important to both 1960s radical feminists and Beauvoir, as is evident in this passage:

> Whether it's a question of a race, of a caste, of a class, of a sex reduced to an inferior condition, the processes of justification are the same: "the eternal feminine" is the homologue of "the black soul" and "the Jewish character." . . . [T]here are profound analogies between the situation of women and that of Blacks: both are emancipating themselves from a same paternalism and the formerly master caste wants to keep them in "their place," that is to say in the place the master caste has chosen for them. (*DS* 1:24)

Beauvoir's analysis of the underlying paternalism common to justifications of both sexism and racism bears striking resemblance to an essay by Alva Myrdal, "A Parallel to the Negro Problem," included as an appendix to the classic text on American racism *An American Dilemma: The Negro Problem and Modern Democracy* (Myrdal, Sterner, and Rose 1944), a book Beauvoir consulted while writing *The Second Sex*.

For Beauvoir ethnocentrism seems to encompass sexism historically in the experience of alterity. Women were not the original, or the only Other: "[Woman] has not represented the sole incarnation of the Other for [man], and she has not always kept the same importance in the course of history" (*DS* 1:234). Drawing on the structuralism of Lévi-Strauss, Beauvoir argues that: "The category of the *Other* is as original as consciousness itself. In the most primitive societies, in the most ancient mythologies, one finds the expression of a duality—that of the

Same and the Other. This duality was not originally attached to the division of the sexes. . . . Jews are 'others' for the antisemite, Blacks for the American racists, indigenous peoples for the colonialists, the proletariat for the class of owners" (*DS* 1:16).

According to Jaggar, the defining feature of radical feminist theory, which set it apart from liberal and Marxist theories "was a conviction that the oppression of women was fundamental: that is to say, it was causally and conceptually irreducible to the oppression of any other group" (Jaggar 12). Echols agrees that radical feminists "expanded the left analysis" of oppression and "argued that women constituted a sex class, that relations between women and men needed to be recast in political terms, and that gender rather than class was the primary contradiction" (Echols 6, 3). Beauvoir's support for this fundamental claim is evident in the following passage from *The Second Sex*, where she acknowledges Marxist insights into the historically changing role of technology and economic factors in shaping women's lives, but criticizes Marxism for failing to recognize the irreducible nature of women's oppression: "Engels does not recognize the singular character of this oppression. He tried to reduce the opposition of the sexes to a class conflict. . . . It's true that the division of work by sex and the oppression that results from it evokes the class division on certain points. But one must not confuse them. . . . The situation of the woman is different, singularly due to the community of life and interests that renders her in solidarity with the man, and by the complicity which he meets in her" (*DS* 1:101). For Beauvoir, "the bond that attaches [woman] to her oppressors is comparable to no other" (*DS* 1:19).

To expand Marxism to include an analysis of gender oppression, and to argue on one level for the primacy of gender contradiction, as later radical feminists would, Beauvoir returns to the philosophical roots of Marxism in Hegel's distinction between immanence and transcendence and his analysis of the master/slave relation. Turning Hegel against himself, Beauvoir argues that his description of the relationship of men, whose warfare and inventions create values that transcend the mere repetition of Life, and women, whom biology destines to immanence, to the passive and dependent reproduction of Life, is more reflective of the absolute opposition of the master/slave relationship than any relationship between men: "Certain passages of the dialectic by which Hegel defines the relation of the master to the slave would better apply to the relation of the man to the woman. . . . Between the male and she there has never been combat. Hegel's definition applies singularly to her" (*DS* 1:112).

Beauvoir described the relationship between men and women as a "caste" relationship defined by struggle: "All oppression creates a state of war; this is no exception" (*DS* 2:561). "[W]oman has always been, if not the slave of man, at least his vassal" (*DS* 1:20). In the past,

> the woman confined to immanence tried to keep the man in this prison as well. . . . She denied his truth and his values. . . . Today, the combat takes on another face. Instead of wanting to enclose man in a dungeon, woman is trying to escape from it herself. She no longer attempts to drag him into the regions of immanence but to emerge into the light of transcendence. . . . It is no longer a question of a war between individuals each enclosed in their sphere. A caste with demands mounts an assault and it is held in check by the privileged caste. (*DS* 2:561–62)

For Beauvoir, a historical analysis is necessary to understand the differences between women and other oppressed groups, and explain why women's liberation has been so long in coming:

> [Women] have no past, no history, no religion of their own; and they have no such solidarity of work and interest as that of the proletariat. They are not even promiscuously herded together in the way that creates community feeling among the American Blacks, the ghetto Jews, the workers of Saint-Denis, or the factory hands at Renault. They live dispersed among the males, attached through residence, housework, economic condition, and social standing to certain men—fathers or husbands—more firmly than they are to other women. (*DS* 1:19)

This situation elicits woman's moral complicity with her oppression, a willingness to accept dependence as a way of fleeing the responsibility of freedom facing any existent. Women are not simply victims in Beauvoir's analysis, as Jaggar charges of radical feminism. Beauvoir argues, in anticipation of the later radical feminist "pro-woman line" (Echols 91–92), that women find both material and ontological advantages from their dependence on men.

But unlike many radical feminists, Beauvoir also holds women morally responsible for complicity with their own oppression once an alternative is presented to them:

> To decline to be the Other, to refuse complicity with the man, would be for women to renounce all the advantages conferred upon them by their alliance with the superior caste. Man-the-sovereign will provide woman-the-liege with material protection and will undertake the justification of her existence; thus she can evade at once both economic risk and the metaphysical risk of a freedom which must invent its ends without aid. . . . The man who makes woman an Other will then meet profound complicities in her. Thus, woman may fail to claim herself as subject because she lacks the concrete means to do it, because she feels the necessary bond that ties her to man regardless of reciprocity, and because she is often well pleased with her role as *Other*. (*DS* 1:21)

The complexity of Beauvoir's analysis of gender difference and women's oppression is evident in her critiques of Marxism and psychoanalysis. Both theories attempt, unsuccessfully, to apply a model derived from men's experience to women. Beauvoir's version of existential phenomenology provides her with the ontological and methodological grounds for reclaiming the specificity of women's experience while avoiding the essentialism of identity politics. Her criticism of the Marxist analysis of woman's situation is both existentialist and feminist. She charges Marxist economic reductionism with denying the reality of woman's lived experience.

Engels's attempt to reduce woman's situation, including her reproductive role, to economic production is "not tenable." Sexuality and maternity are dramas in the lives of individual women that defy integration into society and control by the State. "One cannot without bad faith consider woman uniquely as a worker. Her reproductive function is as important as her productive capacity, as much in the social economy as in individual life. . . . Engels evaded the problem; he limited himself to declaring that the socialist community will abolish the family: it is an abstract solution indeed" (*DS* 1:102).

The practice in the Soviet Union reveals the limits of such a reductionist theory, which fails to recognize the patriarchal power of the State as oppressive to women. "Suppressing the family is not necessarily to emancipate the woman: the example of Sparta and the Nazi regime prove that by being directly bound to the State she can be no less oppressed by the males" (*DS* 1:102). In the interest of rebuilding its population, the Soviet Union was trying to once again "enclose her in situations where maternity is for her the only outlet. . . . These are exactly the old patriarchal constraints that the USSR is resuscitating today. . . . This example shows well that it is impossible to consider the woman uniquely as a productive force" (*DS* 1:103).

For Beauvoir a true socialist revolution must affirm, not deny individualism, and thus acknowledge gender difference in individual experience and the uniqueness of women's situation. "For a democratic socialism where class will be abolished but not individuals, the question of individual destiny will keep all of its importance: sexual differentiation will keep all its importance. The sexual relation which unites the woman to the man is not the same as that which he sustains with her; the link which bonds her to the child is irreducible to every other. She was not created only by the bronze tool, the machine will not suffice to abolish her. Demanding for her all the rights, all the chances of the human being in general does not signify that one must blind oneself to her singular situation. And to become acquainted with it one must go beyond historical materialism that sees in man and woman only economic entities" (*DS* 1:103).

So Marxism, by imposing a male theoretical model of economic production on women's experience, falsifies the experiences of individual women and fails to provide the grounds for challenging patriarchal oppression of women by a male-dominated socialist state. Beauvoir's rejection of the mystification of gender difference by antifeminists and cultural feminists thus does not entail the denial of gender differences in the lives of individual women.

Beauvoir argues that psychoanalysis as well as Marxism reduces women's experience to that of men, thus silencing women. Her argument against essentialist reductionism reflects an existentialist ontology that links her with the new left's "politics of experience" and 1960s radical feminism. It also differentiates her position from that of cultural feminism, and in its combination of cultural critique and celebration of spontaneity and the transgressing of boundaries, aligns her with postmodernism.[3]

Beauvoir criticizes Freud's psychoanalytic theory for attempting to impose a male model onto female experience: "Freud concerned himself little with the destiny of the woman; it is clear that he modelled it on the description of the masculine destiny of which he limited himself to modifying several traits" (DS 1:78). Freud "admitted that woman's sexuality is as evolved as man's; but he scarcely studied it in itself. He wrote: 'The libido is in a constant and regular fashion essentially male, whether it appears in a man or a woman.' He refused to pose the feminine libido in its originality" (DS 1:79).

By relying on a reductive male model of female sexuality, Beauvoir argues, Freud was unable to explain either penis envy or the Electra complex, primary features of his psychology of woman. Freud "supposed that the woman felt herself to be a mutilated man. But the idea of mutilation implies a comparison and a valorization . . . it cannot be born from a simple anatomical confrontation. . . . Freud took [this valorization] for granted when it was necessary to account for it" (DS 1:81).

An adequate explanation of both penis envy and the Electra complex, in which Freud accounts for women's heterosexuality, would require that one leave the confines of the psychoanalytic model and examine the larger social, historical, and ontological dimensions of individual life and woman's oppression:, "Psychoanalysis can only find its truth in the historical context" (DS 1:90). "The fact that feminine desire focussed on a sovereign being [as it does in the Electra complex] gives it an original character; but [feminine libido] is not constitutive of its object, it submits to it. The sovereignty of the father is a fact of the social order, and Freud fails to account for it" (DS 1:82).

Thus for Beauvoir a primary feature of the development of female heterosexuality and the transference of a girl's attraction from her mother to her father, is the father's sovereignty, that is, the social context of woman's oppression. Here we see Beauvoir extending social constructivism to sexuality. Her alternative description of the female libido further undermines the assumption of normative female heterosexuality by postulating an original resistance and repulsion toward men. Psychoanalysts who have approached the female libido only from the male libido, "seem to have ignored the fundamental ambivalence of the attraction that the male exerts on the female. . . . It is the indissoluble synthesis of attraction and of repulsion that characterizes it." Psychoanalysis has failed to acknowledge gender difference in female sexuality: "The idea of a 'passive libido' disconcerts because one has defined the libido on the basis of the male as drive, energy; but neither could one conceive *a priori* that a light could be at once yellow and blue; it's necessary to have the intuition of green" (*DS* 1:91). Beauvoir's social constructivist analysis of sexual difference, and her challenge, albeit limited, to normative female heterosexuality anticipates the later radical feminist critiques of "compulsory heterosexuality."

But in arguing for gender difference, Beauvoir avoids essentialist claims. She lays the groundwork for an appreciation of differences among women in arguing against the reductionism of Freudian psychoanalytic theory: "One must not take sexuality as an irreducible given. . . . Work, war, play, art define manners of being in the world which do not allow themselves to be reduced to any other" (*DS* 1:86–87). Sexuality is one manner among others of ontologically discovering the world. Thus Beauvoir, unlike the radical feminists described by Echols, rejects the a priori primacy of sexual difference. An individual women establishes a unity among her activities as she chooses herself through her work, play, struggles, and sexuality.

Beauvoir criticizes psychoanalytic theory for reducing women to passive objects in the world and for denying women the possibility of authentic choices. "We will situate woman in a world of values and we will give to her actions a dimension of freedom. We think that she has to choose between the affirmation of her transcendence and her alienation as an object; she is not the plaything of contradictory drives; she invents solutions between which exist an ethical hierarchy" (*DS* 1:92). In describing a subject's failure to effect a transference or a sublimation (and surely the most obvious example here is in the "failure" of a woman to become a heterosexual), a psychoanalyst, Beauvoir argues, "does not suppose that they perhaps refused it and that perhaps they had good reasons for doing so; one does not want to consider that their conduct could have been motivated by ends freely posed" (*DS* 1:93).

Freedom is a central theme of *The Second Sex*. If "one is not born a woman" (*DS* 2:13), then with the reality of social intervention comes the possibility of individual action, as Butler argues (Butler 1986). Beauvoir is celebrating woman's freedom, the expansion of her choices, not confinement in a role, whether defined by Freud, or by implication here, essentialist identity politics. In her critique of psychoanalytic theory Beauvoir rejects as inauthentic the pursuit of Being, of a substantive self, which was to become prominent in cultural feminism.

In the psychoanalytic sense "to identify oneself" with the mother or the father is to *alienate oneself* in a model; it is to prefer an alien image to the spontaneous movement of her own existence, to play at being. One shows us woman solicited by two modes of alienation; it is indeed evident that playing at being a man will be a source of failure for her. But playing at being a woman is also a trap. To be a woman would be to be an object, the *Other*; and the Other remains subject in the heart of its abdication. The real problem for woman is refusing these flights in order to accomplish herself as transcendence. (*DS* 1:92–93)

Beauvoir's description of the contemporary struggle as one in which women claim the values of "transcendence" and refuse the limits of "immanence" differentiates her from the cultural feminist position Echols describes as seeking a womanculture where " 'male values' would be exorcized and 'female values' nurtured" (Echols 5). For Beauvoir, women's "demand is not to be exalted in their femininity; they want transcendence to prevail over immanence for themselves as for all of humanity" (*DS* 1:222).

In truth women have never opposed female values to male values. It is men desirous of maintaining the masculine prerogatives who have invented this division. They have claimed to create a feminine domain—realm of life and immanence—only in order to enclose woman there. It is beyond all sexual specification that the existent seeks her justification in the movement of her transcendence. . . . What [women] are demanding today is to be recognized as existents as men are and not to subjugate existence to life, man to his animality. (*DS* 1:113)

But Beauvoir's theory of gender difference is complex. She rejects both the mystification of gender difference and the abstract, gender-free nominalism of liberal modernity as well.

Some feminist critics, such as Iris Young (1990) have charged *The Second Sex* with typifying a nineteenth-century "humanist feminism" that, leaving gender largely unexamined, calls on women to assume men's public roles. Beauvoir does reject the mystification of gender difference typical of both nineteenth-century antifeminists, who argued that women's intellectual and physical inferiority and sensitive natures warranted their exclusion from public life and confinement to the private sphere, and their contemporaries, the "domestic feminists," who argued that women should have access to both education and the vote in order to improve and extend the influence of their special moral sense. But Beauvoir does not deny there are differences.

In the introduction to *The Second Sex*, Beauvoir differentiates her position from modernism, from "the philosophy of the enlightenment, of rationalism, of nominalism; women, to them, are merely the human beings arbitrarily designated by the word *woman*. . . . But nominalism is a rather inadequate doctrine. . . . Surely woman is, like man, a human being; but such a declaration is abstract. The fact is that every concrete human being is always singularly situated. To decline to accept such notions as the eternal feminine, the black soul, the Jewish character, is not to deny that Jews, Blacks, women exist today—this denial does not represent a liberation for those concerned, but rather a flight from reality. It is clear that no woman can claim without bad faith to situate herself beyond her sex" (*DS* 1:12–13).

Beauvoir is a social constructionist who sees women's liberation as requiring the dismantling of the male cultural construct of woman as Other. She certainly wants women to gain access to the public sphere, to escape the confines of women's traditional role of wife and mother, to emerge as an individual. But the public sphere will be transformed in the process: "The future can only lead to a more and more profound assimilation of the woman into the *formerly* masculine society" (*DS* 1:216; my emphasis). She describes how philosophy, for example, has been distorted by men who have taken their own unique perspective as absolute. Her alternative is not to argue for the possibility of an absolute perspective without differences, that is, a return to the nominalism of modernity, but to both critique the male claim to objectivity and to begin constructing a knowledge based on a phenomenological description of women's experience. Hence the title of the second volume "Lived Experience," where Beauvoir tries to move outside the context of men's constructions of woman as Other, which are primarily useful in understanding not women but the men themselves, into women's ways of knowing their own experience.

Beauvoir does not demand access to a gender-free objectivity of modernity, but rather challenges the objective/subjective dualism itself and provides a phenomenological description of how men's perspectives shape their views of women, and reality. Laying the groundwork for women's studies in her feminist cultural critique, Beauvoir argues that men, in defining knowledge from their own point of view, have mistaken that perspective as absolute: "[Man] seizes his body as a direct and normal connection with the world, which he believes he apprehends in its objectivity, whereas he regards the body of woman as an obstacle, a prison, weighed down by what specifies it" (DS 1:14). "She is defined and differentiated with reference to man and not he with reference to her; she is the inessential as opposed to the essential. He is the Subject, he is the Absolute—she is the Other" (DS 1:15).

According to Beauvoir, Lévinas exemplifies this masculinist view in his essay Le Temps et l'Autre where he writes that: " 'Otherness reaches its full flowering in the feminine, a term of the same rank as conscious-ness but of opposite meaning.' I suppose that Lévinas does not forget that woman is also consciousness for herself. But it is striking that he deliberately takes a man's point of view, disregarding the reciprocity of subject and object. . . . Thus his description, which is intended to be objective, is in fact an assertion of masculine privilege" (DS 1:15). Beauvoir would have men, as well as women, claim the subjectivity of their situated consciousnesses, rather than lay claim to false objectivity.

Beauvoir's psychological explanation of men's behavior is derived from her close reading of myths and male-authored texts with which she began her research for The Second Sex. Her analyses of the images of women in the works of Montherlant, D. H. Lawrence, Claudel, Breton, and Stendhal provided the model for Millett's cultural critique in Sexual Politics. Psychologically, men's oppression of women is, in Beauvoir's existential analysis, an inauthentic attempt to evade the demands of authentic human relationships and the ambiguous realities of human existence. For men who would define themselves as pure spirit, women represent an odious link to the absurd contingency of a man's own life: his birth, embodiment, and death. "In all civilizations and in our own day, [woman] inspires horror in man: it is horror of his own carnal contingence which he projects onto her" (DS 1:242).

Woman as Other also seems a privileged prey of men desirous of the confirmation of self found in relationships with others, and yet fearful of the dangers in relationships with their peers. "[Woman] opposes to him neither the enemy silence of nature, nor the hard exigencies of a reciprocal recognition; by a unique privilege she is a consciousness and yet it seems possible to possess her in her flesh. Thanks to her, there is a means of escaping the implacable dialectic of master and slave which has its source in the reciprocity of freedoms" (DS 1:233).

Authentic human relationships, on the contrary, must be constantly created. Beauvoir's vision does not offer a comforting if static social order, but a future of ceaseless struggle in morally challenging relationships. According to Beauvoir, the master/slave dialectic can be surmounted, but only by

> the free recognition of each individual in the other, each posing at once himself and the other as object and as subject in a reciprocal movement. But friendship, generosity, which realize concretely this recognition of freedoms, are not easy virtues. They are assuredly the highest accomplishment of man, the means by which he finds himself in his truth. But this truth is that of a struggle forever opening up, forever abolished; it demands that man surmount himself at each instant. One could say also in another language that man attains an authentic moral attitude when he renounces *being* in order to assume his existence. (*DS* 1:232)

"One is not born, but rather becomes a woman." This familiar quotation (eloquently translated by Parshley) which opens volume 2 of *The Second Sex*, indicates Beauvoir's social constructionism, a position Echols sees as key in differentiating radical feminism from the biological determinism of cultural feminism. In fact Jaggar unknowingly points toward Beauvoir as a theoretical source for the social constructivism of radical feminism in recognizing Monique Wittig as one of the few radical feminists to reject biological determinism; Jaggar cites Wittig's influential 1979 essay "One is not born a woman"—clear reference to Beauvoir.

Judith Butler has argued that Beauvoir's concept of the body as situation "suggests an alternative to the gender polarization of masculine disembodiment and feminine enslavement to the body" (Butler 1986, 45). For Beauvoir, Butler writes, "any effort to ascertain the 'natural' body before its entrance into culture is definitionally impossible, not only because the observer who seeks this phenomenon is him/herself entrenched in a specific cultural language, but because the body is as well. The body is, in effect, never a natural phenomenon" (Butler 46). Butler draws our attention to the conclusion of the biology chapter in *The Second Sex*, where Beauvoir writes: "it is not merely as a body, but rather as a body subject to taboos, to laws, that the subject takes consciousness of himself and accomplishes itself. . . . It is not physiology that can found values; rather, the biological givens assume those that the existent confers upon them" (*DS* 1:75).

If Beauvoir's view, Butler argues, is that the body exists as a locus of cultural interpretations, "then Simone de Beauvoir's theory seems implicitly to ask whether sex was not gender all along," a view radicalized in the work of Monique Wittig and Foucault who both "challenge the notion of natural sex and expose the political uses of biological discriminations in establishing a compulsory binary gender system" (Butler 47). Butler, it should be noted, claims that Foucault, a student of Merleau-Ponty, was not influenced by Beauvoir. But an indirect influence is not unlikely given Merleau-Ponty's long association with Beauvoir.

Beauvoir "suggests," according to Butler, "that a binary gender system has no ontological necessity" (Butler 47). In fact, Beauvoir argues explicitly against the ontological necessity of sexual dimorphism earlier in the biology chapter. Beauvoir argues there against Hegel that "it is in exercising sexual activity that men define the sexes and their relations as they create the sense and the value of all the functions that they accomplish: but [sexual activity] is not necessarily implied in the nature of the human body" (*DS* 1:39). "The perpetuation of the species appears as the correlative of individual limitation. One can thus consider the phenomenon of reproduction as ontologically founded. But we must stop there. The perpetuation of the species does not entail sexual differentiation. If [sexual differentiation] is assumed by existents in such a manner that in return it enters into the concrete definition of existence, so be it. It nonetheless remains that a consciousness without a body and an immortal man are rigorously inconceivable, while one can imagine a society reproducing itself by parthenogenesis or composed of hermaphrodites" (*DS* 1:40).

Butler's analysis provides an alternative reading of existentialist concepts of freedom and choice found in radical feminism, which Jaggar discredits as liberal and idealist (as in one "choosing a sex role" from a transsocial standpoint). For Butler:

> In making the body into an interpretive modality, Beauvoir has extended the doctrines of embodiment and prereflective choice that characterized Sartre's work. . . . Simone de Beauvoir, much earlier on and with greater consequence [than Sartre himself], sought to exorcise Sartre's doctrine of its Cartesian ghost. She

gives Sartrean choice an embodied form and places it in a world thick with tradition. To "choose" a gender in this context is not to move in upon gender from a disembodied locale, but to reinterpret the cultural history which the body already wears. The body becomes a choice, a mode of enacting and reenacting received gender norms which surface as so many styles of the flesh. (Butler, 48)

Beauvoir's rejection of the mystification of gender difference evident in her ontology is based, in part, on her analysis of the historical deployment of an ideology of difference in women's oppression. She concludes from her historical analysis in *The Second Sex* that: "Those epoques that regard woman as the *Other* are those that refuse most bitterly to integrate her into society as a human being. Today she is becoming a fellow *other* only in losing her mystical aura. Antifeminists are always playing on this equivocation. They gladly agree to exalt woman as *Other* in order to constitute her alterity as absolute, irreducible, and to refuse her access to the human *Mitsein* [being-with]" (*DS* 1:120). Beauvoir's intent, here as elsewhere, is not to deny gender difference as women experience it concretely, but to demystify it.

In the nineteenth century, glorification of woman's difference was common to both antifeminists such as Comte and Balzac, as well as utopian socialists such as the Saint-Simonians, who, in a foreshadowing of the goddess worship of contemporary cultural feminism, awaited the advent of the female messiah. But neither, according to Beauvoir, served well the interests of women's liberation: "The doctrines that call for the advent of the woman as flesh, life, immanence, as the Other, are masculine ideologies that in no way express feminine demands" (*DS* 1:217).

Beauvoir's analysis of the historical relationship of socialism and goddess worship provides an interesting context for reading the critiques of cultural feminism in both Jaggar and Echols. Some utopian socialists of the nineteenth century such as Saint-Simon, Fourier, and Cabet called for an end to all slavery and for the ideal of the "free woman." But later followers of Saint-Simon, "exalted woman in the name of her femininity, which is the surest means of her disservice." Enfantin "awaited the coming of a better world from the woman messiah, and the Companions of the Woman embarqued for the Orient in search of the female savior." But for all the glorification of the feminine, with few exceptions, "women held only a secondary place in the Saint-Simonien movement" (DS 1:189). The socialist Flora Tristan, we learn later, also "believed in the redemption of the people by the woman, but she interested herself in the emancipation of the working class rather than in that of her own sex" (DS 1:190). Thus socialism, which Jaggar argued could provide the only clear alternative to goddess worship and cultural feminism, is, ironically, itself a historically problematic root of both.

Beauvoir's historical analysis reveals other limitations of socialism for feminists, problems still apparent in contemporary socialism. There was Fourier, for example, "who confused the enfranchisement of women with the rehabilitation of the flesh. . . . He considered woman not in her person but in her amorous function" (DS 1:189). But the most serious problem for socialist feminism stems from the reductive Marxist analysis that conceives of women's liberation as contained within the proletariat revolution instead of, as Beauvoir argues, requiring women's own collective struggle as a separate development.

In arguing for the importance of recognizing gender difference in experience, Beauvoir does not maintain that the relationship between men and women has been historically unchanging. Her analysis of women's oppression is not a simple analogy, neither trivializing other forms of oppression nor asserting that gender is always the primary contradiction. Class differences figure prominently in Beauvoir's analysis of how the historically different situations of bourgeois and proletariat women have undermined feminist solidarity and activism. For example, in her analysis of the bourgeois French Revolution, Beauvoir argues that neither working-class women, "who experienced, as women, the most independence," nor bourgeois women were able to make many gains: "The women of the bourgeoisie were too integrated into the family to know any concrete solidarity among themselves; they did not constitute a separate caste able to impose their demands: economically, their existence was parasitic. Thus the women who, despite their sex, would have been able to participate in the events were prevented from doing so by their class, while those of the activist class were condemned as women to remain at a distance" (DS 1:184). No analysis that ignores class differences can understand the history of women's oppression and the problems of feminist activism.

Beauvoir criticized the so-called independent French feminist movement at the turn of the twentieth century for reflecting bourgeois interests. But the "revolutionary feminism" of the same era, which "took up the Saint-Simonien and Marxist tradition," also contributed to the internal divisions that were the source of the "weakness of feminism." "Women lacked solidarity as sex; they were first linked to their class; the interests of the bourgeois women and those of the proletariat women did not intersect. . . . Louise Michel pronounced herself against feminism because this movement only served to divert forces which ought to be in their entirety employed in the class struggle; women's lot will find itself well ordered by the abolition of capital." "Since it is from the emancipation of workers in general that women await their freedom, they only attach themselves in a secondary manner to their own cause" (DS 1:205).

Beauvoir reserves her highest praise for the Woman's Social and Political Union established in Britain by the Pankhursts around 1903. Progressive without putting women's issues second; it was "allied with the laborist party," and "undertook a resolutely militant action." "It is the first time in history that one sees women try an effort as women: that is what gives a particular interest to the adventure of the "suffragettes' in Britain and America." In a detailed account, deleted by Parshley from the English edition, Beauvoir pays tribute to their inventiveness: "During fifteen years they led a campaign of political pressure which recalls on certain sides the attitude of a Gandhi: refusing violence, they invented more or less ingenious substitutes" (DS 1:208).

Identifying with an earlier feminist movement, drawing on insights of radical African-American theorists of racial oppression, Beauvoir, in The Second Sex, laid the theoretical foundations for a radical feminist movement of the future and defined a feminist political philosophy of lasting importance.

Notes

1. See Kate Millett's discussion of Beauvoir, for example, in Forster and Sutton (1989), 21–23. See also Echols (1989) who writes that "[Ti-Grace] Atkinson had read Simone de Beauvoir's The Second Sex in 1962, and, like so many other women who helped spark the second wave of feminism, she was profoundly affected by it." Echols elaborates in a footnote: "For instance, Roxanne Dunbar of Cell 16 cited The Second Sex as the book that 'changed our lives.' Shulamith Firestone dedicated her book The Dialectic of Sex to de Beauvoir. And Katie Sarachild called the book 'crucial to the development of the W[omen's] L[iberation] M[ovement]' " (Echols 1989, 167, 337 n. 155).

2. Mistranslations of philosophical terms and unindicated deletions in the English translation by H. M. Parshley are barriers to the philosophical analysis of The Second Sex. For a

critical discussion of these problems, see Margaret A. Simons (1983). Passages from the Simons article are included without quotation marks or citation in the introduction to the most recent edition of *The Second Sex* (Bair 1989, xxii).

3. In fact Linda Singer has argued, in a ground-breaking 1985 article that Beauvoir's "gynocentric" feminism is an "unacknowledged source" of the postmodern discourse "of 'difference' of deconstruction." According to Singer, by "taking the insights of existentialism seriously with respect to its denial of a supervening perspective and its affirmation of the situational character of discourse, Beauvoir begins the project of writing the other side, of giving voice to the discourse of otherness" (Singer 1990, 324–25).

References

Bair, Deirdre. 1989. Introduction to *The Second Sex*, by Simone de Beauvoir, translated by H. M. Parshley, xiii–xxiii. New York: Vintage Books.

Beauvoir, Simone de. 1949. *Le Deuxième Sexe*. 2 vols. Paris: Gallimard; cited in text as DS; all quotations are my translation unless otherwise indicated.

Butler, Judith. 1986. "Sex and Gender in Simone de Beauvoir's *Second Sex*." In *Simone de Beauvoir: Witness to a Century*. Special issue of *Yale French Studies* 72:35–49.

Echols, Alice. 1989. *Daring To Be Bad: Radical Feminism in America, 1967–1975*. Minneapolis: University of Minnesota Press.

Forster, Penny, and Imogen Sutton, eds. 1989. "Kate Millett." In *Daughters of de Beauvoir*, 17–31. London: Women's Press.

Jaggar, Alison. 1983. *Feminist Politics and Human Nature*. Totowa, N.J.: Rowman and Allanheld.

Myrdal, Gunnar, Richard Sterner, and Arnold Rose. 1944. *An American Dilemma: The Negro Problem and Modern Democracy*. New York: Harper.

Simons, Margaret A. 1983. "The Silencing of Simone de Beauvoir: Guess What's Missing From *The Second Sex*." *Women's Studies International Forum* 6, no. 6:559–64.

Singer, Linda. 1990. "Interpretation and Retrieval: Rereading Beauvoir." In *Hypatia Reborn: Essays in Feminist Philosophy*, edited by Azizah al-Hibri and Margaret A. Simons, 323–35. Bloomington: Indiana University Press.

Young, Iris. 1990. "Humanism, Gynocentrism and Feminist Politics." In *Hypatia Reborn: Essays in Feminist Philosophy*, edited by Azizah al-Hibri and Margaret A. Simons, 231–48. Bloomington: Indiana University Press.

14

Beauvoir and the Algerian War: Toward a Postcolonial Ethics

Julien Murphy

Simone de Beauvoir's coauthored book on decolonization in Algeria remains relatively obscure. The 1962 *Djamila Boupacha: The Story of the Torture of a Young Algerian Girl which Shocked Liberal French Opinion* (Halimi and Beauvoir 1962), finds its importance in calling attention to Beauvoir's writings about the Algerian war (1954–62). The war marked a political turning point for her. I argue here that the Algerian war made Beauvoir an engaged intellectual and the book marks this transformation in the canon of her work. Its insertion in a Beauvoir bibliography presents interesting questions concerning her involvement, her relationship to French colonialism, and her activism in behalf of a twenty-one-year-old woman, Djamila Boupacha. By coauthoring the book with Boupacha's defense attorney, Gisèle Halimi, and participating in numerous activities on Boupacha's behalf, Beauvoir used Boupacha's situation to bring to international attention the plight of Algerian rebels and the atrocities of France. She wrote a famous essay for Le Monde on Boupacha's case, organized and headed a political action committee in her defense, and decided that a book should be written about her. By linking her fate with that of Boupacha, who became famous from the book, Beauvoir took up the liberation struggles of her time in ways that challenged her own philosophy of freedom.

Beauvoir's support for the decolonization of Algeria was consistent with her views of freedom in The Ethics of Ambiguity (Beauvoir 1980), published before the war. Of all of the existentialists, she alone had written an ethics by 1954. After her Ethics, her radical politics of liberation continued to evolve as illustrated by the choices she made in support of Algeria and the meanings they held for her. A close examination of her thoughts on Algeria in her autobiographical writings and essays reveals a new context for understanding her notion of freedom and aids an important re-reading of Beauvoir's middle period (1954–63). Moreover, the radical freedom found in these writings provides a powerful tool for analyzing postcolonial societies. I shall argue here three points. First, the war was catalytic for Beauvoir's political consciousness, much as World War II was for her lifetime companion, Jean-Paul Sartre. This is not to suggest that Algeria marked Beauvoir's first political act: she had already published a political novel, The Mandarins, which won the Prix Goncourt Award, and she was a founder of a major political journal, Les Temps Modernes. Rather, Algeria provoked Beauvoir's first acts of political advocacy against colonialism.

Second, the theme of decolonization in Algeria is often missing from scholarly accounts on Beauvoir, and its absence alters how her work is read and understood. Beauvoir's position on Algeria is eclipsed in writings about French intellectuals and decolonization as well. This is unfortunate because Algeria served as a key moment in Beauvoir's political formation, one that would extend her political insights to postcolonial politics. But her writings on Algeria are significant for another reason as well. When seen in the context of her Ethics, they present a radical analysis of her war activities and suggest a postcolonial ethics. In particular, a critical reading shows the practical ethics by which she lived and responded to the Algerian war, an ethics not vulnerable to common criticisms of philosophical humanism.

Third, I argue that there is a radical notion of freedom implicit in

Beauvoir's Algerian writings and that it is more nuanced than the discussions in her *Ethics*. While her concept of freedom has often been interpreted strictly within either left Hegelianism or Sartrean existentialism, it affords much broader and more radical interpretations. It is quite interesting to interpret it in light of feminist ethical theories that stress the interrelatedness of human beings and postmodern theories, Derridian deconstruction in particular. One can find a deconstruction of identities within Beauvoir's writings from this period, afforded by her gender, class, and race analyses. The sense of freedom that emerges after such interpretations offers a view of freedom more problematic and better able to address the complexities of postcolonialism.

Historically, the Algerian war marked the end of imperial France (Lipietz 1991), the last major act of French decolonization, and the collapse of the French left.[1] This last event, which will be explained later, resulted in French intellectuals such as Beauvoir struggling to find if not a political foothold, at least political allies. The war began as an anticolonial uprising and was never a declared war, but it ended French colonialism, which had been deeply rooted in Algeria by the time of Beauvoir's birth in 1908. Some writings, including some on Beauvoir, persist in referring to it as the "Algerian conflict," the "Algerian crisis," or the "colonial problem" (Smith 1978, 9), even though Beauvoir clearly regarded it as a war. French colonization had begun in Algeria as early as 1830, with the Algerians putting up armed resistance until 1871. After that, French colonization in Algeria displaced the Arabic language and many Muslim traditions with French institutions, and many Europeans settled there.

Algeria's rebellion against French colonialism in 1954, more than a century after the initial French conquest, began by rebels waging violent attacks on European colonists and posed no small threat to France's stability as a major power. With its vast land, a population of nine million, primarily Muslims, but also Berbers, Jews, and one million European settlers, its strategic military locations, trading capacity, industry, and the recent discovery of oil, Algeria was integral to the French empire, or so the French government believed. Among the causes of the initial Algerian uprisings in 1954 were difficult economic conditions, a surge of Algerian nationalism, and a growing disparity of wealth between the European colonists or French nationals born in Algeria (called *pied noirs*) and African Algerians. The Algerian war, which would last until the signing of the Evian Treaty in 1962, produced profound effects in

France. France was still suffering from the Nazi occupation and its more recent loss of control over Indochina as a result of the colonial uprising there (1946–54).

Algeria would be Beauvoir's first and most explicit battle for French decolonization, one that would make her painfully aware of the ambiguities of her own position within the colonial structure in ways not experienced in her travels to Algeria before the war to vacation with Sartre and to lecture on existentialism. She had experienced the Occupation a decade earlier and had been deeply affected by it. Like France in World War II, Algeria was an occupied country. However, this time France was the racist occupier, and it took seven years of war to finally end French colonialism.[2] Beauvoir claimed that living in France in the 1950s when it was strongly opposed to ending colonialism was a worse sort of occupation. "Yes, I was living in an occupied city," she wrote during that time, "and I loathed the occupiers even more fiercely than I had those others in the forties, because of all the ties that bound me to them" (Beauvoir 1965, 384–85). Decolonization in Algeria coincided with an important moment in Beauvoir's life. Her work had achieved a sort of maturity and she was approaching age fifty. She had published numerous books, including Le Deuxième Sexe, which made her a somewhat controversial figure in France, and translations of her books gave her prominence abroad. For her, the age of fifty represented the beginning of, if not old age, its discrete preface. She was keenly aware of the steady lapse of her youth and the privileges it had brought her, and she was taking a longer view of history and her place in it. The 1950s were a critical period for her. Her autobiography of the period indicates an implicit radical perspective on decolonization.

Beauvoir's Politics on Algeria

"[L]iving through the Algerian war was like experiencing a personal tragedy," Beauvoir wrote in Force of Circumstance, her autobiography covering the 1950s (Beauvoir 1965, 652). Tragedy suggests a personal relationship to war so painfully profound that it enabled her to see herself quite differently than before. Living through tragedy altered her identity. It also had a moral dimension; certain constructions of goodness and evil were challenged or inverted. Part of the personal tragedy of the

Algerian war for Beauvoir was that she so vehemently disagreed with France's part in it. Until the war, being a French citizen was unproblematic for her. This is not to suggest she completely approved of or agreed with government policies, but that she could reconcile her criticisms with her position as a citizen. Beauvoir was horrified by France's persistence in keeping Algeria French. French officials often argued during the war that France was the friend of the Arabs, and that they would fare better by continuing to be part of the empire. She did not agree. She consistently believed in a free Algeria and never regretted decolonization even when she realized years later that the new government was not the socialist one she envisioned.

Like many people of conscience living in a country waging war, Beauvoir struggled in the mid-1950s to find the best political analysis of the rapidly unfolding events. This was no easy task because the French Left did not present a coherent stand against French colonialism when the war began in 1954. The French Communist party (PCF) had not supported the precursor to the war, the 1945 Sétif riots for independence. Thousands of Muslims were massacred by French troops in the riots. Moreover, the PCF voted in favor of the referendum on special powers in 1956, which transferred additional power to de Gaulle and greatly accelerated the war. Over time, the PCF became supportive of Algerian independence, but not without significant internal opposition. There was some concern that support of the Muslim rebels would alienate the party from the French people. Also, for some, French sovereignty in Algeria was far preferable than allowing America to exercise control there. Nonetheless, communist support for the Front de Libération Nationale (FLN) increased. The French socialists, on the other hand, took a middle position on Algeria, one which favored French control but allowed for some measure of Algerian self-governance. This was opposed by the FLN.

The search for an existential politic can be seen in the war writings of Albert Camus, a former Algerian colonist criticized by Beauvoir for his refusal to support Algerian independence; Franz Fanon, the African psychiatrist and FLN theorist she greatly admired; Jean Genet, the playwright who signed, with Sartre, a manifesto in 1956 in support of Moroccan and Algerian independence and wrote *The Screen*, a play about the Algerian war;[3] Francis and Colette Jeanson, who wrote *Outlaw Algeria* in support of the FLN; and, of course, Sartre.

Sartre and Beauvoir saw themselves as leftist partisans and supporters of the FLN. They shared many political views and activities during the Algerian war, while also pursuing separate activities and causes. Both Beauvoir and Sartre favored social democracy for Algeria. Both strongly opposed the special powers referendum, because it took political power away from French citizens, and both thereafter distanced themselves from the French Communist party. In Beauvoir's final interviews with Sartre, many years later, Sartre claimed: "The [Communist] party did envisage the independence of Algeria but only as one possibility among others, whereas we agreed with the FLN in calling for that independence in the immediate future" (Beauvoir 1984, 367). Later Sartre worked with the party to oppose the OAS (the Organization armée secrète formed in 1961 by French extremists), but saw this coalition as ineffective. Beauvoir described their politics as sympathetic to Marxism while remaining apart from both the French communists and socialists. Nearly twenty years later she wrote,

> On the one side, there were the people who felt close to Marxism, even if they had never belonged to the Communist Party—like Sartre and me and Merleau-Ponty at a certain moment. On the other side, there were people who absolutely rejected it, like Camus and Aron. . . . [We] remained, let's say, fellow-travelers of the Communists. Yet somehow or other, they never stopped insulting us; it was a hard road. What separated us definitely from [the Communists] was the Algerian War. We were very much involved, were what one would call now Leftist partisans of Algerian independence. But the Communists, like the Socialists, had voted to give the government full powers. I was horrified, deeply, by everything I knew about the way in which the French were conducting that War, the torture. . . . It was a very violent, an excruciating experience. (David 1979, 266–67)

The Algerian war was a major focal point for Sartre's political engagement. As Roland Dumas notes in an interview: "The Spanish Civil War passed Sartre by, as did the Popular Front. The Resistance? Yes, but so little . . . He missed all the important political events of his time except the Algerian war, which was, in a way, the meeting of a great cause and a great personality" (Cohen-Solal 1987, 441). His political activities in behalf of the FLN, like those of Beauvoir, were largely those of a famous French intellectual. He spoke out against the war, lent his endorsement to important books (his prefaces to Henri Alleg's *La Question* [1958], which documented war crimes, and Fanon's *The Wretched of the Earth* [1967]), he contributed to Jeanson's underground paper, *Vérités pour*, and gave depositions at the trials of FLN supporters Georges Arnaud and the abbé Davezies. During this time he finished the *Critique of Dialectical Reasoning*; met Arlette Elkaim, an Algerian Jew, and his adopted daughter; and established an international reputation as an anticolonialist. "I've always looked upon colonialism as an action of pure theft," he told Beauvoir, "the brutal conquest of a country and the absolutely intolerable exploitation of one country by another; I thought that all the colonial states would have to get rid of their colonies sooner or later" (Beauvoir 1984, 367).

While Beauvoir never wrote a treatise on colonialism, traces of her views can be found in her war writings and activism. Beauvoir, along with other French intellectuals, struggled with the ambiguities of various political positions on the Algerian war. She acknowledged her humanistic upbringing and its influence on her in her writings: "they should have trained me from childhood to be an S.S.," she wrote in an autobiographical volume, "instead of giving me a Christian, democratic humanist conscience: a conscience" (Beauvoir 1965, 369). Nonetheless, her position was set in sharp contrast to Camus's, who, she felt, was on the side of the *pied noirs*, as evidenced, in part, by his comment to the audience on the occasion of his Nobel Prize: "I love Justice: but I will fight for my mother before Justice" (Beauvoir 1965, 383).[4] She criticized him for not speaking out against the war, for not questioning his own relationship to colonialism deeply enough. He came to represent an unsavory form of humanism: "The fraud lay in the fact that he posed at the same time as a man above the battle, thus providing a warning for those who wanted to reconcile this war and its methods with bourgeois humanism" (Beauvoir 1965, 383).

Camus, Merleau-Ponty, and Fanon died before the war's end, leaving Sartre and Beauvoir all the more central to the French existentialist movement. Beauvoir participated in many activities opposing colonialism, including speaking out publicly against the war. For instance, in 1961 she traveled to Brussels at the invitation of left-wing Belgian socialists and gave a pro-Algerian speech entitled "The Intellectual and the Government" to a large student audience, some of whom were well-known war supporters, while others were secretly assisting Algerians across the border. She took to the streets for antiwar protests, and she and Sartre were threatened with imprisonment for signing the Déclaration sur le droit à l'insoumission dans la guerre d'Algérie, commonly known as Manifesto 121 in 1960, which opposed compulsory military service in Algeria. Sartre called a press conference in Beauvoir's apartment a month later to object to the arrests of some signers. A more moderate appeal, "For a Negotiated Peace in Algeria," was signed by Roland Barthes, Merleau-Ponty, and others. Beauvoir was involved in the court proceedings against Algerian independence fighters and wrote and organized against the war, serving as a character witness for Jacqueline Guerroudj, her former Rouen student who had become a teacher in Algeria involved with the ALN (National Liberation Army). Beauvoir's efforts, joined with those of others on the left, saved Guerroudj from the death penalty. By 1960, the government changed the penal code such that the death penalty could be applied to anyone collaborating with or even in contact with rebel leaders.

Though a leftist partisan, Beauvoir felt that what was required in the case of Algeria was to "fight from the outside," rather than within the narrow confines of party politics. This was also her suggestion for combating the oppression of women. Comparing Algerian liberation with women's liberation, she wrote, "Just take Algeria—it was betrayed by the Socialists just as much as by the Communists. We had to fight against the Algerian war from the outside, from the sidelines, from underground. And similarly women will probably also have to fight from the outside, in the areas where they really want fundamental change" (Schwarzer 1984, 101–2). Refusing nationalism, communism, or middle-class solidarity, the outside became her best political location during the war. She resisted the usual political categories, as much as possible, and struggled to fashion her own ground for political positioning. The politics of the outside or sidelines was contrasted with underground activity, which she greatly admired but felt incapable of. "If one wanted to remain faithful to one's anti-colonialist convictions and free oneself of all complicity with this war," she wrote, "then underground action remained the only possible course. I admired those who took part in such action. But to do so demanded total commitment, and it would have been cheating to pretend that I was capable of such a thing. I am not a woman of action; my reason for living is writing" (Beauvoir 1965, 461).

The roles of women in the Algerian war were the focal point of

Beauvoir's own involvement. Many were in the underground. Rebels such as Djamila Bouhired, Hassiba Ben Bouali, Zhora Drif, Elyette Loup, and Nassima Hablal, were nearly equal partners with men in the FLN, smuggling weapons, throwing grenades, and enduring torture upon capture (Gordon 1968). Their activities, along with their disparate treatment by the French authorities (women were routinely raped by paratroopers and soldiers), deeply affected their supporters, and Beauvoir in particular. Beauvoir's most explicit political action during the Algerian war was taking up the case of Djamila Boupacha in 1960.

A careful analysis of Beauvoir's activities in the Boupacha case (1960–62) reveals a profoundly radical approach to the war and to colonialism. For the last two years of the war, Beauvoir interceded in numerous ways on behalf of Djamila Boupacha, a young Algerian Muslim, accused of planting a bomb, which was defused before it was to explode, at a café near the University of Algiers in 1959. Boupacha had joined the FLN after she learned that all the Muslim girls would be debarred from taking their certificates. Outraged by the racism against Muslims and cut off from her career possibilities, she began working for the FLN. She used the undercover name of Khelida and stole medical supplies from a hospital where she worked, collected intelligence, and hid FLN members in her home. French security forces raided her house one night looking for two prominent rebels. They harassed, attacked, and arrested her along with her seventy-one-year-old father. Boupacha and her father were imprisoned on charges of collaborating with the FLN. She was tortured by electrodes and with cigarettes, beaten, raped with a bottle by French officials, and fell unconscious while imprisoned in a prison in El Bair, where Henri Alleg had been interrogated and tortured, and the French university student Maurice Audin had been strangled. She later was moved to a prison in Hussein Dey and finally brought to Paris for trial. Boupacha had confessed to the charges under torture. Beauvoir got involved in Boupacha's case at the invitation of her lawyer, Gisèle Halimi, Tunisian by birth and a defender of several members of the FLN. Halimi needed help getting an investigation into Boupacha's torture and in pursuing charges against General Ailleret, the military commander in Algiers, and Pierre Messmer, minister of war, for her wrongful detention and torture. Given the serious nature of her charges, Boupacha would easily have been executed, despite the lack of evidence against her, had it not been for the efforts of Halimi and Beauvoir. Their efforts not only educated French citizens but also slowed down the proceedings so that they lasted until the peace treaty was signed, ending Boupacha's trial.

In taking up Boupacha's case, Beauvoir believed that she could best expose the common criminal practices of French officials through an individual situation. Once exposed, the French people could no longer hide behind their innocence in support of French Algeria. The hard part was exposing the truth. Beauvoir believed that people had gotten used to the war atrocities and that the cover-up of explicit evidence was quite thorough. Boupacha's case was able to dislodge many readers from their complacency and present them with evidence. Hence, Beauvoir wrote, "The exceptional thing about the Boupacha case is not the nature of the facts involved, but their publication" (Halimi and Beauvoir 1962, 10). Beauvoir saw her role as rallying public opinion. She eagerly responded to Halimi's request that she write something demanding an investigation into Boupacha's treatment, immediately writing a highly controversial essay which was published in Le Monde in June 1960, entitled, "In Defense of Djamila Boupacha." According to Halimi, Boupacha managed to obtain a copy of the newspaper in prison. Upon reading the essay she exclaimed, "What an article! My, what an article! Every member of the movement should have someone like that behind them" (Halimi and Beauvoir 1962, 73). The attorney general claimed that the essay annoyed the army. The essay was considered so anti-French and dangerous, the government ordered the seizure of all copies in Algiers, bringing even more international attention to Boupacha. The essay was also placed in Boupacha's dossier and condemned for its "scandalous attitude and conduct" at the first hearing on the case (Halimi and Beauvoir 1962, 85). By contrast, François Mauriac had written an article in Express at Halimi's request a few weeks earlier, which she described as "deceptively mild" with "calculated ambiguity." Mauriac's political tone was one of bitter irony, unlike Beauvoir's moral outrage.[5] The seizure of Le Monde provoked an international response in support of Boupacha. Halimi reported letters from Italy, England, Russia, Costa Rica, Egypt, Israel, and elsewhere. Many drew comparisons with Nazi Germany and its silencing of the press and use of torture.

Beauvoir also quickly formed a political action committee, Comité pour Djamila Boupacha, in France, chaired it herself, and held its first press conference the same month. The committee petitioned for the adjournment of Boupacha's trial, protection for her family and friends, and justice for her torturers. The philosophers Gabriel Marcel and

Maurice Merleau-Ponty joined with many notable writers to compose a membership of hundreds. The committee sent the president of the republic telegrams demanding a delay for the trial so inquiries could be made. Beauvoir and others met with key government officials, such as M. Michelet, the minister of justice, and M. Patin, the president of the Committee of Public Safety, whom she accused of promilitarism and racism.

The importance of Boupacha's case involved more than the use of torture by a government that had signed at least four documents prohibiting it. More important, Boupacha's case documented the use of rape by the military. Rape, a form of war torture applied primarily to women, whether vaginal or anal, with a bottle, a gun, or a grenade, had long-lasting negative implications. Beauvoir and Halimi understood not only how Boupacha's case reflected the larger ills of French colonial policy, but equally important, how Boupacha's rape affected her status as a woman eligible for marriage within her culture. As Boupacha put it, "Do you think any man would want me after I've been ruined by that bottle? Our customs are very different from yours. A young bride must be a virgin" (Halimi and Beauvoir 1962, 75). In her tradition, the bloody bridal garment is shown to other men on the wedding night by the groom.

Beauvoir and Halimi had to educate the men of France about the significance of rape. After Beauvoir argued with M. Patin about Boupacha's mistreatment, he responded: "I was rather afraid they'd *sat* her on a bottle, the way they used to do in Indochina with the Viets. . . . That means the intestines are perforated and the victim dies. But that's not what happened" (Beauvoir 1965, 504). It was as if he believed that Boupacha's rape was a relatively "normal" occurrence and patronized Beauvoir for taking up her cause. The behavior of French officials he dismissed. What baffled Beauvoir most was the casual attitude that French officials had about the widespread use of torture. Shortly after the meeting, Boupacha was offered the chance to plead mental incompetence and refused.

To further rally public opinion on the war, the Boupacha committee passed a proposal by Beauvoir that a book or pamphlet be produced describing Boupacha's case. Halimi explained that the book was to be "a weapon in the immediate struggle, and instrument for disseminating the truth as widely as possible, and also constitute a pledge for the future" (Halimi and Beauvoir 1962, 170). While she wrote most of it, she asked

Beauvoir to coauthor it. *Djamila Boupacha: The Story of the Torture of a Young Algerian Girl which Shocked Liberal French Opinion*, appeared in France shortly before the war's end. It was also translated into English and published in London and New York shortly thereafter. The book documented the preparation for and proceedings of the Boupacha trial and includes not only Beauvoir's introduction and her *Le Monde* essay, but accounts of Beauvoir's activities with the Boupacha committee. On the book's cover was Picasso's sketch of Boupacha, signed 21 August 1961, which appeared in several magazines. It also included testimonies by Madame Maurice Audin, Henri Alleg, Andre Philip, Jules Roy, Françoise Sagan, and others. Halimi's careful account of the trial, along with Beauvoir's contributions, shocked French and international readers. In particular, the fact that the French army, despite de Gaulle's denouncement of torture, routinely used torture in Algeria came as a surprise. As Beauvoir put it in her introduction, "For reasons affecting its own interests, and nobody else's, the Army is determined to keep Algeria a slave-state—even though the Algerian people would rather die to the last man than give up their hope of independence" (Halimi and Beauvoir 1962, 20). Beauvoir pleaded with her readers "to refuse to countenance the war" rather than align with "our contemporary butchers." She compared the French atrocities to the Warsaw ghetto and Boupacha to Anne Frank. She cited a million victims of "racial extermination" in internment camps in Algeria. She noted the murders, lynchings, manhunts in Oran and elsewhere and considered Algeria "the second Haiti," condemning not simply the abuses or excesses of the army but the whole system that sanctioned them. She morally challenged her readers to "refuse to countenance a war that dares not speak its true name," and called upon them to "raise heaven and earth to give this gesture of yours effective force" (Halimi and Beauvoir 1962, 21).

Djamila Boupacha would be Beauvoir's only coauthored book, and, as Carol Ascher has pointed out, "one of her first political activities with another woman" (Ascher 1981, 40). It was actually an alliance among three women: Beauvoir, Halimi, and Boupacha, even though Beauvoir never met Boupacha.[6] All three were middle-class and French-educated, but of different religious backgrounds, Christian, Jewish, and Muslim, respectively. Halimi had come to Paris at the age of eighteen for university education and Boupacha had a similar desire after her imprisonment. Beauvoir and Halimi had somewhat different goals. Halimi wanted to free an FLN member from unfair charges. Beauvoir wanted this, but also wanted a moral awakening for France. She used Boupacha's case to enlighten the citizens of France about the war crimes committed in their name with hopes that public outcry would stop the war. The book was among very few accounts of the torture of Algerian women.[7] She claimed to have joined Halimi in coauthorship to share the political fallout from the government and from terrorist extremists. After all, many intellectuals in France were the targets for bomb attacks and she expected that the book might provoke additional violence. Contemplating this, and the threat on her life that happened after the book appeared, she wrote, "I had finally accepted co-authorship with Gisele Halimi in order to share the responsibility" (Beauvoir 1965, 614). There was no small amount of violence happening in Paris connected to the war. The OAS bombed Sartre's flat twice. Just two years earlier, the French police seized a book by seven Algerian men describing their torture while being held by police in Paris and smashed the printing plates (Silvers 1960).[8] A French journalist published with some difficulty another book that gives an account of his torture by French paratroops in Algeria.[9] On the very day in February that Beauvoir and Halimi's book appeared in Paris, her concierge received a phone call threatening Beauvoir's life. Halimi received numerous threats linked directly to the trial. She was even forced into hiding at one point and imprisoned in Algiers on false charges at another time. In addition to terrorism, she risked imprisonment for her anti-French views.

In March 1962, the Evian agreement was signed granting amnesty to all political prisoners and to all accused French officials. Boupacha, who had been brought to France for trial, was freed in April. For several days, she stayed with Halimi, hoping to remain in France to study, but, according to Halimi, the FLN kidnapped her and returned her to Algeria, where she later married.[10] Beauvoir continued to be involved in writing about the war. It was a major theme of her third volume of autobiography, *Force of Circumstance* (La force des choses), which was published in France in 1963. The book charts her increasing commitment to the Muslim rebels as well as the toll of the war on her spirits. At one point, near the war's end, she recounts listening to a radio report on Algerian deaths and prison camps, "Again I loathed it all—this country, myself, the whole world" (Beauvoir 1965, 599). No political event thereafter would match the significance of the Algerian war.

Beauvoir and Her Critics

The Algerian war was a major theme of *Force of Circumstance*, but reviewers routinely skipped over it.[11] Beauvoir herself noted much later that she had written about Algeria with "a heart ablaze with anger," and had "breathed out this anger" in the book, only to find that "[b]y October 1963 the tortures and the massacres were already ancient history that worried nobody" (Beauvoir 1974, 125). Numerous references to the Algerian war can be found in her next volume of autobiography, *All Said and Done* (1974) and in later interviews, including her last interviews with Sartre. In one interview, Beauvoir said that the Algerian war marked an important moment in the development of her life (Wenzel 1986, 25). A final indication of her commitment to Algeria, as noted by her sister, Hélène, was found in the presence of many Algerian women, along with other African women, at her funeral in 1986 (Forster and Sutton 1989, 14). Yet, the significance of the Algerian war for Beauvoir is often erased or diminished in the scholarly literature on Beauvoir. There is no single work devoted to this topic. Even when the topic is Beauvoir's politics, mention of Algeria can be missing.[12]

If Algeria is mentioned at all in Beauvoir scholarship, its mention is brief (Ascher 1981; Appignanesi 1988; Bieber 1979; Biagini 1982; Brosman 1991; Cottrell 1975; Crosland 1992; D'Eaubonne 1986; Evans 1985; Keefe 1983; Okely 1986; Winegarten 1988) and often critical. For example, Anne Whitmarsh claims that the exposure of torture in the Djamila Boupacha case was Beauvoir's most important activity in the Algerian crisis. However, she also claims that the revelations of torture were not instrumental in ending the war (Whitmarsh 1981, 122, 198 n. 6). Clearly, a case can be made to the contrary. To assume otherwise is to believe that public opinion, which involved soldiers deserting the cause for reasons of conscience, had no effect on de Gaulle. This also leaves unexplained why copies of Beauvoir's *Le Monde* essay would be seized in Algiers. Public opinion is always a weapon of war in one way or another and frequently is an important factor in bringing war to an end.

Among those commentators who do discuss the influence of Algeria on Beauvoir, Terry Keefe sees part 2 of *Force of Circumstance* as "entirely dominated by the Algerian War. . . . [H]er handling of it is obviously much more calculated to make a political point . . . than to describe a particular phase of her life." He describes her as having an unanalyzed and nearly pathological obsession "with the idea of being a party to the atrocities committed on the French side" (Keefe 1983, 38–39). Judith Okely attributes Beauvoir's "need to make sense of her life in terms of external political events," not as an achievement of political engagement, but rather as "a compensation perhaps for past naiveté and privileged isolation"; and she claims that Beauvoir's "apparent egocentricism" gets in the way of a "deeper examination of the self" (Okely 1986, 121). Margaret Crosland diminishes Beauvoir's political views by attributing them to meaningless emotional outbreaks. She claims that Beauvoir's "increased political awareness was now focused on the situation in Algeria which upset her so deeply that whole sections of the relevant memoirs . . . become one long moan" (Crosland 1992, 388).

Most critics writing book-length studies of Beauvoir omit reference to her coauthored book on Boupacha. Her political essays from *Les Temps Modernes* remain untranslated. Her role in politics has also been overlooked in scholarship on the French left. It is common to find that the plight of women, including Algerian women, is treated as insignificant. For too many critics, her romantic attachments take precedence over her political beliefs. It is not unusual to find a longer and more detailed discussion of Beauvoir's romantic involvement with the American writer, Nelson Algren, than of her politics on the Algerian war. The displacement of Beauvoir's political involvement in the Algerian war, a decade following the publication of *The Second Sex*, presents a diminished view of her work. One biographer attributes Beauvoir's Algerian activities solely to her relationship with Sartre, claiming that during this time, she "had spent most of her life within various groups formed by men around Sartre's political concerns," and "was spending most of her life in the turbulent 1960s following Sartre everywhere" (Bair 1986, 159, 156). This implies that Beauvoir's involvement was incidental and fails to grant Beauvoir her own political commitments. Beauvoir's pro-Algerian politics should not be dismissed or seen as parasitic upon Sartre's, simply because Sartre was involved as well. Beauvoir and Sartre shared some but not all of their political activities. Beauvoir's advocacy for women rebels, for instance, was a part of her political independence from Sartre and wholly her own. At the same time, her friendship with Sartre, which she greatly valued, should not be ignored. Clearly, their intellectual and political conversations sustained both of them, and as two critics suggest, Sartre gained much from Beauvoir's work (Fullbrook and Fullbrook 1994). It would be hard to argue that Sartre was the political center of their relationship and Beauvoir was merely swept along in his political activity, particularly since even a Sartrean biographer, Annie Cohen-Solal, wonders how much Sartre acted on his own or was swept up in the acts of others. Cohen-Solal attributes Sartre's Algerian activities to his pledge of total support to Jeanson and his political group. She reminds us that although he "lent his name" to Manifesto 121, his letter in behalf of Jeanson's group was actually written by someone else in his name. "So was Sartre really active," she asks, "or simply consenting, managed (and well-managed) by the members of his group and other French intellectuals" (Cohen-Solal 1987, 430)? She concludes that he was a "screen," and, quoting Jean Pouillon, a "national treasure," to be used against de Gaulle by his political friends at strategic moments. This might explain Sartre's tardiness in supporting Algerian independence, which has been noted by one critic who reminds us that there were very few articles on the war in *Les Temps Modernes* until 1957 (Schalk 1991, 101).

In decolonization scholarship, if Beauvoir is mentioned, the mention is similarly brief and critical. David L. Schalk notes Beauvoir's support for Algerian independence and Manifesto 121, in his comparative study of the role of intellectuals in the Algerian and Vietnam wars; but he fails to mention any of her activities in behalf of Djamila Boupacha (Schalk 1991). Rita Maran, who extensively uses the Boupacha case, names Beauvoir among those who failed to expose the ideology behind government sanctioned torture as integral to the "civilizing mission" of French colonialism (Maran 1989, 189). Yet, Beauvoir's outrage and activism against the use of torture to maintain colonialism in Algeria is quite apparent. There is no evidence for Maran's assumption that Beauvoir ignored the dimensions of colonialism in the Algerian war. In Paul Sorum's study, he suggests that "Simone de Beauvoir underwent an emotional and political evolution not unlike [Maurice] Maschino's" (Sorum 1977, 158). Maschino, who wrote for *Les Temps Modernes*, fled to Tunisia to avoid his recruitment to Algeria and struggled with his own French patriotism. While this is a potentially interesting comparison, it does not explain why Sorum spends only a paragraph on Beauvoir, mentioning her again only briefly as a signer of two manifestos (Sorum 1977, 174, 179), or why, in his discussion of torture, there is no mention of Djamila Boupacha. Beauvoir is absent also from other works on French intellectuals (Debray 1981; Judt 1986; Ross 1991) even though it has been noted that she would end her later years with greater influence on French intellectual thought than Sartre (Reader 1987, 73).[13] Her greater influence is attributed to the importance of *The Second Sex* for the feminist movement and the displacement of Sartrean philosophy in later years by French structuralism. Because critics have diminished if not erased the theme of Algeria in Beauvoir's middle-period writings and activism, no analysis has been done about its significance.

Since I will claim that the Boupacha case amounted to radical activity for Beauvoir, it is helpful to address criticism that Beauvoir was a bourgeois French writer absorbed by her romantic relationships and only minimally involved in the Algerian war. This criticism is partially implied in the lack of attention to Beauvoir's writings on Algeria. Even if one attended to this aspect of her life, it could be argued that she dashed off the *Le Monde* essay in a few days, merely lent her name to the Boupacha book, and was primarily a figurehead for the Boupacha committee. The criticism may be common in America because Algeria is barely mentioned in American scholarship on Beauvoir and because American critics and biographers too often portray Beauvoir as an apolitical and primarily literary figure. A recent example of this can be found in the editing of and book reviews for the recent American edition of her *Letters to Sartre*.[14]

Beauvoir's response to the war was not a typical bourgeois response but a radical one. She risked her reputation on the Boupacha book. It could have cost her readers and discredited her in France. It was not a simple decision, and it certainly wasn't a naive one. Beauvoir may have been unprepared for the backlash from *The Second Sex*, but she knew the topic of Algeria was controversial. As a threat to bourgeois politics, she risked much: imprisonment for signing Manifesto 121, the threat on her life for coauthoring the Boupacha book, inner torment that she likened to that of an exile. Her *Le Monde* essay was so controversial that not only were copies seized in Algeria, as mentioned earlier, but the day after, *Le Monde* published a short front-page announcement attributing the government-ordered seizure of the paper solely to Beauvoir's Boupacha essay. Such censorship and attention were quite extraordinary. The author of *The Second Sex* taking on the case of a woman rebel, an African woman rebel, was too much for the French establishment. An analysis of her activities is suggestive for understanding her view of the political and moral content of subjectivity.

An Ethics of Intersubjectivity

Beauvoir's involvement in the Algerian war is interesting not only in light of her earlier work, but also, because so few women intellectuals from that period are on record with their responses to the historical conditions of their time. For philosophers interested in ethics, especially those who have read or taught her *Ethics of Ambiguity* and *The Second Sex*, this study provides another opportunity, namely to put together Beauvoir's war writings and activities with her developing notion of freedom and responsibility.

An analysis of the ethical basis for her anticolonial activism reveals a notion of collective responsibility developed beyond earlier writings. In her *Ethics*, the ambiguity of life situations and interconnectedness of human beings are central notions but do not foreshadow Beauvoir's political challenges to the government a decade later. Nonetheless, she does address colonial violence by questioning the assumption that human beings are in competitive relationships with each other so that some can win only if others lose. As Beauvoir explained there, colonialism perpetuated an insidious form of violence: "And even outside of periods of crisis when blood flows, the permanent possibility of violence can constitute between nations and classes a state of veiled warfare in which individuals are sacrificed in a permanent way" (Beauvoir 1980, 99).

Although the *Ethics* and *The Second Sex* are philosophical accounts of how subjectivities experience freedom and oppression, Beauvoir's view of freedom has long been misunderstood. It is often placed squarely within Sartrean philosophy and is rarely read from within a colonial context. There have been recent debates by critics over whether Beauvoir's view of freedom is compatible with or oppositional to Sartrean philosophy. Much of Beauvoir's *Ethics* agrees with ideas in Sartre's *Being and Nothingness*, more so than Sartre's posthumously published *Cahiers pour une morale*. Both rejected the notions of absolute value schemes and believed that human beings are the creators of values and of history; both emphasized individual freedom as fundamental to human beings and contextual in nature. However, Beauvoir presents a more concrete view of freedom than Sartre's. She understood the severe political and social limitations on individual freedom. Consider Sartre's being-for-itself in *Being and Nothingness* and Beauvoir's female subject in *The Second Sex*. The female subject, although oppressed, is situated within

myth, science, history, politics, and religion. Through these constructions, women either work out limited freedoms or have them snatched
away. Moreover, subjectivity is fundamentally intersubjective for Beauvoir, whereas, while Sartre grants the necessity of being-with-others,
he constructs subjectivity in solipsistic ways: Being is in relation to
Nothingness, subjectivity is Being with Nothingness at its core. This
difference is also expressed in their autobiographies. A comparison of
any of Beauvoir's autobiographies with Sartre's *The Words* (which he
wrote at the end of the Algerian war), contrasts a subjectivity thrown
into a world of political events, friendships, personal thoughts, and
profound connections to others, with a subjectivity that is preoccupied
with itself, insulated from other people.

The significance of this difference on subjectivity cannot be underestimated, particularly in light of contemporary feminism. Some critics read
Beauvoir's language of freedom through Hegelian dialectics and Sartrean
ontology (Butler 1990, 10), while others emphasize the differences
between Sartre's and Beauvoir's conceptions of subjectivity and freedom
(Kruks 1992, 92–97; Singer 1993, 133–43), with claims that Beauvoir's
view of freedom has a better grasp of being in oppressive situations, and
our connections with others. Such controversy over Beauvoir's notion of
freedom shows that much is at stake in critical readings of the *Ethics* and
The Second Sex. In these discussions, Beauvoir and her critics struggle for
new ground. What is the content of moral and political subjectivity?
How can responsibility be defined from the outside? Her writings on
ethical responsibility in her Algerian essays must be added to these
discussions. For in her writings on the Boupacha case, subjectivity is
placed within an intersubjective framework and has a moral basis. The
ethical path requires political action because human freedom is made
possible by a commitment to others. "And it is true that each is bound
to all; but that is precisely the ambiguity of his condition: in his
surpassing toward others, each one exists absolutely as for himself; each
is interested in the liberation of all, but as a separate existence engaged
in his own projects" (Beauvoir 1980, 112). Perhaps there is no clearer
example of how we are bound to others than what she says about the
Boupacha case. There she affirms the collective by affirming the individual. Djamila Boupacha is important because every rebel is important.

In Beauvoir's *Le Monde* essay, she argued that the French people were
complicit in the tortures committed by their government irrespective of
their individual beliefs, morals, and political activities: "For whether we

choose our rulers willingly, or submit to them against our natural inclination, we remain their accomplices whether we like it or not. When the government of a country allows crimes to be committed in its name, every citizen thereby becomes a member of a collectively criminal nation. Can we allow our country to be so described? The Djamila Boupacha affair is the concern of every person in France" (Halimi and Beauvoir 1962, 197).

The relationship between the individual and the social collective has moral implications. Her own ethics recognized her intimate bonds to others. She rejected a framework predicated on the insulation of subjectivities from each other, and instead critically analyzed her relationship to Algerians, imagining how Algerians must have perceived her. Taking up the point of view of others, particularly of Algerian rebels, provided her with a critical perspective. Sartre had argued that the gaze of others objectified us and limited our possibilities.[15] For Beauvoir, the gaze afforded moral possibilities and gave moral content to subjectivity. She might have imagined her individuality would spare her collective responsibility, but instead she was outraged that people were being tortured, raped, and killed for no justifiable reason and felt responsible. She wrote, "I needed my self-esteem to go on living, and I was seeing myself through the eyes of women who had been raped twenty times, of men with broken bones, of crazed children: A French woman" (Beauvoir 1965, 369).[16] Some have questioned the authenticity of this shift in perspective.

Fanon, for one, claimed that French intellectuals were more concerned with their reputation than with the victims of their crimes: "The gravity of the tortures, the horror of the rape of little Algerian girls, are perceived because their existence threatens a certain idea of a French honor. . . . Such shutting out of the Algerian, such ignoring of the tortured man or of the massacred family, constitute a wholly original phenomenon. It belongs to that form of egocentric, sociocentric thinking which has become the characteristic of the French" (Fanon 1967, 71). He never criticized Beauvoir for this, though others might have, particularly those who have not read her autobiographical writings. In these personal writings, there is not the distant perspective described by Fanon. Even the genre in which Beauvoir wrote about Algeria set her apart from male philosophers and protected her from this criticism. Unlike Fanon and other male intellectuals who wrote treatises on colonialism in Algeria (Sartre 1991), Beauvoir's war writings are journalism and autobiography. She abandoned the detached style of the treatise genre to speak directly to newspaper readers or intimately to readers of her life. The direct style hints at the deeply personal way she experienced the war. "I felt the war inside me again," she wrote, "all wars, all the things that divide us, that tear the world apart" (Beauvoir 1965, 359).

She recognized the temptation to be so overwhelmed by the war that one might shut it out. However, she broke through the emotional numbness, writing in *Le Monde*, "The most scandalous aspect of any scandal is that one *gets used to it*. Yet it seems impossible that public opinion should remain indifferent to the present tragic ordeal of a twenty-two-year-old girl called Djamila Boupacha" (Halimi and Beauvoir 1962, 194). It seemed impossible because Beauvoir's moral arguments made it impossible. And again in her introduction to the Boupacha book, after listing many of the horrors in the media, she asks, "Can we still be moved by the sufferings of one young girl?" (Halimi and Beauvoir 1962, 91). That the response to her essay was a resounding yes, indicates her ability to reconnect the reader with the collective, a collective that included rebels as well as patriots. While Beauvoir was a friend of Fanon, what she criticized him for years later were not his remarks on the inauthenticity of French intellectuals but rather his mistaken optimism on the liberation of Algerian women: "And then the thing that really revolts me in Algeria, [after independence] as in all the Muslim countries, is the condition of women. I can't accept the way they oppress their women, veil them, impose forced marriages on them. Fanon thought they would become emancipated after the Algerian war. On the contrary, they have been crushed" (Moorehead 1974, 32). (Or as an Algerian feminist noted, "the [Algerian] war that had just concluded between people was being reborn with the couple.")[17]

Instead of Fanon, it was Halimi, who regarded Beauvoir as emotionally constrained, "I expected a sister-in-arms, I discovered more and more an entomologist" (Halimi 1990, 294). Halimi criticized Beauvoir's relationship to Boupacha as abstract. Beauvoir had never met Boupacha though she had countless opportunities. Halimi remarks in her autobiography, "For her, Djamila was one victim among thousands, a useful 'case' in the battle against torture and the war. . . . For her, was not understanding the nature of the battle more important than the person at stake?" (Halimi 1990, 301). By contrast, Halimi was quite emotionally involved in Boupacha's case, working daily with her in prison, writing letters to her when she was out of the country, sheltering her from the OAS after she was released from prison. But what Halimi missed is the emotional perspective Beauvoir had for her ethics. She felt injustice deeply; the relationship between the French and the rebels was criminal and felt with great emotion. The compromise was an ethical one and felt at an emotional level. Strong emotive language is used in her descriptions: she *felt the war inside her*, war was a *personal tragedy*, the *white heat* of middle-class complicity enraged her. Her activism and beliefs on the Boupacha case, Algerian liberation, and France's use of torture were felt in her body: "It was not of my own free will, nor with any lightness of heart, that I allowed the war in Algeria to invade my thoughts, my sleep, my every mood" (Beauvoir 1965, 365).

As a member of a collectively criminal nation, Beauvoir made little moral separation between herself and the acts of her government and refused to separate her politics from the political economy she participated in. She did not fashion for herself the blameless position of a political dissident. "I'm French," she wrote. "The words scalded my throat like an admission of hideous deformity. For millions of men and women, old men and children, I was just one of the people who were torturing them, burning them, machine-gunning them, slashing their throats, starving them; I deserved their hatred because I could still sleep, write, enjoy a walk or a book" (Beauvoir 1965, 384). Any formal differences between herself and supporters of the war were surpassed by material conditions they shared. In the daily lives of Algerians, she was indistinguishable from French patriots. To be middle-class and French was to be a "profiteer," as she called herself, of educational and class opportunities. This is how she saw herself. "I exploit no one directly; but the people who buy my books are all beneficiaries of an economy founded upon exploitation" (Beauvoir 1965, 652). Her fame and privilege was part of French colonial power. Although at times she saw herself as an "enemy of the middle classes" she also was part of them and shared in their deeds. That is why she claimed that "the horror my class inspires in me has been brought to white heat by the Algerian war" (Beauvoir 1965, 649).

Not only is the dissident who acts not spared from collective responsibility, the bystander who fails to act is also responsible. This is why she argues in her *Le Monde* essay that her readers must act, mindful that even then one is not free from blame. Refusing responsibility for a government acting contrary to her wishes could only be an abstract refusal, a sort of good faith perhaps, in the erroneous belief that beliefs

alone determine responsibilities. To see herself as complicit and a
dissident, while paradoxical, points to the complexity of her situation;
namely, that she was an opponent of Algerian liberation and a benefi-
ciary of French colonialism. Hence, the tragic nature of the war: "I
am an accomplice of the privileged classes and compromised by this
connection; that is the reason why living through the Algerian war was
like experiencing a personal tragedy" (Beauvoir 1965, 652).

Her political response to Boupacha completely altered her relationship
to middle-class culture and she rejected the promise that class privilege
was morally defensible. She admitted that, "Bourgeois culture is a
promise: it is the promise of a world that makes sense; a world whose
good things may be enjoyed with a clear conscience. . . . It was by no
means easy to tear myself away from such splendid expectations" (Beauvoir 1974, 126). Instead, her realization that a clear conscience was
truly not possible transformed her relationship to herself and her past.
She wrote, "As far as I am concerned, my aging became apparent to me
between 1958 and 1962. I was sickened by the crimes that were being
committed in the name of France; I turned nostalgically back to my
past, and I realized that there were many planes upon which I had to say
good-bye to it forever" (Beauvoir 1974, 126).[18] Beauvoir critically
examined her past by writing two books of autobiography during the
Algerian war, Memoirs of a Dutiful Daughter, a book which Boupacha
read while imprisoned in Algeria, and Prime of Life. Such a radical
examination of her life was required by her political development.

Representing Boupacha

I have discussed the moral basis for intersubjectivity in Beauvoir's ethics,
particularly her writings on the war and hinted at ways in which the
moral and political content of subjectivities is constituted through our
bonds to others. Some of these bonds are shared identities, such as
cultural, racial, class, or gender identities. These form the possibility of
a collective, while other identities individuate us. How identities are
transgressed, supplanted, or asserted is a matter too complex for this
study. However, the Boupacha case and its representations, afford us the
opportunity to examine how a few identities were represented and
deconstructed by the Algerian war, for the war was as much a battle over

material conditions such as territory and rulership, as it was over collective identities.

The politics of representation can be analyzed on two levels. Halimi was Boupacha's legal representative in court for her charges of terrorism and her countercharges against her torturers. As her attorney, Halimi described Boupacha's ordeal within the context of the French penal code, particularly the sections prohibiting torture. Boupacha's public statements were generally in court and shaped by that discourse. These statements were transcribed by a court reporter leaving out important details: for instance, although she confessed to the charges while imprisoned, her confession was extracted by torture. The court's transcript can be read as an admission of guilt were it not for Boupacha's request, at the end of her statement, for a medical examination to verify her rape and torture.

The second level of representation is literary. Beauvoir represented Boupacha's case in the court of public opinion, writing in Le Monde and coauthoring a book-length account with Halimi. These representations are all we have of Boupacha, since she has not published any account of her own. Unlike Halimi and Beauvoir, she did not publish an autobiography, though she did write letters to Halimi from prison and wrote a prison diary. Although the literary representations were designed to affect Boupacha's legal case, they are part of a less restrictive discourse. Instead of appealing to penal law exclusively, these representations appeal to moral claims, emotions, politics, and the assumed psychological disposition of the reader. Beauvoir assembles these elements of Boupacha's situation for the reader so that the reader can best perceive it. She did not perceive herself as interpreting Boupacha's situation, "I limited myself, more or less, to transcribing Djamila's own account of the affair [told to Beauvoir by Halimi]" (Beauvoir 1965, 500).

If there is any discourse that is prevalent in the book as well as the essay, it is the discourse of virginity. Doctors, government officials, a psychologist, witnesses, and others address the question of whether Boupacha's virginity was lost or preserved while imprisoned. The gynecological report submitted at the trial documented the perforation of the hymen, suggesting Boupacha's claim of rape was true. Beauvoir noted that Le Monde attempted to censor the word "vagina" from her account of Boupacha's rape. An editor from the newspaper asked that "vagina" be changed to 'womb'. Beauvoir refused because "vagina" was the word Boupacha had used; however, in a later reference describing the rape, "vagina" was changed to "belly." The editor also asked that Beauvoir paraphrase "Djamila was a virgin." Again she refused and the sentence was printed in parentheses (Beauvoir 1965, 501). When the editor remarked that high sources suspected Boupacha's guilt, Beauvoir shot back, "I don't see that that's any justification for sticking a coke bottle into her" (Beauvoir 1965, 501). Virginity is a cultural concept as discussed earlier. One wonders whether Boupacha's claim of rape would have been discussed were she not a virgin. Some suggested she was not. One Algerian journalist wrote in *Echo d'Alger:* "Do not these documents [suggesting that Boupacha hid FLN members in her bedroom] suggest that Djamila Boupacha that supposedly straitlaced and orthodox Muslim girl, really used her bedroom to entertain men in? If that be so, what are we to make of her complaint against the troops whom she alleges to have outraged her" (Halimi and Beauvoir 1962, 88)?

A secondary discourse in the book is the discourse of the body, in particular, the discourse of torture. How could Halimi prove that Boupacha was tortured if there were no witnesses, only accomplices? One newspaper account suggests the complexity of this problem when the government denies it. *Le Monde* claimed that medical examiners considered Boupacha to be in pain but did not address the cause of her physical ailments ("New Charge" 1960, 5). Not only were Boupacha's torturers never held responsible, but even her requests for photographs to confirm their identities were denied. The most compelling proof of her torture was the testimony by fellow women prisoners in Algiers who had also been tortured, in particular, Zineb Laroussi. Laroussi had shared a prison cell with Boupacha and seen her beaten body after torture sessions but the police had threatened her into silence. Fortunately, despite risks to her life, Laroussi supported Boupacha's account when confronted with her in court.

In representing Boupacha, Beauvoir and Halimi needed ways to render a Muslim woman visible to a French culture. French representations of Algerian Muslims had been undergoing transformation even before the war. One writer describes "a closing down of indigenous society [from 1900 to 1954 in Algeria], more and more dispossessed of its vital space and its tribal structures. The orientalizing look—first with its military interpreters and then with its photographers and filmmakers—turns in circles around this closed society stressing its 'feminine mystery' even more in order thus to hide the hostility of an entire Algerian community in danger" (Djebar 1992, 146). By the time Beauvoir took up Boupacha's case, "the feminine mystery" was juxtaposed with the unveiling and militarization of some women rebels who smuggled bombs and who "took those bombs out as if they were taking out their own breasts, and those grenades exploded against them, right against them. Some of them came back later with their sex electrocuted, flayed through torture" (Djebar 1992, 150). Beauvoir and Halimi had the difficult task of describing the rape and torture of many of these rebels, for whom Boupacha became the spokesperson. Moreover, since Boupacha's rape was central to her case, they needed to write about it in ways that did not further objectify Boupacha, or provide a new instance of racist pornography. This was an impossible project and no doubt some read their work in this way. Even so, among the difficult tasks necessary to spare Boupacha her life, was the representation of her subjectivity in ways that avoided her assimilation or her erasure. In their accounts, they stressed the moral prohibition against torture and the dignity of war prisoners, attacked misogynist attitudes toward rape, and challenged notions of French officials that vilified Boupacha. All this was accomplished in part by stressing the middle-class status of Boupacha and her youth. Hence, the subtext of Beauvoir's writings played upon class solidarity and paternalism (the sufferings of a young girl), to attack racist imperialism and misogyny. Her class identity no doubt made her more acceptable to French citizens than if she was poor and uneducated. Similarly, much is made of her youth. Beauvoir herself asks in her essay: "Can we still be moved by the suffering of a young girl?" Part of Boupacha's youth is attributed to being unmarried. In addition, Boupacha appears as an attractive person in photos and in Picasso's sketch. Would it have been different if she were unattractive or an older woman or married? Would a sketch be used? Would her rape have been even more dismissed?

The destabilizing moments of Boupacha's subjectivity represented by Beauvoir had much to do with being caught in the crossfire of culture wars. Boupacha was African, Muslim, an FLN member, an Algerian nationalist, a threat to France. She was represented as an Algerian Muslim girl, a militant young Algerian nationalist (Halimi and Beauvoir 1962, 24), the imprisoned hand-grenade terrorist or the bomb-dropper (Halimi and Beauvoir 1962, 84), the Algerian torture victim (Bair 1990, 487), and a courier for the FLN. By the time of her release from prison, demilitarized representations were used. For instance, one British paper entitled the article on her release: " 'Torture' Case Girl Freed" and then referred to her in the beginning of the article as "a young Muslim typist" (" 'Torture' Case" 1962, 1). In order to render a representation of

Boupacha that did not further her victimization, Beauvoir understood her situation in light of anti-Muslim racism. By the time her thoughts were drawn to the Algerian war, she had visited America, felt her whiteness in Harlem, and seen American apartheid, which she spoke out against in *America Day by Day*. She was appalled by the widespread chauvinism and the depth of racism in France, manifested in the docility of the young men sent off to fight in Algeria and widespread police brutality toward North Africans in France. Many of the more than two hundred thousand Muslim Algerians in France suffered increased hostility (Hollifield 1991). She wrote, "The lives of Moslems were of no less importance in my eyes than those of my fellow countrymen" (Beauvoir 1965, 460). As the African-American philosopher, Angela Davis, noted from her travels in Paris during the war, "While the Algerians were fighting the French army in their mountains and in the Europeanized cities of Algiers and Oran, paramilitary terrorist groups were falling indiscriminately upon men and women in the colonialist capital [Paris] because they were, or looked like, Algerians" (Davis 1974, 122). French patriots desired to maintain psychological and material dominance over the Arabs, including those living in Paris.

Beauvoir understood how racism operated against Muslims in Algeria even before the war. In her *Ethics* she explained, "All oppressive regimes become stronger through the degradation of the oppressed. In Algeria I have seen any number of colonists appease their conscience by the contempt in which they held the Arabs who were crushed with misery: the more miserable the latter were, the more contemptible they seemed, so much so that there was never any room for remorse" (Beauvoir 1980, 101). During the war, she sharply attacked the racism of French patriots who gave "not a thought to what it was going to cost, convinced that 'the loss of Algeria' would make them poorer, their mouths full of slogans and clichés—French Empire, French departments, abandonment, selling out, grandeur, honor, dignity—the entire population of the country— workers and employers, farmers and professional people, civilians and soldiers—were caught up in a great tide of chauvinism and racism" (Beauvoir 1965, 339). At the same time, they were impervious to responsibility ("no one in France raised so much as an eyebrow" ([Beauvoir 1965, 339]), and as long as the press remained uncritical, "the people of France were prepared to accept this war with a light heart" (Beauvoir 1965, 366). She also understood how material conditions were used as the occasion for new racist practices: "It was only when the *pied noirs* rushed into France competing with the French for work and housing that they finally became unpopular; just in time to replace the old one, we watched the rise of a new sort of racism between members of the same race, as if we always needed the Other to hate, in order to be assured of our own innocence" (Beauvoir 1965, 623). Beauvoir needed to ensure that Boupacha was not the hated Other in order to advocate effectively in her behalf. Yet, Boupacha's situation placed her in this role. Were it not for Beauvoir's strong moral language, her use of class solidarity and paternalism, and her avoidance of many aspects of Boupacha's Muslim identity, she may have been unsuccessful.

As Beauvoir and Halimi constructed representations of Boupacha's identity in their writings, they were also aware of how their own identities were undone by the war. It is no surprise that a new philosophy, deconstruction, would emerge from France after the war. Deconstruction, which can easily be applied to Beauvoir's own analysis of her situation during and after the Algerian war, was founded by a former Algerian Jew, Jacques Derrida. The parallels between the theories of deconstruction and the general claims of decolonization are usually not discussed. Yet, they are quite apparent. Deconstruction prepares us to think beyond traditional notions of freedom to a more ambiguous concept of liberation. Such a concept is compatible with Beauvoir's descriptions of subjectivity.

For Beauvoir, like Derrida, notions of identity have much to do with ambiguity and are never resolvable by theoretical categories. In an essay on European cultural identity, Derrida describes himself as an "over-acculturated, over-colonized European hybrid," "someone who, as early as grade school in French Algeria, must have tried to capitalize, and capitalize upon, the old age of Europe, while at the same time keeping a little of the indifferent and impassive youth of the other shore. Keeping, in truth, all the marks of an ingenuity still incapable of this other old age from which French culture had, from very early on, separated him" (Derrida 1992, 7). There is no innocent offering up of a new identity or complete cancellation of an old one. That is why, in the same essay, he calls himself a European intellectual, but not wholly a European.[19] The Boupacha case and the Algerian war disrupted Beauvoir's identity in profound ways. "My own situation with regard to my country, to the world, to myself, was completely altered by it all" (Beauvoir 1965, 365). Halimi too: "Born into a society [German-occupied Tunisia] that had neither French nor Arabic culture, I had inherited nothing but contradictory traditions. A great many superstitions, both religious and folk-loric, taboos handed down from the Diaspora or from pre-colonial times. No written works. The only Language we spoke was Tunisian Arabic, an impure dialect in which words of Italian origin mixed freely with Maltese and Hebrew" (Halimi 1990, 152–53).

In some postcolonial writings, for instance, those of the Algerian writer Marie Cardinal, the difficulty of cultural identity is most apparent. Cardinal describes herself as a French Arab. Her family left Algeria for France before the war, and she writes about living in a France set on destroying her Algerian homeland. The war caused the onset of madness for her: "It seems to me that the Thing took root in me permanently when I understood that we were to assassinate Algeria. For Algeria was my real mother. I carried her inside me the way a child carries the blood of his parents in his veins" (Cardinal 1983, 87–88; Angelfors 1989; Durham 1992). Assia Djebar, an Algerian Muslim, emerged as a young writer during the war. Educated in the French system while under colonial rule, she writes her novels in French. Since the war, she has been critical of the Algerian government and its policy of Arabization, which proclaimed Arabic as the official language and she has commented on the complexities of her identity in postcolonial Algeria: "Who was I? A Berber? An Arab? I was Francophone in my writing, but who or what was I in my life? There was a zone of silence inhabited by words of love I pronounced only in Arabic and kept safe in my memory" (Djebar 1992, 184). Another writer, Hélène Cixous, is a German Jew born in Oran who grew up in the midst of racism and colonialism. "People said, 'the French,' and I never thought I was French. . . . I felt that I was neither from France nor from Algeria. And in fact, I was from neither. . . . I had the 'luck' to take my first steps in the blazing hotbed between two holocausts, in the midst, in the very bosom of racism, to be three years old in 1940, to be Jewish, one part of me in the concentration camps, one part of me in the 'colonies.' " Writing, especially autobiographical writing, is a method of recovery. In Cixous's words, "I lost Oran. Then I recovered it, white, gold, and dust for eternity in my memory and I never went back. In order to keep it. It became my writing" (Cixous 1991, xix, 17, xx).[20] Algeria is also recovered and is a dominant theme not only in Beauvoir's autobiography, as mentioned previously, but Halimi's autobiography as well.

The war had deconstructed not only cultural identities but gender roles, particularly for Algerian women. The abrupt expulsion of women from the veil to the military forged together the roles of men and women in Algerian society. At the same time, the rape and torture of many Algerian women rebels deeply affected the society and was the "cause of painful upheaval, experienced as trauma by the whole of the Algerian collective" (Djebar 1992, 150). Djebar describes the effects of these changes, the repression by men and women of the terror experienced in solidarity during the war, and the renewed emphasis on traditional gender roles following the war:

> The public condemnation of it [rape and torture] through news-papers and legal intervention certainly contributed to the spread of scandalous repercussions: the words that named it became, where rape was concerned, an explicit and unanimous condemnation. A barrier of words came down in transgression, a veil was shredded in front of a threatened reality. . . . What words had uncovered in time of war is now being concealed again under-neath a thick covering of taboo subjects, and in that way, the meaning of a revelation is reversed. . . . As if the fathers, brothers, or cousins were saying: "We have paid plenty for that unveiling of words!" Undoubtedly forgetting that the women have inscribed that statement into their martyred flesh, a state-ment that is, however, penalized by a silence that extends all around. (Djebar 1992, 150–151)

The deconstruction of cultural identities by war not only disrupts our subjectivity but presents us with moral and political challenges. Beau-voir's ethics, in particular, her responses to the Algerian war, indicate possibilities for reconstruction through recognizing our bonds to others. At the same time, it raises questions about history and how we see our own histories. Beauvoir, who turned fifty during the war, saw her own lifeline in terms of historical, not biological moments. When asked, years later, if there were not well-marked stages in women's lives distinct from men's, she replied, "No, I don't think so. I don't think it's due to sex, it's due obviously to politics, events; there were events, I don't know, the Resistance, Liberation, the war in Algeria . . . these are the things that marked eras, at least for me, in any event, and for Sartre as well, and for many of my friends. That's what marked the big epochs in our lives, it's the historical events, the historical involvements one has in these larger events. It's much more important than any other kind of difference" (Wenzel 1986, 25). Part of her radical perspective is her belief that historical events of our time are rites of passage for us.

This essay has taken an unconventional path. An often overlooked book about the rape and torture of a young rebel in Algeria has led to a discussion of subjectivity within a colonial context, in a little-taught ethical treatise and in often overlooked war writings of Simone de Beauvoir. Beauvoir was one of the few women existential philosophers of France. She was the same woman who wrote *The Second Sex*, a book that has had the effect in many countries of decolonizing a nation's women, a book rarely read against its colonial background. While Beauvoir carefully represented Djamila Boupacha in ways that reflected the end of colonialism in Algeria, her own identity was deconstructed by the historical forces around her and her radical relationship to others. An insider in French culture (one of its world-famous authors), she became a political outsider during the Algerian war. A moral voice for France during decolonization, a censored voice at one point, she never denied her bonds to France. A sharp critic of Western bourgeois culture and its colonial past, she did not wholly reject it but acknowledged that French culture had sustained her. In her last autobiographical volume she remarked, "I do not believe in the universal and everlasting value of Western culture, but it has been my food and I love it still. I should not like it to vanish entirely but to be handed on to the rising generation—most of it, at any rate" (Beauvoir 1974, 219).

Notes

1. Raymond F. Betts wrote, "By the time of Algerian independence, the colonies in West and Equatorial Africa had become nations. There is thus something of an overarching irony in the historical realisation that modern French colonial history begins and ends with Algeria, begins and ends with military encounter there" (Betts 1991, 113).

2. This is not to suggest that France was completely well-meaning during World War II. Recent evidence notes that France has taken little responsibility for the deportation of 13,000 both naturalized and foreign French Jews in 1942, and that these activities were not ordered by the German occupiers, but rather freely taken up by the Vichy regime. Mitterand has recently refused to acknowledge this despite a petition signed by Jacques Derrida, Louis Malle, Nathalie Sarraute, Pierre Boulez, and others; see Greeman (1993), 43–45.

3. Edmund White cites correspondence from Genet to Roger Blin, director of *The Screen*, in which Genet claimed that the play was "nothing but a long meditation on the Algerian war." White also cites evidence that explains Genet desired to sign Manifesto 121 but was so viciously attacked in the press as a "thief," a "paederest," and a "police informer," after signing the earlier manifesto, that he supported Manifesto 121 by withholding his signature (White 1993, 491, 411).

4. For a reading of Camus within a colonial context, see Said (1993), 169–85.

5. Mauriac wrote: "A girl called Djamila Boupacha has lodged an official complaint with the examining magistrate in an Algiers court. Dare I waste this column's space on an account of her deposition? Why bother to publish stuff about people having their ribs kicked in, or being electrocuted, or undergoing what they call the bath-torture? We've heard it all so often before, and there's no need to believe what we hear. The plaintiff in this case wants to call a gynaecologist as an expert witness. I hope no reader expects me to say why" (Halimi 1962, 63).

6. Beauvoir's relationship with Halimi continued after Algerian independence. She wrote an introduction to Halimi's 1973 book on the abortion case of Marie-Claire Chevalier in Bobigny and also founded Choisir, an advocacy group for reproductive rights with Halimi, Jean Rostand, and Delphine Seyrig in 1971; see Halimi (1973).

7. Another book, *Pour Djamila Bouhired*, had been published in France in 1957 by two communist supporters of the FLN; see Arnaud (1957).

8. *La Gangrène*, the original version of this account by seven Algerians living in France of their arrests and tortures, had been published in 1959 by Editions de Minuit in Paris.

9. The torture of a French journalist and editor of the *Alger Républicain* by the French Paratroops was published with an introduction by Jean Paul Sartre; see Alleg (1958).

10. Halimi describes Boupacha living in hiding so as to remain in France, but tricked by an appointment set up for her with the Comité Intermouvement Auprès des Evacués, at which she was captured and forced back to Algeria. Halimi saw Boupacha in Algeria a few months later and learned that she held a job at the Ministry of Employment and was married (Halimi 1990, 300).

11. Brigid Brophy wrote, "In it, intellectual analysis and atmosphere are alike suffocated," and "Mlle. de Beauvoir's moral sensibility—simply, perhaps, her imagination—does not impress me as very acute" (Brophy 1965, 1). Olga Carlisle wrote, "Mme. de Beauvoir is highly eloquent in her indignation at the war conducted in Algeria by the French government" (Carlisle 1965, 3). See also Algren (1965), 135.

12. As in Bair (1986).

13. Reader writes, "De Beauvoir may have begun the seventies by being attacked in a feminist journal (*L'An zéro*) for her 'fixation' on Sartre, but she ended the decade (and not for reasons of age or health alone) more in tune with, and influential upon, contemporary French intellectual developments than the man whose 'disciple' she was so often called."

14. An exception is an essay by Hazel Barnes (1991).

15. For a feminist critique of Sartre's gaze, see Murphy (1989).

16. Hélène Cixous takes a similar view of the gaze when she writes: "But in the Society of Crime in which we are citizens of liberty, we do not look each other in the eye—have you noticed?—we avoid looking each other in the eye so that we avoid the risk of seeing ourselves as we are, and being perhaps ashamed or hesitant, or tempted by truth or friendship, in which case our construction would be shaken and deconstructed and that would be the end of our security and our success" (1993, 219).

17. Clarisse Zimra quotes this last line from Djebar's *Les allouettes naïves*, in the afterword to *Women of Algiers* (Djebar 1992, 190).

18. Beauvoir also mentions feeling old age in her fifties in an interview years later: "It was the time of the Algerian war. I was overwhelmed by the course of events. I thought I was getting old and that the political future was overcast at one and the same time. That all led to the sad and disillusioned ending to *Force of Circumstance*" (Schwarzer 1984, 83).

19. Another postmodern philosopher, Jean-François Lyotard, has similarly argued that identities are largely historical and reflect a range of social and material practices. Lyotard held a teaching position in Constantine from 1950 to 1952 and became active in Algerian politics, writing several articles about the war. In early writings published shortly after

Algerian independence, he was critical of the ways in which French colonialism had attempted to prevent an Algerian identity and pessimistic about the FLN's ability to provide alternatives to colonial structures (Abbeele 1991). He observed gripping problems of starvation, unemployment, the corruption of state officials, the war-damaged social and administrative services, and the lack of a coherent ideology to build a new Algeria, concluding, "Nobody, no political group, no social class succeeded in creating a new image of Algeria which Algerians could want as much as they had wanted independence" (Lyotard 1963, 21).

20. For a discussion of the effects of decolonization on Algerian and European Jews, see Friedman (1988).

References

Abbeele, Georges Van Den. 1991. "Algérie l'intraitable: Lyotard's National Front." *L'Esprit Créateur: Passages, Genres, Différends: Jean-François Lyotard* 31, no. 1 (Spring): 144–57.

Algren, Nelson. 1965. "The Question of Simone de Beauvoir." Review of *Force of Circumstance. Harper's Magazine* (May): 135.

Alleg, Henri. 1958. *The Question.* New York: George Braziller.

Angelfors, Christina. 1989. *La Double Conscience: La prise de conscience féminine chez Colette, Simone de Beauvoir, et Marie Cardinal.* Lund, Sweden: University Press.

Appignanesi, Lisa. 1988. *Simone de Beauvoir.* New York: Penguin Books.

Arnaud, Georges, and Jacques Verges. 1957. *Pour Djamila Bouhired.* Paris: Minuit.

Ascher, Carol. 1981. *Simone de Beauvoir: A Life of Freedom.* Boston: Beacon.

Bair, Deirdre. 1986. "Simone de Beauvoir: Politics, Language, and Feminist Identity." In *Simone de Beauvoir: Witness to a Century.* Special issue of *Yale French Studies* 72:149–62.

———. 1990. *Simone de Beauvoir: A Biography.* New York: Simon and Schuster.

Barnes, Hazel. 1991. "Simone de Beauvoir's Journal and Letters: A Poisoned Gift?" *Simone De Beauvoir Studies*, no. 8: 13–29.

Beauvoir, Simone de. 1965. *Force of Circumstance.* New York: Putnam.

———. 1974. *All Said and Done.* New York: Warner Books.

———. 1980. *The Ethics of Ambiguity.* Translated by Bernard Frechtman. Secaucus, N.J.: Citadel.

———. 1984. *Adieux: A Farewell to Sartre.* New York: Pantheon.

Betts, Raymond F. 1991. *France and Decolonization, 1900–1960.* New York: St. Martin's.

Biagini, Enza di. 1982. *Simone de Beauvoir.* Florence: La Nuova Italia.

Bieber, Konrad. 1979. *Simone de Beauvoir.* Boston: Twayne.

Brophy, Brigid. 1965. "Force of Circumstance." Review. *New York Times Book Review*, 9 May:1.

Brosman, Catharine Savage. 1991. *Simone de Beauvoir Revisited.* Boston: Twayne.

Butler, Judith. 1990. *Gender Trouble: Feminism and the Subversion of Identity.* New York: Routledge.

Cardinal, Marie. 1983. *The Words to Say It.* Translated by Pat Goodheart. Cambridge: VanVactor and Goodheat.

Carlisle, Olga. 1965. "Force of Circumstance." Review. *Book Week* (May 9): 3.

Cixous, Hélène. 1991. *"Coming to Writing" and Other Essays.* Edited by Deborah Jenson. Cambridge: Harvard University Press.

———. 1993. "We Who are Free, Are We Free?" *Critical Inquiry* 19, no. 2 (Winter): 1–58.

Cohen-Solal, Annie. 1987. *Sartre: A Life*. Translated by Anna Cancogni. New York: Pantheon.

Cottrell, Robert D. 1975. *Simone de Beauvoir*. New York: Unger.

Crosland, Margaret. 1992. *Simone de Beauvoir: The Woman and Her Work*. London: Heinemann.

David, Catherine. 1979. "Becoming Yourself." [Interview with Simone de Beauvoir]. *Vogue* 169 (May): 266–97.

Davis, Angela. 1974. *An Autobiography*. New York: International.

D'Eaubonne, Françoise. 1986. *Une Femme Nommée Castor: Mon amie Simone de Beauvoir*. Paris: Encre.

Debray, Regis. 1981. *Teachers, Writers, Celebrities: The Intellectuals of Modern France*. London: Verso.

Derrida, Jacques. 1992. *The Other Heading: Reflections on Today's Europe*. Translated by Pascale-Anne Brault and Michael B. Naas. Bloomington: Indiana University Press.

Djebar, Assia. 1992. *Women of Algiers in Their Apartment*. Translated by Marjolijn de Jager. Charlottesville: University Press of Virginia.

Donadey, Anne. 1993. "Assia Djebar's Poetics of Subversion." *L'Esprit Créateur: Post-Colonial Women's Writings* 33, no. 2:107–17.

Durham, Carolyn A. 1992. *The Contexture of Feminism: Marie Cardinal and Multicultural Literacy*. Urbana: University of Illinois Press.

Evans, Mary. 1985. *Simone de Beauvoir: A Feminist Mandarin*. London: Tavistock.

Fanon, Franz. 1967. *Toward the African Revolution: Political Essays*. Translated by Haakon Chevalier. New York: Grove.

Forster, Penny, and Imogen Sutton, eds. 1989. *Daughters of de Beauvoir*. London: Women's Press.

Friedman, Elizabeth. 1988. *Colonialism and After: An Algerian-Jewish Community*. South Hadley, Mass.: Bergin and Garvey.

Fullbrook, Kate, and Edward Fullbrook. 1994. *Simone de Beauvoir and Jean-Paul Sartre: The Remaking of a Twentieth-Century Legend*. New York: Basic Books.

Gordon, David C. 1968. *Women of Algeria: An Essay on Change*. Cambridge: Harvard University Press, Center for Middle Eastern Studies.

Greeman, Richard. 1993. "The French Republic and the Holocaust: French Anti-Semitism, Ethnic Cleansing, and the Nation-State." *Z Magazine*, no. 1:43–45.

Halimi, Gisèle. 1973. *La Cause des Femmes*. Paris: Grasset and Fasquelle.

———. 1990. *Milk for the Orange Tree*. Translated by Dorothy S. Blair. London: Quartet Books.

———, and Simone de Beauvoir. 1962. *Djamila Boupacha: The Story of the Torture of a Young Algerian Girl which Shocked Liberal French Opinion*. New York: Macmillan.

Hollifield, James F. 1991. "Immigration and Modernization." In *Searching for the New France*, edited by James F. Hollifield and George Ross, 113–50. New York: Routledge.

Judt, Tony. 1986. *Marxism and the French Left: Studies in Labour and Politics in France, 1830–1981*. Oxford: Clarendon Press.

Keefe, Terry. 1983. *Simone de Beauvoir: A Study of Her Writings*. Totowa, N.J.: Barnes and Noble.

Kruks, Sonia. 1992. "Beauvoir, Gender, and Subjectivity." *Signs: Journal of Women in Culture and Society* 18, no. 1:89–97.

Lipietz, Alain. 1991. "Governing the Economy in the Face of International Challenge: From National Developmentalism to National Crisis." In *Searching for the New*

France, edited by James F. Hollifield and George Ross, 17–42. New York: Routledge.

Lyotard, Jean-François. 1963. "Algeria." *International Socialism* 13:21–26.

Maran, Rita. 1989. *Torture: The Role of Ideology in the French-Algerian War*. New York: Praeger.

Moorehead, Caroline. 1974. "A Talk with Simone de Beauvoir." [Interview.] *New York Times Magazine*, 2 June:32.

Murphy, Julien S. 1989. "The Look in Sartre and Rich." In *The Thinking Muse: Feminism and Modern French Philosophy*, edited by Jeffner Allen and Iris M. Young, 101–12. Bloomington: Indiana University Press.

"New Charge of Torture in Algeria: Judicial Inquiry." 1960. *Times* (London), 3 June: 5.

Okely, Judith. 1986. *Simone de Beauvoir: A Re-Reading*. London: Virago.

Reader, Keith A. 1987. *Intellectuals and the Left in France Since 1968*. New York: St. Martin's.

Ross, George. 1991. "Where Have All the Sartres Gone? The French Intelligentsia Born Again." In *Searching for the New France*, edited by James F. Hollifield and George Ross, 1–16. New York: Routledge.

Said, Edward W. 1993. *Culture and Imperialism*. New York: Knopf.

Sartre, Jean-Paul. 1991. *Critique of Dialectical Reason*. London: Verso.

Schalk, David L. 1991. *War and the Ivory Tower: Algeria and Vietnam*. New York: Oxford University Press.

Schwarzer, Alice. 1984. *After The Second Sex: Conversations with Simone de Beauvoir*. Translated by Marianne Howarth. New York: Pantheon.

Silvers, Robert. 1960. *The Gangrène*. New York: Lyle Stuart.

Singer, Linda. 1993. "Interpretation and Retrieval: Rereading Beauvoir." In her *Erotic Welfare: Sexual Theory and Politics in the Age of Epidemic*, 131–44. New York: Routledge, Chapman and Hall.

Smith, Tony. 1978. *The French Stake in Algeria, 1945–1962*. Ithaca: Cornell University Press.

Sorum, Paul. 1977. *Intellectuals and Decolonization in France*. Chapel Hill: University of North Carolina Press.

"Torture' Case Girl Freed." 1962. *Times* (London), 23 April:1.

Wenzel, Hélène Vivienne. 1986. "Interview with Simone de Beauvoir." In *Simone de Beauvoir: Witness to a Century*. Special issue of *Yale French Studies* 72:5–32.

White, Edmund. 1993. *Genet: A Biography*. New York: Knopf.

Whitmarsh, Anne. 1981. *Simone de Beauvoir and the Limits of Commitment*. Cambridge: Cambridge University Press.

Winegarten, Renée. 1988. *Simone de Beauvoir: A Critical View*. Oxford: Berg.

Select Bibliography

al-Hibri, Azizah, and Margaret A. Simons, eds. 1990. *Hypatia Reborn: Essays in Feminist Philosophy*. Bloomington: Indiana University Press.

Algren, Nelson. 1965. The Question of Simone de Beauvoir. Review of *Force of Circumstance*. *Harper's Magazine* (May): 135.

Allen, Jeffner. [1982] 1989. "An Introduction to Patriarchal Existentialism: Accompanied by a Proposal for a Way out of Existential Patriarchy." In *The Thinking Muse: Feminism and Modern French Philosophy*, edited by Jeffner Allen and Iris M. Young, 71–84. Bloomington: University of Indiana Press.

Angelfors, Christina. 1989. *La Double Conscience: La Prise de conscience féminine chez Colette, Simone de Beauvoir, et Marie Cardinal*. Lund, Sweden: University Press.

Appignanesi, Lisa. 1988. *Simone de Beauvoir*. New York: Penguin Books.

Ascher, Carol. 1981. *Simone de Beauvoir: A Life of Freedom*. Boston: Beacon.

Bair, Deirdre. 1984. "Women's Rights in Today's World: An Interview with Simone de Beauvoir." *1984 Britannica Book of the Year*, 27–28. Chicago: Encyclopedia Britannica.

———. 1986. "Simone de Beauvoir: Politics, Language, and Feminist Identity." In *Simone de Beauvoir: Witness to a Century*. Special issue of *Yale French Studies* 72:149–62.

———. 1989. "Introduction to the Vintage Edition." In *The Second Sex*, by Simone de Beauvoir. Translated by H. M. Parshley. xiii–xxiii. New York: Vintage Books.

———. 1990a. *Simone de Beauvoir: A Biography*. New York: Summit Books.

———. 1990b. "Simone's Scarlet Letters." *The Guardian*, 15 March.

Barnes, Hazel. 1959. *The Literature of Possibility: A Study in Humanistic Existentialism*. Lincoln: University of Nebraska Press.

———. 1990. "Sartre and Sexism." *Philosophy and Literature* 14:340–47.

Barrett, William. 1958. *Irrational Man: A Study in Existential Philosophy*. Garden City, N.Y.: Doubleday.

Bartky, Sandra. 1982. "Narcissism, Femininity and Alienation." *Social Theory and Practice* 8:127–43.

Beauvoir, Hélène, and Marcelle Routier. 1987. *Souvenirs*. Paris: Séguier.

Beauvoir, Simone de. 1943. *L'Invitée*. Paris: Gallimard. Translated as *She Came to Stay*, by Y. Moyse and R. Senhouse. Cleveland: World Publishing, 1954.

———. 1944. *Pyrrhus et Cinéas*. Paris: Gallimard.

———. 1945a. *Les Bouches inutiles*. Paris: Gallimard. Translated as *Who Shall Die*, by C. Francis and F. Gontier. Florissant, Mo.: River Press, 1983.

———. 1945b. *"La Phénoménologie de la perception* de Maurice Merleau-Ponty." *Les Temps Modernes* 1:363–67.

———. 1945c. *Le Sang des autres.* Paris: Gallimard. Translated as *The Blood of Others,* by Y. Moyse and R. Senhouse. New York: Knopf, 1948.

———. 1946a. "Littérature et métaphysique." *Les Temps Modernes* 7:1153–63. Reprinted in *L'Existentialisme et la sagesse des nations,* 89–107. Paris: Nagel, 1948.

———. 1946b. *Tous les hommes sont mortels.* Paris: Gallimard. Translated as *All Men Are Mortal,* by L. Friedman. Cleveland: World Publishing, 1955.

———. 1947. *Pour une morale de l'ambiguïté.* Paris: Gallimard. Translated as *The Ethics of Ambiguity,* by B. Frechtman. New York: Philosophical Library, 1948.

———. 1948a. *L'Amérique au jour le jour.* Paris: Mohrien. Translated as *America Day by Day,* by P. Dudley. New York: Grove, 1953.

———. 1948b. *L'Existentialism et la sagesse des nations.* Paris: Nagel.

———. 1949. *Le Deuxième Sexe.* 2 vols. Paris: Gallimard. Translated as *The Second Sex,* by H. M. Parshley. New York: Knopf, 1952; Vintage, 1989.

———. 1952. "Must We Burn Sade?" In *The Marquis de Sade,* translated by A. Michelson. New York: Grove, 1966.

———. 1954. *Les Mandarins.* Paris: Gallimard. Translated as *The Mandarins,* by L. Friedman. Cleveland: World Publishing, 1956.

———. 1955a. "Merleau-Ponty et le pseudo-Sartrisme." In her *Privilèges,* 203–72. Paris: Gallimard. Translated as "Merleau-Ponty and Pseudo-Sartreanism," by V. Zaytzeff and F. Morrison. *International Studies in Philosophy* 21, no. 3 (1989): 3–48.

———. 1955b. *Privilèges.* Paris: Gallimard

———. 1958. *Mémoires d'une jeune fille rangée.* Paris: Gallimard. Translated as *Memoirs of a Dutiful Daughter,* by J. Kirkup. Cleveland: World Publishing, 1959.

———. 1960a. *Brigitte Bardot and the Lolita Syndrome.* Translated by B. Frechtman. New York: Reynal and Co., 1972.

———. 1960b. *La Force de l'âge.* Paris: Gallimard. Translated as *The Prime of Life,* by P. Green. Cleveland: World Publishing, 1962.

———. 1963. *La Force des choses.* Paris: Gallimard. Translated as *Force of Circumstance,* by R. Howard. New York: Putnam, 1965.

———. 1964a. Preface to *La Bâtarde* by Violette Leduc, 7–18. Paris: Gallimard.

———. 1964b. *Une mort très douce.* Paris: Gallimard. Translated as *A Very Easy Death,* by P. O'Brian. New York: Putnam, 1966.

———. 1966a. *Les Belles Images.* Paris: Gallimard; Translated as *Les Belles Images.* New York: Putnam, 1968.

———. 1966b. Preface to *Treblinka,* by Jean-François Steiner, 7–11. Paris: Arthème Fayard.

———. 1967. "The Philosopher of the Other Sex in Cairo." *Al Ahram,* 27 February.

———. 1968. *La Femme rompue.* Paris: Gallimard. Translated as *The Woman Destroyed,* by P. O'Brian. New York: Putnam, 1969.

———. 1970. *La Vieillesse.* Paris: Gallimard. Translated as *Coming of Age,* by P. O'Brian. New York: Putnam, 1972.

———. 1972. *Tout compte fait.* Paris: Gallimard. Translated as *All Said and Done,* by P. O'Brian. New York: Putnam, 1974.

———. 1973. Preface to *Avortement: Une Loi en procès: L'Affaire de Bobigny,* 11–14. Association Choisir. Paris: Gallimard.

———. 1975a. "Présentation." *Les Femmes s'entêtent,* 11–13. Paris: Gallimard.

———. 1975b. "Simone de Beauvoir interroge Jean-Paul Sartre." *L'Arc* 61:3–12.

———. 1976a. Preface to *Crimes Against Women: Proceedings of the International Tribunal,* edited by D. H. Russell and N. Van de Ven, xiii–xiv. Millbrae, Calif.: Les Femmes.

———. 1976b. "Simone de Beauvoir: *Le Deuxième Sexe* trente ans après." *Marie-Claire* 209 (October): 15–20.

———. 1979a. "Becoming Yourself." Interview by Catherine David. *Vogue* 169 (May): 266–97.

———. 1979b. *Les Écrits de Simone de Beauvoir.* Edited by Claude Francis and Fernande Gontier. Paris: Gallimard.

———. 1979c. *Quand prime le spirituel.* Paris: Gallimard. Translated as *When Things of the Spirit Come First: Five Early Tales,* by P. O'Brian. New York: Pantheon, 1982.

———. 1981. *La Cérémonie des adieux suivi de Entretiens avec Jean-Paul Sartre, Août–Septembre 1974.* Paris: Gallimard. Translated as *Adieux: A Farewell to Sartre,* by P. O'Brian. New York: Pantheon, 1984.

———. 1990a. *Journal de guerre: Septembre 1939–Janvier 1941.* Edited by Sylvie Le Bon de Beauvoir. Paris: Gallimard.

———. 1990b. *Lettres à Sartre.* 2 vols. Edited by Sylvie Le Bon de Beauvoir. Paris: Gallimard. Edited and translated as *Letters to Sartre,* by Q. Hoare. New York: Little, Brown, 1992.

———, and Gisèle Halimi. 1962. *Djamila Boupacha.* Paris: Gallimard. Translated as *Djamila Boupacha: The Story of the Torture of a Young Algerian Girl Which Shocked Liberal French Opinion,* by P. Green. New York: Macmillan, 1962.

Benjamin, Jessica, and Lilly Rivlin. 1980. "The De Beauvoir Challenge: A Crisis in Feminist Politics," in *Ms. Magazine* (January).

Bennett, Joy, and Gabriella Hochmann. 1988. *Simone de Beauvoir: An Annotated Bibliography.* New York: Garland.

Biagini, Enza di. 1982. *Simone de Beauvoir.* Florence: La Nuova Italia.

Bieber, Konrad. 1979. *Simone de Beauvoir.* Boston: Twayne.

Blackham, H. J. 1965. *Reality, Man and Existence: Essential Works of Existentialism.* New York: Bantam Books.

Breisach, Ernst. 1965. *Introduction to Modern Existentialism.* New York: Grove.

Brosman, Catharine Savage. 1991. *Simone de Beauvoir Revisited.* Boston: Twayne.

Butler, Judith. 1986. "Sex and Gender in Simone de Beauvoir's *Second Sex.*" In *Simone de Beauvoir: Witness to a Century.* Special issue of *Yale French Studies* 72:35–49.

———. 1989. "Gendering the Body: Beauvoir's Philosophical Contribution." In *Women, Knowledge, and Reality,* edited by A. Garry and M. Pearsall, 253–62. Boston: Unwin Hyman.

———. 1990. *Gender Trouble.* New York: Routledge.

Card, Claudia. 1990. "Lesbian Attitudes and *The Second Sex.*" In al-Hibri and Simons, 1990, 290–99.

Chapsal, Madeleine. 1984. "Simone de Beauvoir." In *Envoyez la petite musique.* Collection Figures. Paris: Grasset.

Cixous, Hélène. 1976. "The Laugh of Medusa." *Signs: Journal of Women in Culture and Society* 1:875–99.

———, and Catherine Clément. 1975. *La Jeune Née.* Paris: Union générale d'Editions. Translated as *The Newly Born Woman,* by B. Wing. Minneapolis: University of Minnesota Press, 1989.

Clément, Catherine. 1979. "Peelings of the Real." *Magazine Littéraire* 145 (February): 25–27. Reprinted in *Critical Essays on Simone de Beauvoir,* edited and translated by Elaine Marks, 170–72. Boston: G. K. Hall, 1987.

Cohen-Solal, Annie. 1987. *Sartre: A Life.* London: Heinemann.

Collins, James. 1952. *The Existentialists: A Critical Study.* Chicago: H. Regnery.

Collins, Marjorie, and Christine Pierce. 1976. "Holes and Slime: Sexism in Sartre's Psychoanalysis." In *Women and Philosophy: Toward a Theory of Liberation,* edited by C. Gould and M. Wartofsky, 112–27. New York: Putnam.

Cottrell, Robert D. 1975. *Simone de Beauvoir.* New York: Unger.

Courtivron, Isabelle de. 1986. "From Bastard to Pilgrim: Rites and Writing for Madame." In *Simone de Beauvoir: Witness to a Century.* Edited by Hélène V. Wenzel. Special issue of *Yale French Studies* 72:133–48.

Crosland, Margaret. 1992. *Simone de Beauvoir: The Woman and Her Work.* London: Heinemann.

Dallery, Arleen B. 1985. "Sexual Embodiment: Beauvoir and French Feminism." *Women's Studies International Forum* 8, no. 3:197–208; reprinted in al-Hibri and Simons 1990, 270–79.

David, Catherine. 1979. "Beauvoir elle-même. Propos recueillis par Catherine David." *Le Nouvel Observateur,* 22–29 January, 82–85, 88–90. Translated as "Becoming Yourself." *Vogue* (May 1979): 226–97.

D'Eaubonne, Françoise. 1986. *Une Femme nommée Castor: Mon amie Simone de Beauvoir.* Paris: Encre.

Debray, Regis. 1981. *Teachers, Writers, Celebrities: The Intellectuals of Modern France.* London: Verso.

Dietz, Mary. 1992. "Introduction: Debating Simone de Beauvoir." *Signs: Journal of Women in Culture and Society* 18, no. 1:74–88.

Dijkstra, Sandra. "Simone de Beauvoir and Betty Friedan: The Politics of Omission," in *Feminist Studies* 6 (Summer 1980): 290–303.

Dinnerstein, Dorothy. 1976. *The Mermaid and the Minotaur: Sexual Arrangements and Human Malaise.* New York: Harper and Row.

Echols, Alice. 1989. *Daring to be Bad: Radical Feminism in America, 1967–1975.* Minneapolis: University of Minnesota Press.

Edwards, Paul, ed. 1967. *The Encyclopedia of Philosophy.* 8 vols. New York: Collier Macmillan.

Eisenstein, Hester. 1983. *Contemporary Feminist Thought.* Boston: G. K. Hall.

Eisenstein, Zillah. 1979. "Developing a Theory of Capitalist Patriarchy and Socialist Feminism." In *Capitalist Patriarchy and the Case for Socialist Feminism.* New York: Monthly Review Press, 1979.

Evans, Mary. 1985. *Simone de Beauvoir—A Feminist Mandarin.* London: Tavistock.

———. 1987. "Views of Women and Men in the Work of Simone de Beauvoir." In *Critical Essays on Simone de Beauvoir,* edited by Elaine Marks, 172–84. Boston: G. K. Hall.

Fallaize, Elizabeth. 1988. *The Novels of Simone de Beauvoir.* London: Routledge.

Felstiner, Mary. 1980. "Seeing *The Second Sex* through the Second Wave." *Feminist Studies* 6:247–76.

Ferguson, Ann. 1990. "Lesbian Identity: Beauvoir and History." In al-Hibri and Simons, 1990, 280–89.

Firestone, Shulamith. 1970. *The Dialectic of Sex: The Case for Feminist Revolution.* New York: Bantam.

Forster, Penny, and Imogen Sutton, eds. 1989. *Daughters of de Beauvoir.* London: Women's Press.

Francis, Claude, and Fernande Gontier. 1987. *Simone de Beauvoir: A Life . . . A Love Story.* Translated by L. Nesselson. New York: St. Martin's.

Fullbrook, Kate, and Edward Fullbrook. 1994. *Simone de Beauvoir and Jean-Paul Sartre: The Remaking of a Twentieth-Century Legend.* New York: Basic Books.

Gatens, Moira. 1991. *Feminism and Philosophy: Perespectives on Difference and Equality.* Bloomington: Indiana University Press.

Gerassi, John. 1976. "Simone de Beauvoir: *The Second Sex* 25 Years Later." *Society* 13, no. 2 (January–February): 79–85.

Gilbert, Joseph. 1991. *Une si douce occupation . . . Simone de Beauvoir et Jean-Paul Sartre, 1940–1944.* Paris: Albin Michel.

Gilbert, Sandra, and Susan Gubar. 1979. *The Madwoman in the Attic: The Woman Writer and the Nineteenth-Century Literary Imagination.* New Haven: Yale University Press.

Greene, Naomi. 1980. "Sartre, Sexuality and *The Second Sex.*" *Philosophy and Literature* (Fall): 199–211.

Hardwick, Elizabeth. [1953] 1987. "The Subjection of Women." In *Critical Essays on Simone de Beauvoir,* edited by Elaine Marks, 49–57. Boston: G. K. Hall.

Hartsock, Nancy C. M. 1985. *Money, Sex and Power: Toward a Feminist Historical Materialism.* Boston: Northeastern University Press.

Hatcher, Donald L. 1989. "Existential ethics and why it's immoral to be a housewife." *Journal of Value Inquiry* 23:59–68.

Hayman, Ronald. 1992. "Having Wonderful Sex, Wish You Were Here." *New York Times Book Review* 19 July, 13–14.

Heinemann, F. H. 1958. *Existentialism and the Modern Predicament.* New York: Harper and Row.

Irigaray, Luce. 1974. *Speculum de l'autre femme.* Paris: Editions de Minuit.

———. 1977. *Ce Sexe qui n'en est pas un.* Paris: Editions de Minuit. Translated as *This Sex Which Is Not One,* by C. Porter. Ithaca: Cornell University Press, 1985.

Jaggar, Alison. 1983. *Feminist Politics and Human Nature.* Totowa, N.J.: Rowman and Allanheld.

———, and William L. McBride. 1990. " 'Reproduction' as Male Ideology." In al-Hibri and Simons, 1990, 249–69.

Janeway, Elizabeth. 1971. *Man's World, Woman's Place: A Study in Social Mythology.* New York: William Morrow.

Jardine, Alice. 1979. "Interview with Simone de Beauvoir." *Signs: Journal of Women in Culture and Society* 5:224–35.

Jeanson, F. 1966. "Deux entretiens de Simone de Beauvoir avec Francis Jeanson." In his *Simone de Beauvoir ou l'entreprise de vivre,* 251–56. Paris: Seuil.

Kaufmann, Walter, ed. 1956. *Existentialism from Dostoevsky to Sartre.* Cleveland: World Publishing.

Kaufmann McCall, Dorothy. 1979. "Simone de Beauvoir, *The Second Sex,* and Jean-Paul Sartre." *Signs: Journal of Women in Culture and Society* 5, no. 2:209–23.

———. 1986. "Simone de Beauvoir: Questions of Difference and Generation." In *Simone de Beauvoir: Witness to a Century.* Special issue of *Yale French Studies* 72:121–32.

Keefe, Terry. 1983. *Simone de Beauvoir: A Study of Her Writings.* Totowa, N.J.: Barnes and Noble.

Keller, Catherine. [1985] 1987. "Feminism and the Ethic of Inseparability." In *Women's Consciousness, Women's Conscience: A Reader in Feminist Ethics,* edited by Barbara Hilkert Andolsen, Christine E. Gudorf, and Mary D. Pellauer, 251–63. San Francisco: Harper and Row.

Klaw, Barbara. "The Rewriting of Sexual Identity from Colette's *Chéri* to Beauvoir's *L'Invitée.*" In *The Metaphysical Novel,* edited by Eleanore Holveck and Barbara Klaw. (forthcoming).

Kojève, Alexandre. 1969. *Introduction to the Reading of Hegel.* Translated by J. Nichols. New York: Basic Books.

Kruks, Sonia. 1990. *Situation and Human Existence.* Boston: Routledge, Chapman and Hall.

———. 1992. "Beauvoir, Gender, and Subjectivity." *Signs: Journal of Women in Culture and Society* 18, no. 1:89–97.

Lacoin, Elisabeth. 1991. *Zaza: Correspondence et carnets d'Elisabeth Lacoin, 1914–1929.* Paris: Seuil.

Larsson, Bjorn. 1988. *La Réception des Mandarins: Le Roman de Simone de Beauvoir face à la critique littéraire en France.* Lund, Sweden: Lund University Press.

Lazaro, Reyes. 1986. "Feminism and Motherhood: O'Brien vs. Beauvoir." *Hypatia* 1, no. 2:87–102.

Leclerc, Annie. 1974. *Parole de femme.* Paris: Grasset.

Le Doeuff, Michèle. 1979. "Operative Philosophy: Simone de Beauvoir and Existentialism." *Ideology and Consciousness* 6:47–57. Reprinted in *Feminist Studies* 6(1980): 277–89. Also reprinted in *Critical Essays on Simone de Beauvoir,* edited by Elaine Marks, 144–54. Boston: G.K. Hall, 1987.

———. 1989. *L'Etude et le rouet.* Paris: Seuil. Translated as *Hipparchia's Choice: An Essay Concerning Women, Philosophy, etc.,* by T. Selous. Cambridge, Mass.: Basil Blackwell, 1991.

Leighton, Jean. 1975. *Simone de Beauvoir on Women.* Rutherford, N.J.: Fairleigh Dickinson University Press.

Lerner, Gerda. 1986. *The Creation of Patriarchy.* New York: Oxford University Press.

Lilar, Suzanne. 1970. *Le Malentendu du Deuxième Sexe.* Paris: Presses Universitaires de France.

Lloyd, Genevieve. 1984. *The Man of Reason.* Minneapolis: University of Minnesota Press.

Marks, Elaine. 1986. "Transgressing the (In)cont(in)ent Boundaries: The Body in Decline." In *Simone de Beauvoir: Witness to a Century.* Special issue of *Yale French Studies* 72:181–200.

———, ed. 1987. *Critical Essays on Simone de Beauvoir.* Boston: G. K. Hall.

Marks, Elaine, and Isabelle de Courtivron, eds. 1980. *New French Feminisms.* Amherst: University of Massachusetts Press.

Mead, Margaret. 1953. "A SR Panel takes aim at *The Second Sex.*" *Saturday Review of Literature* 36, no. 8.

Merleau-Ponty, Maurice. 1945a. *Phénoménologie de la perception.* Paris: Gallimard. Translated as *Phenomenology of Perception,* by C. Smith. New York: Humanities Press, 1962.

———. 1945b. "Le Roman et la métaphysique." *Cahiers du Sud,* no. 270 (March) Translated as "Metaphysics and the Novel," by H. Dreyfus and P. Dreyfus, in *Sense and Non-Sense,* 26–40. Evanston: Northwestern University Press, 1964.

Millett, Kate. 1969. *Sexual Politics.* Garden City, N.Y.: Avon Books.

Moi, Toril. 1986. "Existentialism and Feminism: The Rhetoric of Biology in *The Second Sex.*" *Oxford Literary Review* 8:88–95.

———. 1990. *Feminist Theory and Simone de Beauvoir.* Oxford: Basil Blackwell.

———. 1994. *The Making of an Intellectual Woman.* Cambridge, Mass.: Basil Blackwell.

Moorehead, Caroline. 1974. "Simone de Beauvoir: Marriage is a very dangerous institution. A talk with Simone de Beauvoir." *Times* (London), 15 May.

Morgan, Kathryn Pauly. 1986. "Romantic Love, Altruism, and Self-Respect: An Analysis of Simone de Beauvoir," *Hypatia* 1, no. 1:117–48.

Nye, Andrea. "Preparing the Way for a Feminist Praxis," in *Hypatia* 1, no. 1:101–16.

Okely, Judith. 1986. *Simone de Beauvoir.* New York: Random House.

Orphir, A. 1976. *Regards féminins. Condition féminine et création littéraire.* Paris: Denoël-Gonthier. Preface by Simone de Beauvoir, 15–17.

Patterson, Yolanda A. 1979. "Entretien avec Simone de Beauvoir." *French Review* 52:745–54.

———. 1986. "Simone de Beauvoir and the Demystification of Motherhood." In *Simone de Beauvoir: Witness to a Century.* Special issue of *Yale French Studies* 72:87–105.

Pilardi, Jo-Ann [Jo-Ann Pilardi Fuchs]. 1980. "Female Eroticism in *The Second Sex,*" *Feminist Studies* 6 (Summer): 304–13. Revision published in *The Thinking Muse: Feminism and Modern French Philosophy,* edited by Jeffner Allen and Iris M. Young, 18–34. Bloomington: Indiana University Press, 1989.

———. 1991. "Philosophy Becomes Autobiography: The Development of the Self in the Writings of Simone de Beauvoir." In *Writing the Politics of Difference,* edited by Hugh J. Silverman, 145–62. Albany: State University of New York Press.

Rabil, Albert, Jr. 1967. *Merleau-Ponty: Existentialist of the Social World.* New York: Columbia University Press.

Rich, Adrienne. 1977. *Of Woman Born: Motherhood as Experience and Institution.* New York: Norton.

Roudy, Yvette. 1975. "La Seconde Révolution des Américaines." *L'Arc* 61:68–74.

Ruddick, Sara. 1980. "Maternal Thinking." *Feminist Studies* 6 (Summer): 342–67.

Sanday, Peggy Reeves, and Ruth Gallagher Goodenough. 1990. *Beyond "The Second Sex": New Directions in the Anthropology of Gender.* Philadelphia: University of Pennsylvania Press.

Sartre, Jean-Paul. 1943. *L'Etre et le néant.* Paris: Gallimard. Translated as *Being and Nothingness,* by H. Barnes. New York: Philosophical Library, 1953.

———. 1964. *Nausea.* Translated by Lloyd Alexander. New York: New Directions.

———. 1965. *Anti-Semite and Jew.* Translated by G. Becker. New York: Schocken Books.

———. 1960. *Critique de la raison dialectique.* Paris: Gallimard. Translated as *Critique of Dialectical Reason,* by A. Sheridan-Smith, and edited by Jonathan Ree. London: NLB, 1976.

———. 1983a. *Cahiers pour une morale.* Edited by Arlette Elkaim-Sartre. Paris: Gallimard.

———. 1983b. *Lettres au Castor.* 2 vols. Edited by Simone de Beauvoir. Paris: Gallimard. Translated as *Witness to My Life: The Letters of Jean-Paul Sartre to Simone de Beauvoir, 1926–1939,* by L. Fahnestock and N. McAfee. New York: Scribner's, 1992.

———. 1984. *War Diaries: Notebooks from a Phoney War, November 1939–March 1940.* Translated by Q. Hoare. London: Verso.

Schwarzer, Alice. 1972. "Radicalization of Simone de Beauvoir." *Ms. Magazine* (July): 60–63, 133–34.

———. 1977. "Talking to a Friend—An Interview with Simone de Beauvoir." *Ms. Magazine* (July): 12–13, 15–16.

———. 1984. *After the Second Sex: Conversations with Simone de Beauvoir.* New York: Pantheon.

Seigfried, Charlene Haddock. 1984. "Gender-specific values." *Philosophical Forum* 15 (Summer): 425–42.

———. 1985. "*Second Sex:* Second Thoughts." *Women's Studies International Forum* 8, no. 3:219–29. Reprinted in al-Hibri and Simons, 1990, 305–21.

Sicard, M. 1979. "Interférences. Entretien avec Simone de Beauvoir et Jean-Paul Sartre." *Obliques* 18–19: 325–29.

Simons, Margaret A. 1983. "The Silencing of Simone de Beauvoir: Guess What's Missing From *The Second Sex.*" *Women's Studies International Forum* 6, no. 5:559–64.

———. 1986. "Beauvoir and Sartre: The Philosophical Relationship." In *Simone de Beauvoir: Witness to a Century.* Special issue of *Yale French Studies* 72:165–79.

———. 1990. "Sexism and the Philosophical Canon: On Reading Beauvoir's *The Second Sex.*" *Journal of the History of Ideas* 51, no. 3:487–504.

———. 1992. "Lesbian Connections: Simone de Beauvoir and Feminism." *Signs: Journal of Women in Culture and Society* 18, no. 1:136–61.

———, and Jessica Benjamin. 1979. "Simone de Beauvoir: An Interview." *Feminist Studies* 5:330–45.

Singer, Linda. 1985. "Interpretation and Retrieval Rereading Beauvoir." *Hypatia: A Journal of Feminist Philosophy* 3. Special issue of *Women's Studies International Forum* 8, no. 3:231–38. Reprinted in *Hypatia Reborn: Essays in Feminist Philosophy*, edited by Azizah al-Hibri and Margaret A. Simons, 323–35. Bloomington: Indiana University Press, 1990. Reprinted in her *Erotic Welfare: Sexual Theory and Politis on the Age of Epidemic.* 131–44. New York: Routledge, Chapman and Hall, 1993.

Slama, Beatrice. 1987. "Simone de Beauvoir: Feminine Sexuality and Liberation." In *Critical Essays on Simone de Beauvoir*, edited by Elaine Marks, 218–34. Boston: G. K. Hall.

Smith, Janet Farrell. 1986. "Possessive Power." *Hypatia* 1 (Fall): 102–20.

Spelman, Elizabeth V. 1988. *Inessential Woman: Problems of Exclusion in Feminist Thought.* Boston: Beacon.

Stimpson, Catharine R. 1980. "Neither Dominant Nor Subordinate: The Women's Movement and Contemporary American Culture." *Dissent* 27 (Summer): 299–307.

Stone, Bob. 1987. "Simone de Beauvoir and the Existential Basis of Socialism," *Social Text* 17 (Fall): 123–33.

Suleiman, Susan Rubin. 1992. "Life-Story, History, Fiction: Reflections on Simone de Beauvoir's Wartime Writings." *Contention: Debates in Society, Culture and Science* 1, no. 2 (Winter): 1–21.

Thiam, Awa. 1986. *Black Sisters, Speak Out: Feminism and Oppression in Black Africa.* Translated by D. Blair. Dover, N.H.: Pluto.

Wahl, Jean. [1947] 1949. *A Short History of Existentialism.* Translated by F. Williams and S. Maron. New York: Wisdom Library.

Walters, Margaret. 1977. "The Rights and Wrongs of Women: Mary Wollstonecraft, Harriet Martineau, Simone de Beauvoir." In *The Rights and Wrongs of Women*, edited by Juliet Mitchell and Ann Oakley, 304–78. Harmondsworth, Middlesex: Penguin.

Wenzel, Hélène. 1986. "Interview with Simone de Beauvoir." In *Simone de Beauvoir: Witness to a Century.* Special issue of *Yale French Studies* 72:5–32.

———, ed. 1986. *Simone de Beauvoir: Witness to a Century.* Special issue of *Yale French Studies* 72.

Whitmarsh, Anne. 1981. *Simone de Beauvoir and the Limits of Commitment.* Cambridge: Cambridge University Press.

Winegarten, Renée. 1988. *Simone de Beauvoir: A Critical View.* Oxford: Berg.

Wittig, Monique. 1992. *The Straight Mind and Other Essays.* Boston: Beacon.

Willis, Ellen. 1986. "Rebel Girl" [obituary for Beauvoir]. *Village Voice*, May 27.

Young, Iris M. 1985. "Humanism, Gynocentrism and Feminist Politics." *Women's*

Studies International Forum 8, no. 3:173–83. Reprinted in al-Hibri and Simons 1990, 231–48.

————. 1989. "Throwing Like a Girl: A Phenomenology of Feminine Bodily Comportment, Motility, and Spatiality." In *The Thinking Muse: Feminism and Modern French Philosophy,* edited by Jeffner Allen and Iris M. Young, 51–70. Bloomington: Indiana University Press.

Zéphir, Jacques. 1982. *Le Néo-féminisme de Simone de Beauvoir.* Paris: Denoël and Gonthier.

Zerilli, Linda M. G. 1992. "A Process without a Subject: Simone de Beauvoir and Julia Kristeva on Maternity." *Signs: Journal of Women in Culture and Society* 18, no. 1:111–35.

Contributors

JEFFNER ALLEN is professor of philosophy at the State University of New York at Binghamton. She is author of *r e v e r b e r a t i o n s   across the shimmering   CASCADAS* (SUNY Press, 1994), *Lesbian Philosophy: Explorations* (Institute of Lesbian Studies, 1986), and *SINUOSITIES \\ Lesbian Poetic Politics* (fall 1995). She is the editor of *Lesbian Philosophies and Cultures* (SUNY Press, 1991) and coeditor of *The Thinking Muse: Feminism and Recent French Thought* (Indiana University Press, 1989).

KRISTANA ARP grew up in California and now lives in Brooklyn, New York, where she is assistant professor of philosophy at Long Island University, Brooklyn. She received her B.A. from the University of Chicago and her Ph.D. in philosophy from the University of California, San Diego. She has published articles on Husserl and is now at work on a book about Simone de Beauvoir's early philosophical writings on ethics.

DEBRA BERGOFFEN is professor of philosophy and women's studies at George Mason University, where she chaired the Department of Philosophy and Religious Studies and received the university's Distinguished Faculty Award. Professor Bergoffen's writings deal with the questions of truth, subjectivity, and "woman" as they appear in the works of Nietzsche, Freud, Lacan, Sartre, and Beauvoir. She is currently writing a book on Simone de Beauvoir.

KATE FULLBROOK is head of the School of Literary Studies at the University of the West of England, Bristol. EDWARD FULLBROOK is a freelance writer with interests in philosophy, economics, and fiction. Their biography, *Simone de Beauvoir and Jean-Paul Sartre: The Remaking of a Twentieth-Century Legend,* was published by Basic Books in 1994. They are currently working on a volume on Simone de Beauvoir for Polity Press's *Key Contemporary Thinkers* series.

ELEANORE HOLVECK is chair of the Department of Philosophy at Duquesne University. She has recently taught a course on Simone de Beauvoir's philosophy of literature at the Institute of Philosophy, Catholic University of Leuven, Belgium. She received her Ph.D. from the University of North Carolina at Chapel Hill. She is writing a book on the philosophy of Simone de Beauvoir and coediting (with Barbara Klaw) a collection of essays entitled *The Metaphysical Novel.*

BARBARA KLAW is assistant professor of French at Northern Kentucky University. She received her Ph.D. from the University of Pennsylvania in 1990; her dissertation was titled "Men, Women, Power, and Narrative in the Novels of Simone de Beauvoir." She has published papers on Beauvoir in *Cincinnati Romance Review* and *Simone de Beauvoir Studies.* She is currently working on a variety of topics, including a feminist analysis of Rabelais, and Beauvoir's relationship with Nelson Algren and Claude Lanzmann. She is coeditor (with Eleanore Holveck) of the forthcoming *The Metaphysical Novel,* a series of essays on Beauvoir's works, and a contributor to the forthcoming *Simone de Beauvoir and Sexuality,* edited by Melanie Hawthorne.

SONIA KRUKS holds the Robert S. Danforth Chair in Politics at Oberlin College, where she teaches political philosophy and feminist theory. Her books include *The Political Philosophy of Merleau-Ponty* (Humanities Press, 1981; reprinted, Gregg Revivals, 1994) and *Situation and Human Existence: Freedom, Subjectivity, and Society* (Routledge, Chapman and Hall, 1990). She is also coeditor of the volume *Promissory Notes: Women in the Transition to Socialism* (Monthly Review Press, 1989). Her current research involves developing a critical engagement between the ideas of Beauvoir and Sartre and postmodern feminist thought.

MICHÈLE LE DOEUFF is visiting professor at L'Institut Européen de l'Université de Genève. Her principal works include *L'Etude et le rouet: Des femmes, de la philosophie, etc.* (Paris: Seuil, 1989; translated as *Hipparchia's Choice: An Essay Concerning Women, Philosophy, Etc.* [Cambridge, Mass.: Basil Blackwell, 1991]); *L'Imaginaire philosophique* (Paris: Payot, 1980; translated as *The Philosophical Imaginary* [Stanford University Press, 1990]); *Shakespeare: Venus et Adonis,* suivi de *Genèse d'une catastrophe* (Paris: Alidades, 1986); and *Francis Bacon: Du Progrès et de la promotion des savoirs* (Paris: Gallimard, 1991).

CÉLINE T. LÉON is professor of French and humanities at Grove City College. Her publications include articles on Simone de Beauvoir and contemporary French feminism. Along with articles on Kierkegaard, she has recently completed a book, *The Neither/Nor of the Second Sex,* a study of women and the sexual relation in Kierkegaard. She is coeditor (with Sylvia Walsh) of *Re-reading the Canon: Feminist Interpretations of Kierkegaard* (Penn State Press, forthcoming).

JULIEN S. MURPHY is associate dean of the College of Arts and Sciences and associate professor at the University of Southern Maine, Portland. Her book, *The Constructed Body: AIDS, Reproductive Technology, and Ethics* is being published by the State University of New York Press (1995).

JO-ANN PILARDI is associate professor of philosophy and women's studies at Towson State University in Baltimore, where she is also coordinator of women's studies. She has published other articles on Simone de Beauvoir, as well as in the fields of feminist theory and political philosophy.

MARGARET A. SIMONS is professor of philosophy and women's studies at Southern Illinois University at Edwardsville and former editor of *Hypatia: A Journal of Feminist Philosophy*. Coeditor (with Azizah al-Hibri) of *Hypatia Reborn: Essays in Feminist Philosophy* (Indiana University Press, 1990), she is currently researching the influence on Beauvoir of Richard Wright and other theorists of racial oppression, as well as writing a book on Beauvoir and feminist philosophy for Routledge.

KAREN VINTGES is associate professor at the Department of Philosophy of the University of Amsterdam. Her work has been published widely in both professional journals and the media. She has written a book on the philosophy of Simone de Beauvoir, *Philosophy as Passion* (Indiana University Press, 1995).

JULIE K. WARD is assistant professor of philosophy at Loyola University of Chicago. She has published various papers in feminism and ancient philosophy and is currently working on the issue of autonomy and intersubjectivity in the thought of Simone de Beauvoir.

Index